THE OZARKS IN MISSOURI HISTORY

THE OZARKS IN MISSOURI HISTORY

DISCOVERIES IN AN AMERICAN REGION

EDITED BY

LYNN MORROW

University of Missouri Press Columbia and London

University of Missouri Press, Columbia, Missouri 65201
Printed and bound in the United States of America

5 4 3 2 1 17 16 15 14 13

Cataloging-in-Publication data available from the Library of Congress
ISBN 978-0-8262-2006-6

∞™ This paper meets the requirements of the
American National Standard for Permanence of Paper
for Printed Library Materials, Z39.48, 1984.

Design and composition: K.Lee Design & Graphics
Printing and binding: Thomson-Shore, Inc.
Typefaces: Palatino and Giovanni

We dedicate this volume to the National History Day competition of young scholars who have written and will write about Missouri.

National History Day lives and breathes in the classrooms of dedicated teachers. Benefactors and sponsor institutions set an institutional stage to display student work where regional coordinators organize students in front of attentive judges, who vote on presentations and award special prizes.

We all benefit from this extraordinary exercise in thinking, writing, acting, imagining, and talking about our state.

Contents

THE OZARKS IN MISSOURI HISTORY

Introduction

At the annual meeting of the State Historical Society of Missouri in September 1978, Duane Meyer spoke about "The Ozarks in Missouri History." He found that Missouri historians had "largely ignored the Ozarks in describing the mainstream political, economic and social trends in Missouri." He believed that "times are changing," accelerated by booming population growth. In turn, modern developments generated the need for a fresh examination of the hillbilly stereotype of the residents, as well as recognition of new research, writing, and publishing projects emerging in the Ozarks. Conversation about the region was common, professional research and writing was not. The Ozarks seemingly uniform cultural surface had grown complex.[1]

Missouri writers have long described trends in state history, but not in its varied regions. Vernacular areas, like the Ozarks, the Booneslick, Little Dixie, and the Bootheel, are not institutions and do not have discrete political boundaries or official records. By contrast, Appalachian scholars have published a veritable library trying to define the boundaries of their region; and, geographic definitions of the Midwest that include the Ozarks continue to evolve, as well. The Ozarks unique upland location, between the Appalachians and Rocky Mountains, with a famous natural diversity, has attracted a parade of naturalists who ascribe fluid boundaries for interpreters and for government entities seeking to understand geographic space. Famed as a homeland dominated culturally by the Anglo-Saxon, the Scotch-Irish, or, more inclusively, the Ulster migration (Scotch-Irish Protestant, Irish Catholic, and English descendants), even the immigrant population is not clearly understood, while no one doubts resident Ozarkers' ability to adapt to almost any circumstance. Writers must "impose a notion of unity" to make sense of human patterns in geographic spaces. What matters is a framework for discussing the past.[2]

A survey of the *Missouri Historical Review*, for example, reveals that contributors rarely adopted an Ozarks or Ozark terminology until after Duane Meyer's 1978 address, in part, because authors writing about the Ozarks—folklorists, geologists, journalists, and novelists—published elsewhere.[3] Remarkably, the term *Ozark(s)* in a title appears only twice between the first issue of 1906 and one of 1975 in our state's leading historical journal.[4] Consequently, the body of Ozarks history represented in the *Review* is small when compared to that in the Missouri River Valley, but elsewhere in the serial, historians have touched on the region in studies of early travel and exploration, demography, immigration, slavery, the Civil War, Springfield, vigilantes, lead and iron mining, steamboats, and railroad ties floating down rivers. After World War Two historians began commenting on fiction, folklore, and Cherokees in the Ozarks.

The term *Ozark* deserves explanation. Used by colonial hunters as a descriptor for Arkansas Post, the Quapaw Indians, and the Arkansas River, the term migrated with them into the interior of Arkansas and Missouri. Henry Rowe Schoolcraft avoided the term in his famous 1818–1819 travel account, instead using the phrase "western country." But, Major Stephen Long, who undertook explorations of trans-Mississippi lands in 1819–1820, labeled the uplands from the Missouri River into the modern Ouachita Mountains of Arkansas as the "Ozark Mountains." The federal government, represented by Long, created the first, but far from the last boundary outline for the Ozarks. Writers such as Nicholas Hesse, an 1830s German immigrant to Osage County, used Long's map when describing Missouri: "If one has crossed the Ozarks, stretching from Mexico through Arkansas to the Missouri [River] between the Gasconade and Osage Rivers, then the landscape becomes more pleasing." So, when Schoolcraft revised his travel accounts in 1853, he included "Ozark Mountains" in his title, as nineteenth-century cartographers had, by then, embraced the term.[5]

After the Civil War, geologists spearheaded scholarly writing about the Ozark landscape. Garland C. Broadhead assumed the mantle of Missouri state geologist in 1873 and authored dozens of articles and reports helping to promote the popular and scholarly use of the term *Ozark*. Publishers printed maps with the label "Ozark Mountains," showing a summit of land running from the northeast to the southwest, from Rolla to Springfield, and added to it the geologists' term *Ozark Range* or *Ozark Ridge*. The rivers generally flow north and south of the Ozark Ridge. Ironically, the relief along this corridor (i.e., the difference between lower and higher elevations) is gentler than most of the interior Ozarks, thus easier to traverse. The St. Louis and San Francisco Railway (Frisco) followed this old interior pathway, formerly used by fur traders, as did surveyors for Route 66. Local businesses and organizations in the permanent railroad towns made generous use of the adjective Ozark to describe themselves.[6]

St. Louis's corporate institutions became modernization influences, moving into the historic Ozarks along the Frisco and into southeast Missouri via the St. Louis, Iron Mountain Railroad. Two Missourians, Curtis Marbut and Carl Sauer, rode the rails, in the process of publishing benchmark studies that firmly placed the moniker "Ozarks" on Missouri's upland. Marbut's scientifically based *Physical Features of Missouri* (1896), *Soils of the Ozark Region* (1910), and *Soil Reconnaissance of the Ozark Region of Missouri and Arkansas* (1914) set the stage for Sauer's classic, *The Geography of the Ozark Highland of Missouri* (1920). Sauer offered boundaries for a historic Ozarks region and established a spatial model for subsequent work. Ozark boundaries for the physical and biological sciences, however, are more easily discerned than any cultural or historical borders, which remain fuzzy to this day. But, it was journalists, folklorists, and novelists who described a tradition-bound society in image-making portraits to entertain urban readers who revealed the vernacular region to large audiences, including historians. Through their local color writings, images of Ozarks backwoods hillbillies and rugged individualists were well established in the popular imagination by the 1940s.[7]

General readers and professionals took notice of publications featuring the Ozarks. During the 1940s, Minnie Brashear surveyed Missouri literature and concluded that the national movement in regionalism had flowered in the Ozarks. Harold Bell Wright's novels set in southwest Missouri sold millions of copies. They achieved national fame for the region and stimulated an outpouring of fiction and verse in the 1920s and 1930s. Joe Kraus concluded that writings on the customs and folklore of the Ozarks, a sentimentalized rurality called an Arcadian myth, had "caught the public's fancy." Playing to this audience, the State Historical Society of Missouri published Vance Randolph's landmark four-volume *Ozark Folksongs* (1946–1950). The bias of southwest Missouri as a subregional locale in publishing Ozark literature and folksong collecting was unmistakable.[8]

The emergence of tourism and the role of federal and state governments in creating opportunities for commercial investment spawned a widening discussion about the Ozarks. During the 1930s–1950s, the Mark Twain National Forest, the Missouri Department of Conservation, and the Army Corps of Engineers, with its epoch-making reservoirs, brought enormous attention to the Ozarks. Conservation work, flood control, and the subsequent role of commercial recreation produced debates about natural and cultural heritage. In 1952 the climate of discussion brought forth the *Ozarks Mountaineer Magazine* in Springfield. The magazine became a forum for writing about the persistence of cultural traditions despite the dramatic changes in Ozark landscapes.[9] The initiative of the National Park Service in the 1960s to protect and manage America's first free-flowing river park—the Ozark National Scenic Riverways—prompted a popular *Kansas City Star* journalist to call attention to "history made in the Ozarks, the almost overnight (if forty years is overnight) change" to its streams, lakes, and tourism. Two years later, in 1966, Leonard Hall in a "Wildlife in Missouri" essay identified the Ozark Highland as a storied region full of economic promise pending the restoration of habitat.[10]

Duane Meyer proclaimed that "geographers and geologists, unlike historians, have found the Ozarks to be a rich field for work . . . but geography is not history." Moreover, he observed that neither had appropriate research materials been made available. At the Center for Ozarks Studies, Southwest Missouri State University, during the 1970s, staff referred to this phenomenon as the published "I-70 Missouri history." However, since the late nineteenth century, writers had placed stories along the Ozark Ridge. What followed in the twentieth century was a large volume of popular writing about the Ozark Mountains, set in southwest Missouri, so in effect readers have also inherited an "I-44 Ozarks history."[11]

Fortunately, for Ozarks history, Missouri institutions began to build upon Meyer's challenges for Ozarks history. In 1980, the State Historical Society of Missouri and the University of Missouri established the Western Historical Manuscripts Collection office at the University of Missouri-Rolla. Today, nearly 1,700 collections, representing fifty-two counties in southern Missouri, are available for research. A decade later, in 1990, the Office of the Secretary of State established the Local Records Preservation Program, which has centralized tens of millions of executive and judicial government records in the Missouri State Archives, created a branch state archives office in the City of St. Louis, and cosponsored the development of county archives and records centers.[12] In 1996, Missouri State University-Springfield opened its Special Collections and Archives. The result is that twenty-first-century historians have unprecedented access to Ozark primary sources. Archival work in assembling records, maps, photographs, and access through electronic databases for research and interpretation has far outpaced professional writing on the Missouri Ozarks. As this anthology presents, in part, the institutional work in Columbia, Rolla, and Springfield has also brought new contributors to Ozarks history; the founding of large state and federal repositories in Missouri offer similar resources.[13]

Contributors to contemporary Missouri Ozarks history represent a convergence of traditional academics, the recent generation of public historians, that is, those trained in historical methods, but employed by government-funded agencies, and other educated government employees. This mix of backgrounds has centered upon events, trends, and cultural topics that are significant in the region's history that suggest pathways for students in the future. Our historical panorama is in chronological fashion, more or less. The articles display the historian's penchant for change and innovation, not stasis. Most address impacts of modernization upon this rural region, especially increasing access to Ozark towns and hinterlands, via connections to roadways, rail transport, and national commerce.

Missouri's far-flung western fur trade had a secondary theater of operations in the Ozarks. Lynn Morrow highlighted an episode at statehood that included the largest complex of historic emigrant Indian settlement in Missouri, commonly known as Delaware Town and its primary trader, William Gilliss. Popular fascination with the Cherokees notwithstanding, Americans in the Missouri Ozarks had more contact with Shawnees and Delawares than any other Indian culture. The article encouraged decades-long research at Missouri State University on the 1820s history of the Delawares that continues today at its Center for Archaeological Research.[14]

The Gilliss story illuminated judicial case files as important primary sources. Litigation after his death led to a state supreme court case full of depositions about his commercial and private life. They read like oral history, revealing anthropological insights that described events long clouded in folkloric tradition. Central players had direct relationships with Ste. Genevieve, a gateway into the colonial and territorial Ozarks, and a safe "Ozarks domain" for traders that included Delaware Town, home to the largest concentrated population in southwest Missouri until Civil War Springfield. Long-distance commerce traveled a "great interior highway," the "Ozark Ridge" described by geologists and followed by railroads and highways to the southwest (I-44). The contemporary trade of marketing illegal brandy by whites to Indians provided the historical context for the birth of the Yocum Silver Dollar legend, the most famous folkloric tale concerning Ozarks precious ore. Gilliss, a fur trader and man with wide-ranging alliances among the Delaware and Shawnee emigrants, became the wealthiest man in Kansas City, and by all contemporary judgments, a model of success for an American fur trader. The court awarded one-third of Gilliss's estate to his Indian descendants, a landmark decision in Ozarks and Missouri legal history.

Industrial slavery and natural resources is a topic explored by Barbara Green. Missouri's major river counties held, by far, the majority of slaves in the state, but slavery existed in the interior Ozarks, too. Slaves lived in close proximity to their white owners in the Ozarks, working as domestics, farm laborers, or hired out to others. While there were concentrations of slaves in the mineral lead industry in the Ste. Genevieve hinterlands, corporate iron companies owned and hired slaves at Iron Mountain, Pilot Knob, and in smaller numbers at Maramec Iron Works, the site chosen by Green.[15]

Green's focus at Maramec Iron in modern Phelps County was the widespread practice of hiring out slaves, although Maramec records allow a survey of only seventeen slaves, contracted with slaveholders by Maramec owners Thomas James and Samuel Massey. The ironmongers used slaves to construct the frontier industrial site. Later, slaves worked twelve-hour days at wood chopping, mining, as teamsters, haulers of coal, and a few at carpentry and blacksmithing; women washed, cooked, and served, while both genders worked alongside Anglo and German immigrants. Though small in numbers, slave hiring proved profitable.

Most of the slave hires appear to have come from Booneslick counties, but Maramec agents included small-town merchants R. J. McElhany, Springfield, and Charles Eitzen, Hermann. Slave owners issued a permit for the slave to carry on his journey to the iron mine. Contracts often expressed limitations on the labor and treatment of the "owner's property." Masters wanted holidays given at Christmas, humane treatment, a couple kept together, and limited workloads. It is impossible to tell what level of compliance that Massey permitted, but he did allow some to hire themselves out nearby in overtime for cash or clothing.

Nevertheless, the slave hiring business became difficult for both slaves and Massey. Slaves ran away, not to freedom, but back home to their owners. The root cause appeared to be that work, treatment, and life at the iron mines was significantly worse than working at home for their masters. Slave complaints to masters made it more and more difficult for Maramec Iron to hire them. Moreover, labor shortages with the rising cost of slaves in the late antebellum years tended to mitigate the company's search for them. Finally, American black bondage led to the Civil War.

The Ozarks became a dangerous place in the face of the Civil War. Pitched battles and guerrillas have captured the attention of historians, but conventional military operations were the primary occupations of Union soldiers for much of the war. John Bradbury addressed this theme in an interpretive military travel account of northern troops encountering the war-torn Ozarks from Rolla to southwest Missouri and northwest

Arkansas.[16] The soldiers, midwestern prairie farmers at home, made observations that are sometimes exaggerated and punctuated with humor, but full of descriptions for how the timbered, rocky Ozarks impacted their impressions of life in a foreign landscape.

Union soldiers discussed Rolla's unpainted buildings, lack of city planning, poor infrastructure in roads and restaurants, and saloons seen in every direction. The only substantial commerce—in wagons and on the railroad—was military in nature. The army marched through upland prairies, where water was at a premium, and entered county seat towns that offered few amenities. The run-down countryside showed the evidence of war with burned building sites, torn-down fencing, ruined fields and orchards. No wonder locals created a "souvenir trade in human relics" at Wilson's Creek battlefield. The soldiers, like strangers, recorded the "unusual aspects" of a region that was not dominated by commercial agriculture. Given the legacy of pitched battles, armies living off the land, and the outbreak of guerrilla war, "god-forsaken" was the most common description.

Following the war, an irony central to Ozarks history was the emigration of many Union soldiers to the region for economic opportunities. Ex-Union officers became merchants, local politicians, and stockmen in and around Ozarks railroad towns. Principal among these was Springfield.

When formal hostilities ceased in 1865, immigrants flooded southwest Missouri. Agricultural production, manufacturing, mining, and timber economies provided jobs and regional exports. By 1870, when the South Pacific Railroad arrived in Greene County, Springfield assumed a new title, the "Queen City of the Ozarks." However, Charles Piehl described the complexity of local issues during the county seat's postwar years that highlighted the pain of progress in modernization.[17] Key to his tale was the competition in town planning between the railroad town, North Springfield, and the county seat, Springfield, a quiet burg and less robust with its modest town square, located one mile south. Piehl argued that Springfield remained almost as economically weak in the growth of manufacturing and population in 1880 as it had been in 1865. The author recounted how Springfield, a provincial market town poised in 1870 to be integrated into national markets with the arrival of a nearby railroad, struggled against forces beyond its control.

North Springfield became home for shops and was an immediate competitor for new immigrants and investors. Rapid growth encountered inflation, exacerbated by the depression of the 1870s, and continued rivalry between the two towns impeded progress for both. Piehl identified vexing difficulties: low taxes and high county debt, not enough skilled immigrants beyond railroad employees, and high land values and housing shortages for those who did come to Greene County—familiar themes for most boomtown economies.

By the end of the seventies, over 10 percent of the Springfield population had left town. However, in 1881, the arrival of the Kansas City, Ft. Scott, and Memphis Railroad and its close association with the Frisco system brought new trade and demographic growth that finally culminated in the merger of the two towns in 1887, followed by dramatic postmerger prosperity. Piehl's study provided caution for those who champion quick progress from imminent modernization. Springfield, as the region's most influential city, deserves much more study, as do Ozark towns in general.[18]

Railroads bringing people into the Ozarks also brought new organizations, clubs, and institutions, and notably, labor unions. While the Ozarks has long been known as a region without strong unions, Stephen McIntyre wrote about an exception to the rule.[19] Several transportation unions arrived with the South Pacific Railroad in 1870 and the Kansas City, Ft. Scott, and Memphis Railroad in 1881, but craft unions such as cigar makers and carpenters pushed the number of unions to fifteen by 1892. Cigar maker Reuben Wood of Springfield became president of the Missouri State Federation of Labor in 1912.

McIntyre traced Springfield's union reactions to national events. Although workers did not strike during the famous 1877 railroad unrest, populist politicians received notable support in Springfield's northern working-class wards. The expansion of railway economies in the late nineteenth century boosted union membership to 3,000, and the number of local unions rose to three dozen in 1902, initiating a decade-long peak of union presence in the Queen City. Ozark unions had little impact on local political offices, but as a third-party movement, influenced contemporary debates about the future of the city.

In south-central Missouri, elusive visions of rail commerce attracted Roger Grant. His essay revealed that botched efforts in railroad building are also significant events in regional history. They, too, left artifacts, documents, and memories of a future that might have been. His article traced the excitement and dreams of residents in Phelps, Dent, and Texas Counties, the last two entirely lacking market connections to the larger "Ozarks rail grid" and national exchange.[20]

Soap opera elements entertain the reader. Talented promoter E. E. Young boosted an electric rail enterprise, but allowed himself to become snared in criminal diversions of fraud and counterfeiting. "Doc" Perry Herrington, local promoter at Houston, became embroiled in illicit whiskey sales, resulting in front-page scandals. Corporate reorganization of the project for a steam railroad sent grading crews back to work, and the deal included a hydroelectric plant on the Big Piney River near Houston; bad luck followed good intentions when Mother Nature's high water washed out the plant in 1914. Workers did complete Houston's rail depot, and laid a few feet of track at Rolla, but nature's caprice, worse judgment, and a challenging construction project were too many hurdles. A truck line, not railroad, ultimately became a link between Rolla, Licking, Houston, and Cabool. Promotional failure, an important historical reality, rarely receives attention by historians. Grant's example, centered on communities' hopes for rail transport, should provide inspiration for work in the dozens of failed ventures for Ozarks real estate investments, mineral speculation, and recreational and commercial tourism.

Historians have written much about urban and rural conflict, but good will, cooperation, and commercial partnerships are more common. By the 1890s, affluent, urban businessmen and their families traveled into the Gasconade River watershed via the Frisco Railroad, champion booster for rail-borne economies. St. Louis sporting clubs created a foundation in commercial tourism located in the Ozarks backwoods, an exotic setting for urbanites, financially rewarding for resident Ozarkers.

Urban journalists called the well-heeled visitors "true sportsmen." The clubs discovered premier boat-builder and skilled outdoorsman Perry Andres, while the Frisco advertising department anointed Andres as the "Sportsman's Friend." The *St. Louis Globe-Democrat* created a "Rod and Gun" column to follow hunting and fishing exploits, cultural exchanges between urban and rural participants, social events involving both groups, and the urban serial became nationally known for its coverage in the embryonic conservation-minded era.

George Rawlings of sporting goods renown was a leader in the "clubhouse culture" that evolved from an all-male getaway into the nineteenth-century Ozarks to one with women and children in the twentieth. The romantics spent days and weeks in sparse accommodations and skilled guides transported them on the water for float fishing in flatboats that builders quickly refined into stable, reusable vehicles. Lynn Morrow concluded the story with the founding of the Gascondy Club on the Rock Island Railroad that crossed the river and offered a "circle-drive" sporting experience from St. Louis to Arlington on the Frisco, floating downriver to Gascondy and the Rock Island rail station, and later, a return to Union Station.[21]

While affluent St. Louisans reveled along the waterfront world of Ozarks rivers, industrial forces, local Ozarkers, and state government had a different history in the Ozarks southeastern woods. David Benac's study about Missouri's nascent conservation movement paralleled a focus on Progressive-era decision makers and their plans for the future of the marketable forest. He described the traditional uses of the forest in commercial hunting and fishing, annual burning, and as a commons for an open stock range, while showing how corporations exploited the timber, provided jobs, and used the forest as a field lab for progressive thinkers from Yale Forestry School. Whereas the federal government established an Ozark National Forest in Arkansas in 1908, Missouri's competing corporate and local forces for control of Ozarks timberlands kept discussions for a visionary future at the state level.[22]

After the corporations largely cut over Missouri's forests, industry leaders formed the Missouri Forestry Association in 1921. Their secretary, Frederick Dunlap, a professor of forestry at the University of Missouri, became a leading voice trying to negotiate management plans with timber companies and local landowners. However, the industrialists and Ozarkers, and a few vocal proponents for conservation, could not find common ground. As Benac reported, various promotions never effectively engaged locals in common cause; there was no umbrella bureaucracy to sponsor meetings, establish goals, and encourage membership in an association. However, in the 1920s, a new state park system did bring attention to forest policy and conservationists worked to end the widespread woodsburning and overgrazing. But, public support was distant, and faded with the onset of the Depression, leaving the future of stewardship to be decided later.

Back in town, twentieth-century folks who grew up around Pierce City in southwest Missouri heard stories of racial unrest in a dim past. Jason Navarro explored the background of tales heard by high school students in Monett, Aurora, Mount Vernon, and nearby farms.[23]

Navarro tracked one of the thousands of lynchings that have attracted researchers in the last generation, seeking to understand these complicated scenarios that leave deep folkloric and psychological traces in public consciousness. In 1901, over 130 lynchings occurred nationwide, as Pierce City added to the toll. Navarro's article analyzed the context that led to the terror-stricken exodus of Pierce City's two hundred African American citizens in one night.

The discovery of a murdered teenage girl sparked the event. Rewards offered by local banks raised the ante and fueled the frenzy. Law enforcement arrested and jailed two black males, whereupon rioters stormed the jail and lynched one of the prisoners. The frenzied crowd then unleashed a hail of bullets into the dead man's body and nearby buildings, burned houses, and gunned down two more victims in the melee, while terrified blacks fled Pierce City for Joplin, Carthage, and Springfield. When black residents returned days later, white townsmen forced them to sell their property and to leave permanently. Aggrieved blacks filed suits following the violence and destruction, but the courts did not convict anyone or award any damages. Later, courageous widows of lynched men filed unsuccessful civil suits in Jasper County, novel and bold litigation in the Ozarks. The Pierce City episode was one of a cluster of violent circumstances suffered by African Americans in southwest Missouri between 1894 and 1906—their collective exodus left regional towns much whiter than before.[24]

A more favorable and widely popular memory in the Ozarks is the culture of roadside commerce along Route 66. Keith Sculle has written about the national phenomenon of the relationship between automobile travel and place for decades. His essay examined St. Louis commercial ties to the Ozarks via investments in automobile travel and Ozark tourism devoted to travelers' requirements and twentieth-century consumer tastes.[25]

The Pierce Petroleum Company series of complexes, termed "taverns," included gasoline and auto maintenance facilities, as well as lodging, restaurants, restrooms, and bus depots. The first in the Ozarks opened in 1928 at the birthplace of Route 66, Springfield, billed as "the gateway to the Ozark region." A second tavern and large imposing hotel went up next at Rolla, midway between St. Louis and Springfield. The company created a successful advertising plan, including brochures, billboards, and radio, but none so effective and memorable as the architectural styling of its buildings. The popular colonial revival of the era attracted travelers to a "patrician setting" in a rustic Ozarks. A Pennant tavern, one of Missouri's most memorable landmarks, provided a stark contrast to the hillbilly image that had emerged in the regional and national press.

By the Depression, the Sinclair Oil Corporation acquired the system and continued to promote "the famous Ozark Mountain Country" slogan in its tourist brochures. Hard times took a toll on the system, as fewer travelers could afford its upscale amenities, but the Pennant taverns remained as landmarks in the Ozarks "roadside service industry."[26] Like many tourist enterprises, the taverns lasted but one generation. The Springfield and Rolla taverns were razed in 1979 and 1986, respectively. But, in the next essay, we learn about a rare commercial, recreational investment and one that yet remains.

Gary Kremer and Evan Orr tackled a distinctive Ozarks vision in the northwestern Ozarks.[27] In Morgan County, a recreational center, named Lake Placid, began in 1934 when Dr. P. C. Turner and newspaper printer J. M. Sojourner purchased 346 acres. Their idea to serve a black American clientele made them very uncommon investors in the Ozarks. Turner, the primary developer, was a hunter and fisherman and joined the long tradition of sportsmen attracted to the Ozarks outdoors. Similar to resort promotions of the era, they planned the speculative sale of lots near a lake.

A striking aspect of Kremer and Orr's story is the origins of dam construction, far beyond the private means of Turner and Sojourner, who already had a large mortgage on their northern Ozarks land. Turner, superintendent of a segregated hospital, sought help from the Works Progress Administration (WPA) to construct the dam on private property as a "public project" in the severe drought of the Depression. The authors reviewed the Democratic relationships to the Pendergast-controlled WPA construction in Missouri, which commonly spent venture capital for votes, this time perhaps directed at these Kansas City black leaders. Turner's predecessor at the hospital, Dr. William J. Thompkins, allied himself with Pendergast politicians to found his *Kansas City American* newspaper. Investors in the resort believed that Thompkins, a black power broker among midwestern Democrats, had a hand in obtaining funding for Turner.[28] Whatever the case, the creation of a dam that opened a fifteen-acre lake to African Americans in 1937 is remarkable. It is a rare Ozark historic site.

Government influence in the Ozarks occurred in southeast Missouri, too. Dramatic changes described in a Depression-era Ozarks came from Clarence Keathley's personal experience. He recounted progressive efforts to develop schools, public health, roads, agriculture, and forestry, all managed in a matrix of county, state, and federal bureaucracies.[29]

Washington County was "one of the most economically depressed areas in Missouri" despite a long history in tiff mining, predating the Civil War. By the twentieth century, mineral companies provided company housing, "little more than shells with dirt floors," to desperate families grubbing tiff by hand from shallow pits. During the Depression the St. Louis press began frequent coverage of the social problems in the area; by 1939, one-fourth of the county received a measure of state and federal relief. Keathley, a young state bureaucrat, negotiated services and observed the beginnings of what became caseworker assignments in social services.

Public relief combined efforts by the U.S. Forest Service, the Farm Security Administration, the Civilian Conservation Corps (CCC), and local governments. CCC men received medical and dental services, lodging, clothing, and educational programs, while their salaries supported families in the county. In return they planted trees, fought fires, and built telephone lines, but they are often remembered more for constructing roads, building parks, and erecting the once-common fire lookout towers in the forest.

Managers were challenged with the highest illiteracy rate in the state. Children worked the mines and occasionally attended school, but the introduction of a county school lunch program and registered nurses attracted students and alerted administrators who distributed surplus commodities to families. Nurses sponsored public clinics to identify chronic diseases such as problems that required treatment at the Missouri Trachoma Hospital in Rolla. Demand always outpaced staff and resources, but local bureaucrats laid a foundation in trying to improve the quality of life in a very hard-pressed part of the region. Then, everyone participated in and suffered from World War Two.

Transformations of all kinds appeared during the 1950s Ozarks, as elsewhere in America. Milt Rafferty spent a career comprehending historical precedents to become the leading scholar in Ozarks regional studies. Inspired by Carl Sauer, Rafferty implemented methods of cultural geography to explore the Springfield Plain, a subregion within the Ozark Highlands. Tracing tradition, technology, and market changes from the antebellum decades to the late nineteenth century based on data from eight counties, he concluded, as nineteenth-century reminiscences commonly relate, that the earlier pioneer living in the Ozarks was relatively easy.[30]

The introduction of railroad markets after 1870 offered new opportunities with a new era of competitive commerce. In the prairie areas, annual burning of the landscape gave way to fencing and modern agricultural methods, but in the interior hill country subsistence hunting and open-range stock raising persisted in the woods. Land near the railroad lines became more intensively managed by way of smaller acreages and general farming.

A notable feature of the new economy was fruit and vegetable culture that flourished from 1900 to 1940. Landowners planted orchards and strawberries and tomatoes in rockier tracts, sending them to eastern markets via the St. Louis rail portal. Auxiliary enterprises including cooperages and freighting, canneries dotted the landscape, often providing the first paying jobs outside the house to women. Close up to the rail lines, dairies and creameries thrived. Poultry commerce paralleled dairying and, like the canneries, paid wages to women and young people. Disease, drought, and national economic trends spelled the end of significant fruit and vegetable enterprises except near Seymour and Marionville in the 1950s. Springfield continued to flourish as regional nexus in national railroad networks.

Springfield's prominence as a transport hub allowed prairie and hill farmers, large and small, to ship livestock, a phenomenon identified by Rafferty as a significant transition in the Ozarks after World War Two. Farmers converted cutover timberlands to pasture and profits, which gave owners the opportunity for additional lifestyle pursuits, a trend that continues today.

Americans' mobility after World War Two and their quest for recreation brought increasing attention to the Current, Jack's Fork, and Eleven Point Rivers, where the Mark Twain National Forest held vast acreages and the public frequented a handful of state parks. The image of the modern Ozarks had always included spectacular beauty, crystal clear water, and quiet, special places that locals and outsiders alike enjoy claiming as "their own," a personal Arcadia. This sentiment has led members of both groups to leave bequests for their ashes to be scattered in the Current River.[31] Automobiles and good roads allowed increasing numbers of Missourians to visit Ozark waters and to worry about their future.

As the 1960s approached, activists in the national and state conservation movement brought federal proposals to the southeastern Ozarks, where Stephen Limbaugh became a legal participant in a clash of viewpoints about river and land management in the future. The use of eminent domain sparked a historic debate. Condemnation of private property for commerce and transportation for the public good was well known, but serving it for recreation and preservation of natural and scenic beauty was new.

Local residents and conservationists had already refused Corps of Engineer plans for three dams in the Current River watershed. By 1959, politicians and conservation writers made their own proposal—an Ozark Rivers National Monument managed by the National Park Service. By 1964 the preservation concept evolved into the Ozark National Scenic Riverways, but negotiators excluded the Eleven Point from the 65,000-acre plan for federal preservation of the first free-flowing river in the United States. Landowners could sell their property based upon an appraisal; residents could opt for a life estate (the land becoming federal upon their death); or they could do battle in court for what constituted just compensation. The federal government purchased most acreages, but between 1967–1970, attorneys filed condemnation suits on a couple of hundred parcels. Most cases landed in U.S. District Court, Cape Girardeau, where Stephen Limbaugh tried thirty-five before a jury.[32]

Limbaugh outlined the difficulty of establishing a baseline of fair market prices in an area where relatively few property sales had taken place over recent years. Farming was sparse and most buildings had only modest value, but much valuable timber acreage existed as well as sites used for commercial recreation. Calculating "highest and best use" was a severe challenge for attorneys representing anxious landowners. A federal judge tried the first and only case heard locally along the Current River at Van Buren. He awarded $100.00 per acre, a benchmark in subsequent negotiations and trials. The success of conservationists in negotiations for preservation in the Current River watershed proved a model for imitation in the subsequent establishment of the Buffalo River National Park in the Arkansas Ozarks.[33]

The character of writing Ozarks history has dramatically evolved in the last generation, as it should. There is no reason not to expect that improvements lie ahead, as additions and revisions will continue to inform us about our nationally admired Ozarks. When scholars publish books about Missouri's past on emigrant Indians, mining history, the Civil War, railroads, timber operations, tourism, conservation, and federal bureaucracies, understanding the historic Ozarks will play a major role.

Notes

1. Duane Meyer, "The Ozarks in Missouri History," *Missouri Historical Review* (September 1978): 143–149 (hereinafter *MHR*). Additionally, James Olson in his "Local History and the Bicentennial" address to the State Historical Society in 1975 called for "a general awakening to the importance of preserving family records, local and state records"; *MHR* (January 1976): 133. Fortunately, since 1970, local historical and genealogical societies have more than doubled in number, all collecting materials for interpretation. By 1988 Bill Foley proclaimed that "state and local history has won new disciples"; *MHR* (January 1988): 179. In this anthology, authors published nine of the fourteen essays since 1996.

2. The "notion of unity" is from W. K. McNeil's award-winning *Ozark Country* (Jackson: University Press of Mississippi, 1995), xiii. The interweaving of geology and history poses significant regional identity and boundary issues not yet professionally addressed. Arguably, Missourians have traditionally thought of themselves as residents in a particular county, not as a resident of the Ozarks. And, certainly, the citizens in the Missouri and Mississippi River counties do not think they live in the Ozarks. Regional definitions derived from immigration and culture will more sharply define a future Ozarks cultural boundary smaller than its natural one. Historians have contributed few articles to professional journals about Missouri's other regions, as well. For a mature approach to boundaries, see John Alexander Williams, *Appalachia, A History* (Chapel Hill: University of North Carolina Press, 2002), 1–18. The Missouri Ozarks includes some 70–75 percent of the Ozark region, depending on whose boundaries are used.

3. Good places to begin a review of standard works are Vance Randolph, *Ozark Folklore: An Annotated Bibliography,* vol. 1 (Columbia: University of Missouri Press, 1987); Vance Randolph and Gordon McCann, *Ozark Folklore: An Annotated Bibliography,* vol. 2 (Columbia: University of Missouri Press, 1987); and Walter Schroeder, *Bibliography of Missouri Geography: A Guide to Written Material on Places and Regions in Missouri* (Columbia: Department of Geography, University of Missouri, 1977).

4. The two are A. M. Haswell, "The Story of an Ozark Feud," *MHR* (October 1925): 105–109, and John Gould Fletcher, "A Songbag from the Ozarks' Hollows and Ridgy Mountains," *MHR* (April 1951): 252–255. The subject of the former is vigilantes in southwest Missouri that Matthew Hernando examined in his dissertation, "The Baldknobbers of Southwest Missouri, 1885–1889: A Study of Vigilante Justice in the Ozarks" (Louisiana State University and Agricultural and Mechanical College, May 2011).

5. Comments about the Ozark region are drawn from Lynn Morrow, "The Vernacular Ozark(s): Our Placename Revisited," *Elder Mountain: A Journal of Ozarks Studies,* vol. 3 (West Plains: Missouri State University, 2011), 57–73.

6. The Frisco Railway and its permanent railroad towns account for a continuing bias in "southwestern Ozarks history," as urban newspapers, business investors, and travelers had 150 years' access to them and their commerce. The St. Louis-Iron Mountain Railroad in southeast Missouri was equally significant in selected years, but the cyclical nature of the timber and mining economies resulted in more transient institutions (a subject treated by David Benac in this anthology). Cape Girardeau's influence trended south and southwest, and had only minor impact north and northwest into the Ozark upland. Kansas City's influences in the Ozarks came with the Kansas City, Ft. Scott, and Memphis Railroad in the 1880s, but over all, were much less than those of St. Louis.

7. The definitive study on historical image making in the Ozarks is Brooks Blevins, *Hill Folks: A History of Arkansas Ozarkers and Their Image* (Chapel Hill: University of North Carolina Press, 2002).

8. See Vera Zeip, "Geographic Thinking in Ozark Literature" (Master's thesis, Washington University, 1939); Minnie Brashear, "Missouri's Literature Since the First World War," *MHR,* Part I (October 1945): 1–20; *MHR,* Part III (April 1947): 241–265; *MHR,* "The Missouri Short Story as It Has Grown Out of the Tall Tale of the Frontier" (April 1949): 199–219; and Joe W. Kraus, "Missouri in Fiction: A Review and Bibliography," *MHR,* Part II (July 1948): 310–324. *Ozark Folksongs,* collected and edited by Vance Randolph, is in a revised edition in four volumes (Columbia: University of Missouri Press, 1980). Lynn Morrow and Linda Myers-Phinney examined the Arcadian myth in *Shepherd of the Hills Country: Tourism Transforms the Ozarks, 1880s–1930s* (Fayetteville: University of Arkansas Press, 1999).

9. *The Ozarks Mountaineer,* 1952–2012, a notable sixty-year run, ceased publication in December 2012.

10. William Edward Vaughn, "Bill Vaughn's Missouri," *MHR* (January 1964): 140–150, and Leonard Hall, "Wildlife in Missouri," *MHR* (January 1966): 207–215. Hall was a popular journalist for St. Louis newspapers, and both of these articles were annual addresses to the State Historical Society of Missouri.

11. Today, economists locate 36 percent of Missouri jobs within three miles of these two interstate routes, "Highway Construction Could Halt without More Money," *Columbia Missourian,* November 8, 2007. In the late 1970s, I asked senior citizens

in Miller County, "Where is the Ozarks?" They answered, "Down there, around White River," and ignored the nearby Lake of the Ozarks. Robert Flanders put the same question to a retired school superintendent at Pierce City and his answer was the same. Harold Bell Wright's *Shepherd of the Hills* novel still resonated in popular definition for where the Ozarks was located. Modern tourist promotion, however, has claimed a proportionate definitional share for the Lake of the Ozarks. In a larger sense, regarding regional boundaries, the eminent cultural geographer Terry Jordan-Bychkov argued for a core patterning of culture that put the Ozarks in a national context—for him it was Tennessee, the Ozarks, and east Texas in his *The Upland South, The Making of an American Folk Region and Landscape* (Santa Fe, NM: Center for American Places), 2003, 84.

12. For the St. Louis effort, see Kenneth H. Winn, "Making the Case: Using Court Records to Win Friends and Influence Politicians," in *Many Happy Returns: Advocacy and the Development of Archives*, ed. Larry J. Hackman (Chicago: Society of American Archivists, 2011), 279–296. In 1990, there were two local government archives or records centers in Missouri; in the next twenty years, Local Records archivists helped to create or expand some three dozen more.

13. Larry Christensen emphasized sources when he wrote, "Accessibility of sources may be the greatest change in researching and writing Missouri history over the last forty years," *MHR* (October 2006): 46. Additionally, the work in cultural resources management by governments (surveys and reports concerning archaeology, architecture, and history often referred to as "gray literature") has created large repositories for the Ozarks and the state as a whole. Among many are the Missouri Department of Natural Resources, State Park System and Historic Preservation Program, Jefferson City; Ozark Scenic Riverways, National Park Service, Van Buren; Wilson's Creek National Battlefield, Republic; and Fort Leonard Wood, Department of Defense, St. Robert.

14. Delawares and Shawnees had temporary camps and settlements across the Ozarks, c. 1780s–1830s, most notably prior to Delaware Town in the Apple Creek watershed north of Cape Girardeau. MSU archaeologists have conducted several seasons of excavations at Delaware Town and work proceeds to nominate the multiple-village district to the National Register of Historic Places.

15. Barbara L. Green, "Slave Labor at the Maramec Iron Works, 1828–1850," *MHR* (January 1979): 150–164. A recent study of slave hiring is included in Diane Mutti Burke's, *On Slavery's Border, Missouri's Small-Slaveholding Households, 1815–1865* (Athens: University of Georgia Press, 2010). Burke used sources statewide, but concentrated on major river counties, especially Chariton, Clay, Cooper, Marion, and Ste. Genevieve. Bellevue Valley's 1820s–1830s Springfield Furnace and Cedar Creek Forge also await investigation.

16. John F. Bradbury Jr., "'Good Water & Wood but the Country is a Miserable Botch': Flatland Soldiers Confront the Ozarks," *MHR* (January 1999): 166–186.

17. Charles K. Piehl, "The Race of Improvement: Springfield Society, 1865–1881," *MHR* (July 1973): 484–521.

18. More attention to Springfield began last year with Stephen McIntyre, editor, *Springfield's Urban Histories: Essays on the Queen City of the Missouri Ozarks* (Springfield: Moon City Press, Missouri State University), 2012. This work is a significant addition to urban Missouri and Ozarks history.

19. Stephen McIntyre, "The City Belongs to the Local Unions: The Rise of the Springfield Labor Movement, 1871–1912," *MHR* (October 2003): 24–46.

20. H. Roger Grant, "The Ozark Short Line Railroad: A Failed Dream," *MHR* (July 2006): 197–211.

21. Lynn Morrow, "Before Bass Pro: St. Louis Sporting Clubs on the Gasconade River," *MHR* (October 2004): 1–23.

22. David Benac, "Whose Forest Is This?: Hillfolk, Industrialists, and Government in the Ozarks," *MHR* (October 2006): 17–35.

23. Jason Navarro, "Under Penalty of Death: Pierce City's Night of Racial Terror," *MHR* (January 2006): 87–102.

24. For a comprehensive regional study, see Kimberly Harper's masterful *White Man's Heaven: The Lynching and Expulsion of Blacks in the Southern Ozarks, 1894–1909* (Fayetteville: University of Arkansas Press, 2010).

25. Keith A. Sculle, "'Our Company Feels that the Ozarks are a Good Investment . . . ': The Pierce Pennant Tavern System," *MHR* (April 1999): 293–307.

26. It is worth mentioning a Depression irony concerning industrialist and Pennant tavern developer Henry Clay Pierce. In the 1890s he built an $800,000 mansion in St. Louis, but in 1935 administrators of his estate could not find a buyer for $25,000, such was the environmental nuisance in his neighborhood from the city's industrial smoke of modern St. Louis. See Scot McConachie, "Public Problems and Private Places," *Missouri Historical Society Bulletin* (January 1978): 98–99.

27. Gary R. Kremer and Evan P. Orr, "Lake Placid, A Recreational Center for Colored People in the Missouri Ozarks," *MHR* (October 2000): 68–85.

28. Later, Kremer discussed Thompkins in "William J. Thompkins: African American Physician, Politician, and Publisher," *MHR* (April 2007): 168–182.

29. Clarence R. Keathley, "Reflections on Public Welfare in Washington County, Missouri, 1939–1941," *MHR* (October 1987): 51–70.

30. Milton D. Rafferty, "Agricultural Change in the Western Ozarks," *MHR* (April 1975): 299–322.

31. Senator Harry Hawes (1869–1947), a famous Missouri outdoorsman, author, and member of several sporting clubs, began this tradition with his highly publicized funeral on the Current River bridge at Doniphan. In 1954, the Izaak Walton League of America honored him by installing a plaque near Big Spring; a Hawes Campground is nearby, while the former Hawes Clubhouse on the Current River above Doniphan remains.

32. Stephen N. Limbaugh, "The Origin and Development of the Ozark National Scenic Riverways Project," *MHR* (January 1997): 121–132.

33. Will Sarvis expanded Limbaugh's discussion with "Old Eminent Domain and New Scenic Easements: Land Acquisition for the Ozark National Scenic Riverways," *Western Legal History* (Winter/Spring 2000): 1–37, and "A Difficult Legacy: Creation of the Ozark National Scenic Riverways," *The Public Historian* (Winter 2002): 31–52.

Trader William Gilliss and Delaware Migration in Southern Missouri

LYNN MORROW

The early nineteenth century was a time of increased migrations of American Indians on the move west. In the Ozarks, the southern Indian migrations of the 1830s, especially those of the Cherokee, are most well known and often remembered in the region's folklore. But less well known are the migrations and settlements of eastern Indians who preceded the later numerically superior Cherokee. The Delaware, Shawnee, Illinois remnants, and small numbers of southern tribes penetrated the Ozarks in increased numbers during the latter eighteenth and early nineteenth centuries. The Indian immigrants and the Ozarks became a part of each other's history as the Indians' passage left cultural traces in the region. Tribal bands settled in Cape Girardeau District; the watersheds of the Meramec, St. Francis, Black, and Current River country; and groups spread into the White River region and beyond. The Ozarks became the staging area where Indians settled and lived before the Kansas reservations became home to their mid-nineteenth-century generations. The development and naming of the City of Kansas was largely in response to the reservations located west of the city.

Indian migrations into the Ozarks introduced the most profitable trade of the time. As wards of the federal government, the tribes received cash annuities that they spent for trade goods provided by a few white traders. Traders' receipts depended on their diplomacy and skill to monopolize the trade and grow wealthy. A cluster of men, as a result of the Missouri-Ozarks trade, became townsmen and developers in the state. These included the Lorimiers, Menard-Valle interests, the Chouteaus and among others, William Gilliss, a pioneer-entrepreneur of Kansas City where he concentrated his fortune made in the Ozarks Indian trade.

William Gilliss, from Somerset County, Maryland, was borne by a French mother and a Scottish father about 1788. At age fourteen he boarded a ship at Baltimore and ran away to sea. During four years at sea he gained a reputation for physical strength and carpentry and maintained marginal literate skills by reading and writing letters. He entertained himself, and others, by reciting the poems of Robert Burns. In 1806, he left the sea at New Orleans bound for Cincinnati on a keelboat. Once there he began business as a carpenter and builder. Gilliss founded a friendship with William Henry Harrison, who established Gilliss in the construction business. In 1811, Gilliss enlisted in Harrison's command, and apparently spent much time at Fort Meigs in Ohio. Following the War of 1812, Gilliss, accompanied by his mother and brother, moved to Kaskaskia, Illinois, where he immediately became a prominent citizen, purchasing land and building a hotel that was used during the first Illinois legislature meeting in 1818. Adopted the following year into the Delaware tribe, he reputedly became involved in hostilities with the Delawares against the Osages, Pawnees, and others.[1]

By 1820, Gilliss had merchant friends in the Indian trade at Kaskaskia, Ste. Genevieve, and St. Louis. Indian movements through Kaskaskia and Ste. Genevieve lured Gilliss into the lucrative mobile trading markets. The primary markets for Gilliss became the Delaware camps and villages. Associated migrant groups, namely, Shawnee, Peoria, Piankashaw, Weas, Creek, and Kickapoo, substantially augmented this trading business.

The Shawnees, the most common neighbor of the Delawares, shared similar historic experiences in Missouri. Beginning in 1786 with the Shawnee allotment contiguous to the Wyandot and Delaware reserve in Ohio, the Shawnee and Delaware began to have geographical proximity to one another by treaty and grant arrangements.[2] However, members of both tribes were familiar with the trans-Mississippi before 1786. Pierre Laclede of St. Louis had traded with Shawnees as early as 1766,[3] and Kaskaskia merchants had a well-established winter trade with Delawares near the mouth of the Ohio River during the 1770s.[4]

During the 1780s two significant events encouraged the immigration of influential numbers of Delaware and Shawnee across the Mississippi. Louis Lorimier, escaping debts and revenge of the Americans for his support of the British in the Revolution, brought his Shawnee wife, Indian trading experience, and a contingent of loyal and malcontent Shawnee and Delaware to Louisiana Territory. By 1787, Lorimier operated in Ste.

Genevieve District on the Saline River but established himself in Cape Girardeau District six years later. Lorimier received a Spanish grant, and some 1,200 Shawnee and 600 Delaware were awarded a Spanish grant of their own in the Apple Creek watershed. These and other important settlements of historic Indians occurred in the Meramec and James River valleys, on major transportation routes.[5] The Cape Girardeau Indian settlements traded with the Lorimiers and Valles.

George Morgan's colonial effort at New Madrid provided another incentive for eastern Indians to migrate into a frontier trading network. Although Morgan's scheme did not develop according to his designs, it firmly established the New Madrid colony that became an important trading entrepôt. Shawnees, Delawares, and Creeks settled near New Madrid. Moving later into the interior, they established the Muscogee Town complex and trading networks for New Madrid, Little Prairie, and Point Pleasant.[6] These St. Francis River groups worked as stockmen, agriculturists, and hunters who furnished bear oil and pelts to the river trade. In general, the historic emigrant Delaware and Shawnee coupled with the immigration of Scotch-Irish, Germans, and English helped make the Missouri Ozarks region a safe place for new settlements.[7]

Indian removal of Delaware, Shawnee, and others in what is typically called the trans-Mississippi proved to be, in reality, the Ozarks region. The sparse settlement, rough terrain, and abundant natural resources made the Ozarks an ideal "dumping ground" for Indians east of the Mississippi River. Prior to the Osage Treaty of 1808, Meriwether Lewis, governor and superintendent of Indian affairs in Louisiana Territory, gave treaty negotiator Pierre Chouteau instructions that "the land was needed for white hunters and intimately friendly Indians."[8] Over a generation Indians spread throughout the Ozarks followed by traders. Encouraging further movements across the Ozarks, President James Monroe instructed William Clark and Auguste Chouteau "to acquire lands on the west of the Mississippi in order to exchange with such of the Indians on this side as may choose to emigrate to the west."[9] Indian removal policies created an "Ozarks domain" for traders that lasted until 1830.

Eastern Indians and white immigrants, who came to the Ozarks during the first generation of the nineteenth century, were both new settlers. Later written accounts indicate good relationships between the two cultures. The Hancock family in Perry County remembered how their children played with the Indian kids; the Russells in the Belleview Valley reminisced about the "friendly Indians"; Ste. Genevieve entertained the Apple Creek Indians at festivals; and southwest Missourians enjoyed mutual participation in horse races.[10] Only the rhetoric of the War of 1812 threatened this peaceful coexistence. Many whites and eastern Indians intermarried during territorial and early statehood years, which bequeathed a deeply embedded Indian heritage in Ozarkians' gene pool and culture.

After the War of 1812, the Delaware left their eastern Ozarks settlements and drifted westward. While a few accompanied some Shawnee into the Upper and Lower Gasconade Valley, most Delawares moved to the Jack's Fork River valley, James River valley, northern Arkansas, or northeast Oklahoma.

Gilliss, in partnership with Menard and Valle of Ste. Genevieve, established the Delaware trading post on the Upper James River. The locale primarily was dictated by the fact that former Cape Girardeau Delawares had already moved there. The negotiation of the St. Mary's Treaty in 1818 did not specify a particular tract of land for exchange. Officials consulted Governors William Clark of Missouri and James Miller of Arkansas and agreed the James River valley would be a good interim reserve.

In 1821–1822, Chief William Anderson and several hundred Delawares camped south of the Jack's Fork River while on their way to join their

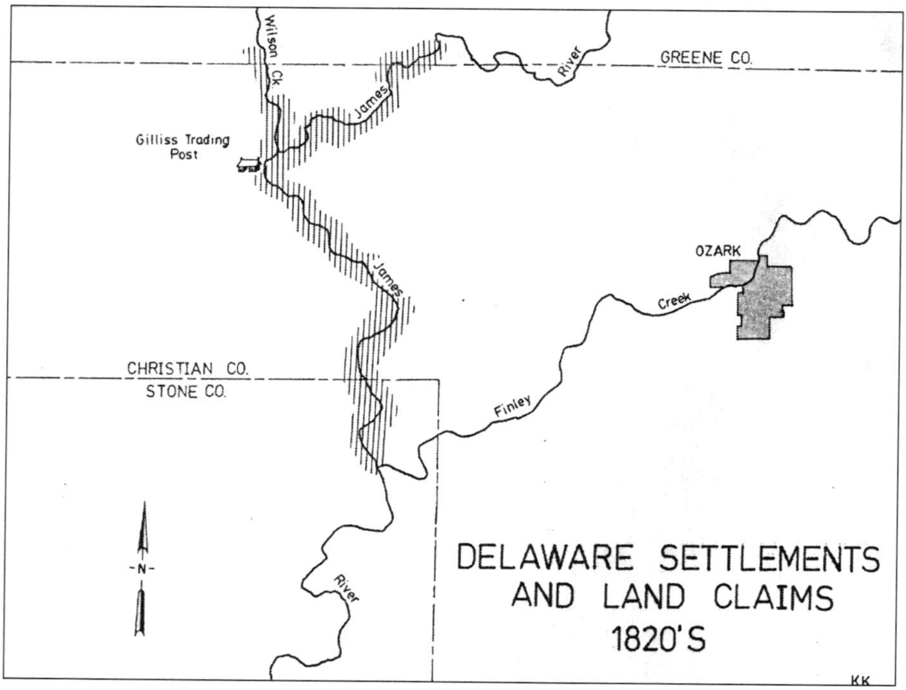

Figure 1. Delaware settlements and land claims early 1820s.
KALEN AND MORROW COLLECTION

brethren in the James River watershed. While there the Delaware fell prey to the usual horse-thieving whites,[11] but more importantly, one of Gilliss's first field expeditions to the Delaware was a visit to Anderson's camp in present Shannon County. Trader William Marshall and Gilliss, both supplied by Menard and Valle, temporarily resided there. Meanwhile, Louis Lorimier Jr. had inherited his father's trading business and followed the Delaware into the White River country. Lorimier built a trading house in southwest Missouri at the mouth of Swan Creek that Gilliss bought in 1822 after Anderson's band had removed to the James River. By 1824, Gilliss's Indian friends began hunting seasonally on the Arkansas and Red Rivers among some 2,000 Delaware, Cherokee, Piankashaw, Shawnee, French, and American hunters.[12]

The Delaware became greatly alarmed at their new location, a "ridiculously small acreage given in exchange for all their valuable possessions in Indiana."[13] Lack of game in the region further aggravated discontent and created continued conflict among immigrant Indians, the Osage, and their allies to the west. However, Delawares continued to arrive in the James River valley, building villages above and below Gilliss's trading post. The Delaware Towns included the largest concentrated population in southwest Missouri until the growth of Springfield at the outbreak of the Civil War. Bands, led by village chiefs, swelled the Delaware numbers in southwest Missouri to some 2,500 by the mid-1820s.[14] The Delaware settlements in the James River valley, northwest Arkansas, and northeast Oklahoma were tribal gatherings not to be equaled after 1829. On the whole, eastern Indian immigrants moving into southern Missouri swelled the regional population to 8,000 by 1824.[15] The immigrant groups, seeking old friends, neighbors, and kin, founded new temporary settlements that attracted traders, whiskey-runners, and squatters waiting to capitalize on Indian improvements once the Indians were removed again.

Gilliss established his trading post on the west side of the James River "up the hill" (Che-wa-y-wek), below the mouth of Wilson's Creek.[16] Down river from the post a mile to a mile and a half stood Captain Ketchum's village. Here lived many of the principals who later gave testimony in the landmark Gilliss probate case. Some of the Delaware women whom Gilliss lived with later resided at Ketchum's, as did John Sarcoxie and John and Henry Conner. John Campbell lived at Chief William Anderson's village. He worked as subagent for Richard Graham, an agent for the office of the superintendent of Indian affairs at St. Louis. Delaware leaders, Patterson, Pipe, Beaver, and Suwaunock each established village sites, too. Not within any Indian village, Gilliss's post was situated between villages. A complex of buildings surrounded the trading post.

Gilliss lived in the north room of a dogtrot cabin, while his black slaves, purchased in St. Louis, lived in the south room. Other buildings included one where slaves Olive and Matilda made cheese; a cabin for Poquas, Gilliss's Delaware wife of 1822; a cabin for hired men; a storehouse for retailing; a large log building for the storage of bales and unbroken packages; and produce cribs and henhouses.

Joseph Philibert, who came with Gilliss as a gunsmith, soon became his chief clerk, friend, and confidant. Numerous other traders, teamsters, hunters, blacksmiths, and interpreters occasionally worked for Gilliss. Philibert proved crucial for Gilliss's trading success from 1822 until 1833 when Philibert returned from "Kansas" to the James River to stay. Philibert transported trade goods west from Ste. Genevieve through Farmington, Caledonia, and the site of modern Steelville to Massey's Iron Works. Then moving southwest along the "great interior highway" he stopped at Jimmy Harrison's by the Little Piney crossing, and rode west across the Big Piney, and crossed the Roubidoux at modern Waynesville. From there he traveled up the Gasconade to the mouth of Osage Fork and on to Pleasant Prairie or modern Marshfield. Then, down the James River valley and across Kickapoo Prairie, the trail ended at the Delaware Towns.[17] When St. Louis replaced Ste. Genevieve as the river entrepôt, this "great interior highway," developed by the Indian trade, continued to be the most important Ozarks interior transportation route. Travel and Indian trade, which shifted to eastern Kansas, helped spell the economic decline of Ste. Genevieve, while St. Louis continued as the major river entrepôt.

Philibert made one to three trips annually for provisions. The Gilliss supply market extended to many river valleys including the Pawnee Fork, Red, Arkansas, Elk, White, Black, St. Francis, and Mingo Swamp. While Philibert ran the James River post, Gilliss and another trader, Boyer, hustled back east to trade with Indians who had not yet moved across the Mississippi. Philibert and Gilliss marketed pelts and skins at least once in New Orleans, and regularly at Ste. Genevieve. They occasionally rendezvoused at Hix Ferry on the Current River and then followed the Natchitoches Trace into the Black and St. Francis River valleys. Here they traded with Illinois remnants and Muscogee Town villages of Shawnee, Delaware, and Creek. Undoubtedly, Philibert and Gilliss took advantage of hospitality offered at a traditional stopover on the Natchitoches Trace, the Widow Harris cabin, some six miles from Hix Ferry.[18]

Administration at the Delaware Towns on the James River did not prove an easy assignment for government agent John Campbell. His management problems taxed his patience and fortitude. Although Campbell visited all the Delaware cabins in the area, he found it disagreeable to board with them. He wanted federally subsidized buildings erected opposite Anderson's village, but the government refused any construction until the Delawares moved to their Kansas reservation. Campbell complained to his superiors about not being paid as an interpreter for the Kickapoos, who visited him at Anderson's village. He ran out of pen, ink, and paper, and when he requested more supplies, he longed for back issues of the St. Louis newspapers to be included with the next dispatch.[19]

The infiltration of traders and squatters all making their own deals with the Delawares alarmed Campbell. First, it appeared "bad policy" for traders to cultivate the Indian land and keep horses and cattle in village environs without paying rent to the Indians. Resident whites and traders cultivated corn on Indian land and sold it to the Indians at exorbitant prices that reached $2 per bushel in 1824. Campbell decried this as a "grand imposition" by the traders who continued clearing more land to support their Indian families. Discouraged from raising corn or stock, the Indians realized their annuities would buy them whatever they wanted. Some Delawares, however, did raise corn, beans, pumpkins, hogs, and more. Traders enticed the Indians to overspend by purchasing goods on credit against next year's annuity payment. Traders who cheated the Indians out of precious supplies compounded credit-buying. Trader John Wilson[20] cheated the Indians out of iron, creating shortages. On one occasion with the delay of government iron shipments, Valle released 300 pounds of bar iron from the Gilliss warehouse for blacksmithing and shoeing horses. Upon the arrival of annuities, political factions within the Delawares divided them. Some chiefs complained to Campbell about unequal shares. Circumstances finally forced Campbell to require William Anderson's signature on all Delaware purchases except for "something to bury the dead" and items for the sick.[21]

Campbell dealt with the whites' thievery of horses from Indians. In turn the Indians stole hogs for food. However, the flagrant liquor sales appeared most vexing to Campbell. When the Delawares settled on their interim land cession on the James River, Chief Anderson permitted some white squatters to remain on their claims, but expelled others. Apparently many of the remaining whites ran a lucrative whiskey and brandy business with the immigrant groups. In 1825, Campbell complained to his superior, Richard Graham, that the Delawares, Weas, and all the White River Indians would "be a lost people before two years." The illegal squatters and liquor traffic proved more than a match for Campbell, who asserted to be powerless without additional help. Campbell ordered two of the principal lawbreakers, a Mr. Denton and Solomon Yoacum, off Delaware land in July 1825, as soon as they harvested their crops and paid rent to the Indians. By the following October, Yoacum had settled just inside the Delaware line near the mouth of the Finley River and had erected a peach brandy still on the opposite side of the line. Yoacum, and a number of "outlaw characters" who settled below him in the James River valley, continued to traffic in illicit spirits.[22]

Competition for the immense Indian wealth often led to charges and countercharges by traders and frontiersmen. During the fall of 1826, trader William Marshall,[23] Gilliss's sometime partner, sometime rival, issued a formal complaint against Gilliss for trading without a license. Gilliss had returned from Ste. Genevieve with Indian trade goods, loaded his packhorses, and "went into the woods to trade." Campbell confronted Gilliss with the issue and replied to Graham that "you have no idea of the high ground this gentleman takes here. He is more than agent." Chief Anderson defended Gilliss, on whose friendship and business relations Anderson had come to depend. Gilliss took his goods to Three Forks of the White River, the seasonal Swan Creek trading post. Then, as later, Gilliss had his own way. Philibert retrieved a license for him at Ste. Genevieve the following year.[24]

Finally Campbell confronted agitators among the Indians. He wrote to Graham: "there is [*sic*] too many persons here acting as agents and advisors."[25] Traders especially promoted their own interests. Some exhorted the Delawares not to exchange their lands again without government promise to pay their debts to the traders; others wanted to be included on the forthcoming land reservations in Kansas; some wanted payment for their buildings; but most Indians promised to support the traders'

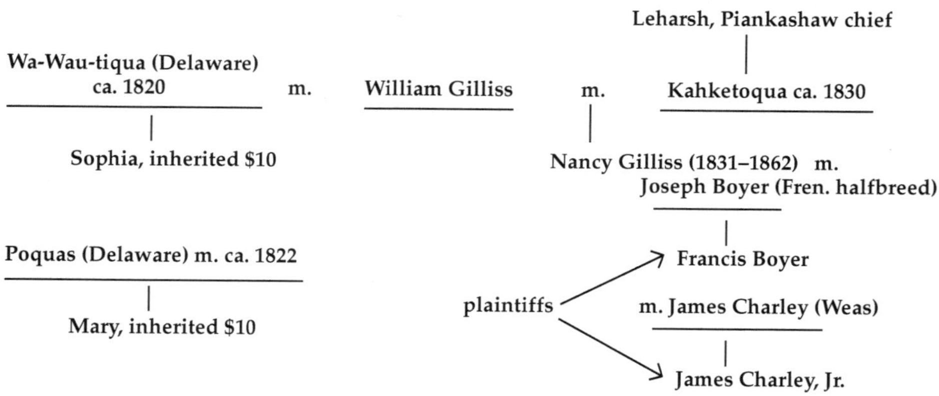

Figure 2. Genealogical basis for the plaintiffs' claim against the Gilliss estate. *Boyer v. Dively,* administrator, Supreme Court case. MISSOURI STATE ARCHIVES

requests, if the traders would continue to help them. With removal of the Delawares imminent in the fall of 1830, Chief Anderson appeared the only tribal leader willing to move. His son, Suwaunock, and others left on hunting trips to Mingo Swamp and the Arkansas River. Months later, some Delaware groups joined Anderson in Kansas.[26]

As soon as the various southwest Missouri Indians removed to Kansas during 1829–1831, Gilliss began buying land in Jackson County. He settled on a thousand acres bordering the Missouri-Kansas line. For the next four decades Gilliss continued his free-wheeling business ventures among the Indians, while he engaged in land and merchant ventures in the development of Kansas City. Gilliss's death on July 18, 1869, proved a significant local event, and one that did not go unnoticed by Piankashaw descendants of William Gilliss.

The half-million-dollar probate case of William Gilliss, contested in litigation for three years, ended in Missouri's supreme court. Attorney Mobillon McGee served the plaintiffs, Francis Boyer and James Charley Jr. The defendants were Gilliss's niece, Mrs. Mary Troost, and administrator Michael Dively. The plaintiffs included half-brothers and sons of Nancy Gilliss, daughter of the Indian marriage between William Gilliss and Kah-ke-toqua. Only Sophia and Mary, two daughters of Gilliss by Delaware women, received any provision in his will other than Mrs. Troost.

The Jackson County Circuit Court established seven issues (which the Johnson County Circuit Court later continued)[27] for the jury to consider in the Gilliss estate:

1. Were William Gilliss and Kah-ke-toqua married ca. 1830; and did they live together as man and wife?
2. Did Gilliss and Kah-ke-toqua have children? Was Nancy Gilliss a child, and only child?
3. Are Francis Boyer, and James Charley, Jr., the only descendants of Nancy Gilliss?
4. Had Kah-ke-toqua and Nancy Gilliss died before commencement of this suit, on October 15, 1869?
5. Did Gilliss, before death, make his last will and testament?
6. Did Gilliss die omitting name and provision for Nancy Gilliss; and did Gilliss die, leaving Boyer and Charley, descendants, unprovided for?
7. Are Sophia Gilliss and Mary Gilliss children of William? Are they provided for in the will?

Despite Gilliss's wishes to be remembered as a wealthy bachelor,[28] and Kansas City's largest landowner and taxpayer, the jury found affirmative all seven issues. The court awarded Boyer and Charley one-third of the Gilliss estate. The majority of the testimony centered on issue number one—were Gilliss and Kah-ke-toqua legally married? Ordinarily, the answer to this question, and many others dealing with Indian trade in southwest Missouri, would be lost to history. In this case, an extraordinary lawsuit, forty years after the facts, recorded a detailed answer.

Testimony in the case centered on companionship relations between the traders and the Indians. The defense, by describing many examples of cohabitation, tried to discount the very possibility that any legal marriage could have taken place between a trader and an Indian in the 1820s James River valley. The plaintiffs' attorney demonstrated, through depositions of contemporary witnesses, the many details leading to the marriage negotiation of Gilliss and Kah-ke-toqua, and the maintenance of that marriage relationship. The court heard testimony from Delawares who had lived in the Current River country, the St. Francis River and Mingo Swamp region, and the White River watershed. Traders who had worked in southern Missouri and in the Kansas City area testified, as well as one of Gilliss's daughters and one of his former slaves. The witnesses firmly established Gilliss as a frontier style sexual free-booter, who used the Indian women for his own gratification and as political pawns in the Indian trade.[29]

Only the testimony of Joseph Philibert continually contradicted the rest, and denied that Gilliss ever had any intimacy with Leharsh's daughter, Kah-ke-toqua. Philibert said, "From the very beginning we [he and Gilliss] were intimate together. We were more like brothers than friends. I was acquainted with his private affairs if he told me the truth. I was acquainted with Gilliss' relations with the Indian women of the tribes with whom he traded."[30] Philibert described domestic relations at the trading post and in the trading business. He enumerated women with whom Gilliss lived, and noted that the Delawares "were not as virtuous as the Piankashaw." He did not know of any Piankashaw having more than one wife, while many Delaware men lived with more than one woman. Indicating the commonness of men and women living together on the James River, Philibert cited Little Jack, a full-blood Delaware, who had a mother and daughter for wives; the war chief, Suwaunock, "had his own cousin, and a strange woman"; and McCullock had Suwaunock's niece and another woman. Above all, Philibert denied any knowledge of Baptiste Peoria's negotiations for Gilliss on the Cow Skin River (Elk River) concerning Leharsh's daughter.[31]

Jack MacLean, a Chillicothe Shawnee, had lived on Crooked Creek in northwest Arkansas with Piankashaw, Peoria, and Weas. He had hunted with Black Bob's Shawnee band and knew Coon Skin McGee, a Shawnee trader and brother of the plaintiffs' attorney. MacLean told how all the traders in the Upper White River country sought Kah-ke-toqua, and how Gilliss won her. Gilliss had been trading on the Cow Skin with packhorses and brought members of the Delaware, Peoria, "Weas and Piankashaw tribes with him when he came for Kah-ke-toqua." Trader A. G. Boone "presumed every Indian trader in the country knew he [Gilliss] had Leharsh's daughter for a wife." Boone, explaining Kah-ke-toqua's attractiveness, described the Piankashaw as fairer skinned than other tribes, wearing more clothes, and being more acculturated to American life.[32]

Peter Menard, the son of the famous Colonel Pierre Menard, who had made his headquarters at the Gilliss trading post, also contradicted Philibert's testimony. Menard explained that Leharsh was "an excellent man, a kind of prophet, from a family of good moral people. Gilliss never could have gotten her [Kah-ke-toqua] as a common strumpet." According to Menard, one or two horses appeared a fair price for a virgin then, but "Gilliss was well off, and knew he would have to pay pretty well to get Kah-ke-toqua."[33]

Baptiste Peoria had been employed by Gilliss as interpreter, part-time trader, and procurer of horses. Later Peoria ran a store in Paola, Kansas, trading with reservation Indians for thirty years. Baptiste stated that there had been a "good many women at the James Fork trading post." He continued that it was customary for the white men to have more than one woman at a time. Peoria had had five or six, but never more than two at one time. The woman's family received one, two, five, or ten dollars, "for a few days or awhile just the same as you [whites] do." Moreover, Peoria had known Leharsh's family on the Black River, Swan Creek, and at the Cow Skin. "Before we came to this country [White River country] Gilliss was after Kah-ke-toqua." While the Piankashaw lived on the Cow Skin, Gilliss had charged Baptiste Peoria to intercede with the old people to get Kah-ke-toqua. The mother, who made the decision whether or not her daughter would marry, said she did not want Gilliss to have Kah-ke-toqua because he would treat her as he did the Delaware women—have a child and then leave. Apparently other kinfolk persuaded the mother, Pah-kong-ke-qua, and she told Baptiste to "go and fetch Mr. Gilliss." On the return to Leharsh's family, Peoria interpreted for Gilliss. According to custom Gilliss gave presents for his bride—a horse, a rifle, goods, blankets, calicoes, side saddle and bridles, and two cloths, one red and one black. The new bride, her mother, and brother accompanied Gilliss on the way back to the James Fork Trading Post. Kah-ke-toqua, her mother, and Gilliss all stayed in Gilliss's house. They ate in the north room and the open entry of the dogtrot in pleasant weather. During all three meals, they ate at the same table. Thus the fact that Gilliss always ate with Kah-ke-toqua and did not openly demean her proved to neighboring Indians that Gilliss considered Kah-ke-toqua his wife.[34]

After removing the Delaware in the fall of 1830, Gilliss helped to distribute rations among the Piankashaw in December, "a time when they were talking about the approaching Christmas." Gilliss then left for Kaskaskia and Ste. Genevieve. He charged Peoria to take Kah-ke-toqua, her mother, and brother to Indian Creek, Kansas. Kah-ke-toqua was pregnant and gave birth to a daughter on Indian Creek. A year or two later Gilliss visited them. Peoria told Gilliss he named Kah-ke-toqua's child, Nancy Gilliss, and he laughed. Gilliss said he would not forget Kah-ke-toqua. In the following years, Peoria occasionally met William Gilliss in Kansas City. Gilliss made inquiry about Kah-ke-toqua and their daughter, and he sent textiles and money by Peoria to them. When Peoria told Gilliss that his child Nancy had married James Charley, Gilliss sent her a half dozen dresses from the Gilliss and Coates store.[35] Peter Labadie, who lived among the Peoria Indians, had been in Kansas City during 1857 and witnessed conversation between Gilliss and Peoria. Labadie remembered Gilliss telling Peoria that "if Nancy needed any clothes or goods [from Peoria's store] to let her have them, and he would make it all right with him."[36]

Gilliss had given closer personal attention to his Delaware children, Sophia and Mary. Accompanied by Gilliss's slaves and their children, they moved together from the James River to Turkey Creek on the Missouri-Kansas line in 1831. Both daughters attended school at Westport and at the Baptist mission. While attending the mission, the children boarded at Isaac McCoy's house. John McCoy and Gilliss were business partners in Kansas City. Gilliss's aunt, a Mrs. Janes, took care of the Delaware children and kept Gilliss's house.[37] Court testimony about the treatment that Gilliss afforded the Indian women and his children proved that Gilliss did not maintain constant personal relationships. The "acquisition" of Kah-ke-toqua represented another Gilliss success in his desire to possess a status symbol that would gain him favor among Indians and whites.

The defense presented testimony that traders did not consider Indians as wives and that prostitution and widespread abandonment of morals appeared the ordinary. Besides, the women became convenient companions who further enriched the traders by sharing their portion of the annuities. Trader Peter Avery said that "most all traders had Indian women, and paid for them in what they dealt in—dry goods, groceries, provisions, or horses."[38]

William Gilliss capitalized on occasions to enhance his commercial interests. At least eight white traders had resided at the Delaware Towns on the James River, but William Gilliss prospered more than the rest. The Indian removal to Kansas cemented Gilliss's career in trade and Indian wardship. Once in Jackson County, Gilliss's business became much easier. With his market concentrated for a generation in a relatively small space, his fortunes multiplied in Westport and Kansas City investments.

The Council Camp treaty on the James Fork in September 1829 and the Castor Hill treaty negotiations in 1832 in St. Louis, attended by Gilliss and Philibert, completed the Delaware and Shawnee abrogation of all rights to improvements and land in Missouri. The federal government awarded $12,000, to be applied to Delaware debts, payable to Menard and Valle of Ste. Genevieve for the benefit of William Gilliss and William Marshall.[39] Gilliss returned to his border trading post, set on a hill above present Southwest Boulevard, overlooking the Kaw Valley, as his Delaware Town post had overlooked the James River valley. By 1838 Gilliss, William Sublette, John McCoy, and others formed a company for the establishment of a new town, which they called Kansas. The first great sale of lots took place in 1846. Buyers included farmers, tradesmen, professional men, laborers, and "William Gilliss, a gentleman, defined as a man with no regular business who lived without labor."[40]

Partly in response to the California gold rush, Gilliss and Dr. Benoist Troost built the famous Gilliss House on the levee in 1849–1850. Old Gilliss House registers recorded 27,000 guests during 1857. The hotel became Kansas City's "first real hotel" and the center of Kansas City's social life until the Pacific opened in 1865. The Gilliss House served as the meeting place for proslavery and antislavery adherents during the violent Missouri-Kansas border trouble. William Gilliss continued to exert an influence in Kansas City development. In 1854, he helped establish the town's first permanent newspaper, the *Kansas City Enterprise*, later becoming the *Journal*; in 1857, he was involved in the incorporation of the chamber of commerce; and two years later Gilliss became a director of a branch bank of the Mechanics' Bank of St. Louis. Gilliss's niece, Mrs. Mary Troost, built the Gilliss Opera House, whose revenues went to support the Gilliss Orphan's Home, a modern survivor on Wornall Road in Kansas City. Near the end of his life, Gilliss performed one last symbolic act: as the oldest citizen of Kansas City, he drove the last spike in the rail of the Cameron Railroad, November 22, 1867.[41]

William Gilliss, as a capitalist in the Ozarks wilderness, founded a fortune in the Indian trade. During the 1820s Ozarks, Indians with cash money provided the major market in merchandising on an unsettled frontier. The trade proved a dependable risk as opposed to other speculation such as land, timber, and mining. Gilliss, the pioneer, turned financier and helped develop a great midwestern city.

A schoolteacher once recalled the image of Gilliss's mansion. She described it as "the great wonder of the town. The white walls gleaming through the trees seemed like marble to us. We could not imagine in those days how anything could be finer."[42] Gilliss aspired to own the finest house in the district, and he did. Indian chiefs, old friends of Gilliss, used to congregate with him in later years at Jim Walker's Indian Store. Blue Jacket of the Shawnees, Journeycake of the Delawares, Armstrong of the Wyandots, and Baptiste Peoria of the Miami recalled old times that brought humor, merriment, and satisfaction to the old men and local onlookers. Gilliss, always seen summer and winter in a black Prince Albert coat, carried a hickory cane with a gold head and spent his later years "in dignified, refined opulence."[43] A local journalist wrote he was "a man of handsome athletic figure, romantic temperament and youthful ardor, it was not surprising that he found charms among the Indian maidens, and by all accounts his affections among them were of a roving and unceremonial disposition." Perhaps Henry Rowe Schoolcraft had the Gilliss-Delaware experience in mind when he stated that the result of U.S. Indian policy had been to "set vampires on the Indians, a set of gentlemen who live off the treasury of the United States."[44] Nevertheless, Kansas City locals thought that William Gilliss had descended from the aristocracy of eighteenth-century Bourbon France.

Notes

1. Newspaper articles concerning Gilliss have been published sporadically. They include columns found in the *Kansas City Star,* April 8, 1887; *Kansas City Times,* May 3, 1902, September 19, 1904; *Kansas City Journal,* April 12, 1909; *Kansas City Star,* October 12, 1912; *Kansas City Times,* August 22, 1916; *Kansas City Star,* November 1, 1925, and *Kansas City Times,* November 29, 1932. All above newspaper citations are located in the clipping file, Missouri Valley Room, Kansas City Public Library, Kansas City, MO (hereinafter KCPL). Unique biographical information is available in the depositions of witnesses in the Gilliss estate case. See Francis Boyer and James Charley Jr., by their next friend M. W. McGee, vs. Michael Dively, administrator of William Gilliss, Missouri Supreme Court cases (January term, 1875), Missouri State Archives, Jefferson City (hereinafter this partition lawsuit is cited as Gilliss probate case). See also notes 17, 27, and 29.

2. Henry Rowe Schoolcraft, *History of the Indian Tribes of the United States . . .* (Philadelphia, 1857), VI: 328. The Louis Rogers "Shawnee Tradition" recorded ibid., IV: 254–256, included a portion of Shawnees living on Delaware hunting grounds in Pennsylvania in the early seventeenth century.

3. Testimony of Pre. Laclede & Shawnee Indians, April 18, 1766, in Ste. Genevieve Missouri Papers, 1759–1876, Vol. II, Indian Affairs #80, Joint Collection, University of Missouri Western Historical Manuscript Collection and State Historical Society of Missouri Manuscripts, Columbia (hereinafter State Historical Society of Missouri).

4. Clarence Alvord, *Kaskaskia Records 1778–1790* (Springfield, IL, 1909), 12–13.

5. In 1809 the first Missouri territorial road, financed by the respective administrative districts, was surveyed and improved. It followed the Shawnee Trail the "whole distance without any deviation from Cape Girardeau courthouse, through Byrd Settlement, Ramsey's heartland, Little Shawnee Town, and the main Indian Town." Survey notes, Col. Valle, Major Haden, and Silas Bent, March 21, 1809, in vertical files, Jackson Public Library, Jackson, MO. See also June Cooper Stacy, *Louis Lorimier* (Cape Girardeau, MO, 1978).

6. See Lynn Morrow, "New Madrid and Its Hinterland: 1783–1826," *The Bulletin of the Missouri Historical Society* 36 (July 1980): 241–250.

7. As John Mathews in *The Osages* (Norman, OK, 1961), 349, pointed out, the "invasion" signaled the end of Osage hegemony in the region.

8. Annie Abel, *The History of Events Resulting in Indian Consolidation West of the Mississippi* in *Annual Report of the American Historical Association for the Year 1906* (Washington, DC, 1908), I: 286–287, footnote k.

9. Paul Nagel, *Missouri* (Nashville, TN, 1976), 87.

10. *History of Southeast Missouri* (Chicago, IL, 1888), 1100, 1113; "Indians Roamed Apple Creek Valley," unidentified newspaper article in vertical files, Regional History Archives, Kent Library, Southeast Missouri State University, Cape Girardeau; various ephemera have recorded the memory of horse-racing by whites and the Indians in Cape Girardeau District and southwest Missouri.

11. William Clark Papers, Volume II, Record of Claims, 1807–1830, National Archives and Records Service microfilm, in NARS Regional Center, Kansas City, MO.

12. Mathews, *The Osages*, 502. The 1812 Louis Lorimier Sr. and 1832 Louis Lorimier Jr. probate cases, Cape Girardeau County Archives, Jackson, MO, are replete with documents that describe the large economic empire of the family, including Indian clients that migrated to the James River. For a fine introduction to Lorimier Sr.'s world, see Herb Meyer, Michael J. McNerney, and Calley Lence, *Historical Background Research in Preparation for Future Archaeological Investigations at the Former Location of Louis Lorimier's Residence and Trading Establishment at Cape Girardeau, Missouri* (Carbondale, IL: American Resources Group, Ltd., November 2002).

13. Abel, *Indian Consolidation*, 290–291.

14. Population figures for 1820s immigrant Delaware in the southwestern Ozarks are difficult to ascertain. See Census of Missouri Territory, November 4, 1816, in Letters Received by the Office of the Secretary of War Relating to Indian Affairs, 1800–1823, NARS, Microfilm Roll 1, 1800–1816; Indians, Missouri Territory, Census 1817, in State Historical Society of Missouri Manuscripts, Columbia; C. A. Weslager, *The Delaware Indian Westward Migration* (Wallingford, PA, 1978), 211; Abel, *Indian Consolidation*, 290; Schoolcraft, *Indian Tribes of the United States*, III, 585, 592; Mathews, *The Osages*, 515.

15. Abel, *Indian Consolidation*, 363.

16. Eliza Bullett deposition, Gilliss probate case. The location of Gilliss's dogtrot house (and complex of associated buildings) is based on Ms. Bullett's comments, which have proved very difficult to verify by archaeological survey. Continuing work by the Center for Archaeological Research at Missouri State University may yet determine a positive location; see Mark A. Rees, Gina S. Powell, and Neal H. Lopinot, "Delaware Settlement in the James River Valley," *White River Valley Historical Society Journal* 41, no. 2 (Fall/Winter 2002): 4–10, 17–23, 26–27, and Sarah Haskins, "The Shawnee and Delaware Indians in Early Missouri, 1787–1832" (Master's thesis, University of Missouri, July 2005).

17. Senator Emory Melton, *Delaware Town and the Swan Trading Post, 1822–1831* (Cassville, MO, n.d.), 11–13. The author is indebted to Marvin Tong, former director of the Ralph Foster Museum, College of the Ozarks, Point Lookout, MO, for a copy of the Gilliss probate case transcript. Senator Melton located the depositions in the Missouri State Archives, Jefferson City, had them transcribed, and used them as a basis for his pamphlet.

18. Archaeologists Dr. James and Cynthia Price have performed extensive historic archaeological investigation into the Widow Harris site, documented by travelers from 1818 to 1834. Its notoriety stems, in part, as a stopover for men engaged in the Indian trade during these years. See Cynthia R. Price and James E. Price, "Pioneer Settlement and Subsistence on the Ozark Border: Preliminary Report on the Widow Harris Cabin Site Project," paper presented to Eighteenth Annual Conference on Historic Site Archaeology, Lafayette, Louisiana, October 26, 1977, and *An Investigation of Settlement Patterns and Subsistence on the Ozark Escarpment in Southeast Missouri During the First Half of the Nineteenth Century, final report submitted to The National Endowment for the Humanities* (Columbia: Department of Anthropology, University of Missouri, February 28, 1978). Hix Ferry is rendered erroneously on maps and newspapers as "Hick's"; however, William Hix established the ferry, c. 1805. In 1823, John Rodney purchased it and in 1828 he sold it to Peyton R. Pitman; see Joan Gould, "*Crossing the Current*, Challenges to Retrieving the Early History of Current River Crossings: Travelers, Ferries, War and Destruction," paper at the Tenth Annual South Central Historical Archaeology Conference, Morrilton, AR, September 27, 2008.

19. John Campbell to Maj. Richard Graham, May 19, 1825, and September 27, 1825, in Richard Graham Papers, Missouri Historical Museum (hereinafter MHM), St. Louis, MO.

20. Captain Martin Hubble, *Personal Reminiscences* (Springfield, MO, 1914), 45–46, reported that John Wilson, who gave his name to Wilson's Creek, also induced voters to name Springfield in honor of his hometown, Springfield, MA. Concern over cultivation of Indian land by traders may be found in John Campbell to Maj. Richard Graham, December 9, 1826, Graham Papers.

21. See John Campbell to Maj. Richard Graham, July 25, 1825, and September 20, 1825, Graham Papers.

22. John Campbell to Richard Graham, October 1, 1825, ibid. This liquor trade resulted in the birth of the Ozarks' famous Yocum silver dollar legend discussed by Lynn Morrow in "The Yocum Silver Dollar: Images, Realities and Tradition," in *The German-American Experience in Missouri, Essays in Commemoration of the Tricentennial of German Immigration to America, 1683–1983,* ed. Howard Wight Marshall and

James W. Goodrich (Columbia: Missouri Cultural Heritage Center, No. 2, 1986), 159–175.

23. William Marshall also had traded with the Delawares in the Current River country. He, like Gilliss, followed the Delawares through Missouri, and to the Kaw Valley, but like Joseph Philibert, Marshall soon returned to live out his life in southwest Missouri, where he continued trading with Indians and whites until his death in 1833. Marshall's published probate case has many primary documents concerning the Indian trade; see Robert Neumann, *William Marshall: Indian Trader of Delaware Town* (Springfield, MO: Greene County Archives, n.d.). James Wilson, a much smaller trader than Marshall or Gilliss, also began trading with the Delawares at Kaskaskia and followed the Delawares to southwest Missouri, but did not engage the Kansas trade.

24. John Campbell to Richard Graham, December 9, 1826, Graham Papers. See also "License to trade at the Three Forks of White River" issued to William Gilliss, November 1, 1827, by Pierre Menard, ibid.

25. John Campbell to Major Richard Graham, December 9, 1826, ibid.

26. Notes from William Clark Collection, 1830, MHM, St. Louis, in personal vertical file of Marvin Tong, Ralph Foster Museum, The College of the Ozarks, Point Lookout, MO.

27. The case began in the Jackson County Circuit Court in October 1869 and stalled until 1872. That year, Mrs. Troost died; Michael Dively was appointed administrator of her estate; and the plaintiffs asked for and received a change of venue to Johnson County. The Johnson County Circuit Court began the case in October 1872 and completed it in February 1873.

28. Norman and Robertson, compilers, *Synopsis of the litigation over the estate of William Gilliss* (Kansas City, MO, 1901). References to Gilliss maintaining bachelorhood are many. For example, Kansas City postmaster Frank Foster claimed it was always understood with acquaintances of Gilliss that he was a bachelor and had never married.

29. The court heard testimony for this case from traders and merchants: A. G. Boone, Peter Menard, John McCoy, William Myers, Joseph Philibert, and Frank Valle. Indian testimony included Eliza Bullet, Mary Gilliss Rogers, John Sarcoxie, Charles Journeycake, and others. Court testimony demonstrated in great detail how Gilliss kept a number of Indian women as consorts or "wives." Considering the anthropological basis for the lawsuit, it is appropriate to indicate some extent of Gilliss's dealings with women. While in Kaskaskia, Gilliss bought a slave Matilda and sired Pamelia and Antoine Gilliss; in the early 1820s, he lived with a Delaware, Wa-Wau-tiqua; in 1822, a Delaware, Poqua, lived with Gilliss on the "Current River," and later on the James River; spring, 1823, he brought Charlotte, a Delaware from the Arkansas River, to the James River for several days; later in 1823 and 1824, Gilliss kept Black Squaw at camp Richwood near Black River Swamp; during 1827 or 1828, he lived with Captain Ketchum's daughter at the James Fork trading post for four to six weeks; summer of 1828, he lived with trader James Wilson's half-breed Delaware daughter on the James River; and in 1829 Gilliss had Baptiste Peoria negotiate the marriage of Kah-ke-toqua, daughter of the Piankashaw chief, Leharsh. The Gilliss/Kah-ke-toqua marriage spawned a daughter, Nancy Gilliss. Her sons, by two marriages, Francis Boyer and James Charley, became plaintiffs in the Gilliss probate trials.

30. Joseph Philibert deposition, Gilliss probate case.

31. Ibid.

32. Jack McLean and A. G. Boone depositions, ibid.

33. Peter Menard deposition, ibid.

34. Baptiste Peoria deposition, ibid.

35. Nancy's first husband, Joseph Boyer, had died. Baptiste Peoria deposition, ibid.

36. Peter Labadie deposition, ibid.

37. Mary Gilliss Rogers and John C. McCoy depositions, ibid.

38. Peter Avery deposition, ibid.

39. Charles Kappler, editor, *Indian Affairs, Laws and Treatises* (Washington, DC, 1904), II: 371.

40. *History of Jackson County, Missouri* (Kansas City, 1881), 396–397, 409. Gilliss's move to the new Indian reservations, relationships with eastern suppliers, and his emerging merchant career on the Kansas-Missouri border was chronicled in *Cher Oncle, Cher Papa, The Letters of Francois and Berenice Chouteau*, ed. Dorothy Brandt Marra, Marie-Laure Dionne Pal, and David Boutrous (Kansas City, MO: Western Historical Manuscripts Collection, 2001).

41. *History of Jackson County, Missouri,* 418, 435–437, 487. For images and more on the famed Gilliss House, see James A. Tharp, "Tumbledown of Gilliss House," *Jackson County Historical Society Journal* (Spring 2004): 14–17.

42. *Kansas City Star,* September 1, 1907.

43. Undated clipping from *Kansas City Star,* 1907, Missouri Valley Room, KCPL.

44. Schoolcraft, *Indian Tribes of the United States,* V: 468, and undated clipping from *Kansas City Star*, 1907, Missouri Valley Room, KCPL.

Slave Labor at the Maramec Iron Works, 1828–1850

BARBARA L. GREEN

In recent years a number of historians have shown an increasing interest in industrial slavery. These scholars have explored the social, political, and economic ramifications of industrial slavery, and they have examined its impact on slaves. Kenneth M. Stampp's *The Peculiar Institution* contains several references to slave use and its effect in industry. Clement Eaton devotes an entire chapter to the emergence and development of southern entrepreneurs and their use of slaves in various enterprises in *Growth of Southern Civilization.* Robert S. Starobin's *Industrial Slavery in the Old South,* to date the standard work on this subject, recounts the extent of slave employment in sundry industries and examines daily living and working conditions of slaves, their resistance and accommodation to slavery and their work routine.[1] However, study in this area, by no means, has been exhausted.

One antebellum industry that continues to attract scholarly interest is the manufacture of iron. Historians have documented the southern iron industry's dependence upon skilled and unskilled labor from its earliest beginnings. Indeed, long before they began looking at iron industries in the antebellum American South, the historian Carter O. Woodson noted that "Africans . . . were the first to learn the use of the valuable metal," and that "the Negro taught the Mediterranean world the use of iron."[2] Since then historians have furnished detailed information about the daily functions of this phase of industrial slavery, especially where the slave has played a prominent role in manufacturing iron.[3] The operations at the Maramec Iron Works from 1828 to 1850 provide a further opportunity to observe this phase of industrial slavery and to examine how slaves fared, according to records produced in the daily operations of this Missouri enterprise.

Although the Maramec Iron Works began its operations with slave labor, its owners never made extensive use of slave workers. They hired only a few black laborers to perform semiskilled or unskilled tasks, and unlike other ironworks in the antebellum South, the black ironworker's role in the manufacture of iron at the Maramec appeared minimal. Despite this limited use of the slave and the reduction of his or her role in the production of iron, the Maramec experience provides a valuable microcosmic study. Many of the characteristics of the slave system and problems encountered at the Maramec Furnace resembled characteristics and problems at other ironworks that operated with extensive slave labor forces.

Thomas James and Samuel Massey, founders of the Maramec Iron Works, were no strangers to the iron industry. The James family had engaged in the industry for three generations. William James, Thomas's grandfather, erected the Antietam Furnace in Maryland in 1764. During the American Revolutionary War, Thomas James Sr. managed an ironworks that manufactured small cannons and swivels for the Continental army.[4] Thomas James entered the iron business in 1810. He ended his partnership with John McCoy and opened the Chillicothe, Ohio, iron store. Prior to that, James and McCoy managed the Scioto Salt Works in Jackson County, Ohio. Over the next six years James acquired part ownership in several furnaces and forges in the state. When James decided to erect an ironworks in Missouri in 1826, he chose Samuel Massey as his partner in the venture. At the time, Massey had eighteen years' experience in the iron business and worked as James's forge superintendent at the Marble Furnace in Ohio.[5] In 1826 the two men traveled to Missouri and subsequently chose Meramec Spring in present-day Phelps County as the site for the new ironworks. Once construction began, James returned to Ohio, leaving Massey to manage the ironworks. Massey served in this position until 1847 when Thomas James and his son, Anvil, bought out Massey's one-third interest in the business.[6]

The year 1828 concurrently marked the beginning of the construction of the ironworks proper and slave hiring at the Maramec. In March, Massey hired several blacks to dig the foundation for the furnace and to quarry sandstone building blocks.[7] During the course of the year, workers completed the blast furnace, refinery, and chafery forges. By 1829 the founder completed firing the furnace. Operations at the Maramec Iron Works began in earnest on January 25, 1829; workers put the first ore in the furnace in February, and the initial production of pig iron came

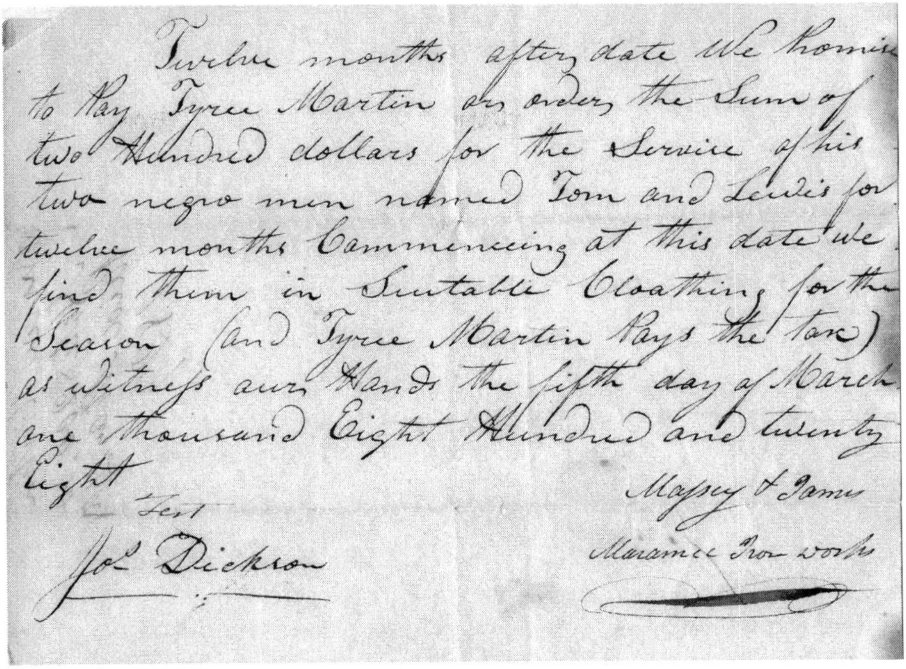

Twelve months after date We promise
to pay Tyree Martin or order the Sum of
two Hundred dollars for the Service of his
two negro men named Tom and Lewis for
twelve months Commencing at this date we
find them in Suitable Cloathing for the
Season (and Tyree Martin Pays the tax)
as witness our Hands the fifth day of March
one thousand Eight Hundred and twenty
Eight

Test
Jos. Dickson

Massey & James
Maramec Iron works

Figure 3. Slave hire agreement between Tyree Martin and Maramec Iron Works.
LUCY WORTHAM JAMES COLLECTION, STATE HISTORICAL SOCIETY OF MISSOURI-COLUMBIA

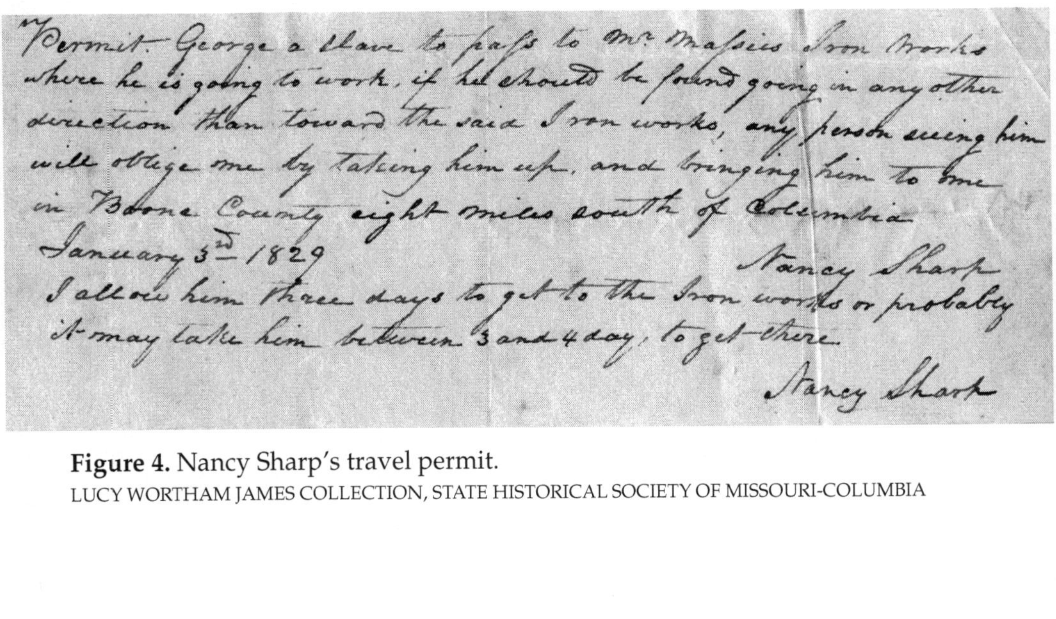

Permit George a slave to pass to Mr Massies Iron Works
where he is going to work, if he should be found going in any other
direction than toward the said Iron works, any person seeing him
will oblige me by taking him up, and bringing him to me
in Boone County eight miles south of Columbia
January 3rd 1829

Nancy Sharp

I allow him three days to get to the Iron works or probably
it may take him between 3 and 4 day, to get there.

Nancy Sharp

Figure 4. Nancy Sharp's travel permit.
LUCY WORTHAM JAMES COLLECTION, STATE HISTORICAL SOCIETY OF MISSOURI-COLUMBIA

shortly thereafter.[8] Bar iron, kettles, and iron supplies for blacksmiths also were produced at the works.

Massey and James then directed their energies toward securing an adequate and skilled labor force to operate the ironworks. James, conducting interviews from his home in Ohio, recruited the highly skilled free white personnel from his Chillicothe Iron Works and sent them to Missouri.[9] In the meantime Massey instructed Charles Eitzen and R. J. McElhany, agents for the Maramec, to begin hiring slaves from owners in the area; these slaves would perform unskilled and heavy work.[10]

Between 1829 and 1850 Massey and his agents completed numerous slave hiring contractual agreements, many of which contained specific terms for those blacks hired. When Tyree Martin rehired his four black men to the works in 1829 he carefully instructed Massey to allow his men to come home for the Christmas holidays.[11] Peter Mason also strongly requested that his slaves be given the customary four days off for Christmas.[12] Two slaveholders, William Slavin and Thomas Tuttle, insisted that their slaves be treated "humanely."[13] Much of the correspondence between Massey and Missouri slave owners offered insight into owners' view of their slaves and the nature of slavery in Missouri. More than one slaveholder described his black man or woman as able-bodied, hard-working, honest, and first rate for business.[14] These positive descriptions are striking contrasts to U. B. Phillips's and Stanley Elkins's descriptions of the slave as lazy, shiftless, childish, dishonest, and requiring great supervision in doing their work. On at least one occasion a slave owner, preferring to hire a couple in order to keep them together, suggested that he would settle for a "fair price."[15] Another slave owner, John Scantlin, appeared not as sensitive in his action regarding a black family. Scantlin wrote to Anvil James about a black woman whose husband was at the Maramec:

> Sir, as my black woman wanst [*sic*] to be near her husband I have thought [it] proper to rite [*sic*] you a few lines[.] If you will buy Mr. Hopkins boy and give me him and $200 you may have the woman and child. Or you may have the woman for the boy and $100 and I will keep the child . . . If we agree I will send the woman and keep the child with me. Ok.[16]

If Scantlin followed through on his plans, the separation of the child from both his parents, even if only temporarily, would be a painful experience for the entire family.

John Hall of Callaway County expressed the concern of many slaveholders when he requested a limited workload and proper clothing for his servant;[17] Nancy Sharp of Columbia voiced concern for her slave's safe arrival at the James furnace. Sharp, acting on word from two of her neighbors, merely had written out a permit for George and sent him on his way. It read:

> Permit George, a slave, to pass to Mr. Massies [*sic*] Iron Works where he is going to work. If he should be found going in any other direction than toward said Iron Works, any person seeing him will oblige me by taking him up, and bringing him to me in Boone County eight miles south of Columbia. January 3rd 1829
> [signed] Nancy Sharp
> I allow him three days to get to the Iron Works or probably it may take him between 3 or 4 days to get there.
> [signed] Nancy Sharp.[18]

She also wrote a letter to Massey informing him of her actions:

> Having received word by Doc't Bennett & Mr. Wall that you would take or hire my boy if I would send him down to you. I have therefore sent him down; be so good as to drop me a line directed to Columbia informing me on what day he arrive[s], in which I would be glad you would make a statement of hire you are in the habbit [*sic*] of giving least some accident might happen. I am a lone woman [and] have a family to provide for, and this is the only negro I have[.] From the best information I have been able to obtain I am under no doubt that you will do me ample justice; don't fail to write as soon as the boy arrives, for I shall be uneasy until I hear from you to know whether he has arrive[d] safe.[19]

By the mid-1830s most of the contracts took these concerns into consideration and resembled the agreement drawn up between Meriwether Bolton and the Maramec Iron Works. The employers hired blacks for a term of one year, from December to December, at a rate of $100 for males and $25–$50 for females. Massey and James contracted to provide bondsmen with bedding and clothing suitable to the weather and at the close of the hiring period to return them home with good clothes.[20] Slave hiring, the careful stipulation of working conditions in contracts and slave owners' continuous voicing of concerns about slaves' welfare prove that slavery in Missouri was more than a marginal institution. Slavery appeared as profitable in Missouri as in the southern states.

Extant sources describe the condition of blacks who arrived at the Maramec. This description included each bondsman's name, age, owner's name, date of arrival, term of hire, and cost of hiring.

The Maramec hired at least eleven black men ranging from the ages of nineteen to thirty for the 1832–1833 term. Most of the men arrived at the furnace before Christmas and were relatively well clothed.

Billy and Harrison, both twenty-three years old, Washington, twenty-one, and Lewis, twenty, arrived at the works with two shirts, a pair of pants, two vests, a jacket, a hat or cap, and shoes, described as "generally good." Twenty-year-old Austin's wardrobe consisted of two old shirts, two pair of old pants, a cap, a jacket, and a good pair of shoes. With the exception of his shoes, his clothes were considered "worn out" and "not much account." Tom, thirty, with the exception of a "good coat," and Harrison, nineteen, also arrived "badly clothed." The wardrobe of Squire, Frank, and Nat appeared in good condition.[21] With the standard cost of hire that term at $100 per year, the employers hired all but two men for that amount; the other two men earned $75 per year.[22]

If the hirelings for the 1832–1833 term arrived with clothes in relatively good condition, the opposite was true of those who arrived for the 1833–1834 term. Most of their clothing was in a miserable state, and only one man, George, had shoes. Peter, Allen, Bob, Dick, Jim, and Martin had no shoes and their few clothes, like George's, appeared worn out.[23] These men also hired out at $100 for the term. The hirelings arrived in mid-July, late August, or early September after harvest. Perhaps this accounts for the poorly clothed condition in which slave owners sent their slaves to the Maramec. They required fewer clothes in the summer.[24]

Women workers at the James furnace received the same terms of hire as the men but for considerably less money. For their masters, Nancy earned $25; Myra, $30, and an unidentified woman, $50.[25] Still another black woman, Darcus earned $20 for a term of six months.[26]

The cost of hire at the Maramec during the 1820s and 1830s appeared quite high in comparison with hiring rates at ironworks in Virginia and other southern states. William Weaver, founder of Buffalo Forge and the Etna Furnace of Virginia, paid $45 to $50 per year to hire bondsmen, with $50 being his upper limit for the best workers. Weaver's hiring rates did not reach $100 until the 1850s.[27]

The Etna Furnace operations, although on a larger scale, appeared similar to those of the Maramec. Weaver's furnace, like practically all southern blast furnaces, used charcoal for fuel and required the hiring of workers to chop wood, haul coal, and mine ore. Weaver's bondsmen, however, also worked as colliers, founders, and general furnace keepers and constituted the bulk of the laboring force. Weaver also conducted farming operations at the Etna Furnace and interchanged slave labor between industrial and agricultural tasks. Weaver's furnace hired from ninety to a hundred slaves each year.[28]

The James furnace hired no more than seventeen slaves, according to surviving Maramec tax lists and census reports. The Slave Schedule of 1850 noted only five adult males and one adult female.[29] By 1860 this figure had dropped to two males and two females.[30]

The Maramec confined slave tasks to one or two phases in the production of iron. Slaves performed most of the heavy manual labor, often working twelve hours a day. Many of the men worked as woodchoppers until white farmers began to perform that seasonal task. Then employers assigned black hirelings the job of mining iron ore and working as drivers or haulers of coal. A few black artisans labored as carpenters and blacksmiths, but the works never employed more than one bondsman as a general furnace keeper.[31] Women at the Maramec usually labored in the boardinghouse where they served as the cooks, washerwomen, and maids for single white men.[32]

Housing, clothing, health care, and food appeared inadequate but typical of that found at most southern ironworks. Slaves lived in temporary huts, which they often built. The dwellings had no windows, one door, log and dirt roofs, log sides, and a fireplace at one side for cooking and heating.[33] Whatever clothing a bondsman received after his arrival at the Maramec often depended upon the slave owner's persistence in forcing Massey and James to fulfill their part of the contract. Available records do not indicate whether slaves needed or received health care.

The slaves at the James furnace received a much more varied diet than those at other ironworks. Basically, it consisted of a weekly ration including one peck of cornmeal, three or four pounds of salt pork, and a quart of molasses. Such food supplements as rice, beans, potatoes, flour, fish, butter, and onions depended upon how near the industry was to transportation facilities.[34] In addition to the basic diet, bondsmen at the Maramec Iron Works enjoyed sweet potatoes, bacon, and beef, with supplements of mutton, ribs, turkey, jowls, rhubarbs, ginger, apples, peaches, tea, and coffee.[35] Despite the varied diet, not all slave owners believed that adequate portions were served. For example, Thomas Horine, of Galena, Missouri, wrote to Massey complaining:

> When Charles came home his plea was that he was not well treated, and that he had been docked since he had been chopping 48 cords [of wood], and that he was allowed only 1/2 lb. of meat per day as to this tale I paid no kind of respect, believing that he was an idle fellow

> and had made it up with a view of getting off from a whipping. John that came in with the boy that accompanied Charles states that he was formerly very well pleased but latterly [sic] they have been very docked in the woodcutting and likewise that they did not have a sufficiency of meat. I asked him if they had no more than 1/2 lb. as stated by Charles, he said he did not know the quantity allowed per week but that it was entirely insufficient to last that time. If it is true that you only allow my boys 1/2 lb. of meat a day you will please add one half more to it and charge the same to my acct. As to their chopping wood I wish them to chop the quantity . . . we agreed upon . . . but not more unless they do it with their free consent . . .[36]

Historian Robert Starobin placed the annual maintenance cost at $85 per slave at the Maramec. Of that amount $36.50 supplied the board or food. The remaining $29 may have been used for clothing and health care.[37] Thomas James estimated that he spent only about $80 per year on each slave, as opposed to $200 a year for free laborers.[38]

Because of the unpleasant working and inadequate living conditions, many slaves protested their plight by running away. Thus, conflicts between slave owners and employers arose. Records indicate that slaves ran away from the Maramec Furnace frequently. In almost every case these slaves returned to the homes of their owners, rather than attempting to escape to free territory. At length, slave owners gave up returning their slaves to the ironworks and made attempts to contact the employers by mail.

One slave owner, Nancy Sharp, wrote to the works repeatedly and finally sent a note to Massey by a friend. She had decided not to risk George's running away again. In a final letter Sharp explained her dilemma and asked that she be released from her contract:

> . . . the boy that I hire to you has come back again and I have wrote to you three times on the subject . . . I now write by Mr. Woods desiring a special answer from you by him . . . It is my wish to take my boy back as it seems he cannot be reconciled to go back to the iron works & if he was to start back I should be afraid I should loose him as I believe he would be shure to run away again . . . I hope you will do me the favor to release me of the contract . . .[39]

Callaway Countians Benjamin Young, William Robinson, Paul Mason, John Holt, and Joshua Ferguson also complained about conditions and treatment of slaves at the ironworks. On one occasion Young indicated that one of his men had returned home ill.[40] Young, Mason, and Robinson wrote Massey and James to find out why their bondsmen had not arrived home for Christmas. Robinson reminded Massey and James that they were still relative strangers in the area. They could ruin their business and lose repute in Missouri by not adhering to the stipulations of the contract.[41] John Holt voiced his anger with Massey over forcing his man, Bruce, to work late at night to keep up with the task done by other hands. Holt felt that he was "at liberty to depart" from the contract and have Bruce returned home with the necessary clothing.[42] Joshua Ferguson appeared equally indignant about the treatment of his slave, Frank, who complained of being forced to work day and night. In a heated letter Ferguson told Massey that he had been hiring Frank out for seven years and had never heard a complaint by or against him in all that time. He charged that the manager and the forgeman for whom Frank worked at the Maramec "had no feeling for a Negro" and that they had "imposed" on Frank. He continued to Massey, "It is your duty to see to it and have it rectified[.] It was you I hired my Negro to and from you I expect justice done."[43] Ferguson sent Frank back to the Maramec Furnace, but six months later Frank returned home sick.[44]

Another Callaway County resident, James Henderson, approached the owners about George, a bondsman who had left the works and was "lurking about Fulton." Reportedly, George was visiting a wife in the area,[45] a common occurrence for a "runaway" slave.[46]

That master-employer conflicts occurred frequently over slave treatment at the Maramec perhaps indicates that conditions at the James furnace were worse than slaves in Missouri previously had experienced.[47] The frequent incidents of runaways also may indicate the lack of an alternative form of resistance open to the bondsmen. The willingness of slave owners to accept their slaves' words about conditions at the Maramec indicates the degree of liberalism in master-slave relationships in Missouri.

Sources on slave discipline and control at the Maramec appear sketchy and inconclusive. Available records reveal the task system as a common method of discipline. The ironworks also employed a daily routine and an overwork incentive system. Allowing the bondsmen time off during the Christmas holidays provided a common means of control and discipline, but Massey and James failed to utilize it effectively.[48]

Cash books, ledgers, and correspondence verify an overtime or incentive system at the Maramec Iron Works. Several instances reflect the use of this system. On one occasion Thornton purchased several items for his wife and himself, including a shirt, shoes, coats, socks, thread, and tobacco.[49] On another occasion Nat received a pair of pants and a pair of shoes for working overtime on Sunday.[50] Cash books also list, from time to time, various amounts of money paid to bondsmen for working overtime.[51]

Records do not reveal the punishment of slaves at the James furnace. By reading correspondence, however, one can infer that the Maramec Iron Works used whipping as a method of punishment.[52] Likewise, employers did not report group slave revolts or resistance at their company. In fact, not one surviving source notes a slave death at the Maramec.

A final point to be reconciled is why James consistently hired free white labor before 1850. The labor force at the Maramec Iron Works was integrated from the beginning of its operations and was comprised of whites almost completely by 1850. At least three reasons account for James's actions.

The cost of hiring slaves at the Maramec Furnace proved erratic after 1832. Fees ranged from $25 to $125 for women, and between $30 and $150 for men.[53] The law of supply and demand, in part, contributed to this fluctuation in prices. Labor shortages confronted Missourians throughout the antebellum period. Slave labor increasingly became scarce, and the purchasing of slaves proved expensive.[54] In 1839 Massey found it difficult to hire slaves at a "reasonable price," and purchased three black men outright for a total of $2,040. He paid $550 for Solomon; $640 for Thornton; and $850 for Tim.[55] By the 1840s male slaves between the ages of eighteen and twenty-five sold for $150 to $500, while the price of female slaves between the ages of fifteen and twenty-two ranged from $375 to $600.[56]

In addition, James desired to hire white laborers to maintain a competitive advantage, or monopoly, in Missouri's iron business. He believed that highly skilled white workers would increase the general efficiency and profitability of the ironworks. James began hiring free laborers as early as 1829, and by 1831 white farmers and German immigrants steadily began replacing black slave workers.[57] This fact influenced directly the cost of hiring or purchasing slaves at the Maramec.

In addition, slave owners' growing reluctance to hire out their slaves affected Thomas James's decision to engage white workers. Living and working conditions and the high incidence of runaways prompted slave owners to seek employment of their bondsmen elsewhere.

By 1850 Missourians experienced an even greater shortage of labor. Along with this shortage came a deficiency of capital, and employers at the Maramec Iron Works found it almost impossible to hire or purchase slaves. Up until then the ironworks had operated with a degree of elasticity, shifting from slave to free labor, depending upon the availability of white laborers and the cost of slave workers. By 1850 this practice had become impractical, and slave hiring and slave labor ceased at the Maramec Iron Works.

It becomes apparent after examining slave labor at the James furnace that this phase of industrial slavery was not contingent upon the quantity of slaves used in the production of iron. Only a small number of bondsmen worked at Maramec while greater numbers of slaves toiled at the other southern ironworks. Whether small or large numbers were worked, certain parallels existed and all of the ironworks suffered the same ills. Working and living conditions appeared comparable. The Maramec had problems with runaways. Its methods of slave control and discipline simulated those at other ironworks where owners had to contend with irate slave owners. Thus, the slave system at the Maramec Iron Works differed from other southern ironworks only in the degree to which its operations were run with slave labor.

Definitive conclusions about the nature of industrial slavery in Missouri cannot be drawn from this study. The incomplete and arbitrary records of the ironworks allow little insight into the slaves own reaction to their bondage. Only a limited view of master-slave relationships may be evidenced from the standpoint of the slaveholders who, while expressing concern for humanity, actually were more concerned about property. Additionally, only an inference regarding the employer-slave relationship can be gained from the correspondence between the slave owners and slave employer. Yet, the surviving sources do allow the reconstruction of the daily operations and the use of slave labor at the Maramec Iron Works.

Notes

1. Kenneth M. Stampp, *The Peculiar Institution: Slavery in the Antebellum South* (New York: Knopf, 1956), 64, 72, 84, 147; Clement Eaton, *The Growth of Southern Civilization, 1790–1860* (New York: Harper and Row, 1963), 221–246; Robert S. Starobin, *Industrial Slavery in the Old South* (New York: Oxford University Press, 1970).

2. Carter O. Woodson, *The Negro in Our History* (Washington, DC: Associated Publishers, 1927), 8.

3. Starobin, *Industrial Slavery;* Charles B. Dew, "David Ross and the Oxford Iron Works: A Study of Industrial Slavery in the Early Nineteenth-Century South," *William and Mary Quarterly* 31 (April 1974): 189–224; and Charles B. Dew, "Disciplining Slave Ironworkers in the Antebellum South: Coercion, Conciliation, and Accommodation," *American Historical Review* 79 (April 1974): 398–418.

4. James D. Norris, *Frontier Iron: The Maramec Iron Works, 1826–1876* (Madison: State Historical Society of Wisconsin, 1964), 14.

5. Ibid., 15–21.

6. Ibid.

7. Agreement between Tyree Martin and Massey and James Maramec Iron Works, March 5, 1828, folder 1469, and Anderson Wood and Samuel Massey, March 26, 1829, folder 1473, in Lucy Wortham, James Collection, State Historical Society of Missouri Manuscripts Collection-Columbia (hereinafter cited as James Collection).

8. Maramec Iron Works Record Book, 1829–1840, folder 117, in Clair V. Mann Collection, State Historical Society of Missouri Manuscripts Collection-Columbia (hereinafter cited as Mann Collection).

9. Samuel R. Finley to Samuel Massey, June 23, 1829, folder 1476, and August Marshall to Samuel Massey, May 18, 1835, folder 1503, in James Collection; Norris, *Frontier Iron*, 37.

10. Charles Eitzen was a wealthy merchant and Republican political leader in Hermann. He made a fortune in the Missouri river trade shipping Ozarks yellow pine lumber and Maramec iron to Booneslick counties, as well as down the Missouri River; *History of Franklin, Jefferson, Washington, Crawford & Gasconade Counties, Missouri* (Chicago: Goodspeed Publishing Company, 1888), 1081; Robert. J. McElhany earned a fortune as a merchant in Springfield, becoming postmaster, a militia major, and bank president; Return I. Holcomb, *History of Greene County, Missouri* (St. Louis: Western Historical Company, 1883), 785–786.

11. Foster Martin to Samuel Massey, October 27, 1829, folder 1477, in James Collection.

12. Peter Mason to [Samuel Massey], July 17, 1834, folder 1498, in ibid.

13. Thomas Tuttle to Samuel Massey, December 27, 1828, and William Slavin to S. Massey, December 27, 1828, both in folder 10, Mann Collection.

14. Rebecca Nichols to S. Massey, October 20, 1828, folder 1472; Anderson Wood to Samuel Massey, March 26, 1829, folder 1473, and July 14, 1829, folder 1476; R. A. Ewing to S. Massey, January 6, 1830, folder 1478; James Barnes to Samuel Massey, September 21, 1832, folder 1489; and Jane Peery to Abram James, December 14, 1843, folder 1555, all in James Collection.

15. Thomas W. Conyers to Massey and James, July 17, 1828, folder 1470, ibid.

16. John Scantlin to Anvil James, April 5, 1849, folder 56, Mann Collection.

17. Anderson Wood to Samuel Massey, August 18, 1829, folder 1477, and John Hall to Samuel Massey, undated, both in James Collection; William Nash to Samuel Massey, December 20, 1828, William Slavin to Samuel Massey, December 27, 1828, Thomas Tuttle to Samuel Massey, December 27, 1828, all in folder 10, Mann Collection.

18. [Travel) permit, January 3, 1829, by Nancy Sharp, folder 1473, James Collection.

19. Nancy Sharp to Samuel Massey, January 3, 1829, folder 1473, ibid.

20. Agreement between Meriwether Bolton and Iron Works, December 27, 1832, folder 1241, ibid. At the time, Meriwether Lewis Bolton was building an extraordinary stone Greek Revival mansion, completed c. 1833, overlooking the Osage River near modern Wardsville. The house is on the National Register of Historic Places, file in Missouri State Archives, Jefferson City.

21. Maramec Iron Works Record Book, 1829–1840, folder 117, Mann Collection.

22. Ibid.

23. Ibid.

24. Ibid.

25. Thomas Tuttle to Samuel Massey, December 27, 1828, folder 10; agreement between William Welden and Maramec Iron Works, April 22, 1831, folder 117, both in Mann Collection; agreement between Meriwether Bolton and Iron Works, December 27, 1832, folder 1241, in James Collection.

26. Agreement between Ruth Luper and Massey and James, March 10, 1831, folder 117, Mann Collection.

27. Dew, "Disciplining Slave Ironworkers in the Antebellum South," 398.

28. Ibid., 396–397.

29. Tax Lists for 1834, 1835, and 1838, in folder 1496, 1500, and 1513, respectively, James Collection; U.S. Census, 7th Report, 1850, Slave Schedule, "Crawford County, Missouri," 175.

30. U.S. Census, 8th Report, 1860, Slave Schedule, "Phelps County, Missouri," 577.

31. Jane A. Thompson to James, December 28, 1843, folder 1555, James Collection; Norris, *Frontier Iron*, 39.

32. Norris, *Frontier Iron*, 39.

33. Ibid., 43.

34. Starobin, *Industrial Slavery*, 50–53.

35. Cash Book, vol. 11, September 27, 1847–July 31, 1849, pp. 6–8, 10–14; Ledger, vol. 14, August 1, 1849–January 12, 1850, p. 54; Ledger, vol. 18, January 1, 1851–January 31, 1852, p. 118; Ledger, vol. 126, February 1, 1844–July 29, 1845, pp. 200–203; Ledger, vol. 128, December 14, 1847–March 31, 1849, pp. 281–364; Ledger, vol. 138, August 1, 1850–September 30, 1852, pp. 82–83, 458, 539, 558, 582; all in James Collection.

36. Thomas M. Horine to Massey and James, July 23, 1829, folder 11, Mann Collection.

37. Starobin, *Industrial Slavery*, 296.

38. Norris, *Frontier Iron*, 40.

39. Nancy Sharp to Samuel Massey, June 10, 1829, folder 1475, James Collection.

40. B. Young to Samuel Massey, May 5, 1829, ibid.

41. Benjamin Young to [Samuel Massey], January 1, 1835, folder 1500, Paul Mason to Samuel Massey, July 17, 1834, folder 1498, and William Robinson to Massey and James, December 28, 1843, folder 1555, all in ibid.

42. John Holt to Samuel Massey, July 31, 1829, folder 1476, ibid.

43. Joshua Ferguson to Samuel Massey, January 16, 1831, folder 18, Mann Collection.

44. Ibid., June 22, 1831, folder 19, Mann Collection.

45. James S. Henderson and Co. to Samuel Massey, May 7, 1835, folder 1503, James Collection.

46. Starobin, *Industrial Slavery*, 83. Diane Mutti Burke's *On Slavery's Border, Missouri's Small Slaveholding Households, 1815–1865* (Athens: University of Georgia Press, 2010), chapter 5, includes a significant discussion of marriage and family.

47. Ibid., 111.

48. Ibid., 75–115; Dew, "Disciplining Slave Ironworkers in the Antebellum South," 406–411.

49. Day Book, vol. 45, October 1, 1845–February 7, 1849, James Collection.

50. Le[d]ger, vol. 122, May 1, 1833–December 25, 1834, p. 527, in ibid.

51. Cash Book #2, pp. 143, 230, and Cash Book, vol. 82, January 1, 1853–May 31, 1856. See also Wood Book, vol. 71, December 26, 1828–November 24, 1829, and Anderson Wood to Samuel Massey, March 26, 1829, all in James Collection.

52. Thomas M. Horine to Massey and James, July 23, 1829, folder 11, Mann Collection.

53. Journal B, vol. 3 [cash book #3], March 10, 1831–April 30, 1833, pp. 408–409; Ledger D, vol. 6 [cash book #6], May 1, 1833– December 31, 1840, p. 36, both in James Collection.

54. Lee Meriwether, "Labor and Industry in Missouri During the Last Century," *Missouri Historical Review* 15 (October 1920): 163–175; Walter Houf, "Fifty Years of Missouri Labor, 1820–1870" (Master's thesis, University of Missouri-Columbia, 1958).

55. Store Account-Boonville, August 10, 1839, f. 32, Mann Collection.

56. John Calvert to G. P. Hardy, 8 September 1844, f. 44, ibid.

57. Norris, *Frontier Iron,* 15–22, 41.

"Good Water & Wood but the Country Is a Miserable Botch"

Flatland Soldiers Confront the Ozarks

JOHN F. BRADBURY JR.

Professor William Shea has examined the image of Arkansas during the Civil War in a perceptive essay entitled "A Semi-Savage State." After studying hundreds of Yankee accounts, Shea concluded that Arkansas did not meet the standards of volunteers who compared it to their own agricultural homelands in the Midwest. Their largely negative impressions still affect the state's reputation today. In this essay Shea concerned himself only with Arkansas; however, to get there, Union troops marched through southern Missouri. By geographical extension many of Shea's observations about Union soldiers in Arkansas, especially regarding their reactions to the landscape, also apply to the Ozarks of Missouri.[1]

As in Shea's study, the sources for reactions to the Missouri Ozarks include hundreds of letters, diaries, newspaper accounts, and reminiscences by United States volunteers who served in the hills. The sources prove especially rich for the first two years of the war, when the region was the most strategically critical and both sides committed their greatest efforts to the area. Despite rugged terrain that impeded military operations, thousands of Union soldiers in the Army of Southwest Missouri and the Army of the Frontier marched to the battlefields of Pea Ridge and Prairie Grove. By the time they were drawn off to other theaters, midwestern volunteers in four Union armies ultimately had triangulated all of southwestern Missouri and had reached as far south as Fayetteville and Van Buren, Arkansas. The men traveled nearly all of those miles on foot, giving them plenty of opportunity to study the terrain and express their opinions of the landscape. The men appreciated the extensive oak and pine forests and abundant springs of clear water, but as it did in Arkansas, the novelty of the wilderness hill country soon wore off.

The greatest number of Union troops moved into the Ozark Highland from St. Louis and three railroads ending at Ironton, Rolla, and Sedalia. As the fighting developed along the western flank of the Ozarks between Springfield, Missouri, and Fayetteville, Arkansas, the direct military line from St. Louis through Rolla into southwestern Missouri became the main artery of federal control. The road followed an old path from St. Louis known to geographers as the interior ridge route through the northern Ozarks. In the 1830s it had served as the state road from St. Louis to Springfield and was the northern branch of the Trail of Tears. The Frisco and Burlington Northern Railroads have followed the same corridor across the Ozark Highland, as have Route 66 and Interstate 44. The route passed along the divide between watersheds, through terrain densely covered with oaks, relatively level but poorly watered, and disappointing to travelers who looked for Ozark "mountains." Southwest of St. Louis, the road crossed stony ridges and unremarkable post oak and prairie flats that did not always present the area in its best light.[2]

The volunteers spent the first one hundred miles of the journey from St. Louis aboard trains of the Southwest Branch of the Pacific Railroad, following the ridge path to its railhead at Rolla. Before stepping off the cars at the Rolla depot, the troops had passed through miles of rough and undeveloped country. The rocks along the railroad line impressed one Iowa soldier, who wrote: "Every formation described in geology here has its representative, apparently. There were red, blue, black, gray, yellow, white, green, purple, speckled, brindled, and porphyritic rocks . . . it is an awful mean country, Missouri is." Other soldiers called it desolate, "rantankerous, half-manufactured" territory "hardly worth fighting for," with soil "shallow and strong," and "poor enough to starve a cat." An Iowa infantryman expressed similar sentiments, "Of all the unearthly, desolated regions, this takes the palm." Still another Iowan who stepped off the train stated his considered opinion: "I am very much disappointed in Missouri, so far as I have seen it. Of all the God-forsaken countries, this is the worst. The whole section of the country, from St. Louis to here, is not worth the life of a single northern soldier, and were it not for the vital principles involved, would not pay for half an hour's defense. As our good-natured Major remarked the other day, it is an absolute crime to kill a secesh in this part, for no greater punishment could be inflicted on him, than to compel him to live here."[3]

Situated on the ridge route equidistant from St. Louis and Springfield, the railhead town of Rolla was barely old enough to be strategically important. No one had lived in the immediate area prior to 1845, although the Maramec Iron Works had opened in 1829 only a few miles to the east. Railroad construction along the interior ridge route resulted in the creation of Phelps County in 1857, with the designation of Rolla as the county seat. The town's military significance derived from the fortuitous circumstances that left it as the terminus of the Southwest Branch from 1860 to 1866 and the counterclockwise progression of the first half of the war in the Ozarks. Thousands of Union troops passed through the railhead during the war because of its position on the federal line of communications. But anyone expecting an impressive town at this strategic spot was disappointed, and it was a rare soldier who had a kind word for the place. An Irish volunteer in the Seventh Missouri Infantry, sent as a reinforcement to the railhead, grumbled, "We have been very fortunate in getting good quarters, until we came to this God-forsaken place." Another Missouri soldier described the location as "a poor post oak ridge, worn bare by soldiers of everything but roots." A former printer turned infantryman from Bloomington, Illinois, told readers of the hometown newspaper: "Rolla was a Peruvian chieftain who was killed by Pizarro. If Pizarro were here now, Rolla would kill him."[4]

The four-year-old town of about six hundred citizens sported a motley collection of seventy-five unpainted buildings scattered along the railroad tracks in what one soldier said resembled "the effects of a recent earthquake." The new two-story brick courthouse and county jail were the only buildings of any note. Siege guns in an earthen fortification overlooked everything. The army's log headquarters building was usually awash in a sea of choking dust or churned mud. A newspaper correspondent who stepped off into mud at the depot said, "There was the feeling that the place was a mortar bed and the inhabitants were preparing to make bricks." Rolla had "miserable" hotel accommodations, mixed with a collection of "oyster shops, eating houses, and other traps for the hard earned wages of the soldier." Looking closer, the men found it "mean and dirty" and every other door marked "saloon." The town looked busy enough: freight and forage were stockpiled everywhere, dozens of the army's quartermaster and commissary warehouses lined the tracks, and hundreds of horses and mules occupied the government's corrals or pulled ponderous supply wagons through the streets. But it was a warborn flush; the army created the only business. Take away the war, said an Iowa City soldier in 1862, and Rolla was "an exotic without the surrounding to support it."[5]

Most of the troops ultimately marched out of Rolla toward Springfield. Initially level, the land becomes increasingly rugged at the crossings of the Little Piney, Big Piney, Roubidoux, and Gasconade, all of which notch through the ridge trail. Marching up and down the Gasconade hills, the soldiers invariably thought it the poorest, roughest country they had ever seen and the spring-fed streams the coldest and clearest they had ever waded. For infantrymen toiling along the primitive road, the Ozarks provided a monotonous panorama of "scrub-oaks, up hill, limestone rocks; down hill, creeks, deserted cabins." Iowan Nathan King called it "Opossum Country" and claimed that there were not two acres of tillable ground within five miles. On the whole, said an Illinois infantryman, the region was "a miserable, rough, rocky, broken, worthless wilderness" and remarked that "what ever induced these people to locate in this wilderness is more than I can conceive."[6]

The troops marched through the "miserable" village of Waynesville, said to be one of those places necessary "for horse racing, quarrels & fights and where bad whiskey and poor tobacco is offered for sale at reasonable prices for approved credit or country produce." By the middle of 1862, a garrison of federal volunteers and local militia entirely occupied the town's score of buildings and the brick courthouse. The armies did not linger long, but a few soldiers did take time to explore the springs and "curiosities" in the caves along Roubidoux Creek and the Gasconade River, leaving their names "in haunts never tread by human foot." The huntsmen found the abundance of wild game impressive, and one Illinois soldier saw his first wild turkeys. West of the Gasconade the country becomes gentler as the road ascends the Springfield Plain. The volunteers reported occasional patches of good land, "seldom interspersed with the beauty given to them by the enterprise of a thriving community of men," but judged only a tenth of the land fit for agriculture.[7]

Fifty-five miles west of Rolla the soldiers discovered Lebanon, the seat of Laclede County, a town so alternately plundered by both sides as early as the beginning of 1862 that it was entirely destitute of even the most common domestic goods. According to Iowa captain Henry Ankeny, "Lebanon has been a better town than Rolla was when we first went there, but all now is gone for a generation to come." Colonel E. A. Carr warned General Samuel Curtis that he and his staff "must not expect the luxuries of Rolla" when they arrived in Lebanon. One of Curtis's infantrymen found the town especially cheerless in January 1862: "The streets are a gore of mud, the houses mostly dilapidated and scattered, and presenting a dismal and ominous appearance when visited on a cold cheerless, sunless winter day."[8]

Nine months later, the other climatological extreme prevailed in the drought-stricken hills. Away from the Gasconade, good water was scarce on the ridge road, and this caused long, dry marches between campsites. Parched soldiers straggling into Lebanon had to skim the scum from the only pond that had not dried up. Finally, twelve miles east of Springfield at Mill Springs, thirsty marchers found plenty of fresh water.[9]

At Springfield the troops arrived at the gateway to the Southwest and the first town worthy of the designation within two hundred miles on the ridge road from St. Louis. The town developed in the 1830s at the intersection of the St. Louis Road with the all-important avenue (later the Telegraph or "Wire" Road) linking settlements on the Missouri and Arkansas Rivers. Soon, Springfield developed a thriving regional trade based on the agricultural fertility of the Kickapoo and Grand Prairies that border the city to the west and the north. Its trade associations extended through Fayetteville to the Arkansas River at Van Buren and Fort Smith, the White River via Forsyth, and the Missouri River via Bolivar, Warsaw, and Cole Camp. Commercial connections to St. Louis passed through the Missouri River towns until construction of the Southwest Branch Railroad commenced in the mid-1850s. By 1861 Springfield boasted nearly two thousand citizens in several hundred buildings around the Greene County Courthouse, with churches, a female academy, a bank, blacksmith and machine shops, wagon and harness manufactories, and merchants offering the latest variety of goods. The soldiers liked the place; "pretty" is the word most often used in their diaries and letters. Even Major William G. Thompson, who called the country in the Gasconade hills "God-forsaken," wrote to his wife, "The truth is I would like to live in Springfield."[10]

In June 1861, German soldiers in Nathaniel Lyon's flanking column, known as the "Southwest Expedition," were the first U.S. troops to enter Springfield and also the last to see the town in pristine condition. After changing hands before its permanent occupation by federal forces in February 1862, the town became the principal military depot in southwest Missouri and northwest Arkansas. Soldiers arriving later found the army using the public buildings for headquarters and offices, the provost marshal occupying a church, and prisoners filling the courthouse and the female academy. Four earthen artillery fortifications ringed the town. But, like Rolla, Springfield flourished in an unnatural way. Government wagons, teams, soldiers, and refugees thronged the streets; recruiting broadsides plastered the public square; and every man of military age either wore the insignia "U.S." or was guarded by one who did. A *New York Times* correspondent characterized the traffic in August 1862: "The public square is crowded almost constantly with army wagons. The arrival and

Figure 5. A public funeral on the square of Springfield honored soldiers who died as a result of Major Charles Zagonyi's charge. Union soldiers burned the old courthouse (*right*) and later used the new courthouse (*left*) as a military hospital. STATE HISTORICAL SOCIETY OF MISSOURI-COLUMBIA

departure of trains, the great piles of boxes in front of the Commissariat, the hum of busy life within, the crowd who daily go in and out of the Post and Division Quartermaster's Departments . . . The frequent mounting and dismounting at headquarters, the passage of squads of guarded 'Butternuts' through the streets, the activity at sutlers' stalls, and the occasional arrival of an ambulance with a paymaster inside, all conspire to give a very decided business air to the town."[11]

But Springfield also provided many soldiers with their first glimpse of the "barbarous touch" of war. By 1863 it bore scars from Major Charles Zagonyi's charge, the passage of thousands of soldiers from several armies, and Colonel John S. Marmaduke's raid. Its ruination, "the fruits of treason," stood in stark contrast with the evidence of obvious former prosperity.[12]

As long as the armies operated around Springfield and in the upland prairies of southwest Missouri and northwest Arkansas, the midwestern soldiers professed to see some opportunities for the "husbandman." The agriculturally inclined sized up the land and remarked on the fine orchards and the profusion of wild grapes. They wrote home of prairie lands available for five or ten dollars an acre and observed that the natives tended to settle only on the forested fringes of the prairies. Some believed that an infusion of "Yankee thrift" and "industry" would render the prairies the most productive land in the area. Parts of the country even appealed to the men. General Francis J. Herron's brigade encamped in October 1862 along Crane Creek, "a limpid stream furnishing the troops with excellent water, and beyond all this is a precipitous forest covered bluff, which forms a fine background to this striking picture. The blue smoke from the hundreds of camp fires hangs heavily over the scene, adding beauty to the landscape." The soldiers found Mount Vernon and Neosho "well built" and "pretty," but a sheet covered the sign of the Union Hotel at Neosho and Confederate flags flew from the building.[13]

The Army of the Frontier's artillery opened the Prairie Grove campaign by dueling the cannon of General Thomas C. Hindman's Confederates on the rolling prairie at Newtonia, Missouri, in October 1862. Iowa major William Thompson wrote that he had only the vaguest idea of his location but said, "It is in the prettiest spot I ever seen in MO., and at the same time in the most out of the way place imaginable." The ridge and prairie terrain allowed the men to see the battle lines fully spread out with all the military panoply—a rare sight in the heavily timbered Ozarks. After the battle the Ninth Kansas Cavalry rode to Sarcoxie and found it full of wounded soldiers from General James G. Blunt's Kansas division. Soldier Albert Greene thought their suffering to be strikingly incongruous in such a setting: "Sarcoxie was a dreamy old village comfortably situated among vines and shrubbery and overhanging fruit trees, with a single street that wound here and there to accommodate the course of a lovely little river of sparkling water, on the low bank of which it stands. Through openings . . . could be seen cultivated fields with white houses and green blinds, and big barns and cattle in pastures beyond."[14] Even at Prairie Grove, Arkansas, where the price of the view turned out to be considerably higher, the troops agreed with old soldiers who claimed that "a more beautiful field of battle" could not be found.[15]

The historic nature of the site, not the landscape, drew soldiers to the Wilson's Creek battlefield as they passed by on the Telegraph Road. Veterans of the battle as well as men who had yet to face enemy fire made pilgrimages to the site. Numerous graves and the pile of rocks marking the place of Lyon's death provoked many expressions of patriotic sentiment regarding the late general and the horrors of war. Bones, hair, and hides were strewn over the site, especially around the mass grave of Sigel's men. The chaplain of the Thirteenth Illinois Infantry called the field a "regular Golgotha." Much less piously, a grisly souvenir trade in human relics from the battle also developed.[16]

Federal armies moved from the upland prairie of southwestern Missouri into the White River Hills and the foothills of the Boston Mountains of Arkansas twice in 1862. South of Springfield the land briefly retains its pleasant rolling qualities, and many of the soldiers still thought the talk of Ozark mountains was just "humbug." Along the way, the midwesterners saw formerly prosperous farms where apples, peaches, and sweet potatoes had abounded, and some of them saw cotton under cultivation for the first time. Cassville, with a courthouse, a mill, a blacksmith shop, and business houses and homes, looked as though it may have been a "live" town, but when the army first arrived, it appeared old, dilapidated, and virtually deserted. It was even more so after troops burned some of its buildings and all of its fence rails. For much of the war, sick and wounded soldiers filled the remaining buildings.[17]

Beyond Cassville, the Telegraph Road passes through an increasingly rugged landscape of heavily forested ridge tops, isolated knobs and balds covered with broken chert, and narrow, fertile stream valleys. As it approaches the state line, the road traverses a series of hills through Keetsville, Missouri, then enters a narrow, rugged defile, continuing through Cross Timbers to Elkhorn and Cross Hollow, Arkansas. Every mile southward led to more difficult terrain in which the army's wagon trains invariably fell behind. Benjamin McIntyre considered the country "a freak of nature," with piled-up limestone ridges in apparent random order, but the roads on the stony ridge tops stayed dry, "piked by nature" with rocks suitable for paving city streets and levees. The men appreciated their dry shoes but lost more than they gained when the footwear began to disintegrate from the stress of rocks and miles. Because they found it nearly impossible to pitch tents on the ridges, the soldiers leveled the rocks on their camping grounds before rolling up in blankets.[18]

Keetsville, on the Butterfield Stage route before the war, contained "a dozen shanties which looked like a funeral procession in honor of Keets, whoever he may have been. The neighbors called the place 'Chicken-Thief.' Another hamlet a few miles southward was known as 'Scarce-o'-Grease!'" Although Keetsville through Cross Hollow was the most dangerous stretch on the Wire Road, the entire area was considered a "grand stamping ground for bushwhackers." Commanders worried about the increasing threat to their lengthening supply lines—with good reason after Confederates jumped a wagon train and attacked Keetsville in February 1862. Troops marching through the area in the following fall found everything in ashes, burnt by "Mountain Feds" in retaliation for depredations against mail and dispatch riders. Farther south, Union troops had burned parts of Bentonville after the killing of one of Benton's Hussars, a battalion-strength unit of the Missouri Cavalry. The graves of Confederate soldiers and the remains of rebel encampments along the way led Union troops to consider the relative defensive merits of positions at Cross Timbers, Cross Hollow, Elkhorn, and Sugar Creek.[19]

The armies of both the North and the South lived off of the land between Springfield and Fayetteville in 1861–1863. As early as April 1862, the country along the roads appeared "about eat up, starved out, burned out, and demolished generally." Broken-down orchards, fields overgrown in weeds, and stone chimneys marking ruined cabin sites were the rule rather than the exception. The flatland volunteers rarely remarked about crossing the arbitrary boundary between Missouri and Arkansas, although it does seem to have been obligatory for regimental bands to strike up "The Arkansas Traveler." One Indiana soldier noted having to march back into Missouri to find ground level enough for battalion drill, but the Ozarks in both states looked much alike. As one correspondent wrote, the region "is a mixture of Arkansas and Missouri, with a doubtful preponderance of either." According to a Wisconsin soldier, "This Arkansas country is a hard looking spot, but no worse than Missouri . . . It is perfectly wretched."[20]

In March 1862, the Army of the Southwest won the Battle of Pea Ridge in this difficult country but withdrew into Missouri the following month to shorten the line of supply. Six months later, the Army of the Frontier resumed the Union advance into northwest Arkansas. Based once again in Springfield and following familiar routes, the army reached Fayetteville and the foothills of the Boston Mountains.[21]

Fayetteville, the key military position in northwest Arkansas, was a town of one thousand residents and, like Springfield, had grown up along the corridor linking Missouri and Arkansas river settlements in the 1820s and 1830s. It prospered on the local trade of the White River valley, the north slope of the Bostons, and the prairie area of northwest Arkansas, and commercial connections with the Arkansas River, Indian Territory, and Missouri. By the beginning of the war, Fayetteville, the social as well as the military and economic center of northwest Arkansas, boasted Arkansas College, schools, churches, and fraternal societies.[22]

Until late February 1862, the town served as the headquarters for Confederate armies cooperating with Missouri secessionist forces. As they retreated before the Army of the Southwest, southern forces sacked and burned parts of the town, which still smoldered when Union cavalrymen first arrived. After the Confederate defeat at Pea Ridge, Fayetteville became the center of a dangerous no-man's-land through the summer of

1862, with the advance federal post at Elkhorn Tavern. In the fall, Union troops advanced from Springfield and Kansas to form the Army of the Frontier. They battled with Thomas C. Hindman's Confederates at Newtonia, Missouri, and at Cane Hill and Prairie Grove, near Fayetteville, before the year ended.[23]

Union troops arriving in Fayetteville in the fall of 1862 discovered a seminary, three print shops, and files of newspapers. By that time the formerly impressive town had been badly scarred by arsonists and the routine wear and tear of thousands of soldiers on the move. In addition, for months following the battles at Pea Ridge and Prairie Grove, virtually every building in and around Fayetteville held sick and wounded soldiers of both armies, often in frightful conditions.[24]

Fayetteville was the limit of permanent occupation by the Army of the Frontier in 1862–1863. At the end of the long logistical tether from St. Louis, federal reinforcement and supply through Rolla and Springfield proved tenuous, and the Confederates pitched into the town whenever the opportunity arose. When the army pulled out, Fayetteville was left to a garrison of native Union loyalists organized into regiments of federal volunteers. The garrison evacuated the post and northwestern Arkansas altogether after a daylong attack by Confederates on April 18, 1863, and did not return until the following September. Arkansas Confederates attacked again in October and November 1864. The garrison survived and became the nucleus for a farm colony system instituted by Colonel M. LaRue Harrison through the summer of 1865.[25]

Union troops campaigning in northwestern Arkansas typically appreciated fertile agricultural enclaves in the mountain coves but abhorred the rugged regions and the "desolate" hills they most often traveled. One soldier even made the distinction between the land around Fayetteville and the rest of "the Ozarks." A few prosperous villages earned honorable mention, mostly in connection with how much they reminded the soldiers of home. The community at Robinson's Crossroads southeast of Bentonville gratified Benjamin McIntyre, who for months had seen only middling villages: "This is a thrifty neighborhood and there is several fine dwellings near by and the vicinity presents many farms such as I have not seen since I came into the service. There is also a fine church and schoolhouse at this place which are things seldom met with in our former travels." In contrast, the nearly deserted and entirely unimpressive town of Huntsville was only a few miles away.[26]

Military authorities declined to operate in strength in the Boston Mountains for any extended period after the winter of 1862–1863. Federal armies could fight in the Boston Mountains south of Fayetteville, and even reach the Arkansas River, but the cost of overland supply from Springfield proved enormous. Ultimately, the topography of the Ozarks frustrated Union attempts to develop a successful path from southwest Missouri and northwest Arkansas toward Little Rock. The logistical cost was too high and the demands from other active fronts too pressing for the Union army to remain in strength in the Ozarks. After winning two critical battles near Fayetteville in 1862, both the Army of the Southwest and the Army of the Frontier drifted eastward on the north side of the White River before exiting the Ozarks for other theaters.[27]

The flatland volunteers were thankful to move on after skirmishing with the Confederate cavalry at Cane Hill, and especially after enduring the "fastness" of the Bostons during the raid on Van Buren, Arkansas, at the close of 1862. The Army of the Frontier struggled over truly mountainous country on that winter expedition from Fayetteville to the Arkansas River and back. Cliffs, deep ravines, and innumerable crossings of Cove and Lee's Creeks contributed to the soldiers' misery, although the Van Buren raid proved militarily successful. Union columns included artillery often pulled by soldiers as well as draft animals. Because of the season and the topography, even the cavalry deigned to lend the infantry their assistance. As they marched, probably very few of the volunteers maintained the equanimity of Benjamin McIntyre, who wrote, "Each step [presents a] new incident for the poet, the painter and Scholar." He went on to describe the mountain "steeps" as a blend of the picturesque and the sublime "mingled in happy confusion" that rivaled western scenery. Probably all of the troops could have agreed with McIntyre's statement, "For anyone but a Soldier in our Situation there would have been food for thought."[28]

As the armies withdrew from the vicinity of Fayetteville, the troops moved eastward into the White River hills of Arkansas and Missouri, encountering the least inhabited and most rugged parts of the area. The most trying physical conditions often accompanied the experience. The country made a believer of Iowa captain Henry G. Ankeny, who wrote his wife, "I had thought the Ozarks were a Myth—but they are surely a reality." When cavalryman S. S. Marrett reached the White River, he wrote, "It is the roughest country it has ever been my fortune to travel." Major William Thompson of the Twentieth Iowa Infantry found the geography so confusing that he confessed to being unsure where he was, nor did he think the enemy knew. He expressed the opinion of many of the flatland volunteers when he said: "It would take (the) Rebels a month to find us if they were a mile from us. We have good water & wood (rails), but the country is a miserable botch." Thompson professed relief at the prospect of leaving the White River country, even if it meant going to Vicksburg: "It would take a peck of Bullets to hurt me I think." The rugged, ransacked countryside tested Benjamin McIntyre's magnanimity in the winter of 1862–1863 as the army maneuvered from point to point merely to feed itself and its animals. After a January march from Huntsville to Carrollton, Arkansas, McIntyre noted that he had "never seen a grander display of natures rough handy work than I have seen displayed in the last three days and I even wonder what the great law giver could have intended this roughness of nature for."[29]

As the armies moved east, so did the main line of supply from Springfield, utilizing the old White River Trace through Ozark to Forsyth. Troops marching through Ozark, the seat of Christian County, found a "live place" with twenty families, several "pretty" residences, and a good mill, all "pleasantly situated" on a bluff overlooking Finley Creek. There were also a log blockhouse for the garrison and "a fine covered bridge," the first span the men had crossed since leaving the railhead at Rolla. Ozark looked the worse for the wear when the Army of the Frontier passed through in spring 1863, with the charred remnants of the blockhouse and the stubs of telegraph poles marking the passage of Marmaduke's Confederate raiders.[30]

A difficult and dangerous crossing of the White River was at Forsyth, the site of one ferryboat disaster and numerous individual drownings. Not a single inhabitant remained in town when the Army of the Frontier arrived, and the courthouse had cannonball holes in it, but the condition of the few remaining houses was generally good and the setting admirable. Each successive army damaged Forsyth. By the time the Army of the Frontier left, soldiers had torn down most of the buildings for ferryboats and fortifications.[31]

Both the Army of the Southwest and the Army of the Frontier ultimately moved north and eastward across the southern tier of Missouri counties, traveling routes on the divides between the watersheds of the White, Gasconade, and Current Rivers. In the spring of 1862, the victors of Pea Ridge marched through the interior via Cassville, Cape Fair, Galena, Vera Cruz, and West Plains, before moving to Batesville, Arkansas, and exiting the Ozarks in the direction of Little Rock. Marching dispersed in three divisions a year later, the Army of the Frontier took a more northerly path through Huntsville, Arkansas, and Forsyth, Hartville, Houston, and Salem, Missouri. Nearly all the infantrymen marched to the railheads at Rolla and Ironton or to the Mississippi River landing at Ste. Genevieve before leaving the Ozarks in June 1863.[32]

In their journeys eastward across Missouri, the men first encountered the same "loathsome and God-forsaken" topography of steep ridges covered with scrub oak and narrow valleys with occasional fertile glens. But as they marched eastward, the camping sites were closer together and the roads not as stony as the ones in southwest Missouri and northwest Arkansas. The deserted towns, however, looked about the same. Mountain Grove had seven houses, a carding mill, and a seminary "of no particular style of architecture except to use as much lumber as possible." A few miles farther, soldiers marching into West Plains found a formerly respectable county seat ruined, with a courthouse destroyed in an 1862 skirmish. After the Army of the Southwest arrived, it was "as if a plague had hit" West Plains when hundreds of men fell ill from camp fever and dysentery. When the army moved on, every building in town housed sick soldiers. By mid-war West Plains looked "awful"; by 1865 not a building remained.[33]

The Gasconade bottoms appeared fertile, but Benjamin McIntyre said that most of the country was of "the post oak kind—not barren and yet not productive." Another soldier described the country as decidedly secondhand and said that even the rocks appeared to have been worn out elsewhere before being dumped in Missouri. The men found the large pineries in Texas County along the Big Piney River "a novel and picturesque sight," although picket duty at night in the tall pines was "notoriously lonesom." The army had first penetrated this country in November 1861 with an expedition from Rolla to clear out guerrilla bands threatening the railhead. The Texas County expedition marched through deep woods in rough and broken country, crossing Little Piney Creek. Aside from the tramp of marching, the only noise was "an occasional oath from some luckless wight as he measured his length upon the stony road." The same rugged terrain caused the Army of the Frontier's "grand review" in the spring of 1863 to turn into a "grand humbug" due to the lack of enough level land for a parade.[34]

Farther east, the Current River hills proved even tougher. Cavalrymen who plunged into them, chasing guerrillas who periodically threatened the army's supply lines, "underwent great hardship and fatigue, and traveled in one of the roughest countries this side of the Mountains of the Moon . . . all hills and no valleys." The troops liked the Dent County seat of Salem, which seemed to them a "pleasant village" with many fine residences and much prettier than Rolla. Benjamin McIntyre said, "Salem judging from appearances of today has been a lively gay little town and presents an aspect different from any of the interior towns." Located only thirty miles from the railhead at Rolla, rations, supplies, and even

Figure 6. Union troops guard the railroad terminus at Pilot Knob.
STATE HISTORICAL SOCIETY OF MISSOURI-COLUMBIA

newspapers arrived on schedule, so it may have been full stomachs as much as anything that sweetened the soldiers' attitude toward the town. McIntyre noted that the troops enjoyed the soldier's lifestyle as never before, "and for the first time since our enlistment the government does not compel us to steal sustenance for our teams." An Iowa cavalryman simply said that the regiment was "in the land of hard bread & bacon . . . camped in a beautiful place, with plenty of large shade trees, good water & so near to Rolla that we lack nothing for our selves or horses." Finally, at Rolla and Pilot Knob, the troops heard railroad whistles for the first time in many months and hundreds of miles.[35]

By the time the men marched to board the cars at the depots, they had circumnavigated on foot nearly the entire area dominated by Union troops in southwestern Missouri and northwestern Arkansas. As they did throughout Arkansas, soldiers in the northern Ozarks freely expressed their opinions of and disappointment with the landscape. Mostly midwestern agriculturalists, the volunteers measured the hill country in light of what they had known back home. Clearly, the Ozark region did not meet their expectations. Wilderness solitude, good hunting and fishing, and country living were not the features they expected or desired. As Shea points out, the soldiers from the American heartland felt like strangers in a strange land. They reacted to the unfamiliar as do tourists, more likely to record the unusual than the ordinary, especially the negative. Of course, there are many parts of the Ozarks that agriculturalists can never love, especially those accustomed to planting crops right up to the front doorstep. Soldiers from the flatlands around Aurora and Bloomington, Illinois, voiced especially vociferous complaints.[36]

Certainly, some of the descriptions are examples of "trash" talk employed by troops in every army to describe their surroundings. Other narratives, such as Jenks's "War Letters" and "Boswell's Letters," written by former printers turned soldiers and serialized in hometown newspapers, are obviously literary and journalistic exercises meant to engage as much as to inform the folks back home. Humor and sarcasm are spread with a broad brush. The soldiers' accounts, however, are not merely hyperbole or evidence of cultural bias, although there is plenty of both. Even Missouri soldiers weighed in against the Ozarks. Given the circumstances of the 1860s, there was considerable room for improvement in the region. Most of the Ozark Highland was indeed largely undeveloped and uninhabited; parts of the region were true wilderness. Where it was populated at all, much of the area remained at the frontier subsistence level. Only a few towns were a generation old, most of the smaller villages even less than that. Although most still stood when the armies passed through, the rural villages and county seat towns were mostly deserted and entirely plundered by mid-war and were about to undergo the ordeal by fire that left them nearly wiped out by war's end. Springfield, Fayetteville, and Batesville were the only towns worthy of the name in the Ozark Highland and also the only ones that pleased Union troops. These towns reminded the soldiers of home.

Finally, it was wartime, hardly the time to experience the Ozarks. Parts of the Ozark Highland were definitely enemy territory where Union soldiers were unwelcome guests. The troops toured the region under the most disadvantageous circumstances, and their objectives did not include scenic attractions. Even when unthreatened, the armies kept on the move. Geography confined them to the network of flinty ridge roads, taking the midwestern prairie farmers through some of the least productive parts of the section. Additionally, the Pea Ridge and Prairie Grove campaigns occurred during the winter, making a hard country even more difficult. The most arduous physical conditions often accompanied the experience. The exigencies of military service, the primitive road network, and other logistical difficulties kept wagon trains laden with tents, food, supplies, and amenities lagging behind the troops. Exhausted soldiers often waited hours for baggage wagons to arrive before setting up camp. Such experiences were enough to blight the appeal of any area. Undoubtedly, the troops embellished their complaints some in the telling, but soldiers such as those in the Army of the Frontier, who marched thirty-five miles a day for three consecutive days to enter combat on the battlefield at Prairie Grove, surely earned the right to say whatever they pleased.

As they prepared to leave the Ozarks, many of the volunteers probably entertained sentiments similar to those registered by "Boswell" of the Ninety-fourth Illinois many months and hundreds of miles earlier. The young soldier from Bloomington stepped off the train at Rolla in September 1862 determined to see the fight to its finish. He spent a day in town before composing his fifth "War Letter" to the *Bloomington (Illinois) Pantagraph.* Make no mistake, he wrote, "If the Southern Confederacy is like the part of Missouri we passed through, Jeff Davis is a most consummate ass for wanting it, and Uncle Sam is ditto for not letting him have it."[37]

Notes

1. William L. Shea, "A Semi-Savage State: The Image of Arkansas in the Civil War," *Arkansas Historical Quarterly* 48 (Winter 1989): 309–328.

2. Milton D. Rafferty, *The Ozarks: Land and Life* (Norman: University of Oklahoma Press, 1980), 105; Carl O. Sauer, *The Geography of the Ozark Highland of Missouri* (Chicago: University of Chicago Press, 1920), 223; James R. Shortridge, "The Expansion of the Settlement Frontier in Missouri," *Missouri Historical Review* 75 (October 1980): 76; Steven D. Smith, *Made It In the Timber: A Historic Overview of the Fort Leonard Wood Region, 1800–1940* (Normal, IL: Midwestern Archaeological Research Center, 1993), 23; Henry R. Schoolcraft quoted in Gerard Schultz, *Early History of the Northern Ozarks* (Jefferson City, MO: Midland Printing Company, 1937), 101–102, 104; *Guadal P'a: The Journal of Lieutenant J. W. Abert, from Bent's Fort to St. Louis in 1845,* ed. H. Bailey Carroll (Canyon, TX: Panhandle-Plains Historical Society, 1941), 113. Abert called the route "too well known" to describe in his journal.

3. W. H. K. to editor, *Council Bluffs (Iowa) Nonpareil,* September 7, 1861; F. O. W. to editor, *Aurora (Illinois) Beacon,* November 7, 1861; Henry G. Ankeny to wife, August 25, 1861, Florence Marie Ankeny Cox, compiler, *Kiss Josey For Me* (Santa Ana, CA: Friis-Pioneer Press, 1974), 19–20; Jeff to editor, *Iowa City Republican,* October 8, 1862; C. D. to editor, *Indianapolis Daily Journal,* February 20, 1862; "War Letter From Jenks," *Dubuque (Iowa) Daily Times,* October 7, 1862; Sigma to editor, *Dubuque (Iowa) Daily Times,* October 5, 1862.

4. G. T. to editor, *St. Louis Daily Missouri Democrat,* August 20, 1861; Philander Draper to wife, September 24, 1862, Draper-McClurg Family Papers, Western Historical Manuscript Collection, University of Missouri-Columbia (hereinafter cited as WHMC-Columbia); "Boswell's Letters-No. V," *Bloomington (Illinois) Daily Pantagraph,* September 18, 1862.

5. Ankeny to wife, August 25, 1861, *Kiss Josey For Me,* 19–20; Samuel Prentis Curtis, "The Army of the South-West, and the First Campaign in Arkansas," *Annals of Iowa* 4 (April 1866): 641; Samuel R. Curtis to wife, December 30, 1861, "Frontier War Problems," *Annals of Iowa,* 3rd ser., 24 (April 1943): 309; Charles Carleton Coffin, *The Boys of '61* (Boston: Estes and Lauriat, 1885), 51; Peter Wilson to brother, January 13, 1863, "Peter Wilson in the Civil War, 1863–1865," *Iowa Journal of History and Politics* 40 (October 1942): 339–340; Henry Carroll to family, October 1, 1862, Henry S. Carroll Letters, U.S. Army Military History Institute, Carlisle, Pennsylvania; Willis to editor, *Woodstock (Illinois) Sentinel,* October 2, 1861; Jeff to editor, *Iowa City Republican,* October 8, 1862.

6. Entries. November 1, 1861; January 18, 21, 1862, Nathan King Diary, State Historical Society of Iowa, Des Moines; H to editor, *Woodstock (Illinois) Sentinel,* February 12, 1862; entry, February 17, 1862, Lyman G. Bennett Diary, L. G. Bennett Collection, Western Historical Manuscript Collection, University of Missouri-Rolla (hereinafter cited as WHMC-Rolla); One of the Boys to editor, *Aurora (Illinois) Beacon,* February 13, 1862; Letters from the 36th Regiment, *Aurora (Illinois) Beacon,* February 6, 1862.

7. Entry, September 18, 1862, Nannie M. Tilley, editor, *Federals on the Frontier: The Diary of Benjamin F. McIntyre, 1862–1864* (Austin: University of Texas Press, 1963), 14; Sergeant Knapp to editor, *Burlington (Iowa) Hawkeye,* June 9, 1862; H. J. B. Cummings to wife, January 31, 1862, H. J. B. Cummings Letters, State Historical Society of Iowa, Des Moines; F. O. W. to editor, *Aurora (Illinois) Beacon,* January 30, 1862; Jeff to editor, *Iowa City Republican,* November 19, 1862; On Foot to editor, *Aurora (Illinois) Beacon,* February 6, 1862; entry, February 15, 1862, Bennett Diary; Typo to editor, *Keokuk (Iowa) Constitution,* September 30, 1862. For Waynesville, see Terry Primas, "Civil War Comes to Pulaski County, Post Waynesville 1862–1863," *Old Settlers Gazette,* Issue 30, July 28, 2012: 32–49.

8. Entry, January 4–5, 1862, Henry P. Mann Diary, WHMC-Rolla; Brigade to editor, *Chicago Times,* March 8, 1862; Ankeny to wife, February 2, 1862, *Kiss Josey For Me,* 42; E. A. Carr to assistant adjutant general, January 26, 1862, *The War of the Rebellion: A Compilation of the Official Records of the Union and Confederate Armies,* ser. 1, vol. 8 (Washington, DC: Government Printing Office, 1883), 527; letter in the *Animosa (Iowa) Eureka,* n.d., cited in William E. Corbin, *A Star For Patriotism* (Monticello, Iowa: privately published, 1972), 98–99.

9. "Boswell's Letters-No. VII," *Bloomington (Illinois) Daily Pantagraph,* September 29, 1862; Colonel Ira M. Gifford to editor, *Dubuque (Iowa) Daily Times,* November 25, 1862; entry, September 20, 1862, *Federals on the Frontier,* 15–16.

10. Sauer, *Geography of the Ozark Highland,* 139, 219–220; Shortridge, "Settlement Frontier," 77–78; Charles K. Piehl, "The Race of Improvement: Springfield Society, 1865–1881," *Missouri Historical Review* 67 (July 1973): 486–489; entry, May 1, 1862, Samuel P. Herrington Diary, U.S. Army Military History Institute; E. P. M. to editor, *Waukegan (Illinois) Weekly Gazette,* July 12, 1862; J. K. M. to editor, *Bloomington (Illinois) Daily Pantagraph,* October 14, 1862; G. W. Howser to Woodson Horine, October 20, 1862, W. W. Horine Papers, McLean County Historical Society, Bloomington, Illinois; William G. Thompson to wife, September 25, 1862, *The Civil War Letters of Major William G. Thompson of the 20th Iowa Infantry Regiment,* ed. Edwin C. Bearss (Fayetteville, AR: Washington County Historical Society, 1966), 25.

11. Vox to editor, *Keokuk (Iowa) Constitution,* October 14, 1862; A. W. B. to editor, *New York Times,* August 31, 1862.

12. Henry Voelkner to mother, October 31, 1861, Henry Voelkner Letters, WHMC-Columbia; A. W. C. to editor, *Woodstock (Illinois) Sentinel,* November 20, 1861; letter of J. Christian Miller, *Amboy (Illinois) Times,* December 5, 1861; entries, March 12, 13, 1862, Henry Seaman Journal, Civil War Times Illustrated Collection, U.S. Army Military History Institute; entry, February 22, 1862, Bennett Diary; Thompson to wife, September 25, 1862, *Civil War Letters of Major William G. Thompson,* 25. An excellent overview of Springfield is William Garrett Piston and John C. Rutherford, "Quinine and Courage: The Battle of Springfield, January 8, 1863," in *Springfield's Urban Histories: Essays on the Queen City of the Missouri Ozarks,* ed. Stephen L. McIntyre (Springfield: Moon City Press, Missouri State University, 2012), 15–57.

13. A. W. C. to editor, *Woodstock (Illinois) Sentinel,* November 27, 1861; entries, September 23, 25, 1862, *Federals on the Frontier,* 17–19; Sergeant Knapp to editor, *Burlington (Iowa) Hawkeye,* June 9, 1862; "War Letters From Jenks-No.3," *Dubuque (Iowa) Daily Times,* October 21, 1862; unsigned letter, c. September 1862, in *Seneca, Missouri: The Little Town on the Border* (Seneca, MO: Seneca Historical Committee, 1982), 2: 112.

14. "From the 20th," *Cedar Valley (Iowa) Times,* October 23, 1862; Thompson to wife, October 6, 1862, *Civil War Letters of Major William G. Thompson,* 30; Albert Robinson Greene, "Campaigning in the Army of the Frontier," *Collections of the Kansas State Historical Society* 14 (1915–1918): 290.

15. Chester Barney, *Recollections of Field Service With the Twentieth Iowa Infantry Volunteers* (Davenport, IA: Gazette Job Room, 1865), 138.

16. S. L. P. to editor, *Mount Pleasant (Iowa) Home Journal,* April 19, 1862; T. J. R. to editor, *Keokuk (Iowa) Daily Gate City,* November 5, 1862; J. Christian Miller to editor, *Amboy (Illinois) Times,* December 5, 1861; George Root to mother, October 14, 1862, George W. Root Civil War Letters, 1862, State Historical Society of Wisconsin, Madison; Albert J. Rockwell to family, November 26, 1862, Albert J. Rockwell Letters, State Historical Society of Wisconsin, Madison; David Lathrop, *The History of the Fifty-Ninth Regiment Illinois Volunteers* (Indianapolis: Hall and Hutchinson, 1865), 73. Southern troops were also fascinated with the battlefield. See Griffin Frost, *Camp and Prison Journal* (1867; reprint, Iowa City: Camp Pope Bookshop, 1994), 4.

17. Lathrop, *History of the Fifty-Ninth Illinois,* 82–83, 104–105; entry, February 16, 1862, Mann Diary; "From the South-Western Anny," *Des Moines Daily State Register,* November 6, 1862.

18. Lyman G. Bennett, "Route of the Army of the Southwest" [Cassville to Washburn's Prairie], and diary entry, March 5, 1862, Bennett Collection; entries, October 13, 14, 1862, *Federals on the Frontier,* 26–27; Barney, *Recollections of Field Service,* 67–68; W. J. Lemke, editor, *Captain Edward Gee Miller of the 20th Wisconsin: His War 1862–1865* (Fayetteville, AR: Washington County Historical Society, 1960), 9; Thomas to editor, *Davenport (Iowa) Daily Democrat & News,* February 18, 1863; Lathrop, *History of the Fifty-Ninth Illinois,* 80–81.

19. Albert D. Richardson, *Beyond the Mississippi: From the Great River to the Great Ocean . . .* (Hartford, CT: American Publishing Company, 1867), 214; A. W. Bishop, *Loyalty on the Frontier, or Sketches of Union Men of the Southwest* (St. Louis: R. P. Studley and Company, 1863), 12; Thompson to wife, October 20, 1862, *Civil War Letters of Major William G. Thompson,* 42; Jacob D. Brewster to wife, October 29, 1862, James W. Pohl, editor, "From Davenport to Vicksburg: The Odyssey of a Soldier in the

Civil War," *Annals of Iowa* 40 (Winter 1971): 499; "War Letters From Jenks, No. 5," *Dubuque (Iowa) Daily Times,* November 8, 1862.

20. "From the Fourth Iowa Cavalry," *Mount Pleasant (Iowa) Home Journal,* April 16, 1862; Samuel M. Hartley to editor, *Rock Island (Illinois) Weekly Argus,* March 12, 1862; Daniel H. Jones to wife, in *Belvidere (Illinois) Standard,* March 24, 1863; "War Letters From Jenks-No. 3," *Dubuque (Iowa) Daily Times,* October 21, 1862; entry, March 31, 1862, Herrington Diary; William L. Shea, "A Continual Thunder," in *Rugged and Sublime: The Civil War in Arkansas,* ed. Mark K. Christ (Fayetteville: University of Arkansas Press, 1994), 24; "Letter from Boswell," *Bloomington (Illinois) Daily Pantagraph,* February 9, 1863; George W. Root to wife, October 19, 1862, Root Civil War Letters.

21. William L. Shea and Earl J. Hess, *Pea Ridge: Civil War Campaign in the West* (Chapel Hill: University of North Carolina Press, 1992). For the foreseeable future, this work will be the standard source for the battle and the crucial campaign that began at Rolla and ended at Helena, Arkansas. A preliminary study by Earl J. Hess, "Battle in the Brush: Davis' Division at Pea Ridge, March 7, 1862," *Indiana History Journal* 8 (May 1983): 12–20, describes the tactical realities of fighting on the rugged and heavily wooded battlefield. There are no similar comprehensive studies of the Prairie Grove battle or the campaign that brought the armies to fight there.

22. William Baxter, *Pea Ridge and Prairie Grove; or, Scenes and Incidents of the War in Arkansas* (Cincinnati, OH: Poe and Hitchcock, 1864), 10–12; *History of Benton, Washington, Carroll, Madison, Crawford, Franklin and Sebastian Counties, Arkansas* (Chicago: Goodspeed Publishing Company, 1889), 238–247.

23. Michael A. Hughes, "Wartime Gristmill Destruction in Northwest Arkansas and Military-Farm Colonies," *Arkansas Historical Quarterly* 46 (summer 1987): 171–175; Kim Allen Scott, "Witness for the Prosecution: The Civil War Letter of Lieutenant George Taylor," *Arkansas Historical Quarterly* 48 (Autumn 1989): 260–271; William S. Bums, *Recollections of the 4th Missouri Cavalry,* ed. Frank Allen Dennis (Dayton, OH: Morningside Press, 1988), 25; Tom Feathers, "The History of Military Activities in the Vicinity of Fayetteville, Arkansas," *Flashback* 3 (April 1953), no pagination.

24. Entry, December 9, 1862, Francis Springer Journal, Illinois State Historical Library, Springfield; entry, January 2, 1863, *Federals on the Frontier,* 90–91; E. N. B. to editor, *Cedar Valley (Iowa) Times,* November 13, 1862; William L. Shea, editor, "The Aftermath of Prairie Grove: Union Letters from Fayetteville," *Arkansas Historical Quarterly* 47 (Winter 1988): 345–361.

25. Hughes, "Wartime Gristmill Destruction," 176–182; Richard N. Current, *Lincoln's Loyalists: Union Soldiers from the Confederacy* (Boston: Northeastern University Press, 1992), 75–78, 168–170; Feathers, "The History of Military Activities."

26. W. S. Brooks to father, in *Fairfield (Iowa) Ledger,* February 25, 1863; entries, December 6, 1862, January 8, 1863, *Federals on the Frontier,* 56, 95.

27. William D. Butler, "The Ozarks as a Barrier during the Civil War" (Master's thesis, University of Missouri-Columbia, 1983), 79. Butler identifies the lack of forage for livestock as the single most limiting factor for armies operating in the interior of the Ozarks.

28. Thomas E. Wright, "The Capture of Van Buren, Arkansas, During the Civil War: From the Diary of a Union Horse Soldier," *Arkansas Historical Quarterly* 38 (Spring 1979): 80–88; Michael A. Mullins, *The Fremont Rifles: A History of the 37th Illinois Veteran*

Volunteer Infantry (Wilmington, NC: Broadfoot Publishing Company, 1990), 170; entries, December 30, 31, 1862, *Federals on the Frontier,* 86–87.

29. Ankeny to wife, April 7, 1862, *Kiss Josey For Me,* 55–56; S. S. Marrett to wife, April 18, 1862, S. S. Marrett Papers, Special Collections Library, Duke University, Durham, North Carolina; Lathrop, *History of the Fifty-Ninth Illinois,* 110; Thompson to wife, November 6, 16, 1862, *Civil War Letters of Major William C. Thompson,* 57–58, 66; entry, January 12, 1863, *Federals on the Frontier,* 98–99.

30. Charles H. Lothrop, A *History of the First Iowa Cavalry Veteran Volunteers* (Lyons, IA: Beers and Eaton, 1890), 87; Thomas to editor, *Davenport (Iowa) Daily Democrat & News,* November 21, 1862, March 21, 1863; entry, November 11, 1862, *Federals on the Frontier,* 45.

31. "Return of Gen. Curtis's Anny to South-West Missouri," *Waukegan (Illinois) Weekly Gazette,* April 26, 1862; Ankeny to wife, April 14, 1862, *Kiss Josey For Me,* 59–60; Jonathan Dwight Stevens to wife, February 13, 1863, Jonathan Dwight Stevens Papers, State Historical Society of Wisconsin; N. E. D. to editor, *Mount Pleasant (Iowa) Home Journal,* March 21, 1863; Charlie to editor, *Keokuk (Iowa) Weekly Gate City,* April 10, 1863. For an extended review of the Forsyth episode, see John F. Bradbury Jr., "The Army of the Frontier at Forsyth, 1863," Part I, *White River Valley Historical Quarterly* 10, no. 8 (Summer 1990): 4–7, 15; Part II, 10, no. 9 (Fall 1990): 3–9; Part III, 10, no. 10 (Winter 1991): 3–7.

32. It is no surprise that the soldiers liked Batesville, a prosperous port town in a beautiful setting on the White River. They also enjoyed several weeks of pleasant spring weather and signs of Union sentiment among the local populace. See Shea, "A Semi-Savage State," 319–321; Nola A. James, "The Civil War Years in Independence County," *Arkansas Historical Quarterly* 28 (Autumn 1969): 256–257; and John P. Morrow Jr., "Impressions of the War Years," *Independence County Chronicle* 3 (October 1961): 14.

33. Lathrop, *History of the Fifty-Ninth Illinois,* 112–115; J. W. Hankins to editor, *Mount Pleasant (Iowa) Home Journal,* May 23, 1863; "Letter from Boswell," *Bloomington (Illinois) Daily Pantagraph,* March 21, 1863; Thomas to editor, *Davenport (Iowa) Daily Democrat,* April 15, 1863; William Forse Scott, *The Story of a Cavalry Regiment: The Career of the Fourth Iowa Veteran Volunteers from Kansas to Georgia, 1861–1865* (New York: G. P. Putnam's Sons, 1893), 38–39; William Robinson to editor, *Indianapolis Daily Journal,* May 20, 1862; John Walter Lee to family, February 3, 15, 1863, John Walter Lee Letters, State Historical Society of Iowa, Des Moines.

34. Entries, April 29, 30, May 1, 2, 1863, *Federals on the Frontier,* 143–145; H. R. H. to editor, *Quincy (Illinois) Daily Herald,* May 23, 1862; entry, December 28, 1862, Aquilla Standifird Diary, WHMC-Rolla; Chasseur to editor, *Council Bluffs (Iowa) Nonpareil,* November 23, 1861; E. P. M. to editor, *Waukegan (Illinois) Weekly Gazette,* May 2, 1863.

35. C. D. to editor, *Burlington Iowa Hawkeye,* March 10, 1862; Sigma to editor, *Dubuque (Iowa) Daily Times,* October 31, 1862; G to editor, *Madison Wisconsin State Journal,* June 4, 1863; entries, May 2, 19, 1863, *Federals on the Frontier,* 145, 151; William O. Gulick to mother, May 26, 1863, Max Hendricks Guyer, editor, "The Journal and Letters of Corporal William O. Gulick," *Iowa Journal of History and Politics* 28 (October 1930): 588.

36. Shea, "A Semi-Savage State," 310–311.

37. "Boswell's Letters-No. V," *Bloomington (Illinois) Daily Pantagraph,* September 18, 1862.

The Race of Improvement

Springfield Society, 1865–1881

CHARLES K. PIEHL

Late-nineteenth-century Springfield, Missouri, grew on a fragile base. Like so many American towns after the Civil War, it was vulnerable to forces beyond the control of its citizens, especially to the economic accomplishments or failures of capitalists in distant cities. Seldom were residents of Springfield able to influence the broad and impersonal powers that affected them. At times, certain men were able to take advantage of outside forces, and they prospered as a result. On the whole, however, the hope of Springfield citizens to control their own present and future course remained little more than a dream.

The frustrated ambition of Springfield residents is clearly evident in the fifteen years following the Civil War. In that period, the dream of Springfield's rapid growth and improvement, of uniting the people in a drive to advance prestige and fortune, dominated the concerns of the town. But to build Springfield into a large and influential city overnight required more stable conditions than the town or the nation seemed able to produce in the postwar years.

Part of the problem was derived from the several thousand individual fortunes comprising the fortune of Springfield as a whole. A few citizens looked far enough beyond their own concerns to identify their future with the town's. Many more, however, were not so motivated and stayed in Springfield only as long as it profited them. By its impermanence this group of profit-seeking individuals made stability impossible and the goals of achievement more difficult to attain. A second part of the reason that a unified, fast-growing city could not be created related to the nature of nineteenth-century progress. Indicators of advancement such as railroads, manufacturing, and population increase—the yardsticks by which a town's growth could be judged—contributed to the very instability that inhibited the development of the ideal community in Springfield. By trying to achieve all these goals simultaneously, the men who dreamed of a prosperous, powerful, and unified city actually worked against themselves. After fifteen years of racing to improve itself, Springfield society in 1880 remained almost as weak and as vulnerable to outside forces as it had been in 1865.

The Civil War provides more than a convenient dividing point in the history of Springfield. Convinced that the town's progress had been retarded a decade by the conflict, Springfield residents in the postwar period were determined to make up the lost time. Even though much of their society had to be completely rebuilt after the war, precedents for progress, improvement, and social institutions were found in the prewar years.

Until the 1850s, Springfield's economic and social concerns had extended only as far as the surrounding agricultural region of Greene County. Though the largest town in southwest Missouri, Springfield was basically a local trading center. Until a branch of the State Bank of Missouri was established in 1845, the leading business firms in the town could be classified as either "merchants" or "grocers."[1] Getting the farmers' produce to larger markets and returning with manufactured goods took precedence over even the most basic small manufacturing. Abundant agricultural land in Greene County offered the greatest opportunities for personal advancement in the early years. Speculations on, and improvement of, open lands were common and profitable practices.

Without adequate transportation to large markets, especially St. Louis, Springfield could not expect to be more than a small town serving the trading needs of the surrounding country. Between 1838 and 1848, the population increased from about 300 to only 344, of which 108 were slaves.[2] Wagons and stages traveled to the Missouri River at Boonville and to St. Louis as well as south into Arkansas, but their service was expensive and unreliable. Proposals to deepen rivers running into Greene County failed to receive statewide support, forcing Springfield residents to place all their hopes for cheaper transportation on the railroad. The belief in the railroad panacea laid the foundation on which Springfield began to grow.

The proposed line to southwest Missouri received almost universal support in Springfield. In 1845, four years before the line was chartered, county residents held railroad meetings to express the local desire for better transportation. The commitment of county and town residents to the railroad became more obvious in 1854 when Greene Countians purchased $100,000 of stock in the proposed road. By 1860 goods from the East arrived more easily as work on the railroad, which began in St. Louis, moved steadily southwest.[3]

Springfield in the 1850s had experienced its first rapid growth and acquired its first manufacturing. In a decade, the population tripled, and by 1858 the town supported an iron foundry, a lumber planing mill, and two tobacco factories. Retail business became increasingly diversified, and a permanent group of professionals was attracted to Springfield.[4] The economy of the town was expanding on the expectation of the railroad.

Springfield society also grew more complex within a few years. During the forties, town government very nearly had ceased to function. At one point the town trustees simply stopped meeting. However, the expectation that Springfield would grow more rapidly as railroad construction approached the town necessitated a more active government in the 1850s. Springfield reincorporated in 1851 with a full set of officials and a workable administration. Even so, the town populace and the county expressed concern for the reputation Springfield would acquire as it grew. Among the first to actively promote public regulation were temperance advocates eager to ensure the morality of the growing town. The physical, as well as the moral, condition of the town received attention. In 1859 the council spent $417 for better streets and sidewalks around the town square, and work began on a new county courthouse and jail.[5]

Springfield churches grew along with the town in the 1850s. Baptist and Episcopal groups joined the three Presbyterian and Methodist congregations already in town. Between 1850 and 1860, the Southern Methodist Church grew from 87 to 207 members and embarked on a $25,000 building project.[6] Other new church structures were built or planned during the decade in anticipation of continued progress.

By 1860 Springfield was almost a miniature copy of what its natives hoped it would become. Rapid growth made the town attractive for settlement. The people could choose from among several Protestant denominations. Fraternal orders as well as temperance groups formed in the fifties, offering further associations for Springfield residents. A core of permanent citizens provided the town some stability to develop a firm business and manufacturing base. What Springfield needed most was the railroad, which by 1860 had reached Rolla, 120 miles to the northeast.

Springfield's competing political newspapers recorded the growth of the town in the 1850s. But while the journals told of events in southwest Missouri, they were also debating the national crisis that led to war in 1861. With the coming of the Civil War to Missouri in that year, construction of the railroad halted, and Springfield's progress, which had been continuous for over a decade, also stopped. The war demonstrated for the first time the fragility of Springfield's society.

Five years of fighting and military occupation distinctly affected the town and its society. Some of the most bitter fighting in Missouri took place in Greene County from 1861 to 1863 with Springfield often the center of contention. Confederate and Union troops alternately occupied and employed the town as a supply and quartering area, taking what they needed and destroying what might aid the enemy when they left. As a result, churches and the courthouse as well as small factories, many businesses, and homes were turned over to soldiers. By the end of the war, the foundry, the planing mill, and many shops had been destroyed.[7]

More difficult to assess than the physical damage was the damage to the society. George Ward Nichols, a *Harper's Magazine* journalist, visited Springfield at the end of the war and described its inhabitants and merchants as "strange, half-civilized people" covered with dirt and grease and dressed in homespun. Nichols wrote:

> These men were temporary or permanent denizens of the city and were lazily occupied in doing nothing. The most marked characteristic of the inhabitants seemed to be an indisposition to move, and their highest ambition to let their hair and beards grow . . . When people moved in this lazy city they did so slowly and without method. No one seemed in haste.

This somewhat unfavorable and exaggerated description of Springfield citizens at least gives some idea of the unsettled nature of the society and the decay of its previously ambitious life.[8]

There were changes in the composition of Springfield's population during the war years. When Union troops recaptured the area in 1862, outspoken slaveholders, many living in Springfield, fled to the South and took their slaves. An 1865 census of Greene County shows that less than one-third of the 1860 Negro population remained in the county. The same census mentions a large class of men listed as "refugees."[9] This group was composed largely of soldiers who remained in the area after the fighting ended and their units disbanded. They became the first postwar immigrants into southwest Missouri and Springfield. A portion of the population of the town, then, was made up of this unattached group that came after many of the respectable, settled, slaveholding families left during the war.[10] While there was no great decrease in the number of residents in Springfield, the composition of the citizenry had been altered. Those who remained from the prewar years faced the task of once more uniting diverse and unattached residents in promoting the interests of Springfield.

By the end of the war, A. F. Ingram's newspaper, the Springfield *Missouri Weekly Patriot,* speaking for those who were concerned about rebuilding Springfield, began advocating growth and improvement to surpass the achievements of the 1850s. First, town society would have to be reoriented toward the North, for that was where true progress was supposed to emanate. Part of this redirection had already occurred as a result of the war and occupation by Union soldiers. "They will render important aid in building up our country [southwest Missouri] and restoring her to her former prosperity," said the *Missouri Patriot.*[11] Springfield's region needed men of good character similar to Union veterans and had a great deal to offer them, the paper noted:

> The disbanding of a large army has naturally thrown upon the country a great number of mechanics and laborers, whose subsistence depends upon their daily labor . . . The field now open to this class is large, no portion of our country offering greater inducements than Southwest Missouri . . . If submitted to the proper test, [Springfield] will put to shame the claims of more arrogant communities . . . Every stage is crowded, and the roads are lined, with this class of people; seeking homes and investments in our favored land; we bid them welcome. Warm hearts and strong arms will receive you, and hand in hand we will enter the road of greatness and glory.[12]

Ingram also printed and endorsed a statement by the Missouri State Board of Immigration calling for vigorous local efforts to attract "industrious people of the older States of the East, or of the countries of the Old World; so that Missouri may regain what she has lost in the race of improvement with her neighboring free sister States during four years of desolating war."[13]

Springfield sought anyone from the North or the East, regardless of how many would come or whether the town could absorb the influx. Such movement was bound to bring not only all kinds of laborers, but also men eager to invest their money. A gazetteer of the region noted with a degree of favorable prejudice that: "Men of large capital can find here chances for profitable investment, while the honest, industrious mechanic with small means will find opportunities to increase them."[14] Undoubtedly, these types of northerners were the preferred immigrants.

Springfield residents were also concerned with removing the remnants of the slave society that had existed in Missouri before the war. Unionists in Springfield were not all radical emancipationists. When black servitude ended and the South was defeated, however, the radicals in Springfield pressed to the fullest the association of slavery with economic backwardness. Pennsylvania's *Pittsburgh Daily Commercial* noted that slavery in Missouri had been powerful enough "to hinder the wholesome immigration which the natural resources of the land invited."[15] After passage of the radical state constitution in November 1865, Ingram noted that this ensured the flow of immigration of "industrious and intelligent" farmers, mechanics, and manufacturers from the North. Anything but the strongest radical control in Missouri would discourage these people "and immigration would continue to flow chiefly from Kentucky, Tennessee and other Southern States, as it was before slavery was abolished."[16]

No matter how much the "unflinchingly radical Republican" *Missouri Patriot*[17] favored this change in the complexion of town society, the fact remained that many people in Springfield, including the editor of the *Patriot* himself, had come from Tennessee. Most residents in southwest Missouri before the war, and some immigrants shortly afterward, had migrated almost directly west across the states of the Upper South. For example, an 1876 survey reported only one of eighty people who had settled in Springfield's Campbell Township before 1840 had been from the North. Tennessee provided half of the remaining seventy-nine, while Kentucky, North Carolina, and Virginia furnished most of the rest.[18] This migration across the Upper South to southern Missouri continued until the Civil War and was the major source of Springfield's population growth in the 1850s.

Springfield's close links with the South in postwar years also were noticeable in the number of town leaders from that region. The bank, the Republican newspaper, the congressional seat, most of the town offices, and many of the retail stores were controlled by people born in Virginia, Tennessee, or Kentucky. In addition, the town merchants revived the Arkansas trade that had developed before the war. In exchange for finished goods, wagon drivers from northwestern Arkansas regularly brought lumber and raw cotton to Springfield. During the postwar years, when dealers in Arkansas had access to merchandise from St. Louis only through Springfield, wholesale merchants made sizable profits from the South in spite of its alleged backwardness.[19]

Despite these continued ties with the South, Springfield's newspaper disclaimed any resemblance between southwest Missouri and the South. Unlike the South, it was said, Missouri would quickly forget the sectional strife and disorderly life of the antebellum and war years. While willing to admit that Greene County had been divided over the war and experienced destruction, the *Missouri Patriot* insisted that the area, unlike the old Confederate states, was united in favor of progress. "Although this part of Missouri has suffered terribly by the ravages of the war, it is recovering more rapidly perhaps than any other portion of the State, there being perfect peace and harmony among its inhabitants."[20] Letters printed in the paper reflect this same theme of renewal and harmony. One from Lawrence, Kansas, compared Springfield with areas farther west, saying it had all the advantages with none of the drawbacks. The writer urged citizens to regain Springfield's prewar accomplishments while pushing forward in order to catch up with the North.[21]

Thus, in spite of Springfield's continued links with the South, the North seemed to offer greater opportunity for united pursuit of prosperity and harmony. The self-assurance of newspaper rhetoric, however, did not reflect the real uncertainty of postwar years. The most important connection to the North, the railroad, remained unfinished. Believing that the project was essential for their future well-being, the people of Springfield increased their great faith in the benefits of the railroad. Hope of its rapid completion provided the basis and stimulus for a growing society between 1865 and 1870.

The *Marshfield Yeoman* described the railroad as "the one great absorbing interest to the people of Southwest Missouri—a question that overshadows all others."[22] This concern made good economic sense to the people of Springfield. Many were convinced that their area was blessed with a peculiar abundance of resources that not only could be shipped out on a railroad but would also naturally serve the future needs of manufacturing in Springfield. The rail line would bring streams of people, many of whom would settle in Greene County, townspeople thought. The railroad would contribute to the prestige of Springfield as a northern instead of a southern city, end several decades of anticipation of progress, and show the rest of the state the importance of Missouri's forgotten southwest corner.

The most important line, the Southwest Branch of the Pacific Railroad, would run from St. Louis. In 1865, 115 miles remained unconstructed. A road to the West in the direction of Kansas City would be the next step for railroad men in Springfield. This, as well as a route leading to the Mississippi River at Memphis, were not yet being built. The first priority, nevertheless, remained the line to St. Louis. After its completion, great changes would occur in Springfield. The editor of the *Patriot* wrote in August 1865:

> Before much progress can be made . . . it will be necessary to have our Southwest Branch of the Pacific Railroad completed to the western border of our State, to transport our products to market. This great desideratum, so long and ardently hoped for by the people of the

> Southwest, we hope to see consumated [*sic*] speedily, now that slavery is removed and progress takes the place of conservatism.[23]

Four and a half years of waiting remained before the first train arrived in May 1870. In the meantime, Springfield experienced a period of reckless growth and suicidal extravagance with uninterrupted migration, plentiful money, booming commerce, and rising property values. Delays in completion of the railroad line often seemed as much a misfortune for the town as the Civil War. Prosperity, while welcomed by the natives, made them wonder whether the boom would last. They feared immigrants might move on if the railroad plans did not turn into reality.

Delays in railroad construction were largely beyond the control of Springfield's residents. Management and ownership problems crippled the railroad project throughout the postwar years. The bankrupt Pacific Railroad was bought by General John C. Fremont in 1866. His company, the Southwest Pacific Railroad, in which there had been unbounded confidence, quickly spent its resources and failed after building only twelve miles of road. Finally, in 1868, the South Pacific Railroad assumed control and completed construction to Springfield, only to be merged soon afterward with the Atlantic and Pacific Railroad Company.[24] Springfield men traveled to New York, St. Louis, Jefferson City, and Washington, attempting to speed the progress of construction. "They are becoming impatient," the *Patriot* reported in 1865 of the townspeople.[25] By 1870, they were glad the railroad had arrived in the area but they remained disgruntled by the delay.[26]

The benefits of the railroad as it turned out, however, were experienced in Springfield before the first train arrived. The period before 1870, in fact, proved more satisfactory for Springfield's anticipated growth into an important city than did the next decade. The 1870s brought problems to the town that few people considered before the railroad arrived.

Besides the problems that would surface in the seventies, serious difficulties had already appeared in the late 1860s. The delay of building the road from St. Louis had caused many residents to weigh benefits of railroads against disadvantages. In particular, many Greene County residents had objected to the continuing requests for money to influence decisions and speed construction of railroads to the city. In 1869 Andrew Pierce, president of the Atlantic and Pacific Railroad, proposed that Springfield businesses pay $25,000 to divert the railroad survey. His request was denied and the railroad went north of town.[27] This rejection, later attributed to "the stinginess and selfishness of some of the moneyed men of old Springfield," led to the creation of North Springfield.[28] Also in 1869, vot-

Figure 7. North Side Frisco Shops, Springfield, Missouri.
POSTCARD, POSTMARKED 1908, SPRINGFIELD, KALEN AND MORROW COLLECTION

ers defeated proposals for county subscriptions to help build the Fort Scott, Springfield, and Memphis Railroad and the Kansas City and Memphis Railroad. This action, as it turned out, meant that a second railroad would not come to Greene County until 1881.[29] Adding to the bitterness related to recurrent financial requests was the fact that railroad management difficulties complicated the settlement of land in Greene County owned by the rail line. The predicament of not knowing who owned vacant land when potential purchasers were numerous amounted to a real "calamity to this whole section of the state," as the editor of the *Patriot* noted. The people of Springfield, eager for their share of the open land, certainly agreed with him.[30]

Rapidly increasing land values and widespread land speculation in the period between 1866 and 1870 were among the most obvious indications that the railroad was near. In 1866, the newspaper had published frequent warnings against selling land at anything higher than "fair prices." Restraint, the editor explained, was particularly important at a time when sales were so numerous. This problem became especially apparent in Springfield because of the great need for housing lots in the fast-growing town. Lot speculators trying to make a quick profit would only retard the growth of the entire town, noted A. F. Ingram. "City property is too high here, and our population and prosperity would be greatly increased if the evil were remedied. If it is not, immigrants will go where property is cheaper." Ingram's proposal was that half the lots in the city be sold at cost.[31] Three years later, H. E. Havens of the *Patriot* estimated that land in the Springfield area was selling at prices three times greater than similar land elsewhere in southwest Missouri "simply because we have an immediate *prospect* for at least one road, while they have no prospect of any." A completed railroad, Havens wrote, would add at least another twenty dollars per acre to land values.[32] Of course some men in Springfield gained a great deal from these inflated values. As the newspapers indicate, however, this extravagant speculation threatened to ruin the town if it were not controlled. Yet, speculation on land values naturally took place, for everyone wanted a share of the rapid growth in the town. It would be difficult for the railroad to satisfy such uncontrolled optimism.

Population increase was believed to be an important sign of the advent of Springfield's greatness. People expected great gains as a result of the railroad. "A very large immigration is contemplating moving here," wrote A. F. Ingram in 1865.[33] Judge Sempronius H. Boyd proudly submitted to the newspaper a letter from Jefferson City, which stated, "You will have an influx of population exceeding any immigration that has heretofore gone to any of the new States or territories, and we are determined that you shall have your railroad."[34] Predictions such as these were matched by reports of the great migration to Springfield. "Our own section is attracting great attention, and considering the great distance we are from rail or river communication with the East, cannot complain of the proportion of this desirable population falling to our share," noted the *Patriot* in 1865.[35] Northerners were being attracted to Springfield. In 1866 Ingram reported that: "Immigration is pouring in" from "Iowa, Illinois, Ohio, Pennsylvania, Connecticut, Wisconsin, Central and Northern Missouri." Such migration would ensure prosperity for southwest Missouri and the Union.[36]

Germans were among the foreigners most often included in the groups of desirable immigrants sought by Springfield. The faith the residents placed in the railroad was reinforced by reports that railroad executives were going to Germany to attract settlers to southwest Missouri.[37] A Springfield paper encouraged the town's residents to accept Germans as readily as American-born immigrants. "We regard them as the most thrifty and desirable citizens, and should be glad to welcome them to our midst. No other class of population would do more to develop the country," the paper noted.[38]

Germans came, but not in the numbers predicted. In 1870 there were 185 German-born residents out of a total population of 21,550 in Greene County.[39] Half-price tickets on the railroad and stage from St. Louis, however, attracted many other people to Springfield. Between 1865 and 1870 Springfield's population grew steadily. Some men arrived as part of railroad construction crews. Others were speculators expecting a greater boom when the railroad arrived. If these men could be convinced to stay in Springfield and not merely pass through, the town would be on its way toward becoming a great city.

Despite the importance accorded to the railroad and to immigration for Springfield's future greatness, the 1870s were extremely disappointing years, bringing frequent reminders that Springfield society was still weak and vulnerable to forces and decisions beyond its control. In particular, the founding of a rival town, an economic panic and a lingering depression stalled plans for a second railroad, delayed many public and private improvements, slowed population growth, and ended the general economic abundance of the late 1860s.

In the late sixties men in Springfield believed that a good society resulted from business prosperity, which, in turn, depended on attracting the right type of merchants to the town. Getting rich was an acceptable goal, but only under the proper aura of work and community spirit. This attitude explains the disdain expressed in the newspapers, not only toward laggards, but also toward underhanded speculators whose wealth would be gained at the expense of others. Attracting the right type of businessmen appeared to have been a major concern in the decade and a half after the Civil War. "Few persons perhaps fully realize," noted the *Patriot,* "how much the prosperity of a town, and of the country about it, depends upon the character of its merchants."[40] If Springfield's residents were to build "a great commercial and manufacturing city in our midst,"[41] they would have to attract the right kind of business and a desirable sort of citizen.

To attract these businesses and citizens, the people of Springfield believed that a number of problems needed to be solved. Frequent letters to the newspaper complained of the poor roads leading into Springfield. The recurring incidents involving broken wagon wheels and injured horses reminded residents of the town's frontier reputation and prompted appeals for county court action and volunteer duty to repair ruts.[42] Increasing concern was expressed for the physical appearance of the town itself. In Springfield's early years, a three-acre plot of barren land in the center of town had been reserved for a park to be landscaped when the city achieved appropriate proportions. Meanwhile, however, the condition of this "public square" alternated between dust and mud, depending on the weather. The *Patriot* editorialized:

> We have frequently urged upon our City Fathers the propriety of remedying its vacant, cowyard appearance by enclosing it with a neat fence and ornamenting it with trees, shrubbery, and flowers. But it still remains neglected, a disgrace to our city, and a subject for the ridicule of strangers.[43]

Photographs taken in the 1870s show the huge public square still empty, except for a firebell tower in the center.[44] Another perennial city council debate involved the best means for improving streets and sidewalks and of keeping them free of garbage.[45]

A more serious problem during the years of rapid population growth developed from the shortage of housing and business places worthy of the great city Springfield hoped to become. Shortly after the war, A. F. Ingram noted that the high rents being charged those living in sheds and dilapidated old houses would certainly discourage settlement of the town. "Mechanics and day laboring men are a necessary part of the institutions of a city," he observed, "but they like to live in comfortable houses,

Figure 8. Bird's-eye View of Springfield, Missouri, looking west from Woodruff Building. POSTCARD, POSTMARKED 1912, SPRINGFIELD, KALEN AND MORROW COLLECTION

and would be willing to pay reasonable rents."[46] Perry Baricklow, editor of the *Cassville Republican,* visited Springfield in 1867 and acknowledged that it would be "unquestionably the Metropolis of Southwest Missouri." He praised its geographic location and the fact that it was spread out. "The streets are wide and regularly laid out, but are badly kept," he complained. "Many of the houses in the business part of the city are in a dilapidated condition, and altogether the town presents rather a shabby appearance."[47]

Such criticism by an out-of-town newspaper could be used to great advantage by those urging that brick structures replace old wooden buildings. Others suggested town improvements of the 1860s and 1870s—street lighting, a fire department, gas lines, and streetcar tracks—were advocated by those aware of Springfield's image. Town law and order was equally important for a good image. When police enforcement seemed too lax or too aggressive, letters and editorials reminded the city marshall and council of the need for sensible control of "quarreling, drunkenness, and other immoral practices" to preserve the city's good name.[48]

Springfield citizens, who wanted to attract better merchants by improving the town, faced an agonizing problem that stemmed from the strong desire for personal economic gain on the part of most businessmen. Businessmen who would ultimately benefit from improvements in town life often opposed the taxation necessary to undertake even small public projects. These men felt that high taxes might discourage people from coming to the town as much as unsanitary streets and dilapidated buildings. In fact, when immigration slowed down and workers left the city early in the 1870s, taxation received the blame.[49] The debate over the needs of Springfield dealt largely in terms of economic gain. A compromise existed throughout the postwar years. Men continued to favor improvements, but they preferred private financing rather than taxation. Public action would be unnecessary if individual businessmen would see the opportunity before them. Men who had money to put into housing, the *Patriot* argued, "would most assuredly find it a paying investment, and one that would advance the interests of our city."[50]

Prosperity was threatened and confidence in Springfield's future was shaken, however, by events related to the building of the rival town of North Springfield. The new town resulted from a fantastically successful venture in speculation undertaken at the expense of the old town. It was not outsiders but several Springfield residents who joined in what seemed to many a betrayal of their town's interests. Their actions created an atmosphere of suspicion that lasted for ten years.

The original 1852 railroad survey through Greene County had run about one mile to the north of Springfield's town square. During the rapid growth before and after the Civil War, most buildings were constructed south, east, and west of the town. Getting the road built seemed a greater concern than readjusting the survey through the center of town. Meanwhile, in the late 1860s, three Springfield residents—Congressman S. H. Boyd, Dr. Edwin T. Robberson, and Charles E. Harwood—had worked out a plan to capitalize on the original survey. Both Boyd and Robberson came from well-established Springfield families; Boyd had served as a prewar mayor of the town. Already partners in a real estate business, Harwood and Boyd approached Robberson, who owned five hundred acres of land on the original survey, with their plan. As business partners, these men would suggest to the railroad that it maintain its original survey. As an incentive they would propose the following: forty acres of land would be given to the railroad to construct shops; a strip of land three hundred feet wide would be deeded for railroad yards; Harwood, Robberson, and Boyd would lay out a town site of at least two hundred acres, erect a depot, and organize a town company with one-half the stock owned by the railroad.[51]

While representatives from Springfield were trying to get the survey changed by carrying petitions to St. Louis and Boston, railroad officials recognized the advantages of letting the original survey stand and accepted the offers of the three speculators. To settle the matter, Andrew Pierce representing the railroad came to Springfield and demanded $25,000 from Springfield businesses in order to change the survey. Within a few years, when the rival town was successful, this would not seem such an exorbitant amount. Under the circumstances, however, Springfield men, led by banker C. B. Holland, demanded that the charter stating that the railroad would be built through Springfield be honored. Pierce reportedly replied angrily, "I'll damned soon show you where I'll build!" and accepted the plans for North Springfield.[52]

In one sense rivalry between the two towns was natural. Not only did North Springfield attract the long-awaited railroad, but for several years, it also seemed to draw new residents more easily than the old town. By the time the first train arrived, the new town included four hundred permanent inhabitants. Railroad shops comprised the principal economic element of North Springfield. By mid-1870, however, thirty other businesses were established in the town. Some Springfield merchants even moved their affairs to North Springfield. To accommodate the constant flow of people through the new town, the three-story Ozark House, believed to be the largest hotel in southwest Missouri, was constructed.[53]

Men who remained in the old town attributed lagging business to a conspiracy of real estate men and railroad executives who created and sustained North Springfield. The new town appeared to be blocking further progress in Springfield. A letter to the *Patriot* accused North Springfield of joining the railroad in opposition to plans for a competing main line to Springfield. The writer called on residents of Springfield to oppose outside interference that would favor North Springfield. "When we give money to another railroad enterprise," the letter concluded, "we must at least have a depot for our convenience and advantage, and not for the interest of a few men at North Springfield who are trying to enrich themselves by divesting business from us and depreciating our property."[54]

In another sense, however, the rivalry was natural only in that it demonstrated by its ridiculousness the fragility of Springfield society's values. The towns were only one mile apart, but few men saw the possibility of merging them or that the towns could work together for common goals. The majority of men in both towns thought primarily of how their grand designs were being frustrated. Using both private and public funds, expensive improvements were attempted in order to boost the prestige of each town and, thus, attract more settlers. Great financial risk was involved, especially in the depression years after 1873. While many of the projects—the streetcar line, the college, the second railroad, and manufacturing enterprises—actually would assist in bringing the two towns together, their original purpose was to aid private fortunes by advancing the prestige of the individual towns.[55]

The economic impact of competition from North Springfield would not have been so great if economic depression had not hit Springfield after the panic of 1873. Business had been declining in Springfield even before the failure of Jay Cooke's New York bank in the fall of that year and the money crisis that followed. In the optimism of the late 1860s the newspaper had pronounced the town's major bank so secure that "even a systematic 'run' upon its vaults could not disturb its operations."[56] By 1871, however, when Springfield merchants organized a board of trade to revive the town's economy, business "was duller and the prospects gloomier than they had been for years."[57] The Springfield Manufacturing Company, for instance, which seemed to be a promising attempt at large-scale factory production of farm machinery, came into financial difficulties soon after its opening in 1871.[58]

Some of these problems could be blamed on competition from North Springfield. Nevertheless, the overall economic picture was equally frustrating to those who thought that Springfield's economic base was strong. Excessive taxation was believed responsible for part of the economic difficulty, especially loss of an abundant labor supply. "More than five hundred mechanics and laborers have been driven from Springfield within the year and a half past" because of high taxes, noted the *Patriot*.[59]

Still optimism remained, though it was somewhat restrained. As long as Springfield maintained control of its own capital, noted the *Patriot*, it would withstand economic pressures from the outside. Even though some merchants had closed their establishments because of credit problems, "the aggregate business of the city cannot be crippled," the editor argued. In spite of this, he warned, the immediate future "is likely to be a period of great stringency in money matters."[60] The problem of caring for the increasing number of Greene County indigents necessitated moving the poor farm from its rural location to a larger site near the eastern city limits of Springfield. The county court was also asked to pay the standard fee for burial of paupers more frequently.[61]

The banks of Springfield remained open during the money crisis that followed the panic. The *Patriot* warned people against hoarding money. Those who had money to spend should continue, confident that "in a week business will be resumed in all quarters, and commerce will continue to go forward as usual." In the very same issue, however, several stores announced that goods would be sold for cash only. Other businessmen advertised that "panic prices" were forcing them to sell merchandise at cost.[62]

For about three years Springfield's progress was noticeably affected by the national depression. Immigration virtually halted, and every part of the city had empty residences and shops as people left to look for better opportunities elsewhere.[63] North Springfield faced similar problems since many people connected with railroad construction moved on when the line was extended southwest toward the Indian Territory in 1874. And as late as 1876 the newspaper reported that Springfield still was not attracting settlement from the "constant stream of people passing through this city for Texas."[64]

Town image and prestige remained the chief concern, even in the most difficult depression years. Maintaining these values residents believed would attract immigrants and restore prosperity. Private debt increased as a result of construction when money was not available. Newly organized Drury College, founded just before the depression, was able to collect money for only a small percentage of its $100,000 subscription because of the money crisis. Yet in 1874, the school decided to build a $30,000 building with only $11,000 in resources. In spite of three lawsuits over unpaid construction bills, the Ladies Hall was completed. Drury College had gained the confidence of townspeople by giving them a school to point out to prospective immigrants.[65]

Improvements too risky for private enterprise were undertaken with public money. The gasworks, franchised by Springfield in 1874, were completed the next year at a cost of $60,000. This and other public improvement projects, including inducement payments to attract manufacturing, explained why the debt of the county increased 165 percent between 1873 and 1876.[66] It was argued that improvements similar to these, including the proposed water works, omnibus line, and fire department, would pay for themselves when they drew immigrants to the city in the better times that were ahead.[67] Presumably they would then become private ventures.

Springfield's misfortune in the 1870s was attributed to uncontrollable circumstances: the greed of a few railroad and real estate men who created North Springfield and the failure of eastern banks that caused the depression. In the last half of the decade, however, the city seemed to be regaining control of its own future by beginning to develop large-scale manufacturing necessary for any great city. In the period after the Civil War, when Springfield had grown quickly, the dream of rapid industrialization had been voiced frequently, and steps were taken to bring large-scale industry to town. An iron foundry was rebuilt; a plow factory was established; and wood planing, wool, and cotton mills opened within a few years. A small "manufacturing district" even developed.[68] Men generally conceded that the railroad was necessary for large-scale manufacturing since it alone would bring sufficient workers. "Labor is the source of all wealth," wrote A. F. Ingram in 1866.[69] Impatient over railroad construction delays, an impassioned correspondent to the *Patriot* called for manufacturing instead of "trading horses and swapping jack-knives." Only then would railroads see the real prospects for Springfield.

> The Southwest has all the material advantages . . . and means of becoming in manufactures, the New England of the West. She can furnish everything desired or required in these great industries that have already built up Massachusetts. . . . Give way then, gentlemen, traders, and dealers. Turn a little of your energies and means in the direction of making something . . . Let's make a firm stand for the Southwest, for Springfield as the center manufacturing point. Stand up for . . . the foundry, your wagon and carriage makers, and everyman who has put his means and energy into manufactories, and you will draw after you railroads, as naturally as ducks take to water.[70]

But the advantages of the railroad were offset by the economic problems of the early 1870s. Edward Thompson's foundry was the only major manufacturing effort to continue uninterrupted production through the panic and depression. Recovery, however, was already beginning in 1872 when things appeared worst. In that year, the city council decided by a vote of five to one to issue $22,000 in bonds to aid certain "infant industries."[71] In addition, the Springfield Cotton Mill and H. F. Fellows' wagon factory began operations in 1872. By 1878, the foundry employed forty, the wagon factory fifty, and the cotton mill one hundred men and women.[72] These enterprises and smaller manufacturing efforts were given much of the credit for Springfield's recovery from the depression. In 1876 the county court, recognizing the cotton mill's benefits for the town, canceled $25,000 in back taxes owed by its operators.[73] When the railroad finally was being built to Kansas City, Springfield's residents believed they had a good start in manufacturing and that the new rail line would make the factories more successful by offering competition to the line from St. Louis.[74]

"Business is reviving in our midst and our business men are beginning to feel that we are starting up hill again," noted the *Springfield Patriot-Advertiser* in 1876. "We hope there will be no disappointment in expectations so reasonably entertained. We have been down at hard pan long enough, and would, we think, appreciate at its true worth a season of prosperity."[75] Confidence seemed completely restored by 1878 when the *Springfield Spiritual Offering* boasted:

> Nearly all stores are of brick, and very creditable in appearance, as fine as those of any medium city in the United States. The city is growing steadily, improvements are constantly in progress, and the country can support a city three times the size of Springfield. Its resources are not half developed. Here is a promising field for capital, and not a chance of failure in any well-directed effort.[76]

Although not everything in Springfield revolved around success and failure in business, even noneconomic aspects of town life reflected economic concerns. Development of social institutions in the town, such as the public school system, a private college and voluntary organizations including churches, was affected and inhibited by the efforts to make Springfield a booming manufacturing center. For example, the school system established after the Civil War was intended as another attraction to draw immigrants to Springfield and ensure the town's good name. None of the small private schools of the 1850s had survived the war. As a result, stated a letter to the newspaper, town morality and good reputation had deteriorated. "Intellectual cultivation of this community" could remedy this immorality, the writer noted.[77] The movement for education always was seen as part of the drive for material progress. "While the vast mineral resource of Southwest Missouri is to be developed by the great Southern Pacific Railroad," noted W. B. Jones at the first meeting of the Young Men's Association, "the vast intellectual resources shall be developed also."[78] Schools were promoted as a useful inducement to bring settlers to the area. The association of schools with profitable business in Springfield was explained by a teacher who argued:

> Our good schools will attract the best and most intelligent class of immigrants, and will induce them to pay much higher prices for homes amongst us. One of the first questions, indeed, that an intelligent and enterprising man from the North or East asks, when seeking a home in any particular locality in the West, is "have they good schools there?" If we wish such men to settle among us—in a word, if we wish to prosper, we must have good schools.

Further, he noted, as much as $20,000 a year was spent outside the community by citizens who sent their children to eastern schools. Good public schools would bring many times that amount into the town.[79] The argument over taxation for public schools in the spring of 1867 had divided the town between those who believed schools would help make a moral, and therefore, attractive community and those who thought such taxation was "illegal, unjust, infamous" and placed oppressive financial burdens on townspeople.[80] The advocates of schools were generally successful, and bond issues for building construction passed in 1868, 1871, and 1880. Public schools remained an important attribute for Springfield in its rivalry with North Springfield until 1886, when North Springfield established a system of its own.[81]

Initially, Drury College apparently differed from the public schools. Besides the general and commercial educational programs, students at Drury read Homer and Cicero and learned French, trigonometry, and zoology. Of course this impressive course of study was almost totally unrelated to the value the townspeople placed on the college. Most Drury students came not from Springfield nor even from Missouri, but from the states of the Northeast and New England. Apart from providing temporary teachers and ministers for southwest Missouri's schools and churches, the college served almost no immediate practical purpose for the town.

In reality Drury was a "booster college."[82] Its primary purpose was to add prestige to the town and to promote town interests by legitimizing its status as a true city. The booster spirit was strong in Springfield. The enterprising pledge drives of C. E. Harwood and his brother, the Reverend James H. Harwood, enabled Springfield rather than Neosho or Carthage to be selected by the Association of Congressional Churches as the site of the school. Convinced that a college would be good for the community, residents pledged over $100,000 in 1872, when the town's business was certainly not at its best.[83]

The school's supporters, however, wanted spectacular results from their investment, which could not easily be achieved. "Little popular interest was taken in our work at the time," Drury president Nathan Morrison wrote of the first day of school. He added:

> The former enthusiasm of the people had largely died out. The "great expectations" as to the opening importance of the college had not been met. The first building was too modest . . . The community was disappointed by the meagre external outfits of the College. They had expected, justly or unreasonably, the erection of fine buildings, whose architectural pretensions would dignify their city.[84]

In order to "save the institution from ruin," Morrison decided to construct a prestigious building, even though the school lost most of its pledgers in the depression. The scheme worked, community support and confidence were regained, and by 1878 the *Springfield Leader* boasted that the school could be compared to Vassar.[85] Instead of Drury's classical curriculum, the simple fact of the college's existence served the same purpose as Springfield's public schools, only on a grander scale.

The churches, like the public schools, were supposed to indicate Springfield's concern for morality. However, since the churches also claimed to serve as social organizations for the people, their purpose was not solely to enhance the image of the town. All churches were expected to offer universal concern for various aspects of morality in Springfield. When temperance people appealed for support, when residents expressed a need for religious instruction in the city jail, when public schools or Drury College were promoted, the call was generally for "Christian unity." Interdenominational organizations such as the YMCA and the Greene County Bible Association existed in addition to the various congregations, performing tasks of religious instruction on a larger scale than could the individual churches.[86] All levels of education were supposed to contribute to Christian and democratic ideals, which were more important than any particular theology or church affiliation.[87]

Even though the churches seemed to offer some moral leadership in Springfield, they did not perform adequately the function of contributing stable social order in the midst of the town's frantic drive for growth. Some congregations traced their history to the prewar period. In reality, however, no congregations had remained intact through the Civil War years. When the Baptist church reorganized in 1866, only fifteen prewar members could be found.[88] During the war, the Southern Methodist church had lost most of its Confederate-sympathizing members. In 1865 and 1866 Southern Methodists throughout Greene County became involved in violent disputes with the county's Northern Methodists over control of church buildings.[89] The two Presbyterian churches as well as the Episcopal congregation suffered disruption and division resulting from the war. The Episcopal rector, Theodore Holcombe, was the only clergyman to serve in Springfield throughout the war years.

In the prosperous half decade after the war, religion advanced along with the town. Not only were older congregations reorganized and churches rebuilt, but with the financial assistance of whites, independent black Presbyterian, Baptist, and Methodist groups were formed. In 1869 immigrants from New England established a Congregational church, and about the same time a resident Catholic priest arrived.[90] Some churches retained their ministers for as long as four years during the late 1860s. Not only could congregations financially support their own clergy instead of a missionary preacher, but ministers themselves saw Springfield as a growing city with abundant opportunities for their work.

However, the good fortunes of the Springfield churches after the war declined in the 1870s, following the economic fate of the town. With immigration virtually ended and business declining, the churches ceased to attract many new members. North Springfield, in contrast, was growing rapidly between 1870 and 1874, and its Christian, Northern Methodist, and Catholic churches soon became the largest congregations in the Springfield area.[91] At the same time Baptist, Presbyterian, and Congregational churches in Springfield turned increasingly to "revivals of religion" and "protracted meetings" to attract new members.[92]

A major difficulty of almost all Springfield churches during the 1870s was the impermanence of their ministers. Christ Church Episcopal had seven different rectors in the 1870s; six ministers served the Baptist church; and the Cumberland Presbyterian church witnessed the loss of ten preachers during the decade.[93] The Congregational church was fortunate to have various faculty members from Drury College to substitute during the frequent vacancies. The congregation, however, desired a permanent clergyman so much that in 1876, when the Reverend Joseph C. Plumb requested a release to go to Joplin, the congregation refused two times and only after a bitter dispute complied with his third request.[94] With their rapidly fluctuating memberships and impermanent clergy, the churches hardly proved to be stable social institutions for the people of Springfield in times of prosperity or depression.

During the 1870s, when Protestant congregations were having difficulties, the Roman Catholic church of Springfield seemed to be flourishing. Numerically, this was quite true. By 1881, the parish had five hundred members, making it the largest church body in Springfield or North Springfield. Except for a brief drop in membership around 1873, the increase had been steady since its founding in 1868.[95] Yet the Catholics suffered from the same unsettled conditions as the Protestants.

Springfield's Catholics could not agree on how important a parochial school was for the future of their parish. Operation of a separate school proved expensive and competed with Springfield's recently established public schools. Frequently parents chose to send their children to the public schools rather than pay the tuition at the parish school. Therefore, the Catholic school was always in financial trouble.

Equally distressing were the disputes between Springfield and North Springfield Catholics. This conflict was partly ethnic in nature since North Springfield's Catholics were predominantly Irish and Springfield's Catholics generally had German backgrounds. The dispute also reflected the fact that North Springfield's Catholics, who had arrived with the railroad, challenged the parish leadership of the more established merchants of Springfield. Disputes over the control of church property resulted, with the priest unable to mediate the conflict. In 1882 the parish divided.[96] Rapid immigration of new residents, which had enabled the creation of a Catholic parish in Springfield, prevented the development of a stable social organization among the town's Catholics. Instead of uniting in a common purpose, the group broke apart with each section seeking its own interests.

The rudimentary labor unions of Springfield also failed to provide much real order for the workingmen of the town. For one thing, they were small. Over half of the men in North Springfield were directly employed by the railroad, yet the two railroad unions—the Brotherhood of Locomotive Firemen and the Brotherhood of Locomotive Engineers—had a combined membership of about eighty in 1881. Many of these members were not even residents of the city but rather of other towns along the line.[97] Furthermore, the railroad men of Springfield did not have an identity that separated them from the rest of the townspeople.

During the 1877 national rail strike, the railroad workers seemed to support demands for a restoration of wages. At a town meeting attended by trainmen and Springfield merchants, opposition by town businessmen to a proposed strike, however, convinced workers to stay at their jobs. In practice, the labor unions seem to have had little more practical social activity than the numerous fraternal orders of both Springfield and North Springfield. Membership in these lodges offered residents an elaborate system of rank and degree. Nevertheless, participation in fraternal organizations remained a place to withdraw from the rest of life in Springfield. Except for an occasional open house party or patriotic parade, lodge activity presumably was quite isolated.[98]

Unlike Springfield's fraternal orders, the Grange and temperance groups had stated purposes for their organization that related to the conditions of town life. The Springfield Patrons of Husbandry had 380 members in 1873. While many of these men came from the surrounding rural area, a group of farmers resided in town throughout the 1870s. Among these men, anti-railroad and anti-manufacturing sentiment remained strong. However, beyond opposition to using county money to subsidize manufacturing, their voices seldom were heard on matters relating to the promotion of town progress.[99]

Temperance proved to be one of the most popular issues. Successful on a small scale in Springfield immediately after the war, the temperance movement revived in the mid-1870s. In 1866, the city council had limited the number of saloons in Springfield as a step toward reducing crime, establishing "law and order," and making a good name for the town.[100] By the 1870s temperance emerged as a more voluntary effort among Springfield citizens. Aware that thirteen of the first thirty business places in North Springfield had been taverns, a Temperance Alliance formed in Springfield in 1873 to solicit signatures and assure that their town would not share in the evil reputation of the new town.[101] In response to charges that a good share of the residents of Springfield had been morally corrupted, the *Patriot's* editor remained confident. "We had supposed we were a comparatively moral community, and still indulge in the same belief."[102]

The citizens of Springfield did not boast about their cultural activities and entertainment as readily as they announced their morality. People recognized, however, that some sort of "amusement" was necessary to supplement the ordinary life of the town. An occasional animal show traveled through Springfield and won the praise of the residents. No matter how much "good moral entertainment" the Hippo-Olympiad Circus provided or how educational the Mammoth Menagerie proved to be, such shows were infrequent.[103] The town, however, developed its own style of entertainment and culture. The winter balls given at the courthouse or a lodge hall were often considered the major social events of the season. Despite the sponsorship by certain "social clubs," the balls were generally open to all who wished to attend.[104]

Lectures and readings of literature provided what A. F. Ingram called "rational amusement" and "intellectual entertainment" for residents who cared for learning. "A taste for literary pursuits will be encouraged in the young," he noted, "instead of a passion for base and groveling sports."[105] One literary group, in fact, supported a library and a regular lyceum before Drury College was founded. After 1875, intellectual life in the town revolved primarily around the college and its faculty. Some of this influence extended to the rest of the town, even if only on a small scale. "The inspiration given here to musical culture by my colleague at the organ there," President Nathan J. Morrison of Drury said in an 1881 address, "has improved the quality of the music in the churches of Springfield 100 per cent."[106]

Even though no movement for a better cultural life existed, some people expressed displeasure with unrefined popular tastes. The editor of the *Patriot-Advertiser* criticized the "offensive demonstrations" during a minstrel show at the opera house. In the next week's issue the paper commended the Choral Union for its presentation of a patriotic "Centennial Cantata," but regretted that the performance did not please the audience as much as some cruder types of music. A former rector of the Episcopal church believed that Springfield ought to have an exhibition of paintings. He recognized, however, that the idea would have little chance of success. "Such an Exhibition would elevate the taste of all who engaged in it, and be a rich source of intelligent pleasure," he wrote to a church member, "and yet you know that it would appeal only to the more intelligent few."[107] This type of culture was clearly unnecessary for the improvement of Springfield envisioned by most people.

By 1880 Springfield had almost completely recovered from the economic difficulties of the early 1870s. The opening of the rail line from Kansas City to Springfield in 1881 eased much of the rivalry with North Springfield and helped create a new mood of cooperation that eventually led to a merger of the communities in 1887. The consolidated city had a population in 1890 of almost 22,000, about three times the 1880 combined population of Springfield and North Springfield. As the towns began to grow in the late 1870s, businesses there experienced new prosperity. Springfield citizens in 1880 and 1881 seemed to have more reason to be optimistic about the future of their town than in the preceding decade.

In reality, however, Springfield society in 1880 still showed signs of instability. About eight hundred residents of the town moved away between

1878 and 1880, years when the town was beginning to prosper once again. This group did not simply represent migrating laborers and their families, but rather it was composed to a large degree of artisans, merchants, and some of the town's professional men.[108] In addition to losing over one-tenth of its population within two years, Springfield lacked firmly rooted social institutions to provide a stable base for its society. In Springfield, the schools, churches, and other voluntary associations had been primarily products and agencies of rapid growth and not social institutions offering order for town residents. There were, in fact, few structural definitions for society in Springfield that offered permanence to a social order. Except for the concerns of morality and town prestige, people lived in the town as individuals, free to succeed or fail in business and to participate in most aspects of town life.

One notable exception, however, stands out. Most blacks in Springfield assumed the lowest positions on the occupational scale and a segregated social position. Jobs for black men usually involved some type of common labor while black women worked mainly as servants and maids. Younger black women sometimes found jobs in the cotton mill, and a few men worked as artisans.[109] Generally, however, the range of occupations open to Springfield's blacks was severely limited. The school board provided public instruction for black children, which was eagerly accepted. And money from white congregations helped construct separate black Protestant churches, denoting that the town's religious life generally was divided. In 1868 Springfield residents admitted that blacks would eventually participate more fully in their society. Their primary concern, however, was that black children obtain sufficient education and religious training so that the abundant freedom of the community would not become license.[110]

Political position served principally as a reward for Springfield's prosperous businessmen, for success was admired by the voters. As a result, when settlers from the Northeast established profitable businesses in the town after the Civil War, people from that group began to be elected to city and county offices, previously held only by men from the Upper South. The division of Democrats and Republicans offered no clear pattern, especially after the debates over issues of the war and Reconstruction cooled down. Even though the rapid settlement of North Springfield by railway workmen made that city predominantly Democratic for several years, thereby giving the intertown rivalry a political tone, Republican politicians avoided nativist appeals. The Republican newspaper, however, charged that the Greene County Democrats were guilty of nativism in their attempts to attract the votes of foreign-born citizens.[111] Local partisan issues usually involved the public debt and blame for railroad construction delays. No matter which party controlled the city or county government, the other party supported efforts to gain prosperity for the town.

Politics in Springfield, like so much of town life, was unorganized and made little difference in the creation of a metropolis. The community's populace remained fragmented during times of prosperity as well as years of depression. Dreams of growth and improvement and fears that Springfield might be left behind by national progress remained the dominant concerns. Yet when railroads and factories were constructed, a great city did not result overnight. Such improvements only made the town more disorganized. Throughout the postwar years, Springfield's society consisted of several thousand individuals who knew they had to live together to succeed but who did not understand the problems they would have to confront to achieve their goals. Individual residents of Springfield—and the town as a whole—remained disoriented in nineteenth-century America and vulnerable to forces beyond their control. Whether a stable society would have been enough to bring about orderly and reasonable progress in the town during these years is impossible to tell. As it turned out, however, Springfield society between 1865 and 1881 moved blindly toward the future, with only a faint hint of direction or self-control.[112]

Notes

1. Return I. Holcomb, *History of Greene County, Missouri* (St. Louis, MO: Western Historical Society, 1883), 188.

2. Ibid., 733, 736; Samuel S. Vinton Jr. to his father, Samuel Vinton Sr., Baltimore, MD, 1843, in Charles Sheppard Private Collection, Springfield, stated: "Uncle David [David D. Berry, Springfield's first merchant] is a-coining money. People from all over the country come in to trade at his store. They say they are poor but will put down $25, $40, or $50 cash for purchases. We have no beggars here abouts like you do back East."

3. Holcomb, *History of Greene County,* 211–212, 255, 267.

4. Floyd Calvin Shoemaker, *Missouri and Missourians: Land at Contrasts and People at Achievements* (Chicago, 1943), II: 571–572; Holcomb, *History of Greene County,* 256.

5. Ibid., 232, 736, 738–739.

6. George M. Jones, *St. Paul Methodist Episcopal Church, South, Springfield, Missouri, 1831–1924: A Brief History* (Springfield, MO, 1924), 12.

7. Holcomb, *History of Greene County,* 740. For an excellent description of wartime Springfield, see William Garrett Piston and John C. Rutherford, "Quinine Courage: The Battle of Springfield, January 8, 1863," in *Springfield's Urban Histories: Essays on the Queen City of the Missouri Ozarks*, ed. Stephen L. McIntyre (Springfield: Moon City Press, Missouri State University, 2012), 15–57.

8. George Ward Nichols, "Wild Bill," *Harper's New Monthly Magazine* 34 (February 1867): 274.

9. Holcomb, *History of Greene County*, 480.

10. Ibid., 740.

11. Springfield *Missouri Weekly Patriot*, July 13, 1865.

12. Ibid., September 14, 1865.

13. Ibid., June 15, 1865.

14. Nathan H. Parker, *Missouri As It Is in 1867: An Illustrated Historical Gazetteer of Missouri* (Philadelphia, 1867), 258.

15. Quoted in Springfield *Missouri Weekly Patriot*, July 6, 1865.

16. Ibid., November 30, 1865.

17. The description of the newspaper's political stance during Reconstruction was offered by an editor a decade later. *Springfield Patriot-Advertiser*, October 11, 1876.

18. John R. Williams, compiler, *An Illustrated Historical Atlas Map of Greene County, Missouri* (Springfield, MO, 1876), 2.

19. Holcomb, *History of Greene County*, 795–796; eventually Springfield's wagon manufacturers made the hardwood lumber trade with Arkansas extremely profitable. This relationship of wagon makers with Arkansas Ozark wood dealers became so important that Springfield's wagon manufacturing has been described as one of Arkansas's industries. F. P. Rose, "The Springfield Wagon Company," *Arkansas Historical Quarterly* (hereinafter *AHQ*), 10 (Spring 1951): 98.

20. Springfield *Missouri Weekly Patriot*, October 19, 1865.

21. Ibid., September 21, 1865.

22. Quoted in ibid., February 6, 1865.

23. Ibid., August 31, 1865.

24. See Margaret Louise Fitzsimmons, "Missouri Railroads during the Civil War and Reconstruction," *Missouri Historical Review* (hereinafter *MHR*), 35 (January 1941): 188–206.

25. Springfield *Missouri Weekly Patriot*, November 23, 1865.

26. For a discussion of the contradictory opinions concerning the arrival of the railroad in Springfield, see H. Craig Miner, "Hopes and Fears: Ambivalence in the Anti-Railroad Movement at Springfield. Missouri, 1870–1880," *Missouri Historical Society Bulletin* 27 (January 1971): 129–146.

27. Alanson Mason Haswell, "The Building of a City—Springfield," *MHR* 19 (April 1925): 399–400.

28. Holcomb, *History of Greene County*, 839.

29. Jonathan Fairbanks and Clyde Edwin Tuck, *Past and Present of Greene County, Missouri* (Indianapolis: A. W. Bowen and Company, 1915), I: 191.

30. Springfield *Missouri Weekly Patriot*, November 21, 1867.

31. Ibid., February 22, March 29, 1866.

32. Ibid., September 16, 1869.

33. Ibid., June 8, 1865.

34. Ibid., August 19. 1865.

35. Ibid., Supplement, October 12, 1865.

36. Ibid., March 8, 29, 1866.

37. Ibid., September 28, 1865.

38. Ibid., October 3, 1867.

39. Lewis W. Spitz, "The Germans in Missouri: A Preliminary Study" (Master's thesis, Washington University, 1930), 147.

40. Springfield *Missouri Weekly Patriot*, January 2, 1868.

41. Ibid., September 16, 1869.
42. See especially ibid., August 10, 17, 1865, February 20, 1868.
43. Ibid., November 28, 1867.
44. See Virginia Hogg, "The Urban Pattern of Springfield, Missouri" (Master's thesis, Washington University, 1934).
45. Springfield *Missouri Weekly Patriot,* September 14, 1865, December 26, 1867, September 16, 1869.
46. Ibid., August 24, 1865.
47. Quoted in ibid., November 28, 1867.
48. Ibid., January 18, March 15, 1866, October 10, December 19, 1867.
49. Ibid., March 28, 1872.
50. Ibid., June 8, September 4, August 24, 1865.
51. Haswell, "The Building of a City—Springfield," 398–399; Holcomb, *History of Greene County,* 839.
52. Haswell, *MHR,* "The Building of a City—Springfield," 399–400; Holcomb, *History of Greene County*, 839–840.
53. Haswell, *MHR,* "The Building of a City—Springfield," 400–401.
54. Springfield *Missouri Weekly Patriot,* August 11, 1870.
55. Haswell, "The Building of a City—Springfield," 401–402. Two historians of Greene County made their positions clear in 1883: "Although North Springfield still retains its autonomy, and the right of local self-government, of which right it is very jealous, yet it does not require much of a prophet to predict that at no very distant day it will lose its identity as a distinct town and be merged into and become a very important part of the great city of Springfield. But any movement looking to the consolidation of the two towns must be begun by the old town. North Springfield is too important a municipality *per se,* and too capable of managing well its own interests, to beg that it may be swallowed up by some other big town in order that it may be 'protected.'" Holcomb, *History of Greene County*, 844.
56. Springfield *Missouri Weekly Patriot,* January 9, 1868.
57. Holcomb, *History of Greene County*, 775.
58. Rose, "Springfield Wagon Company," 98.
59. Springfield *Missouri Weekly Patriot,* March 28, 1872.
60. Ibid., November 21, 1872.
61. Fairbanks and Tuck, *Past and Present of Greene County,* I: 177.
62. Springfield *Missouri Weekly Patriot,* October 2, 1873.
63. Holcomb, *History of Greene County*, 778–779.
64. Springfield *Missouri Weekly Patriot,* October 18, 1876.
65. Nathan J. Morrison, *A Sketch of the Origin and Statement of the Present Condition of Drury College* (Springfield, MO, 1881), 9–10; Springfield *Missouri Weekly Patriot,* December 30, 1875.
66. George S. Escott, *History and Directory of Springfield and North Springfield* (Springfield, MO, 1878), 128; Springfield *Missouri Weekly Patriot,* December 30, 1875; *Springfield Patriot-Advertiser,* November 2, October 18, 1876.
67. Ibid., December 21, 1876.
68. Springfield *Missouri Weekly Patriot,* August 24, September 14, 1865, February 15, April 5, April 26, 1866, February 13, 1868.
69. Ibid., January 23, 1866.
70. Ibid., September 16, 1869.

71. Holcomb, *History of Greene County,* 775–776.
72. Escott, *History of Springfield,* 113.
73. *Springfield Patriot-Advertiser,* December 14, 1876.
74. Escott, *History of Springfield,* 109.
75. *Springfield Patriot-Advertiser,* October 26, 1876.
76. Quoted in Escott, *History of Springfield,* 111–112.
77. Springfield *Missouri Weekly Patriot,* October 19, 1865.
78. Ibid., March 22, 1866.
79. Ibid., October 26, 1865, February 22, 1866.
80. Fairbanks and Tuck, *Past and Present of Greene County,* I: 410; Springfield *Missouri Weekly Patriot,* August 24, 1865, October 31, 1867.
81. Fairbanks and Tuck, *Past and Present of Greene County,* I: 410.
82. See Daniel J. Boorstin, *The Americans: The National Experience* (New York, 1965), 152–161.
83. Fairbanks and Tuck, *Past and Present of Greene County,* I: 421–423; Shoemaker, *Missouri and Missourians,* I: 552; Morrison, *Drury College,* 3–7.
84. Ibid., 8, 10.
85. Escott, *History of Springfield,* 115–116.
86. Springfield *Missouri Weekly Patriot,* February 20, 1868; *Springfield Patriot-Advertiser,* December 14, 1876.
87. Fairbanks and Tuck, *Past and Present of Greene Co.,* I: 421, 423; Morrison, *Drury College,* 12.
88. M. M. Richardson, *A Brief History of the First Baptist Church of Springfield, Missouri, 1852–1927* (Springfield, MO, 1927), 11.
89. *History of Greene County,* 501–503; Jones, *St. Paul M. E. Church, South,* 16.
90. A. M. Haswell, *The Story of the First Congregational Church of Springfield, Missouri, 1869–1929* (Springfield, MO, 1929), 8–10; Escott, *History of Springfield,* 124–125.
91. Springfield *Missouri Weekly Patriot,* December 30, 1875.
92. Haswell, *Story of the First Congregational Church,* 17; *Springfield Patriot-Advertiser,* October 26, November 16, 1876.
93. Holcomb, *History of Greene County,* 805; Richardson, *History of 1st Baptist Church,* 2; Paul R. Talbot, *Christ Church, Springfield, Missouri, 1859–1924* (Springfield, MO, 1924), 1.
94. Haswell, *Story* of *the First Congregational Church,* 17.
95. John E. Rothensteiner, *History of the Archdiocese of* St. *Louis* (St. Louis, 1928), II, 257; Escott, *History* of *Springfield,* 124; M. Lilliana Owens, *Loretto in Missouri* (St. Louis, 1965), 118.
96. Holcomb, *History of Greene County,* 847–848; Owens, *Loretto in Missouri,* 120–121.
97. Escott, *History of Springfield,* 158; Holcomb, *History of Greene County,* 849–850. For a review of Springfield's unions, see Stephen L. McIntyre, "'The City Belongs to the Local Unions': The Rise of the Springfield Labor Movement," in this volume.
98. *Springfield Patriot-Advertiser,* July 26, 1877; Holcomb, *History of Greene County,* 556.
99. Ibid., 542–545.
100. Springfield *Missouri Weekly Patriot,* February 1, March 29, April 5, 1866.
101. Haswell, "The Building of a City—Springfield," 401; Springfield *Missouri Weekly Patriot,* August 28, September 11, 1873.

102. Ibid., September 11, 1873.

103. Ibid., October 3, 1867.

104. Ibid., January 4, 1866, October 24, 1867; *Springfield Patriot-Advertiser,* November 30, 1876.

105. Springfield *Missouri Weekly Patriot,* December 19, 1867.

106. Morrison, *Drury College,* 14.

107. C. F. Robertson to Marie L. Burden, July 3, 1879, quoted in Talbot, *Christ Church,* 19.

108. William Kearney Hall, compiler, *Springfield, Greene County, Missouri: Inhabitants in 1880* (Champaign, IL, 1966), 300–318.

109. Data on occupations is abstracted from Hall, *Springfield Inhabitants,* 1880.

110. Springfield *Missouri Weekly Patriot,* February 20, 1868.

111. Ibid., March 21, 1872.

112. For a recent continuation of Piehl's discussion, see Angela Wingo Miller's "Retail Rivals: Springfield's Commercial Street versus the Public Square, 1870–1945," in *Springfield's Urban Histories: Essays on the Queen City of the Missouri Ozarks,* ed. Stephen L. McIntyre (Springfield: Moon City Press, Missouri State University Press, 2012), 87–112.

"The City Belongs to the Local Unions"

The Rise of the Springfield Labor Movement, 1871–1912

STEPHEN L. MCINTYRE

When E. J. Smith, an organizer for the Cigar Makers International Union (CMIU), visited Springfield, Missouri, in early 1903, he found a vibrant local labor movement that consisted of fifty-four unions. After surveying the economic and political landscape of the city, Smith concluded: "The city belongs to the local unions if they will all join hands and get out and hustle; it only needs the asking."[1] Smith's assessment was insightful. During the next few years, the combined efforts of local unions and an active Socialist Party turned organized labor into a significant economic and political force that city leaders could not disregard.

Unfortunately, Missouri historians have ignored the Springfield labor movement, primarily focusing instead on unions in St. Louis.[2] Two recent books have shifted the focus from St. Louis to smaller communities, but the labor movement in Kansas City, St. Joseph, Joplin, and Springfield remains largely unexamined.[3] Organized labor in Springfield grew and gained influence between 1871, when the city's first union was chartered, and 1912, when Reuben T. Wood, a young socialist cigar maker and Springfield labor leader, assumed the presidency of the Missouri State Federation of Labor. He was elected in large part because of the Springfield labor movement's statewide reputation for aggressive organizing and socialist political activity. Although Springfield socialists never succeeded in electing any candidates, their presence forced local political and business leaders to accommodate many of the demands of the city's growing labor movement.

The roots of this labor radicalism can be found in the late nineteenth century, when many of Springfield's early-twentieth-century labor leaders first joined unions and experimented with third-party politics. In 1870, the year the railroad arrived in Springfield, the city's population totaled 5,555. Thirty years later the population had increased to 23,267, ranking it the fifth largest in the state. The growth of railroads during this period made Springfield an important processing and shipping center for the region's agricultural products. Manufacturing also expanded, with a 35 percent increase during the 1890s, making the city the state's fourth-largest manufacturing center by 1900. The city's largest employer in this period was the St. Louis and San Francisco Railroad, whose division headquarters and repair shops were located in Springfield. By 1899 the railroad's machine and repair shops provided employment for about 2,500 residents.[4]

Railroad engineers organized the city's first union in 1871, followed by the cigar makers in 1879. As the economy improved and trade unions revived nationally following the depression of the 1870s, unions in the city increased, with workers in six more trades establishing locals during the 1880s. By 1892, Springfield was home to at least fifteen unions, six of them in the railroad trades.[5]

Often exclusive, craft unions generally ignored the concerns of workers in other trades. But several developments during the last two decades of the century worked to promote broader working-class solidarity in Springfield. In 1886 local unions joined together to form the Springfield Central Labor Union. Although records of the organization's activities in this era are virtually nonexistent, it would become a crucial vehicle through which workers pursued political objectives during the early twentieth century. In 1891 the Central Labor Union, in conjunction with the locals of the cigar makers and carpenters, joined seventeen other unions from across the state in founding the Missouri State Federation of Labor to work for legislative goals.[6]

The establishment of six local assemblies of the Knights of Labor in Springfield during the 1880s also fostered greater working-class unity. Workers created the first local assembly in Springfield in 1881 and another in 1882. By 1883 more than 10 percent of the nonagricultural workforce in Greene County belonged to the Knights. An even higher percentage of workers within the city may have been Knights. Four more assemblies appeared in Springfield in 1885–1886 as railroad workers nationwide poured into the Knights during major strikes against Jay Gould's southwest system. At its peak in Springfield in July 1886, the Knights' district assembly counted 1,353 members, making it a force to be reckoned with in a town of about 20,000.[7]

Local assemblies of the Knights were usually mixed, composed of workers from a number of different trades. This proved true for five of the Springfield locals, with the sixth not reporting on the subject. Such assemblages served to break down the craft exclusivity of trade unions and foster a greater sense of class solidarity among members. The Knights also differed from other nineteenth-century labor organizations in their inclusiveness. Unlike trade unions, which usually ignored the needs of unskilled, African American, and women workers, the Knights admitted all three groups into the order, albeit black and women workers often belonged to locals segregated by race and sex. Whether women joined the Knights in Springfield has not been ascertained, but by 1886 the city had one assembly composed primarily of black workers. Although the Knights had declined nationwide by the early 1890s, the order's impact endured because many future labor leaders had been members of the organization.[8]

Many railroad workers who had been Knights found their way into the American Railway Union (ARU) in 1893 and 1894. Eugene Debs, former secretary-treasurer of the Brotherhood of Locomotive Firemen and a future Socialist Party presidential candidate, joined with other former members of the railroad brotherhoods to found the ARU in 1893. They established an industrial union open to all white railroad workers. Railroad employees in the West, especially the less skilled who were not members of any of the railroad brotherhoods, flocked to the ARU during its first year. Springfield quickly became an important site of ARU organizing, joining Chicago, Minneapolis, St. Paul, and Portland, Oregon, as the only cities in the nation with two locals. Only St. Louis, with three locals, surpassed the organization in these cities. By the summer of 1894, the ARU had enrolled about 150,000 members nationwide, a figure that nearly equaled the membership of all American Federation of Labor (AFL) unions combined.[9]

Springfield railroad workers participated in the Pullman strike during July 1894 and witnessed firsthand the use of U.S. marshals to force movement of the trains. The collapse of the strike after the intervention of the federal government and Debs's subsequent six-month jail sentence on a contempt of court conviction led Debs to conclude that only independent political activity by workers could overcome the united power of corporations and the state. Debs had endorsed the People's Party in March 1894, prior to the Pullman strike, and he helped found the Socialist Party in 1901.[10] Whether or not railroad workers in Springfield in the 1890s came to similar conclusions about the need for independent political activity remains unknown, but third-party candidacies had seen limited success in the city during the previous two decades, making such a break with Democrats and Republicans at least plausible for the workers.

The Greenback Party, which rose to prominence in large part due to hostility toward the railroads, first exposed workers to a significant third-party challenge in Springfield in the late 1870s. In 1869, Greene County voters had rejected a proposal to issue $400,000 in bonds to support railroad construction but then saw the county court issue the bonds a year later. A movement to refuse payment on the bonds emerged in the early 1870s, leading bondholders to sue for nonpayment in a number of court cases in the mid-1870s. In 1877 anti-railroad sentiment increased due to the nationwide railroad strikes. Although railroad workers in Springfield did not strike, they met and demanded restoration of their slashed wages and expressed sympathy for strikers, including those involved in violent confrontations with authorities in Pittsburgh. Some of those attending the meeting also expressed support for the Greenback Party.[11]

A year later local Greenback Party candidates won both of the county's state representative seats and one of three county judgeships. Springfield's mayor, Homer F. Fellows, ran a close third for state senate on the party's ticket. Some Springfield workers may have supported the party due to the pro-labor provisions of its 1878 national platform, which included planks calling for a reduction of hours, the establishment of state and federal bureaus of labor statistics, an end to prison contract labor, and restriction of Chinese immigration. In 1880 the party continued to demonstrate strength in the county, with the Greenback presidential and gubernatorial candidates each receiving 24 percent of the vote. Ira Hazeltine, a Springfield Greenbacker who ran as a Greenback-Republican fusion candidate, won election to the U.S. Congress.[12]

During the 1880s, the Knights of Labor became active politically in Springfield, a city in which closely contested elections gave an organized bloc of working-class voters the potential to affect the outcome of elections, if not to elect their own candidates. The local Republican Party responded by beginning to court working-class voters, in some cases by nominating workers for office. In the 1886 municipal elections, the Knights supported a Republican city council candidate in the Third Ward, turning the race in the normally solidly Democratic ward into a close, but losing, contest.[13]

The Knights also supported Greenback candidates in this period, although by 1884 the party no longer posed a serious threat of electing candidates in Greene County. Nonetheless, the presence of Greenback candidates who could tip the balance in favor of one or the other of the established parties continued to concern local politicians. In 1886, Fellows ran again on the Greenback ticket, seeking election to Congress. During

Figure 9. Homer F. Fellows organized the Springfield Wagon Company and served as mayor for two terms. He was involved in establishing a street railway system and the city waterworks. STATE HISTORICAL SOCIETY OF MISSOURI-COLUMBIA

the 1877 railroad strikes, Mayor Fellows had received a cool reception among workers when he spoke against the strikes, commenting: "Labor, like every other commodity, is worth just what it will bring." By the 1880s, however, Fellows's sympathies for labor had increased. As president of the Springfield Wagon Company, he voluntarily instituted the eight-hour day in 1886, without reducing wages. Although the company was not unionized, such actions by Fellows won him the admiration of the local Knights, who endorsed his unsuccessful candidacy for Congress.[14]

The Springfield Knights began to field candidates on their own United Labor Party ticket in 1887. Such independent political activity by the organization became common nationwide between 1885 and 1888, with the Knights' demands including the eight-hour day for municipal employees, minimum wage laws, and increased public expenditures for education and poor relief. The Knights also entered politics in response to their defeat in the 1886 Great Southwest railroad strike. They believed political power would allow them to defeat unfriendly politicians, including judges, and restrain the use of the police in future strikes.[15]

Although the Knights entered the Springfield municipal elections in April 1887, no United Labor candidates were elected. The following spring the Knights again fielded a United Labor ticket, this time with somewhat better results. In the city's Sixth Ward, located on the working-class north side, the United Labor candidate for city council finished second in a three-way race, receiving 34 percent of the vote compared to the victorious Republican's 40 percent. Most citywide United Labor candidates did not fare well, except in the race for city assessor. The Republicans had nominated an African American, J. H. McCracken, for the office. The Democrats chose not to run a candidate, leaving the United Labor nominee, railroad engineer John Berry, as the sole opposition to McCracken. Initially, the local press reported a narrow three-vote majority for McCracken, but the city council later certified Berry the victor with a majority of 260 votes, for reasons unexplained in the local press. Berry assumed office with McCracken threatening to contest the election results, but the press reported no further consideration of the issue by city officials.[16]

In 1887 members of the Knights of Labor, the Greenback Party, the farmers' alliances, the Grange, and various antimonopoly movements met in Cincinnati to found another third party—the Union Labor Party. The party platform, which aimed to appeal to both farmers and workers, opposed the monopolization of land by speculators—a central theme of political economist Henry George's critique of American society in *Progress and Poverty,* published in 1879—and the importation of Chinese labor and endorsed arbitration of strikes, elimination of child labor, government ownership of the railroad and telegraph industries, a graduated income tax, direct election of senators, and women's suffrage. Most of the party's support came from western farmers, with urban workers in the East largely ignoring this new electoral alternative. Midwestern workers were somewhat more sympathetic, as evidenced by the support of party candidates by the Milwaukee and St. Louis labor movements.[17]

In Springfield organized labor at least flirted with the new party. Party leaders created an infrastructure in the city, with two Union Labor Party Clubs and a party newspaper, the *New Crusade,* in existence by 1888. Notices of Union Labor Party club meetings were published in local newspapers alongside trade union notices. Frederick Mayfield, a local labor figure, edited the *New Crusade* and served as secretary of the Central Labor

Union, Knights of Labor Local Assembly 6315, and Union Labor Party Club No. 1. Controversy swirled around the party in Missouri, with Springfield papers reporting just days before the 1888 election that the party's gubernatorial candidate, Ahira Manning, might be replaced for failure to conduct an acceptably active campaign. The *Springfield Leader* reported: "This leaves the party in a deplorable condition within a week of the election. All sorts of charges of boodle and sell out are made in the rank and file of the party."[18]

The Union Labor Party enjoyed little success nationally or in Springfield. Alson Streeter, the party's presidential candidate, received only 1.3 percent of the vote nationally and 3.6 percent in Missouri. In Springfield, Streeter also fared poorly, garnering only 3.3 percent of the vote citywide and 5.4 percent in the working-class Sixth Ward where a United Labor city council candidate had received strong support the previous spring. Party candidates for state and local office fared little better with Springfield voters.[19]

Figure 10. Commercial Street, Springfield, c. 1889.
STATE HISTORICAL SOCIETY OF MISSOURI-COLUMBIA

The populist insurgency of the 1890s gained much greater support in Springfield. Nationally, the People's Party backed a number of labor causes and in turn received far greater support from organized labor than had the fledgling Union Labor Party. Although in serious decline by the 1890s, the Knights of Labor formally endorsed the party, as did Eugene Debs. Samuel Gompers, the AFL president, opposed offering the federation's support, but workers in many parts of the South and West warmly embraced the party, as did many AFL affiliates. The Missouri State Federation of Labor and eleven other state federations endorsed the party, as did nearly two dozen city centrals, including those in Kansas City and St. Louis.[20] No evidence exists on the relationship between organized labor and populism in Springfield, but populist candidates fared well in the working-class wards.

In the 1892 presidential election, People's Party candidate James Weaver received 8.5 percent of the vote nationally and 7.6 percent in Missouri. Lawrence Christensen and Gary Kremer have argued that one of the reasons for populism's poor showing in Missouri was the party's failure to attract working-class voters. This proved to be true in St. Louis, but Weaver's vote totaled 12 percent in Springfield, far exceeding the statewide average. The People's Party candidate ran particularly well in Springfield's four northern working-class wards, receiving 11 percent in Wards Five and Six, 14 percent in Ward Seven, and 26 percent in Ward Eight.[21] Regardless of whether or not organized labor in Springfield endorsed the People's Party, the populist message resonated well with many of the city's workers.

William Jennings Bryan, the Democratic and Populist candidate in the 1896 presidential election, won a narrow victory in Springfield, with a margin of only eighteen votes. His victory represented a reversal of fortune for the Democratic Party in Springfield; Republicans had carried the city in the two previous presidential elections. Bryan won in three of the four northern working-class wards and lost in the other ward by a narrow margin. In the preceding two presidential elections, these wards had voted mainly Republican, perhaps indicating a change in allegiance due to Bryan's endorsement by the Populists.[22]

The lack of evidence on organized labor's relationship to populism in Springfield may stem from the declining fortunes of the city's unions during the 1890s. Springfield was home to sixteen unions in the early 1890s, but unions declined in strength and number with the onset of a serious economic depression in 1893. By 1896 as few as two unions may have survived in the city.[23] With so few unions, organized labor received little attention in the local press during the populist insurgency. Despite this decline, Springfield workers gained significant experience with trade unions, labor reform, and third-party political activity during the late nineteenth century. These collective influences would shape organized labor in the city during the next decade.

Nationwide, AFL craft unions enjoyed a revival between 1897 and 1904 due to economic recovery following the mid-1890s depression. Membership nationally quadrupled to more than two million during this period. Springfield's labor movement enjoyed similar explosive growth during this period. The number of unions in the city increased rapidly between 1896, when only two unions may have remained, and the end of 1902, when the Missouri Bureau of Labor Statistics reported that thirty-six unions existed in the city. According to state statistics, twenty-four new local unions were organized during 1902. By the end of 1904—the first year for which the state compiled membership numbers for Springfield—the city had 2,311 union members. In 1910, Springfield trailed only the state's three largest cities, St. Louis, Kansas City, and St. Joseph, in union membership while surpassing all three in union density, primarily due to the large number of unionized railroad workers in the city.[24]

The number of unions in Springfield between 1900 and 1912 may have far exceeded the figures presented by the state. The labor bureau counted thirty-nine unions in 1903, 1907, and 1909, but other sources suggest a higher number. The aforementioned CMIU official who visited Springfield in 1903 noted fifty-four unions in the city. Newspaper reports for the years 1906 to 1912 routinely reported the presence of between forty-three and forty-seven unions.[25]

Union membership may also have exceeded the bureau's estimates. State figures for the years 1904 to 1911 show union membership peaking in Springfield at 2,311 workers in December 1904, yet the local press reported union membership at 5,000 in 1906. The latter figure may represent an exaggeration on the part of labor leaders, but it seems unlikely that they would claim membership twice their actual numbers. In part the discrepancy may be explained by the possibility that local labor leaders included railroad telegraphers in their figures. The telegraphers' union maintained its district office in Springfield, but most of the 600–800 members of that union resided in towns throughout the state. The Bureau of Labor Statistics stopped including the telegraphers in its calculations for Springfield in 1910, and the figures presented in this article have been adjusted to exclude the telegraphers for all years. Even if one subtracts as many as 800 telegraphers from the local estimates of union membership, local reports remain nearly 2,000 members higher than state reports. The state may also have understated union membership by using a reporting date of

December 31, a time when construction union membership was undoubtedly low. Local press reports in 1907 suggest that construction unions may have had 300 to 400 more members during construction season than when the state collected its data in December. Given these differences, it seems reasonable to estimate that union membership in Springfield peaked at more than 3,000 workers during the century's first decade.[26]

Three institutions gave voice to the demands of organized labor in Springfield—the Central Trades and Labor Assembly, the labor press, and the Socialist Party. The Central Trades and Labor Assembly had been organized as the Central Labor Union in 1886, but its effectiveness increased with the growth of unions in the early twentieth century. Most of the locals in the city belonged to the assembly, which claimed 3,000 members in its affiliated unions in 1907.[27] The assembly sought to unite existing locals and organize new locals to expand labor's presence in the community. Weekly meetings served to educate the approximately 100 delegates with speakers or debates on important local issues. Although the assembly did not endorse political candidates, it took positions on issues such as tax levies and the commission form of government in city elections and pressured city officials to pay prevailing union wages and avoid the use of convict labor.[28]

The labor movement displayed its power annually on Labor Day, which the *Springfield Republican* characterized as a "big event in Springfield."[29] Each year from 1905 to 1912, between 1,500 and 5,000 trade unionists marched in a Labor Day parade sponsored by the labor assembly. Family and friends joined union members in a city park after the parade for a picnic, games, and a visiting speaker, producing crowds estimated by the press as large as 20,000 people, but more often numbering between 6,000 and 10,000. Such public displays in a city that claimed 35,000 residents in 1910 reminded other members of the community of organized labor's numbers and solidarity and buttressed the labor assembly's claim to speak for Springfield's workers.[30]

The existence of local labor newspapers also gave unions a heightened visibility in the city. By 1905 a weekly labor paper titled the *Sunday Tradesman* was being published with the endorsement of the Central Trades and Labor Assembly. Although the assembly removed the endorsement for unreported reasons a few years later, the *Tradesman* continued to label itself a labor paper until it ceased publication in 1912. That same year the labor assembly helped launch a new weekly paper, the *Springfield Laborer,* which continued publishing until 1920.[31]

An active Socialist Party offered Springfield workers an alternative to the two major parties and gave organized labor a stronger political voice in the city. Socialism's roots in Springfield can be traced to the late nineteenth century, when socialist ideas, if not institutions, circulated in unions and working-class neighborhoods. Following the 1877 railroad strikes, the Workingmen's Party, which in 1878 changed its name to the Socialist Labor Party, gained momentum in a number of cities, including St. Louis, where socialists elected candidates to the school board and city council. The party never ran candidates for office in Springfield, but local newspapers reported that advocates of the party resided in the city. Yet the lack of a viable Socialist Party in Springfield did not prevent the spread of socialist ideals. As historian Julie Greene has noted, during the late nineteenth century, "it was the idea and the culture of socialism, not its institutional expression, that persuaded so many."[32]

In Springfield, trade unions, particularly the cigar makers' local, spread socialist ideas. Nationally, socialists had a strong presence within the Cigar Makers International Union throughout the late nineteenth century. When Socialist Labor Party delegates at the 1894 AFL convention proposed a plank calling for "collective ownership by the people of all the means of production and distribution," 68 percent of cigar makers nationwide endorsed the plank in a union referendum. Members of Springfield's Local 23 frequently voted for J. Mahlon Barnes, a Philadelphia socialist, for CMIU president and unanimously endorsed the AFL collective ownership plank.[33] Whether other unions in Springfield were home to socialists in the late nineteenth century is uncertain. Following the defeat of the Pullman strike and then of populist hopes in 1896, Debs and other American Railway Union leaders became socialists. It seems likely that, given the large number of railroad workers in Springfield and the existence of two ARU locals in the city, at least some railroad unionists followed Debs's path to socialism. The Central Labor Union did elect socialist leaders during the late nineteenth century, suggesting that socialist sympathies extended beyond the CMIU.[34]

J. A. Wayland's *Appeal to Reason,* a national socialist newspaper that began publishing in Kansas City, Missouri, in 1895 before moving to Girard, Kansas, in 1897, introduced many workers to socialist ideas. Wayland's paper circulated widely in Kansas, Oklahoma, Texas, and Missouri, particularly in rural areas and small towns and cities that lacked their own socialist press. By 1900 the paper's circulation was 140,000; it eventually reached 750,000 at its peak in 1913. The efforts of a volunteer army of more than 80,000 "salesmen-soldiers" who sold subscriptions to the paper across the country brought about the increase in circulation. Several of these salesmen soldiers resided in Springfield, where the *Appeal to Reason* had a small but loyal following by 1900. Springfield was also home to socialist writer and editor Henry Mulford Tichener, some of whose articles appeared in the *Appeal*. The *Appeal* and other socialist papers played a vital role in circulating socialist ideas at the turn of the century when the two most important socialist parties—the Socialist Labor Party and the Social Democratic Party—were small and had little or no presence in Springfield and other small towns and cities. When the Socialist Party surveyed its membership in 1908, 52 percent of the respondents reported that they had been converted to socialism by reading literature such as the *Appeal to Reason*.[35] Consequently, even with no viable party in Springfield at the turn of the century, socialist ideals gained a hearing through local unions and the socialist press.

After the founding of the Socialist Party in 1901, the socialist movement grew significantly. Nationally, workers composed the majority of the party, with members of organized labor highly represented. Socialists elected to local political office in the early twentieth century also came primarily from the working class. The Socialist Party in Springfield, which commenced activity by 1903, displayed similar membership characteristics. Skilled workers composed 74 percent of party officials and candidates in Springfield between 1905 and 1911 and 68 percent of party membership in 1914. Railroad workers made up a large percentage of the local party—53 percent of party leaders and candidates and 40 percent of identified party members. Machinists alone accounted for 26 percent of party officials and candidates and 15 percent of the identified party membership.[36]

As in most cities, the Springfield Socialist Party had close ties to the local labor movement. By the early twentieth century, socialists had a strong presence in the CMIU, several railroad unions, and probably other local unions as well. Socialists also controlled Springfield's Central Trades and Labor Assembly during the early twentieth century. In 1908, Gompers, upset with the Republican Party, sought to guide the AFL toward an alliance with Bryan and the Democrats. The Springfield labor assembly wrote Gompers to object to his "partiality shown in mentioning only two parties when there is another in the field which demands your attention and the attention of every man who labors for a living." Featured speakers at Springfield's Labor Day events frequently attacked Gompers's political strategy and advocated socialism. At the 1905 Labor Day celebration, William Brandt, an influential St. Louis cigar maker and socialist, told the assembled crowd to go into "class politics" because "our emancipation will not come until we own the job instead of the job owning us." Chris Rocker, a St. Louis socialist, condemned Gompers's alliance with Democrats in his 1908 Labor Day speech.[37]

The Springfield local aligned itself with the right wing of the party, which embraced electoral politics as a means of achieving social and political reforms that would gradually lead to socialism. This wing of the party, which attracted many skilled trade unionists, was more conciliatory toward the AFL than the left wing, which supported the Industrial Workers of the World and embraced political work primarily as an educational tool. With immigrants comprising only 4.5 percent of the population in 1900 and 3.2 percent in 1910, and with little large-scale manufacturing, the left wing of the party, which emphasized organization of immigrant industrial workers through industrial unionism, did not speak to the economic realities of the city's largely native-born, skilled craft workers.[38]

In 1904 the national Socialist Party adopted a municipal program that called for public ownership of utilities and expanded city services, particularly in working-class neighborhoods. Although party leaders recognized the limited nature of these demands, most believed that local political campaigns served as a vital means of educating and recruiting party members. The Springfield local embraced this program and adopted platforms calling for municipal ownership of utilities, including street railways, gas, electricity, water, and telephone; municipally owned bakeries, ice plants, parks, bathhouses, hospitals, and dispensaries that would provide drugs at cost; increased support for public schools, including enlargement of school buildings, decreased class size, free schoolbooks, and higher teacher salaries; an eight-hour day and union wages for city workers; public jobs for the unemployed; and democratic reforms such as the initiative and referendum and recall of elected officials.[39]

Springfield socialists propagated their message through the socialist press, frequent visiting speakers, and local election campaigns. Salesmen soldiers continued to sell the *Appeal to Reason* in Springfield, and nearby Fair Grove had a socialist paper—*The News*—from 1905 to 1908.[40] Eugene Debs appeared in Springfield on several occasions, and Mary Harris "Mother" Jones visited the city at least once. Both spoke to packed houses in local theaters. Other less-prominent socialist speakers also frequented Springfield regularly, with five visiting the city in 1909 alone.[41]

Beginning in 1903, Springfield socialists regularly ran candidates for local and state offices and supported Debs's presidential campaigns. The prospects for electoral success appeared to be good in the city. The Socialist Party experienced its greatest success in midwestern towns and cities with populations between 10,000 and 50,000 that had well-organized labor movements and whose workers were culturally homogeneous. Springfield, with a population of 23,267 in 1900 and 35,201 in 1910, a high percentage of unionized workers, and a very small immigrant population, seemed to offer the right conditions. Furthermore, the party's call for municipal ownership of utilities potentially appealed to middle-class voters in Springfield because of repeated conflicts between citizens and the privately owned street railway and telephone companies.[42]

These favorable conditions produced some strong showings by socialist candidates but no electoral victories between 1903 and 1912. In presidential elections Springfield voters gave Debs stronger support than voters statewide or nationally, with the highest vote totals in Wards Five through Eight on the working-class north side. Yet Debs never polled more than 8 percent of the Springfield vote in the 1900–1912 elections and no more than 11 percent of the combined vote in the north side wards. Socialist candidates for state representative from Greene County's First District, which encompassed the city of Springfield, fared little better than Debs. The socialist vote in the district steadily increased from 4.5 percent in 1906 to 7.8 percent in 1912 but offered little hope of impending victory. Socialist mayoral candidates in Springfield also polled poorly, never obtaining more than 10 percent of the vote.[43]

Springfield socialists fared best in city council elections on the north side but did not elect any socialists to the council. On two occasions a socialist ran second in a three-way race, with the best such result in Ward Eight in 1906, when the party's candidate received 34 percent of the vote. In 1911 the socialist candidate in that ward received 45 percent of the vote in a two-way race.[44]

From one point of view the socialist experiment in Springfield can be deemed a failure. The party elected no candidates between 1903 and 1912, even in the heavily working-class, unionized wards. Yet the significance of the Springfield Socialist Party may best be measured not by election victories, but by its impact upon the local political scene. Socialist electoral activity combined with a well-organized and active labor movement gave labor leaders considerable influence with the established parties as each vied for the labor vote.[45]

The substantial Springfield labor vote greatly interested local political leaders. In 1910, Springfield's population included 10,516 males of voting age. Using the most conservative estimate of labor union membership provided by the Missouri Bureau of Labor Statistics, the city had 2,292 male union members that year. Although a few of these men were not yet of voting age or immigrants without voting rights, it seems likely that union members made up at least one-fifth of Springfield voters. Trade unionists did not vote in unison at all times, but local Democratic and

Republican politicians viewed such a large organized bloc of voters as an important constituency to be courted. It was not uncommon for politicians to praise organized labor publicly, as Democratic mayor James Blain did in 1907 when he told a Labor Day gathering that unions had been responsible for a decline in child labor and helping workers get a fair deal from their employers. Although the Central Trades and Labor Assembly did not formally endorse candidates, political discourse during local election campaigns frequently centered on which office seekers were friends or enemies of organized labor.[46]

The use of police and the courts to break strikes caused great concern among the ranks of organized labor in most cities. When Reuben Wood campaigned for city marshal in 1908, he commented that he had "always been opposed to police and soldiers because of the way they have been used as a club over the heads of laboring men." In Springfield, the political power of organized labor produced police and judges who remained more neutral than in many cities. During strikes, police arrested strikers involved in violence against strikebreakers, but they also arrested strikebreakers who violated the law. Molders at United Iron Works, the most heavily capitalized industrial firm in the city and the fourth-largest industrial employer, went on strike on May 1, 1906, as part of a nationwide molders' strike for the nine-hour day. The company responded by hiring two armed guards and importing forty nonunion molders from St. Louis whom the company also armed. During the strike, which stretched into the summer, police arrested at least one striking molder for assaulting a strikebreaker but refused to allow strikebreakers to roam the city armed, arresting five of them for carrying weapons while intoxicated. United Iron Works sought an injunction against forty-one striking union molders and a union leader in late May, claiming that the men had tried to intimidate their replacements. In June a Greene County judge issued a permanent injunction against one molder but dismissed the case against the other forty-one defendants. Al P. Tatlow, the elected Springfield city attorney, represented the union in the case.[47]

Organized labor and local socialists proved effective at pressuring city officials to provide public works employment for the unemployed during the depression that followed the Panic of 1907. With unemployment high in the winter of 1907–1908, both the Central Trades and Labor Assembly and the Socialist Party called upon the city government to hire the unemployed to work on city streets. Such demands had been made by the AFL since the 1890s, and they became a growing part of the Socialist Party's national municipal strategy to politicize unemployment. The day after Springfield Socialists called for such public works jobs, the city council voted to employ one hundred men on city street work. During the spring election season, the chairman of the Springfield Republican Party launched the municipal campaign by commenting: "We should adopt every method possible to give as many men employment on our streets as the revenue will permit." Springfield certainly was not alone among cities in making use of public works to aid the unemployed. Many cities had established large-scale programs during the depression in the 1890s, and numerous municipalities again expanded public works employment during the recession of 1907–1908. Unlike many cities where conservatives criticized public works employment as an example of creeping socialism and many social workers opposed the efforts, no such public criticism appeared in Springfield, perhaps a mark of labor's political influence with both parties.[48]

Well aware of organized labor's power, city leaders frequently sought labor's input on important issues facing the community. In 1908 citizens complained about a twenty-five-year franchise the city council planned to offer Ozark Bell Telephone Company. Council members appointed five organizations—the Springfield Club, the Commercial Club, the Elks, the Retail Merchants Association, and the Central Trades and Labor Assembly—to investigate the proposal. Ultimately, the city council accepted the recommendation of the groups to reject the franchise agreement. In 1910 when city officials began plans to secure a second-class city charter for Springfield, the head of the Central Trades and Labor Assembly joined the mayor, a city councilman, a state senator, and representatives from the Springfield and Commercial Clubs on the planning committee. The committee's proposed charter incorporated a key demand of organized labor and socialists—an eight-hour day for city employees and employees of city contractors.[49]

Organized labor's political influence extended to elected state officials as well. In an analysis of voting patterns in the Missouri House and Senate between 1907 and 1939, historian Gary Fink determined that representatives from Springfield, St. Joseph, and Hannibal and senators from Springfield, St. Joseph, and Sedalia were the most supportive of organized labor's interests in the state legislature. Conversely, no bloc of legislators from St. Louis or Kansas City could be counted on to support labor's concerns in the General Assembly. Fink cites three factors that contributed to the election of pro-labor representatives in smaller cities—capable labor leaders who involved themselves in politics, a large number of railroad workers whose unions were politically active due to the nature of their industry, and an active Socialist Party that imparted a political consciousness to workers. With regard to Springfield, Fink concluded that the local labor movement was "considered a force to be reckoned with by politicos of the city."[50]

It proved also to be a force in the Missouri State Federation of Labor (MSFL). Springfield had long exercised considerable influence in the organization through the perennial service of Henry A. W. Juneman as a convention delegate. Juneman had moved from New York City, where he worked with Samuel Gompers organizing cigar makers, to Springfield in the 1870s. A committed socialist, Juneman helped organize Springfield's CMIU local in 1879, served as secretary-treasurer of the Central Labor Union and secretary of the city's first Knights of Labor Assembly during the 1880s, and was a delegate to the founding convention of the MSFL in 1891. Juneman was widely admired and influential in the state labor movement and recognized by many labor leaders as a mentor.[51]

In 1912, Juneman and other Springfield delegates to the MSFL convention lobbied for the election of Reuben Wood as federation president. Having served as an officer of his CMIU local and as president and vice president of the Central Trades and Labor Assembly and having stood for office three times as a Socialist, Wood had extensive experience in the Springfield labor movement. At the convention, Wood's presidential bid also gained the support of many Socialist delegates from St. Louis. Cigar makers from across the state, who had played a critical role in the federation from its beginning, also likely supported his candidacy. In an election one delegate recalled as being "spirited and close," Wood defeated J. B. Conroy, a much better known St. Louis union leader, by a narrow margin. Despite Wood's relative anonymity statewide, the Springfield labor movement's successes were well known, thus making possible his election.[52]

Wood's victory represented the culmination of the Springfield labor movement's rise to power between 1871 and 1912. That power was predicated upon both effective organization of most trades in the city and a willingness to experiment with third-party politics. Although such third-party campaigns rarely produced electoral victories, they nevertheless encouraged elected officials to grant concessions to the city's labor movement in an effort to preempt a leftward electoral drift by workers. Such a result suggests the need for more careful consideration by historians of the relationship between unionization and politics in Missouri's smaller communities.

Notes

1. *Cigar Makers' Official Journal* 28 (March 15, 1904): 3.

2. The only work to devote any significant attention to the Springfield labor movement is Gary Fink, *Labor's Search for Political Order: The Political Behavior of the Missouri Labor Movement, 1890–1940* (Columbia: University of Missouri Press, 1973).

3. On Sedalia, see Michael Cassity, *Defending a Way of Life: An American Community in the Nineteenth Century* (Albany: State University of New York Press, 1989). On Ilasco, near Hannibal, see Gregg Andrews, *City of Dust: A Cement Company Town in the Land of Tom Sawyer* (Columbia: University of Missouri Press, 1996).

4. Craig Miner, "Hopes and Fears: Ambivalence in the Anti-Railroad Movement at Springfield, Missouri, 1870–1880," *Bulletin of the Missouri Historical Society* 27 (January 1971): 146; Morey W. McDaniel, "A Comparison of Springfield and Joplin, Missouri" (B.A. honors thesis, Wesleyan University, Middletown, CT, 1961), 14–17; *Twenty-First Annual Report of the Bureau of Labor Statistics and Inspection of the State of Missouri* (Jefferson City: Tribune Printing Co., 1899), 190; U.S. Bureau of the Census, *Twelfth Census of the United States . . . 1900, Manufactures* (Washington, DC, 1902), vol. 8, part 2: 477; Lawrence Christensen and Gary Kremer, *A History of Missouri, Volume IV, 1875 to 1919* (Columbia: University of Missouri Press, 1997), 92–93.

5. Return I. Holcomb, *History of Greene County, Missouri* (St. Louis: Western Historical Co., 1883), 849–850; *Cigar Makers' Official Journal* 5 (March 10, 1880): n.p.; *Hoye's City Directory of Springfield, Missouri,* 1888–1889 (Kansas City: Hoye Directory Co., n.d.), 293; *Springfield Daily Herald,* January 20, 1888; *Hoye's City Directory of Springfield, Missouri, 1892–1893* (Kansas City: Hoye Directory Co., 1892), 419–420.

6. Neal Moore, "Ozarks Labor History," *Springfield Union Labor Record,* March 1, 1984; Stephen McIntyre, *With One Voice: A Century of Service to Missouri's Workers* (Jefferson City: MO, AFL-CIO, 1991), 17.

7. Jonathan Garlock, *Guide to the Local Assemblies of the Knights of Labor* (Westport, CT: Greenwood Press, 1982), 243; Nelson Lichtenstein et al., *Who Built America? Working People and the Nation's Economy, Politics, Culture, and Society* (New York: Worth Publishers, 2000), 2: 93; Ruth Allen, *The Great Southwest Strike* (Austin: University of Texas Press, 1942), 256.

8. Leon Fink, *Workingmen's Democracy: The Knights of Labor and American Politics* (Urbana: University of Illinois Press, 1983), 3–15; Garlock, *Guide to the Local Assemblies,* 243.

9. Shelton Stromquist, *A Generation of Boomers: The Pattern of Railroad Labor Conflict in Nineteenth-Century America* (Urbana: University of Illinois Press, 1987), 79, 84–85; Bruce Laurie, *Artisans into Workers: Labor in Nineteenth-Century America* (New York: Noonday Press, 1989), 205.

10. H. F. Rice, "The Great Pullman Strike of 1894," *Springfield Union Labor Record,* April 25, 1963; Nick Salvatore, *Eugene V. Debs: Citizen and Socialist* (Urbana: University of Illinois Press, 1982), 147, 188; Laurie, *Artisans into Workers,* 209–210.

11. David Thelen, *Paths of Resistance: Tradition and Democracy in Industrializing Missouri* (Columbia: University of Missouri Press, 1991), 64; Edwin L. Lopata, *Local Aid to Railroads in Missouri* (New York: Arno Press, 1981), 107; Holcomb, *History of Greene County,* 555–556; *Springfield Patriot-Advertiser,* July 26, 1877; *Springfield Weekly Leader,* July 26, 1877. When the national railroad strike reached Pittsburgh in July 1877, many local citizens sided with striking railroad workers, prompting

railroad executives to request that the state militia be sent to the city. Following the militia's arrival, violent confrontations occurred between its members and strikers and local residents. Ultimately, twenty Pittsburgh citizens were killed by militia rifle fire during the conflict, leading to attacks on railroad property by thousands of Pittsburgh citizens. During the ensuing battle, twenty additional civilians and five militia members died. Lichtenstein et al., *Who Built America?* 13–14.

12. *Springfield Patriot-Advertiser,* November 7, 1878; *Missouri State Almanac and Official Directory 1879* (St. Louis: John J. Daly and Co., 1879), 98; *Missouri Official Directory 1881* (St. Louis: John J. Daly and Co., 1881), 45, 80; Jonathan Fairbanks and Clyde Edwin Tuck, *Past and Present of Greene County, Missouri* (Indianapolis: A. W. Bowen, 1915), 1: 522; Holcomb, *History of Greene County,* 558, 560–561, 752; Paul Kleppner, "The Greenback and Prohibition Parties," in *History of U.S. Political Parties,* vol. 2, *1860–1910, The Gilded Age of Politics,* ed. Arthur Schlesinger Jr. (New York: Chelsea House, 1973), 1558–1564.

13. *Springfield Express,* October 24, 1884, April 10, 1885, April 9, 1886; *Springfield Daily Herald,* April 7, 1886.

14. *Springfield Express,* October 17, 24, 31, 1884; *Springfield Patriot-Advertiser,* July 26, 1877; *Springfield Leader,* July 26, 1877; Steven Lee Stepp, "'The Old Reliable': The History of the Springfield Wagon Company, 1872–1952" (Master's thesis, Southwest Missouri State College, 1972), 72–73.

15. Leon Fink, *Workingmen's Democracy,* 25–31; *Missouri Official Directory, 1887–1888* (Jefferson City: Tribune Printing Co., 1888), 200, 204.

16. *Springfield Daily Leader,* April 5, 1887; March 30, April 4, 7, 1888; *Springfield Express,* April 6, 1888; *Hoye's City Directory . . .* 1888–1889, 31.

17. Andrew D. McNitt, "Union Labor Party," in *Encyclopedia of Third Parties in America,* ed. Immanuel Ness and James Ciment (Armonk, NY: M. E. Sharpe, 2000), 3: 569–571; *Missouri Official Manual, 1889–1890* (Jefferson City: Tribune Printing Co., 1889), 236–237; *St. Louis Post-Dispatch,* November 7, 1888.

18. Hoye's *City Directory . . .* 1888–1889, 293–294; *Missouri Official Manual, 1889–1890,* 193; *Springfield Daily Herald,* January 20, September 2, 1888; *Springfield Leader,* October 30, 1888; *Springfield Republican,* October 30, 1888.

19. McNitt, "Union Labor Party," 571; *Missouri Official Manual, 1895–1896* (Jefferson City: Tribune Printing Co., 1895), 11; *Springfield Daily Leader,* November 12, 1888.

20. Julie Greene, *Pure and Simple Politics: The American Federation of Labor and Political Activism, 1881–1917* (New York: Cambridge University Press, 1998), 53–54; Philip S. Foner, *History of the Labor Movement in the United States,* vol. 2, *From the Founding of the American Federation of Labor to the Emergence of American Imperialism* (New York: International Publishers, 1955), 300–320; Salvatore, *Eugene V. Debs,* 147; Elizabeth Sanders, *Roots of Reform: Farmers, Workers, and the American State, 1877–1917* (Chicago: University of Chicago Press, 1999), 84–85; Richard Schneirov, *Labor and Urban Politics: Class Conflict and the Origins of Modern Liberalism in Chicago, 1864–97* (Urbana: University of Illinois Press, 1998), 343–344.

21. *Missouri Official Manual, 1895–1896,* 12, 19; Foner, *History of the Labor Movement,* 2: 309; Christensen and Kremer, *A History of Missouri,* 142.

22. Martin Gerald Towey, "The People's Party in Missouri" (Ph.D. diss., St. Louis University, 1971), 98, 105–106, 164; *Missouri Official Manual, 1895–1896,* 11–12, 19; *Missouri Official Manual, 1897–1898* (Jefferson City: Tribune Printing Co., 1897), 10, 20.

23. *Cigar Makers' Official Journal* 28 (March 15, 1904): 3.

24. Lichtenstein et al., *Who Built America?* 158; *Thirty-Third Annual Report of the Bureau of Labor Statistics . . . 1911* (Jefferson City: Hugh Stephens Printing Co., n.d.).

25. *Cigar Makers' Official Journal* 28 (March 15, 1904): 3; *Springfield Republican,* September 4, 1906, March 25, 1908, September 3, 1911, September 3, 1912.

26. *Twenty-Seventh Annual Report of the Bureau of Labor Statistics and Inspection . . . 1905* (Jefferson City: Hugh Stephens Printing Co., n.d.), 363; *Report of the Bureau of Labor Statistics . . . 1911,* 145; *Springfield Republican,* July 13, 28, 1906; May 1, 5, 1907.

27. *Report of the Bureau of Labor Statistics . . . 1911,* 145; *Springfield Republican,* March 23, 1907, March 25, 1908.

28. *Springfield Republican,* March 23, 1907; March 6, 13, May 1, 1909; January 22, 1910.

29. Ibid., July 13, 1906.

30. Ibid., August, 19, September 5, 1905; July, 28, September 4, 1906; June 21, 1907; September 8, 1908; September 7, 1909; September 1, 3, 1912; *Springfield Leader,* September 7, 1908; September 5, 1910; September 4, 1911; September 2, 1912.

31. *Missouri Official Manual, 1905–1906* (Jefferson City: Hugh Stephens Printing Co., n.d.), 335; *Missouri Official Manual, 1907–1908* (Jefferson City: Hugh Stephens Printing Co., n.d.), 508; *Missouri Official Manual, 1909–1910* (Jefferson City: Hugh Stephens Printing Co., n.d.), 613; *Missouri Official Manual, 1911–1912* (Jefferson City: Hugh Stephens Printing Co., n.d.), 608; *Missouri Official Manual, 1913–1914* (Jefferson City: Hugh Stephens Printing Co., n.d.), 623; Fairbanks and Tuck, *Past and Present,* I: 523; *Springfield Republican,* July 25, 1908.

32. *Springfield Times,* August 20, 1877; Stephen L. McIntyre, "'Communist Progress': The Workingmen's Party and St. Louis Educational Politics, 1877–1878," *Missouri Historical Review* 95 (October 2000): 23; Greene, *Pure and Simple Politics, 55.*

33. Patricia A. Cooper, *Once a Cigar Maker: Men, Women, and Work Culture in American Cigar Factories, 1900–1919* (Urbana: University of Illinois Press, 1987), 23, 27–28; *Cigar Makers' Official Journal* 20 (January 1895): 10–11; *Cigar Makers' Official Journal* 21 (November 1895): 18, 21; *Cigar Makers' Official Journal* 21 (March 1896): 10–13; *Cigar Makers' Official Journal* 26 (March 1901): 4; *Cigar Makers' Official Journal* 27 (November 1901): 11; *Cigar Makers' Official Journal* 28 (March 1903): 15.

34. Stromquist, *Generation of Boomers,* 96; Salvatore, *Eugene V. Debs,* 153–163; Gary Fink, *Labor's Search,* 28; *Springfield Republican,* September 7, 1909, September 6, 1910, September 16, 1913.

35. Elliott Shore, *Talkin' Socialism: J. A. Wayland and the Role of the Press in American Radicalism, 1890–1912* (Lawrence: University Press of Kansas, 1988), 75–76, 81–83; James R. Green, "The 'Salesmen-Soldiers' of the *'Appeal* Army': A Profile of Rank-and-File Socialist Agitators," in *Socialism and the Cities,* ed. Bruce M. Stave (Port Washington, NY: Kennikat Press, 1975), 14, 16, 34; Peter H. Buckingham, *Rebel Against Injustice: The Life of Frank P. O'Hare* (Columbia: University of Missouri Press, 1996), 22; *Appeal to Reason,* July 28, August 11, 18, September, 29, October 6, 1900; March 9, 1901.

36. Richard W. Judd, *Socialist Cities: Municipal Politics and the Grass Roots of American Socialism* (Albany: State University of New York Press, 1989), 29. Calculation of numbers of party officials and candidates is based on forty-one names taken from newspaper reports in the *Springfield Republican,* 1905–1911. Of these, the author identified thirty-five by examining Springfield city directories and the U.S. censuses for 1900 and 1910. Calculation of party membership is based on ninety-eight socialists

who signed a petition in support of a candidate for Springfield postmaster, located in the Ewing Y. Mitchell Jr. Papers, microfilm roll 27, folder 951, Western Historical Manuscript Collection, University of Missouri-Columbia. Of these, the author identified eighty-one by examining Springfield city directories and the U.S. censuses for 1910 and 1920.

37. *Thirty-Second Annual Report of the Bureau of Labor Statistics . . . 1910* (Jefferson City: Hugh Stephens Printing Co., n.d.), 354–355; William H. Bush to Samuel Gompers, August 20, 1908, AFL Papers, serial 11, file A, box 8, State Historical Society of Wisconsin; Gary Fink, *Labor's Search,* 21, 27; *Springfield Republican,* September 5, 1905, September 8, 1908, September 7, 1909; *Appeal to Reason,* December 25, 1909. The secretary of the Missouri Socialist Party reported in the *Appeal* that one of the largest unions in Springfield had elected all socialists as officers in 1909 but failed to note which union. The eight largest unions in Springfield in 1909 were railroad unions, with the largest being a machinists local.

38. Greene, *Pure and Simple Politics,* 220; James Weinstein, *The Decline of Socialism in America,* 1912–1925 (New Brunswick, NJ: Rutgers University Press, 1984), 3–9; *Thirteenth Census of the United States . . . , 1910 Abstract . . . with Supplement for Missouri* (Washington, DC: GPO, 1913), 626.

39. See, for example, *Springfield Republican,* March 6, 10, 31, 1908.

40. *Appeal to Reason,* April 10, 1909; *Missouri Official Manual, 1905–1906,* 335; *Missouri Official Manual, 1907–1908,* 508.

41. *Springfield Republican,* August 18, 1905; June 20, July 10, 1906; July 9, 1910; *Appeal to Reason,* February 27, June 26, August 1, September 11, November 13, 1909; January 8, March 19, July 9, 1910.

42. Judd, *Socialist Cities,* 25; *Twelfth Census of the United States . . . , 1900, Population,* 1: 240; *Thirteenth Census . . . 1910 Abstract,* 626; *Springfield Republican,* March 6, 10, 31, 1908.

43. *Missouri Official Manual, 1907–1908,* 635; *Missouri Official Manual, 1909–1910,* 833; *Missouri Official Manual, 1911–1912,* 827; *Missouri Official Manual, 1913–1914,* 1139. The local press irregularly reported city election results. For the 1906 mayoral election results, see *Springfield Republican,* April 4, 1906.

44. *Springfield Republican,* April 5, 1905, April 4, 1906, April 3, 1907, April 8, 1908, April 7, 1909, April 5, 1911; Judd, *Socialist Cities,* 22–29.

45. Richard Schneirov offers a model for such analysis of Chicago labor and socialist politics, arguing that labor's political power can best be measured by the increased influence in the Democratic and Republican Parties produced by periodic socialist and labor party insurgencies, rather than by third-party electoral victories. See Schneirov, *Labor and Urban Politics,* 366.

46. *Thirteenth Census . . . 1910 Abstract,* 627; *Report of the Bureau of Labor Statistics . . . 1911,* 102; *Springfield Republican,* September 3, 1907; March 24, 25, 29, 1908; April 1, 1911.

47. *Springfield Republican,* May 11, 30; June 19, 20, 30; July 12, 15, 20; September 26, 1906; March 3, 1908; July 4, 1909.

48. *Springfield Republican,* April 4, 1906; April 3, 1907; January 18, March 3, 5, 26; April 8, 1908; Judd, *Socialist Cities,* 35; Udo Sautter, *Three Cheers for the Unemployed: Government and Unemployment before the New Deal* (Cambridge: Cambridge University Press, 1991), 96, 100; Leah Hannah Feder, *Unemployment Relief in Periods of Depression: A Study of Measures Adopted in Certain American Cities, 1857 through 1922* (New York: Russell Sage Foundation, 1936), 214–217.

49. *Springfield Republican,* March 11, 24, 25, 1908; December 10, 17, 1910; January 15, 1911.

50. Gary Fink, *Labors Search,* 193–194.

51. Ibid., 28; *Springfield Union Labor Record,* April 25, 1963, March 1, 1984; *Cigar Makers' Official Journal* 5 (August 10, 1880): 4; *Cigar Makers' Official Journal* 7 (September 15, 1882): 3; *Hoye's City Directory of Springfield,* 1892–1893, 419; *Springfield Republican,* September 7, 1909, September 6, 1910, September 16, 1913; *Proceedings of the Thirty-Second Annual and Third Biennial Convention of the Missouri State Federation of Labor,* 1928, 53.

52. *Cigar Makers' Official Journal* 79 (August 1955): 7; *Springfield Union Labor Record,* July 28, 1955; *Springfield Leader,* September 20, 1912.

The Ozark Short Line Railroad

A Failed Dream

H. ROGER GRANT

Between the end of the Civil War and the beginning of World War I, the construction of thousands of miles of railroad lines bolstered the economic life of the United States. Isolated "island communities" diminished, and commercialism blossomed. Much of this railroad expansion took place between the end of the hard times of the 1870s and the devastating Panic of 1893. In 1880 slightly more than 93,000 miles of railway were in operation; a decade later the figure exceeded 163,000 miles. Never before or since have so many new rails been spiked down in a ten-year period. And there was a final burst of building activity. In 1900 the national railroad map showed 193,346 miles of track; sixteen years later, it peaked at 254,251 miles. Much of the addition consisted of trackage built by major carriers as feeders and by independent short lines. During this time, residents of communities that lacked access to railroads, what was popularly dubbed the "steamcar civilization," realized that they likely had one final chance to obtain rail service. Hundreds of places, commonly called "inland towns," scrambled to attract the iron horse or perhaps the cars of an electric interurban, a recently introduced and popular transportation alternative.[1]

For decades, citizens of Missouri experienced railroad fever. Residents understood the necessity of having access to railways. "Among the great material forces and factors of modern growth and development in this country the railroad stands first and foremost," opined the editor of the

Ava Douglas County Herald in 1909. "It has converted the wilderness into a garden and led the van of civilization wherever it has gone. It has converted villages into cities and built churches and school houses where none were known before." And, the journalist from Ava added, "It has been the evangel of progress, of religion and of education, of material prosperity and moral betterment wherever its whistle is heard." This desire for modern transport produced considerable railway mileage. On the eve of the Civil War, the state's network stood at 817 miles and by the close of World War I reached 8,529 miles, although sections of the Ozarks region lacked extensive rail service.[2]

It is hardly surprising that one of the last frontiers in America, the sprawling Ozarks of south-central and southern Missouri, with large stands of pines and hardwoods, abundant water, valuable minerals, and moderate climate, became the site of an array of proposals and some construction during the twilight of railroad building. Several trunk roads, most notably the St. Louis-San Francisco (Frisco) and the Missouri Pacific, already operated both main and branch lines in the region, and several largely lumber-carrying "tramways" offered additional, albeit limited, service. Arguably the most painful attempt to expand the Ozarks rail grid involved efforts between 1908 and 1914 to construct the Ozark Short Line, initially under the corporate banner of the Missouri, Inland and Southern Railway (MI&S), then sponsored by the Missouri, Arkansas and Gulf Railway (MA&G), and finally by the Rolla, Ozark and Southern Railway (RO&S). Although the project was never completed, workers cleared and graded portions of the route between Rolla and Houston, assembled ties and bridge timbers, built two depots, and laid some rail.[3]

For good reason, residents of Dent, Phelps, and Texas Counties had long complained about inadequate railroad service. By the early years of the twentieth century, they had to make do with the main line of the Frisco, which ran through St. James, Rolla, and Dillon between St. Louis and Springfield; a branch line that linked Cuba and Salem; and another Frisco route (the Kansas City, Fort Scott and Memphis) between Springfield and Memphis, Tennessee, that served such Ozark communities as Mansfield, Cabool, and Willow Springs. In 1904 citizens who lived to the north rejoiced when the Chicago, Rock Island and Pacific Railroad (Rock Island) forged a secondary main line between Kansas City and St. Louis, providing rail service to Belle, Eldon, and Meta. But there remained a massive hole in the railroad map south of Rolla and Salem and north of Cabool and Willow Springs. Typical complaints came from the *Houston Herald* in 1908: "Houston, being off the railroad, is subject to many inconveniences, and not the least of these is the exorbitant charges at the station at Cabool both for express packages and boxes shipped from here to other points . . . In many instances the shipping charges on small packages are far greater than the value of the packages, and in many instances are beyond all reason." A railroad would bring considerable benefits to the area, including easier access to St. Louis. "Best of all would be the development of the resources of the country," observed a rival Houston newspaper. "Many desirable citizens would locate among us, giving us the advantage of their capital and of enterprises, not now practicable, if there was convenient means of transportation."[4]

Although earlier proposals to pierce the greater Houston area had been floated, extending back to the 1880s, the failed dream of the Ozark Short Line had its start about 1908. That summer the *Houston Texas County Star* reported that a "conference on the railroad question" had taken place in Rolla and that possibilities for connecting Rolla with Houston by rail appeared encouraging. By November the newspaper told of prospects for an "Electric Road from Mtn[.]Grove to Rolla or St. James via Houston and Licking." Indeed, representatives of the Houston Commercial Club had already canvassed the locality and indicated that a "bonus of $20,000 or more can be raised" for what was then known as the Inter-Ozark Electric Railroad. By January 1909, area residents continued to beat their drums

Figure 11. An artist's rendering of the proposed electric line between Rolla and Licking. POSTCARD, POSTMARKED 1909, ROLLA, JOHN BRADBURY COLLECTION

for the project, contending: "There is no doubt but it would be a paying proposition from the start, as a short line from Mtn. Grove or Cabool to Rolla would put passengers from the south into St. Louis about five or six hours earlier, to say nothing of the reduced cost of travel and shipping." And more was expected: "All land and property within a reasonable distance of the road would be advanced in many cases to two or three times their present value."[5]

Talk of an electric, or traction, rather than a traditional steam railroad was hardly surprising. Although the nation had already experienced two great bursts of intercity electric railway construction in 1901–1904 and then 1905–1908, it would not be until 1912 that the interurban map had mostly jelled. In fact, the longest traction road in Missouri, the seventy-nine-mile Kansas City, Clay County and St. Joseph Railway, did not open until 1913. During the time citizens of Rolla, Licking, and Houston contemplated an electric road, several other projects were rumored in the greater Ozarks, including an interurban between Jefferson City, Carthage, and Joplin; another between Columbia, Jefferson City, and Rolla; and still another between Mansfield, Ava, and Gainesville. The continuing success of the pioneer Southwest Missouri Electric Railway, which built a network of lines out of Joplin, may have stimulated such proposals.[6]

Enthusiasts for an electric interurban between Rolla and Houston conceived of more than a rural trolley line reminiscent of the cheaply built traction roads in most of New England and parts of the Midwest. Rather, their Ozark route would be "well graded and well constructed in every department. Built on standard gauge, full cars of freight and stock can be hauled." It was expected that the interurban would dispatch fast, frequent passenger runs and that the road would ultimately be more economical to operate than a steam railroad. Moreover, excess electricity, generated by on-line hydroelectric plants, could be sold to commercial and residential customers. And some backers mistakenly believed that "steam roads control money in the East and can shut off small [steam] roads in bond sales."[7]

Every successful railroad project, whether electric or steam, needed a sparkplug. The Ozark Short Line found Elbert E. Young, better known as "E. E.," a highly motivated promoter seemingly capable of turning dream into reality. Information on Young's background is sketchy. He was born in 1884 on a farm near Licking, the son of Mr. and Mrs. Charles W. Young. He subsequently lived in the Pacific Northwest, then briefly in Alaska, and later in San Francisco. By 1909 the handsome Young, who stood slightly more than 5 feet, 10 inches, weighed about 145 pounds, and had black hair and light blue eyes, was married and fathered a child. The

Houston Texas County Star described Young as being "a railroad promoter and is said to be a builder of railroads." Another account mentioned that he hailed from Spokane, Washington, and had been "identified with great development corporations of the Northwest, but his heart and his hope has [*sic*] never slackened for opening up and development of his old home of Texas County." Still another newspaper believed that "he has amassed a fortune of $200,000." These published reports likely contained elements of truth, but there is no evidence that Young had become wealthy while in the American West.[8]

In early 1909, Young became identified with the electric interurban proposal. "[Young] has taken hold of the enterprise and promises to push it to completion," reported the *Houston Herald*. "Knowing the need of a railroad through this part of the state and knowing the large territory to be developed, he has interested the western capitalists in building this road." Young quickly held meetings with civic groups and prominent individuals along the proposed route, spending most of his time in Houston, Licking, and Rolla. He immediately sensed that public interest throughout much of the future service territory was keen, especially in Texas County. The *Houston Texas County Star* editor noted, "Houston wants a railroad; wants it badly; will pay any reasonable sum to get one." This part of the Ozarks was potentially a railroad promoter's paradise.[9]

Young told railroad-hungry residents that his project lacked great complexities. He underscored the advantages of a "high speed electric interurban" and indicated that financing was feasible. Although the estimated cost was initially reported to be a whopping $2.5 million, the public would only need to subscribe to stock in the amount of $250,000. Young urged civic groups to create canvassing committees so that stock subscriptions might be raised. "This is no hot-air talk," he asserted, "but a red-hot proposition."[10]

The next step for Young involved incorporation. In May 1909 he filed legal papers with the Missouri secretary of state for the Missouri, Inland and Southern Railway Company, modestly capitalized at $400,000, and paid the state treasurer $225 to incorporate, apparently money from his own pocketbook. For reasons that are not totally clear, the MI&S would not stretch between Rolla and Cabool or even Houston. "That the railroad shall be constructed from Rolla in the county of Phelps, . . . to Licking, in the county of Texas . . . that the length of the road, as near as may be, is forty miles; and that the names of the counties in this state through or into which it is intended to be made are Phelps, Dent, and Texas." The incorporators, in addition to Young, who listed his residence as Licking, were three other Licking men, a backer from Lecoma, Missouri, and two who hailed from Spokane, Washington, giving credence to Young's earlier business ties to "western capitalists."[11]

It is highly unlikely that Young had ruled out service to Houston. The strategy of the MI&S seemed to be to open the northern segment and later push to the south. Furthermore, money raising in the Houston area had fallen short of an expected goal of $50,000, with only slightly over $30,000 committed to a railroad. "Citizens of Houston have subscribed liberally but farmers are holding back," observed the somewhat annoyed editor of the *Houston Herald* on May 13, 1909. Moreover, Young faced a competing project. In July 1909 a group of Houston citizens, led by Dr. Perry Andre "Doc" Herrington, a young, dynamic, and entrepreneurial druggist, won incorporation of the St. Louis and Houston Mineral Belt Railway Company. According to papers filed with the secretary of state, this electric railroad, also capitalized at $400,000, "shall be constructed from, at or near Cabool, in the County of Texas . . . to Houston, county of Texas . . . that the length of the road as near as may be Sixteen (16) miles." By September the St. Louis and Houston had a small force in the field conducting a preliminary survey, likely made possible when nine backers, including Herrington, each took $3,500 of the road's stock.[12]

The local press believed that the St. Louis and Houston would join a much greater project. Several accounts indicated that the "Herrington Road" would become part of a proposed steam railroad that would be built between St. Louis, Salem, Gainesville, and Harrison, Arkansas, and would ultimately meet the Atchison, Topeka and Santa Fe Railway at Paris, Texas, perhaps even reaching the Gulf of Mexico. The wackiness of this longer scheme failed to dampen optimism for some type of railroad, steam or electric, to serve Houston and Texas County.[13]

Undismayed by events in the Houston area, Young, officially president of the MI&S, forged ahead. Supporters took heart when the company hired Hugh Palmer, chief engineer of the Chicago, Kankakee and Champaign Electric Railway and the Yorkville and Morris Railroad, two mostly paper interurbans in Illinois, "to make all surveys, draw all specifications and superintend the entire construction." Palmer publicly indicated his approval of the MI&S. "I can very safely say that the road is bound to meet all its obligations in the way of bond interest and operating expenses, and besides to be in a position to pay a dividend on its capital stock soon after the cars start running." Reports circulated that surveyors had entered the field and that "work of construction will begin by September 15."[14]

Yet all was not well with the MI&S project. In late May, Young told individuals who gathered at a promotional meeting in Licking that it would be necessary to raise "$15,000 more in order to guarantee the road." The reason was simple: "This was made necessary to Licking on account of dropping out all the territory south of this place and building the road just to Licking, at least for the present." The need for more financial support from Licking was only one concern. In early June, the Dent County sheriff arrested Young. The June 10 *Salem Monitor* revealed that he had "committed fraud in some land deals in this country when he was a citizen of Salem not long ago." Young quickly posted bond and resumed his railroad work. Yet this widely reported event may have damaged the credibility of the MI&S president and project, although the burning desire for rail service surely worked to his advantage. Several weeks later the press indicated that Young had become gravely ill. "The malarial fever . . . has developed into typhoid of the worst form," yet the exact nature of his health was not fully known. Considering his recent brush with the law, perhaps the "malarial fever" may have been more mental than physical. By mid-August, however, Young had recovered and told the *Licking News*, "During the past month this railroad question has not been from my mind one hour at a time, while awake, regardless of my illness."[15]

The MI&S was hardly stillborn. By July the surveyors had completed their preliminary assignments and seemed satisfied with their work. "The engineers declare that the grade is all that could be desired," announced the *Rolla Herald-Democrat*. The only negatives were Coon Hill, south of Rolla, where the anticipated grade would be 1.5 percent, steep but not disastrous, and another 1.5 percent grade at Salem Lane near Licking. The railroad would connect with the Frisco on the east side of Rolla, extend in a generally southerly direction to reach "what is known as the Ozark divide," a relatively level ridge (the route of present-day U.S. Highway 63) near Elk Prairie in Phelps County, and then pass through the Dent County villages of Lecoma, Victor, and Lenox and the Texas County hamlet of Maples to Licking. The *Rolla Times* described the profile as looking "like a prairie roads," and this assessment had merit. But as late as the end of 1909, Young announced that he still wanted "some additional survey work."[16]

Some individuals already liked what was happening. The promotional efforts of Young and his associates had an impact on real estate activities. In July 1909 the W. S. Nichol Realty Company of Licking advertised "20 farms on and near line of proposed new railroad from Cabool to Rolla to sell at bargain prices." Others expected prices for agricultural and town lots to increase, even soar, if a railroad shattered the area's isolation.[17]

Yet the MI&S failed to attract the financial support that backers wanted. In July 1909 an unsigned letter in the *Licking News* indicated that "only one third of the stock subscribers had paid their five per cent . . . To each

Figure 12. Harrington's railroad grading teams assembled at Licking.
POSTCARD VIEW, 1913, JOHN BRADBURY COLLECTION

one the amount is small, but all of it to Mr. Young is of great importance, besides this dallying and indifference threatens the very existence of the road." Added the writer, "Mr. Young has spent much time, done lots of hard work, used up a tremendous amount of nerve force, contracted obligations, surely as much for the benefit of the community as for himself, and to be treated this way is the unkindest cut of all." Still, most farmers along the route planned to donate land for rights-of-way, a common way that many electric interurbans and steam short lines solved this potentially expensive problem.[18]

Throughout the summer and early fall of 1909, fund-raising languished. In October a disgusted Young told stockholders, "Now, if you want this road all you will have to do is to come up and subscribe or donate your part, and if you do not do this, why, the road will not be built and you will still be left in the 'sticks.'" He issued this ultimatum: "I will abandon the enterprise and you will see that you will never get another proposition as liberal as the one I have secured for you."[19]

About the time Young harangued actual and potential investors, he scored a modest triumph. Somehow the MI&S president brought in A. C. Harrington of Indianapolis, a consulting engineer who represented an eastern trust company interested in purchasing MI&S bonds. Initially, Harrington was not too enthusiastic about the Ozark Short Line. After an on-site examination, he changed his mind, but he told Young and MI&S backers that the road should be steam rather than electric. Harrington correctly concluded that a steam road "would be cheaper to construct and would have the advantage of conveying transferred cars with less trouble." Talk of an interurban largely subsided, and Houston area residents became interested in rejoining the MI&S scheme. Indeed, Young indicated that the road would terminate in Houston, not Licking.[20]

Press coverage of the Harrington connection may not have revealed the entire story. Harrington and colleagues at Carnegie Trust Company of New York City, together with Young and his investor friends, may have anticipated Rock Island support. Perhaps this sprawling carrier would push a branch southward from its newly opened Kansas City to St. Louis route at or near Belle to Rolla, forging a direct connection with the MI&S or, even better, the Rock Island might buy or lease the MI&S, whether projected, partially built, or fully operational. The *Houston Herald* categorically stated that "the Rock Island was behind the [MI&S] enterprise." The system map of the Rock Island revealed numerous appendages to main and secondary lines, including some recent additions in Arkansas and Texas. At this time, management was changing due to a powerful group of speculators who ended the company's short-term control of the Frisco, and after 1910 the Rock Island concentrated on additional betterments, including line expansion.[21]

The altered plans of the MI&S raised hopes. Since only $150,000 needed to be raised and all stock subscriptions were to be null and void unless construction commenced by a prescribed time, likely June 1, 1910, "the proposition looks good, so let our citizens get together and get to work."[22]

As 1910 unfolded, residents of Phelps, Dent, and Texas Counties had reason to believe that the Ozark Short Line was headed toward success. "Conditions are becoming brighter and better each day and there is a greater feeling of confidence and certainty among our citizens," reflected J. A. Prigmore, editor of the *Licking News*. "Don't become discouraged, friends, this road is certain to be built."[23]

Young reaffirmed his intentions to bring the MI&S into operation: "We are in shape and will begin grading within sixty days from the time the subscriptions are all in . . . This will be a winner, it must be, I'll work here as long as I have life if the people here will stick to me." The pronouncement closed oddly: "Yours until death, E. E. Young."[24]

Early in 1910, plans were announced for formation of the Inland Construction and Realty Company, a firm that would manage building and equipping the MI&S and also develop real estate, particularly through town lot sales. For decades such ancillary organizations offered promoters a rich opportunity to reap profits from the construction phase. Significantly, Inland Construction brought together the area's two leading railroad promoters: Young served as corporate secretary, and "Doc" Herrington, "the man who does things," assumed the presidency. The Houston druggist now would contribute more of his energy to the MI&S in addition to the on-and-off-again St. Louis and Houston project.[25]

Inland Construction pushed ahead vigorously. The firm arranged for a town lot sale in Licking to be held on July 4–5, 1910, telling potential buyers about the unusual terms: "Not a Red Cent to be paid until the M. I. & S. is built." An Inland Construction representative explained: "If the road is built the lots will be worth more than you pay for them, thereby making a profit off of the building of the road, besides encouraging one of the greatest enterprises ever launched in this country. If the road should not build you will not take the lots but it is foolish to consider this . . . under the circumstances." As an added incentive, the company would "give away one dozen of the best residence lots in Licking to the holders of the lucky numbers." The results of this real estate promotion were impressive, generating between $30,000 and $40,000. "This is a big boost to the railroad," concluded the *Licking News* in the latter part of July, "and seems to make the railroad a certainty."[26]

Inland Construction continued to peddle property. The company conducted a lot sale at Lenox on July 23 and held one at Anutt, a village in Dent County, on July 29–30. Arrangements for similar events at Lecoma and Elk Prairie and then in Houston were also publicized. Inland Construction did well at both Lenox and Anutt, although organized sales in the other communities never transpired. The Anutt event attracted a large audience, estimated at more than a thousand. "There were several stands on the grounds, where you could get any kind of refreshment you desired, also a swing for the young people and several other kinds of entertainment," including the popular Victor Cornet Band. Not surprisingly, Young spoke to the assembled crowd, reassuring listeners that trains would soon arrive. Inland Construction sold forty-five parcels for $6,300 and gave away a residential lot in an advertised drawing.[27]

Coinciding with the labors of Inland Construction, the MI&S pushed forward with construction. Because of their low level of stock subscriptions, Young threatened Rolla residents with a northern terminus near Dillon, "where town site and terminal grounds will be donated," but he relented. In July the intermittent building process on the previously announced survey began north of Licking—a sensible choice since it was the easiest part of the route and the best section to make a show of progress. A crew working with a dozen teams cleared the right-of-way and started to shape the roadbed. The following month a few more workers appeared in the vicinity of Elk Prairie. By November the *Rolla Times* reported, "At first they [the construction men] did not do very good grading but they made every fill and every cut necessary until they passed through Lecoma." And the *Times* added, "They quit work one half mile south of town and have now gone back over the work they had done and made fills higher where it was necessary and cuts deeper until they are getting it in good shape." Laborers also installed several concrete culverts and cleared a route several additional miles south of Lecoma. About the same time, the *Rolla New Era* believed that "about twelve miles of roadbed is [*sic*] now ready for the ties . . . and a force of men are working every day." A later edition of the *Times* expected that "a large part of the road bed" would be ready for rail laying by January 1911.[28]

While construction reports encouraged backers of the MI&S, the actions of prominent promoters generated negative newspaper coverage. In December 1910 a Dent County jury found Young guilty of the earlier charge of fraud. Remaining out of jail on bond, he appealed the verdict. A few months later a U.S. Secret Service agent arrested Young, his brother-in-law Bode Payne, and Carl Evers, an MI&S compatriot, on charges of counterfeiting. The government contended that Evers had made several hundred dollars of fake currency and that Young and Payne had committed criminal possession of "bad money." Young remained free on bond. Herrington, too, faced legal problems, having recently been convicted for illicit alcohol sales. All of these events prompted the *Houston Republican* in its edition of March 16, 1911, to editorialize in a humorous vein: "With several convictions against Dr. Herrington for selling whisky and the promoter of the railroad to Licking under arrest for counterfeiting, we wonder that the Appeal to Reason [a Socialist Party newspaper] doesn['']t charg[e] that the Plutocratic Legal Department is conspiring to keep Texas County from getting a railroad."[29]

The growing legal scandals that plagued the MI&S surely explain Young's resignation as president in April 1911 and the reorganization of the property. Gilbert Lay, a bank cashier from St. Clair, Missouri, succeeded Young, and the new Ozark Short Line, which paid its $1,028 incorporation fee to the state treasurer on April 12, 1911, was the Missouri, Arkansas and Gulf Railway. "Many of the names appearing on the list of officials of the new company are well known here," observed the *Houston Texas County Star.* "They are not only financially responsible but they have a reputation for integrity which will greatly strengthen the project." The MA&G absorbed the assets of Young's firm. The *Houston Herald* reported, "The company bought the right of way, the donations, real estate and all assets of the Missouri, Inland and Southern Railway Company." Moreover, the MA&G, capitalized at $2 million, had bigger plans. Rather than linking Rolla with Houston, the replacement company planned to build a 125-mile line southward from Rolla through Willow Springs to the railroad-starved community of Bakersfield in Ozark County. In an early map, the MA&G route bypassed Houston, running to the east through the Texas County villages of Raymondville and Yukon.[30]

The relationship between Herrington and the MA&G is mystifying. The new corporation's officials may have determined to bypass Houston because Herrington had decided to push ahead with the St. Louis and Houston, using steam rather than electricity, between the Texas County seat and Cabool. In early 1911, Houston journalists showed a newfound optimism, with the editor of the *Herald* stating in his January 12 issue, "You can wager your old hat that Doc Herrington will build this railroad." Using his own resources, Herrington purchased eleven "heavy" mule teams, constructed a large animal barn, and contracted for cross-ties to be hewn from local stands of oaks. In February the Herrington forces staged a "railroad parade" through Houston, led by a traction engine, "showing people that the preparations for building the railroad was [*sic*] not all a bluff." And in May, Herrington purchased a husky Peerless traction engine that would "be used in moving the dirt for the new railroad."[31]

Then a monumental shift occurred. Herrington took renewed interested in the Ozark Short Line. In July 1911 the *Houston Republican* reported that he had taken a contract for grading part of the MA&G between Rolla and Licking. The *Houston Herald* indicated that Herrington "at least for the present [has] given up the proposition of a railroad from Houston to Cabool, the latter place not taking a very active interest in the matter." Since he needed to purchase additional railroad-building tools and equipment, Herrington sold $1,000 worth of ties that he had stockpiled for the St. Louis and Houston.[32]

The change in railroad-building strategy neither alarmed nor angered Houstonians. Although stock subscription agreements would need to be altered, backers concurred that a rail outlet through Rolla was preferable to one via Cabool. "We believe this will be highly satisfactory to everyone," concluded a Houston editor, "for we realize that a connection with the St. Louis market is what we want and need so badly."[33]

With Herrington and his supporters behind the MA&G, the public was generally optimistic about the proposed route, which would again terminate in Houston. "The road has now passed the experimental stage . . . and the officers are setting down to business," surmised the *Rolla Times* in July 1911. In early August the *Houston Herald* reported that Herrington "received here a shipment of 19 dump cars, tent, [cooking] range, blacksmith outfit, etc., and . . . his great 30 horse power traction engine left to begin the construction work on the railroad between Rolla and Licking."[34]

Work on the Ozark Short Line advanced during the remainder of 1911. In Rolla the Frisco installed a switch near the future yards and depot located on a ten-acre parcel owned by the company. Soon thereafter the MA&G completed 2.5 miles of grade from the Frisco interchange to the south. Even though officials had not finalized a route survey south of Licking, limited construction began in Houston, and the town held a gala event in honor of the proposed line. That September afternoon became a time to remember.

> The band played, the stores closed, and every body went to the northeast corner of Mart Coyle's pasture to see work started on the new railroad which is to be built from Houston to Licking to join the one from there to Rolla. The school was dismissed and most of the children attended . . . The exercises consisted of an address by Mayor Carmical, followed by prayer by Rev. J. J. Carty. Mrs. Coyle then threw the first shovel of dirt, after which the plow teams started. Mayor Carmical turning the first furrow, followed by Garwitz's [traction] engine and the graders.[35]

Once dirt had been turned in Houston, the "Herrington Construction Company" divided efforts between the immediate Houston area, where some grading occurred and preparations were made to construct a steel bridge across the Big Piney River, and the Rolla-to-Licking segment. This unusual division of efforts may have stemmed from the desire of Herrington and MA&G backers to attract badly needed financial support from Houston residents.[36]

While the increased railroad activities may have surprised doubters, the return of E. E. Young to the railroad scene surely astonished many. In November a judge sentenced Carl Evers and Bode Payne, the two men charged with counterfeiting along with Young, to jail terms but dropped Young's indictment due to lack of evidence. A few months later, Young became general manager of the MA&G.[37]

Events would soon either make or break the Ozark Short Line. Because of winter conditions, construction slackened. "Owing to the severe weather only a small force of men could be kept employed," observed a Houston newspaper in January 1912. March press reports, however, indicated renewed activities. "A car load of grading machinery of the latest and most approved kind was unloaded at Rolla this week with which to do the grading on the Missouri, Arkansas & Gulf Railroad," announced the *Rolla*

Herald. "The work of grading is being pushed with all possible speed." In June the Frisco delivered two carloads of steel rails to the MA&G switch. Two depots also took shape, first in Rolla and then in Houston, and the company hired an immigration agent for development work.[38]

As the year progressed, the MA&G faced mounting problems. Fund-raising became paramount. Apparently, local residents had contributed all that they could (or were willing to), and the sale of bonds to outside parties never produced the hoped-for results. Efforts to attract foreign investors came to naught, and toward the end of the year, company coffers were nearly empty. Part of the woes involved some bad luck that had befallen Herrington—spring floods had temporarily knocked out his hydroelectric plant on the Big Piney River outside Houston. By summer the generating facility was "operating better than ever before," and Herrington resumed railroad construction. Then in September another flood struck. Instead of damaging the impoundment dam, the raging waters scoured out a new course, necessitating putting the stream back into the old channel. A few weeks later a fire erupted at the plant. These events left Houston in the dark and Herrington in a financial bind. Power was eventually restored, but another flood in January 1913 damaged the facility. "This is another hard blow for Dr. Herrington," commented the *Houston Herald,* "coming as it does on the top of his other misfortunes and losses." In 1914 the *Houston Republican* recalled that the last flood was too much. "The doctor's means are so exhausted that he is forced to sell his railroad equipment and abandon the [MA&G] proposition."[39]

Once again Young confronted legal problems. In the wake of serious money woes, the MA&G general manager sought to cash $28,000 of promissory notes that were not to be redeemed until the railroad opened. In December 1912 directors of the MA&G won a court injunction that prevented Young from receiving these funds. About the same time, Young illegally cashed a note for $100 that had been made out to Carl Kimmel, a company director from Lecoma, and he soon found himself in the Phelps County jail. A trial swiftly followed. After a guilty verdict, the judge sentenced Young to a two-year term in the state penitentiary. In May 1913 the twenty-nine-year-old "promoter" became inmate No. 14681 in the Jefferson City facility.[40]

As 1913 dawned, the MA&G project was in shambles. Construction and fund-raising had ceased, yet the railroad was much more than a "paper" scheme. About fifteen miles had been graded, one account indicated "two miles of track laid," and there were depot buildings in Rolla and Houston. Shareholders remained hopeful. At the annual meeting held in March, the *Rolla New Era* reported, "It was the consensus of opinion among stockholders and directors now that the affairs had been straightened out to resume work towards the completion of the road at an early date." That was wishful thinking.[41]

The Ozark Short Line saga was not yet over, even though Young had been incarcerated and Herrington had moved to Lewistown, Idaho, after another run-in with law officers over the illegal sale of whiskey and losing his light plant through a foreclosure. The MA&G was sold on December 29, 1913, for only $100 on the steps of the Phelps County Courthouse. "It is generally supposed that Mr. [W. T.] Denison bought the road for a syndicate of Rolla financiers and that the road will be built next summer," optimistically observed the *Rolla Times*. The sale, however, did not include the Rolla depot and about three-quarters of a mile of track, suggesting that the earlier report of two miles of rails having been installed to be false. The exemption of the depot and track may have been due to bondholder liens.[42]

In early 1914 the Ozark Short Line gasped its last breath. On April 15, 1914, a group of Rolla-area investors filed incorporation papers for the Rolla, Ozark and Southern Railway Company. These men had in mind a truncated line: "That the railway shall be constructed from Rolla, in the County of Phelps . . . to Anutt, Dent County . . . that the length of the road, as near as may be, is eighteen (18) miles." Capitalization was modest, only $200,000. Press reports were again optimistic. "It seems that something is about to be done at last on our long wanted railroad," commented J. A. Prigmore of the *Licking News*. "While the company is chartered under a different name, it is virtually the same company and men who are the most interested in the building of this road . . . While the charter was only taken to Anutt, which is about half way between this place and Rolla, there is no doubt that the road will continue right on down the ridge through Licking and on to the South."[43]

A railroad never linked Rolla with Licking, Houston, Cabool, or Bakersfield. Houston could claim the only depot in Missouri without ever having an operating railway, and Rolla had an unused depot not far from the Frisco main line that became a private residence. There were other physical remains, including sections of the graded rights-of-way and Rolla streets bearing the names Missouri, Arkansas, and Gulf.[44]

Though the concept of the Ozark Short Line was hardly far-fetched, much went wrong. Financial shortcomings stand out as the major stumbling block. If adequate outside funding had materialized, perhaps underwritten by the Rock Island, chances for a successful outcome would have dramatically improved. Although local enthusiasm existed, the number of individuals who were able to contribute was limited. The area contained only a small population; Rolla, the largest community, claimed about

3,000 residents; Houston, 1,000; and Licking, 500. Surely, too, the repeated legal problems that Young faced damaged the project, perhaps prompting some to view him as nothing more than a flimflam man. Although Herrington's difficulties with illegal liquor sales were an annoyance, this energy-packed and resourceful entrepreneur failed to focus on either the Houston and Cabool or the Houston and Rolla projects. If Herrington had pushed the former, a smaller, less-expensive proposition, the likelihood of rail service for his hometown would have improved. The Houston-Cabool line probably would have paralleled the fate of the nearby Kansas City, Ozark and Southern Railway (KCO&S), a road that linked Mansfield, located on the Frisco's Memphis line, with Ava, the Douglas County seat, fifteen miles to the south.[45]

The KCO&S strikingly resembled the Houston-Cabool proposal. Although originally projected in 1908 as an interurban that could exploit cheap electric power generated from proposed nearby hydroelectric plants, the line opened as a steam road in early 1910. Local promoters used public stock subscriptions and a bonus from Ava to finance the modest costs of construction and the few pieces of rolling stock. At first the KCO&S seemed successful. "They are now running two trains a day and the traffic is increasing so fast they will soon put on another train." But business soon dropped, in part because of unattractive freight rates and poor service. In time this jerkwater line slipped into bankruptcy. A reorganization in 1919, which created the Ozark Southern Railway, kept the operation alive, but the railroad shut down in the mid-1930s.[46]

If the KCO&S had not opened when it did, prospects for a functioning railroad between Mansfield and Ava would have dimmed. Indeed, the longer the Ozark Short Line remained unfinished, the greater the opportunity for other forces to work against a triumphant outcome. By 1914 lumbermen had harvested much of the area's commercially valuable trees, and lumber and wood products would have constituted a sizable portion of the company's freight traffic. Significantly, the motor age was also rapidly evolving, both with trucks and automobiles. By then Houstonians, for example, could use the commercial services of three two-ton Kissel trucks that operated regularly between Houston and Cabool. Even though a network of good roads had not yet appeared in Phelps, Dent, and Texas Counties, longer car trips became practical. In July 1914 a Houston resident drove his Maxwell to Rolla, taking three hours and thirty-five minutes to travel this fifty-five-mile route. "Formerly with a good team," observed the *Rolla Herald*, "it was an all day trip and some times parties would use part of two days in making the trip." Area newspapers enthusiastically embraced the good roads movement and agitated for a long-distance, all-weather highway, which would be known as the Ozark Trails Route.[47]

Motor vehicles and good roads doomed most steam and electric short lines in Missouri and elsewhere. Railroads that lasted beyond World War I often failed during the Great Depression. Promoters and backers of the Ozark Short Line can hardly be damned for lacking clairvoyant powers. Perhaps some proved gullible in their enthusiasm for E. E. Young's scheme, but all backers of this project can be admired for struggling to improve a challenging transportation situation.

Notes

1. *Historical Statistics of the United States, Colonial Times to 1957* (Washington, DC: U.S. Bureau of the Census, 1960), 427, 429.

2. *Ava Douglas County Herald,* September 9, 1909; Paul W. Gates, "The Railroads of Missouri, 1850–1870," *Missouri Historical Review* (hereinafter *MHR*) 26 (January 1932): 126–141; Edward J. White, "A Century of Transportation in Missouri," *MHR* 15 (October 1920): 152. At times, though, Missourians complained about railroad monopolies and political entanglements. They also found failed railroad ventures troubling.

3. A Houston newspaper editor explained the meaning of the Ozark Short Line, writing "not that the line is to be short, but it means a short line to southern Missouri." *Houston Herald,* May 4, 1911.

4. Ibid., December 24, 1908; *Houston Texas County Star,* December 24, 1908.

5. *Rolla New Era,* March 14, 1885; *Houston Texas County Star,* August 20, November 26, 1908; *Houston Herald,* January 9, 1881; January 31, 1909; *Licking News,* January 29, 1909; July 29, 1910.

6. George W. Hilton and John F. Due, *The Electric Interurban Railways in America* (Stanford, CA: Stanford University Press, 1960), 3, 186, 368–369; H. Roger Grant, "The Excelsior Springs Route: Life and Death of a Missouri Interurban," *MHR* 65 (October 1970): 37–50; *Houston Herald,* December 10, 1905; *Electric Railway Journal* 35 (February 19, 1910): 336.

7. *Houston Herald,* February 25, March 4, 1909.

8. *Licking News,* February 26, 1909; "State Penitentiary Register," 1911–1913, roll 5230, 8 A-B, Missouri State Archives, Jefferson City; *Houston Texas County Star,* February 25, 1909: *Rolla Herald-Democrat,* March 11, 1909; *Houston Herald,* February 25, 1909.

9. *Houston Herald,* March 11, May 6, 1909; *Houston Texas County Star,* February 25, 1909.

10. *Licking News,* February 26, 1909.

11. "Articles of Incorporation of the Missouri Inland and Southern Railway Company," copy in Western Historical Manuscript Collection, University of Missouri-Rolla (hereinafter WHMC-Rolla); *Railroad Age Gazette* 46 (June 4, 1909): 1187. The selection of Rolla as the northern terminus disappointed residents of nearby St. James. In early 1909 the *St. James Journal* reported that the community had created

a committee to bring the electric railroad to town. That prompted the *Licking News* to editorialize: "St. James is not asleep on the railroad proposition, and when the proper time comes she will be up for action." *Licking News,* March 12, 1909.

12. *Licking* News, May 21, 1909; *Houston Herald,* April 22, May 13, September 23, 1909; March 12, 1987; "Articles of Incorporation of the St. Louis & Houston Mineral Belt Railway Company," copy in WHMC-Rolla.

13. *Licking News,* May 21, June 11, 1909.

14. Ibid., May 7, 14, 1909. It is difficult to know if Hugh Palmer was a credible participant, although he was unquestionably an interurban enthusiast. He later served as the electrical engineer for the Cienfuegos, Palmira and Cruces Electric Railway and Power Company in Cuba. See *McGraw Electric Railway List* (New York: McGraw-Hill Co., 1918), 207.

15. *Salem Monitor* quoted in *Houston Republican,* May 21, June 10, 1909; *Licking News,* July 30, August 13, 1909.

16. *Rolla Herald-Democrat* quoted in *Licking News,* July 2, 15, November 12, 1909; *Houston Herald,* June 17, 1909; *Rolla Times* quoted in *Houston Herald,* June 24, 1909; *Houston Herald,* December 12, 1909.

17. *Licking News,* July 23, 1909.

18. Ibid., July 16, 1909.

19. Ibid., October 15, 1909.

20. Ibid.

21. *Houston Republican,* December 23, 1909; *Houston Herald,* September 22, 1910; William Edward Hayes, *Iron Road to Empire: The History of 100 Years of the Progress and Achievements of the Rock Island Lines* (New York: Simmons-Boardman, 1953), 177–189.

22. *Houston Herald,* November 25, 1909.

23. *Licking News,* January 21, 1910.

24. Ibid., March 18, 1910.

25. Ibid., January 28, 1910; *Rolla Herald,* February 3, 1910; *Houston Texas County Star,* January 12, 1916.

26. *Licking News,* March 18, June 10, July 15, 22, 1910; *Houston Herald,* July 28, 1910.

27. *Houston Herald,* July 22, 29, August 5, 1910; *Licking News,* August 5, 1910; *Rolla Herald,* August 18, 1910.

28. *Rolla Times,* June 16, 1910, quotation in November 17, 1910; November 24, 1910; *Rolla Herald,* June 2, 1910; *Licking News,* September 23, 1910; *Rolla New Era* quoted in *Houston Herald,* November 17, 1910; *St. Louis Globe-Democrat,* December 4, 1910.

29. *Houston Herald,* December 15, 1910, January 19, March 2, 1911; *Houston Republican,* March 16, Apri1 6, 1911.

30. *Houston Texas County Star,* April 27, 1911; *Houston Herald,* April 27, 1911 ; *Houston Republican,* April 27, 1911; "Articles of Incorporation of the Missouri, Arkansas & Gulf Railway Company," WHMC-Rolla; *Missouri, Arkansas & Gulf Railway: Ozark Short Line* (Rolla, MO: Missouri, Arkansas & Gulf Railway, 1911), 2.

31. *Houston Texas County Star,* January 12, 1911; *Houston Herald,* January 12, May 4, 1911; *Houston Republican,* February 9, May 25, 1911.

32. *Houston Republican,* July 21, 1911; *Houston Herald,* July 20, 1911.

33. *Houston Herald,* July 20, 1911.

34. *Rolla Times* quoted in *Houston Herald,* July 20, 1911; *Houston Herald,* August 3, 1911.

35. *Houston Republican,* September 7, 1911; quotation in September 21, 1911; October 12, 1911; *Houston Herald,* September 14, 1911.

36. *Houston Republican,* October 19, 1911; *Houston Herald,* November 23, 1911.

37. *Houston Republican,* November 30, 1911; *St. Louis Republic,* January 7, 1912; *Licking News,* July 5, 1912.

38. *Houston Herald,* January 25, April 4, 1912; *Licking News,* February 16, July 5, 1912; *Rolla Herald* quoted in *Houston Republican,* March 7, 1912; *Houston Republican,* August 1, 1912. In late fall 1912 workers finished the Houston depot. "This structure is built with concrete, with commodious waiting room, etc.," observed the December 5, 1912. *Houston Republican,*" and we must say it is a better depot than graces many of our neighboring towns."

39. *Houston Herald,* March 28, August 29, September 26, November 7, 1912; January 23, 1913; *Houston Republican,* January 22, 1914.

40. John F. Bradbury Jr., "The Ozark Short Line: Electric Railway from Rolla to Houston," *Newsletter of the Phelps County Historical Society,* n.s. 16 (October 1997): 6; *Houston Herald,* November 26, December 19, 1912; February 20, 1913; *Rolla Tines,* May 29, 1913; "State Penitentiary Register," Missouri State Archives.

41. *Houston Herald,* March 13, 1913; *Rolla New Era* quoted in *Houston Republican,* March 20, 1913.

42. *Houston Herald,* March 12, 1987; *Houston Republican,* May 21, 1914; *Rolla Times* quoted in *Licking News,* January 2, 1914.

43. "Articles of Incorporation for Standard Gauge Railway: Rolla, Ozark & Southern Railway Company," WHMC-Rolla; *Licking News,* April 24, 1914.

44. Bradbury, "Ozark Short Line," 1, 10.

45. *Missouri, Ozark & Gulf Railroad,* 10–11.

46. *Street Railway Journal* 31 (May 2, 1908): 35; *Railway Age Gazette* 45 (June 19, 1908): 209; *Houston Herald,* December 17, 1908; *Ava Douglas County Herald,* March 17, 1910; April 20, 1911; quotation in *Licking News,* June 10, 1910; *Houston Republican,* January 26, 1911; *Poor's Manual of Railroads* (New York: Poor's Manual Co., 1921), 2089; William D. Edson, compiler, *Railroad Names: A Directory of Common Carrier Railroads Operating in the United States, 1926–1989* (Potomac, MD: by the author, 1989), 95.

47. Bradbury, "Ozark Short Line," 10; *Licking News,* March 28, 1913; July 2, August 6, 1915; July 13, 1917; *Houston Republican,* July 17, 1913; *Rolla Herald* quoted in *Houston Herald,* July 2, 1914. The growing commitment to better public roads also involved the Ozark Short Line. The idea was floated that grading the railroad right-of-way should be finished but, rather than install ties and rails, the roadway should be used as a highway, *Licking News,* July 4, 1913.

Before Bass Pro

St. Louis Sporting Clubs on the Gasconade River

LYNN MORROW

A century before the modern Bass Pro Shops headquartered in Springfield, Missouri, captured the imagination of midwestern sportsmen, St. Louis businessmen had already become regular seasonal tourists throughout the Gasconade River watershed. Rail excursions on the St. Louis and San Francisco Railway (Frisco) later made the village of Arlington in Phelps County a gateway to the Ozark outdoors. These beginnings of outdoor recreation, incidental at first, then evolving into commercial notice during the 1890s, brought corporate leaders into a dialogue with small-town businessmen and especially with skilled Ozark guides. These native naturalists served as mythic pathfinders for their urban guests. The backcountry men were culture brokers who ushered city folks into an idealized primitive experience, even if only for a few days. Guides like Perry Andres at Arlington knew the techniques for successful excursions into the woods. His ability to handle guns and gigs and his boat-making skills established a model for urban sportsmen to imitate. The Frisco, promoter of all Ozark economies, capitalized upon and marketed these images to sporting clubs. Newspapers, urban and rural, supported the idealization of an Ozark Arcadia available to the traveler not far from a Frisco depot. By the early twentieth century, a few thousand St. Louisans had walked the streets of a bustling Arlington, relaxing a remote distance from smoky, smelly, and industrialized St. Louis.

The *St. Louis Globe-Democrat*, the *Sportsman* and the *Fish and Game Protector* magazines, and urban and rural weeklies carried reports of weather and fishing and hunting conditions, news of local events, and stories by city folks about their adventures in the Ozark countryside. Urban serials promoted the Gasconade River for an important quality observed by professional anglers: it remained unpolluted by sawdust from the great sawmills that poisoned the water and ruined fishing on the Current, Black, and Eleven Point Rivers. The number of fish in the Gasconade amazed all who patronized the stream.[1]

Tourists viewed the land differently from the natives, created their own folklore about landmarks, and conferred Arcadian sentiments on Ozark place-names. Americans dreamed of a rural Arcadia where virtue, rest and relaxation, and the regeneration of the spirit were possible. Editor and outdoor writer Charles Meade of the *St. Louis Globe-Democrat* wrote about "romantic Potato Hollow," "Pumpkin Hill," "Onion Hollow," and the towering bluff known as "Lover's Leap" where the Little Piney enters the Gasconade River in his "Rod and Gun" column. In spring 1902, weary urbanites beheld a flag at Lover's Leap, planted the summer before by an adventuresome lady from Kirkwood, that "still flutter[ed] in the breeze as a starter for all those lovers who want to leap over the trees to the Gasconade or Piney." Visitors walked the land, treed squirrels, and gathered mushrooms, frogs, and mulberries. They fished for bass and jack salmon (walleye), and at night the Arlington boys taught them how to run a trotline.[2] Old gobblers, a favorite of many hunters, fussed on the steep hillsides within hearing distance of Arlington's Gasconade Inn. The "Rod and Gun" column invited sportsmen to relax upon arrival at Arlington and "take a pull from the bottle" at trainside with guide Perry Andres, who became a sportsman's folk hero.[3]

The ideal existence, according to true sportsmen, required a cultivated style—an expectation planned for by urban romantics. The increasing popularity of recreation on the rivers brought inquiries to editors for advice on how to arrange an outing. Reports from Arlington to St. Louis readers gave hints on planning for camp life in the country. "Rod and Gun" warned neophytes to "not neglect a single detail."[4]

Meade cautioned: "Don't go out to rough it too much, unless you are an old-timer, who is seasoned to the business." He published a list of provisions and necessities for a party of six persons and associated guides for a six-day float trip but qualified his list by saying that it could be reduced "more than half in variety" and still afford a healthful supply. Meade's recommendation included more than three dozen items such as weapons, meat, vegetables, condiments, and medical supplies. He emphasized that the traveler should include "a small package of mustard plasters, and such other emergency remedies as you may suggest . . . Adding a bottle of aqua ammonia and a little oil of lavender, the outfit will get along all right. The lavender is a great mosquito preventive, while the ammonia is a good cauterizer for insect bites, especially the little chigger . . . The natives . . . say that green pennyroyal rubbed on the person will prevent the chiggers or ticks from getting familiar with the human anatomy." At the campfire, he continued, "Cook plenty of fish when they are fresh . . . Bacon gravy is much better than lard . . . Get a big side of bacon that is sweet . . . fry it out to put with a small quantity of lard and you will have a mixture that will add to the flavor of the fish . . . Take a gun . . . Squirrels are mighty fine eating . . . [and] a little rifle to nip the frogs . . . if you do not like to gig them at night."[5]

True sportsmen did not forget the women. Meade continued: "Teach them to shoot the little .22 so they can get some of the summer sport of frogging . . . Teach the women how to cast a fly." The sport will "put the color on a lady's cheek as quick as a proposal of marriage." And do not forget to take for the ladies "a 5-pound box of candy and some chewing gum." Contentment demanded "a good comfort and blanket for each person; also a pillow."[6] Tourists, fully supplied and armed with guns and

Figure 13. Camp Comfort, Pulaski County.
POSTCARD VIEW, 1907, KALEN AND MORROW COLLECTION

cameras, drew notice from the press. Over the years, the *Globe-Democrat,* considered one of the nation's most influential commentators on conservation and the outdoors, continued to promote floats on Ozark streams, spreading the word through midwestern newspapers.[7]

Correspondents from Arlington responded in kind, promoting their idyllic hamlet as a bustling depot prepared for sport. After all, they had a proprietary interest in seeing that readers of the St. Louis sporting pages knew where to go. L. F. Pillman, a businessman in Arlington since 1887, wrote in March 1903 that the new season had already begun. He confirmed that all guides had sufficient supplies of minnows to put the one- and two-day fishermen immediately in the waters. Guide Mark Brooks had hosted Springfieldians and caught so many trout that he had to "store them away in a lifeboat." Andres, "the Sportsman's Friend," had made "extensive improvements on his property" and prepared for fishing parties. Guides Glover Courson and Alfred Miller had booked several St. Louis groups for early outings. Pillman's Gasconade Inn, newly opened under the management of E. F. Strawhun, was ready to receive overnight guests.[8] Moored at Arlington was fisherman Billy Moore's and Pillman's gasoline launch, the *Pride of the West,* "a marvel of speed" traveling a mile and a half upriver in one hour.[9] All in all, Arlington expected its best season yet.

Events involving well-known guides received considerable attention in St. Louis. At Arlington on a Sunday afternoon in July 1903, Andres and other local men were involved in a violent fracas in which the guide and another man were shot and others stabbed.[10] Andres's wounds were considered mortal. During the following weeks, the *Globe-Democrat,* with the help of Perry's wife, Ettie, carried progress reports on the Sportsman's Friend. Remarkably, in only one month, Andres's wounds healed enough for him and Courson to travel to St. Louis to schedule more business. An upshot of this unsavory affair was the rise in Andres's reputation among St. Louisans. Like Hawkeye in the *Leatherstocking Tales,* Andres met adversity at the risk of his life. His survival earned him a new title, "Old Ironsides," that delighted St. Louis correspondents.[11]

Sporting St. Louisans looked forward to visits from the "Gasconade Guides." Andres and his associates rode the Frisco to downtown St. Louis, where they attended the theater, purchased Stetson hats, pampered themselves at tonsorial parlors, ordered the latest outdoor gear at Rawlings Sporting Goods, and drummed up business with old clients. Andres regaled St. Louis clubmen with Ozark tales and his homespun poetry. Vernacular poetry was a regular feature of the literary outdoors romance, and the rivers performed as leading actors in the sentimental verse. These simple expressions of outdoor living formed a genre of fraternal humor, entertainment, and satisfaction. Readers expected it, and "Rod and Gun" did not disappoint them. During the Progressive era, such poetry was a popular medium for men, women, and children who went "flowering, floating, and fishing" on the rivers.[12]

St. Louis sportsmen relied upon Andres for his expert advice. In 1901 the prominent Red Horse Club asked him to seine suckers and catch turtles for a club banquet. They wanted to celebrate the election of a member to local political office in Gasconade sporting style. When the Laclede Hunting and Fishing Club took an option on six thousand acres in southeast Missouri, they asked Andres to consult on the organization of a game preserve.[13]

St. Louisans, in turn, promoted the Big Piney and Gasconade Rivers to their friends. Andres knew that the hundreds of pounds of fish exported from Arlington to St. Louis by these affluent sportsmen represented free advertising for his business. Additionally, these true sportsmen practiced a version of an emerging conservation ethic in Missouri. For example, Charley Robinson, a Webster Groves real estate dealer, led a 1902 float trip from Slabtown down the Piney to Arlington. His group caught 305 bass and released all but 30, which had an aggregate weight of ninety pounds. Robinson's group was a portent of changing attitudes on Ozarks rivers, but a dramatic transformation in the hunting and fishing habits of Missourians lay in the distant future.[14] The year 1904 proved to be a good one for Arlington merchants, with St. Louis businessmen bringing their out-of-state clients into the Ozarks. The increased tourist traffic to Arlington, a spin-off of the St. Louis World's Fair, caused Andres to complain that his own travels to the fair suffered—too many travelers wanted his services. The Sportsman's Friend operated camps scattered over 65 miles, from Arlington to Indian Ford in Maries County and from Arlington up the Big Piney into Texas County—a total of 165 river miles. The single most important item, of course, was the boat. Perry Andres's brother, Tilden, and cousin, Russ Andres, built and guided quality flatboats that carried 1,500 pounds of supplies and gear. The emerging trade and need for reusable boats prompted craftsmen to build stable watercraft, eliminating the historical need to sell temporary boats at the end of a float or for importing boats freighted from St. Louis on the Frisco. The Andres associates were the leading boatbuilders on the Frisco route.

Over the years, a growing diversity of tourist-sportsmen traveled to Arlington, bringing middle-class "clubhouse" resort culture to the Ozarks. Business groups and social clubs made annual outings, and some clubs purchased land in the area. Other changes occurred as well. During the

1890s, male sportsmen dominated the trade. But that changed in the early twentieth century—wives, girlfriends, and children came along as summer visitors. The broadening audience of gender and age required different types of recreation; women and children were not going to ride tie rafts to gig fish as male adventurers did. The presence of families eroded the traditional all-male memberships in clubs and opened the resorts to general visitation by rail-borne tourists.[15]

Railroad managers were crucial in the promotion of Arlington and the extension of the trade to include both men and women. To focus customers' attention, the Frisco ticket office in St. Louis hung a large promotional painting of the Ozark outdoors near the counter. Frisco agent Sam Hughes; C. C. McCarty, passenger agent for the Illinois Central; Brainard Allison, advertising manager for the Missouri Pacific and St. Louis, Iron Mountain lines; and W. J. Leahy, of the Chicago and Rock Island, served as public advocates of the sporting culture. As women increasingly traveled to the country, railroad managers encouraged outfitters to provide the best gear and boats. Regular Arlington customers like George H. Rawlings, Colonel Dick Fleming, Hugh Pattison and his large entourage, and Louis Dennig and his "band of Budweisers" from Anheuser-Busch Brewing Company had long demanded quality gear. Thus, Perry Andres happily announced the construction of a new supply of boats for the benefit of the boys from St. Louis. Not bashful, the Sportsman's Friend declared that his boats were comfortable enough that his "'old fishing friends feel like living in them.'"[16]

Across the river from Arlington, the Jerome Hunting and Fishing Club exemplified the changes in outdoor recreation. In late 1899, B. H. Rucker and his old St. Louis fishing pal, Olney "Pop" Fuller, decided to build a resort open to the general public. Fuller, facing retirement as a businessman in Maplewood, owned 95 percent of the newly incorporated club in January 1900. As president, Rucker served as the local manager. Club membership included St. Louisans of public reputation such as judges Waiter F. McEntire and Willis H. Clark, attorneys Richard M. Johnson and Jeptha Howe, Dr. Otto Forster, and such well-known Izaak Waltonians as Ed Wickham, Harry C. Smith, H. W. Harris, ex-senator Fred Espenschied, and the Honorable George W. Allen.[17] Professionals such as these typically founded the sporting clubs. They held their club business meetings in downtown St. Louis, where they planned outings to their Americanized version of Eden.[18]

Sited "north and west of the Frisco railroad bridge, overlooking the [Gasconade] river," the Jerome Club represented a transitional club in Missouri Ozarks sporting history. The corporation completed its clubhouse in early 1901. From its founding, the club welcomed the general public, including women—a sure sign that tourism at Arlington would be different from what it had been in the 1890s. Club rules required only that women abide by the same obligations as the male members. Members paid a $5.00 annual fee; daily rates were $1.00. Any member could bring or send friends to enjoy the facility; the special railroad rates, however, applied only to club members. Visitors staying at the clubhouse had ready access to guides, boats, and bait.

One member of the Jerome Club worked as the premier publicist, George H. Rawlings, general manager of the Rawlings Sporting Goods Company. A recognized enthusiast of Ozark fishing, Rawlings appeared regularly on Ozark waters and came to be considered one of the old guard on the Big Piney and Gasconade Rivers. Rawlings's guests included important promoters such as J. B. Parkell, advertising manager for the Frisco, and C. C. Spink, publisher of the *Sporting News*—St. Louisans who had influence in writing and advertisement.

In keeping with the innovative policies of the Jerome Club, Rawlings brought his wife, Ella, for her first fishing trip. Pop Fuller dug angleworms for Mrs. Rawlings and other women. Rawlings pronounced his wife a fearless boat handler and a fisherwoman of whom any sportsman would be proud. Mrs. Rawlings was a bit bashful about demonstrating her swimming abilities before the watchful eyes of the natives, but she and George frolicked in the rippling Gasconade just the same. The Rawlings couple introduced business associates and friends to the club and advertised Arlington fishing conditions, based on telegrams received from Andres, in the downtown St. Louis store. Young sales clerks at the Rawlings store added to the fame of the club. One of the youngsters, drawing upon a reliable quote from Davy Crockett, summarized their fun: "'Couldn't furgit it if we would; an' wouldn't furgit it if we could.'"[19] The *Globe-Democrat* advertised this new trend of inclusive accommodations for the "comfort and entertainment of the feminine portion of the members' families." Meade complimented the enthusiasm of the ladies who were "becoming comrades by the camp-fire, in the clubhouse, the field and upon the waters where game and fish are sought."[20]

The Jerome Club, like most sporting clubs, had a short-lived first generation of membership. The better-known members moved on in a few years to other new clubs and newly discovered sporting grounds. By 1903 the exit of affluent members led the Jerome Club into debt and an uncertain future. In 1904, Fuller built a few cabins around the club and advertised private cottages for families. He spent much of his retirement at Jerome, occasionally visiting the Rawlings store to regale listeners with tales about the Ozarks. By the end of 1905, however, the clubhouse and its charter were for sale. The corporation dissolved, and a few of the members purchased the property and continued its operation as a public place but omitted annual membership dues. This cycle of incorporation and dissolution, followed by passage from urban to rural ownership, became common in the history of sporting club properties throughout the Ozarks.[21]

Hugh Pattison, a veteran of sporting safaris on the nation's railroads, became a leader in sporting history on the Gasconade River. A St. Louis businessman renowned for his Irish tavern, restaurant, and bowling alley, he belonged to twenty-five sporting clubs, including the famous Venedy Club organized in 1881 in East St. Louis, Illinois. In January 1902, he investigated possibilities for a new club on the Gasconade and, by late winter, settled upon a site at Fish Dam Ford, upstream from Arlington and Jerome. His resort plan included apartments for women in a cozy and comfortable camp.[22]

Pattison, Emile Remmers, superintendent of the St. Louis poorhouse, and their associate William Hussig closed a deal in March that was representative of the new tourist culture in the Ozarks. The St. Louisans took a five-year lease, with the option to purchase in five years, on 37.5 acres "near the Dixon bridge," seven miles from the Frisco depot in Dixon. The land, located between two hills, included springs, woods, and "a shack, 12 x 28" (probably a two-room, board-and-batten house), which they remodeled into a kitchen and dining room. New construction added an 18′ x 35′ two-room house as apartments for women. The club contracted with the manager of Dixon's Frisco Hotel to care for members at twenty-five cents per meal and twenty-five cents for lodging, and a liveryman agreed to a $1.50 hack rental per tourist and another $1.50 for transporting freight. The Frisco office in St. Louis cooperated by making available a $4.00 round-trip ticket, "the cheapest rate on the road." Pattison and Remmers completed improvements at the Dixon Club within a month. The $25.00 membership cost to join and the annual $5.00 fee, paid in advance, also purchased a complimentary membership in the Venedy Club for those who fancied flatwater duck hunting. A month later, in May 1902, Frisco agent Sam Hughes announced that the state government hatcheries had dumped fish near Crocker, upstream from the Dixon Club. The Frisco railroad, the Missouri Fish Commission, Dixon merchants, and sporting St. Louisans all rejoiced.[23]

Farther upstream, four miles from Crocker at Schlicht's Mill, Frisco railroad sports leased property and set up Forest Lodge (sometimes called the Frisco Clubhouse) to accommodate twenty people in a completely screened building. "Rod and Gun" promoted the lodge as the answer for "those who have wanted to 'camp out,' but dreaded the living in tents" and the disagreeable features of "roughing it." Travelers disembarked at Schlicht Station, only one mile from the springs, where Schlicht's Mill store stocked supplies—milk, butter, eggs, meats, groceries, and even fishing tackle. Squirrel, quail, and rabbit abounded in the countryside on John A. Schlicht's nine-hundred-acre farm, continually improved since 1876 and actively cared for by his son, Charles. The Frisco Club permitted nonmembers to stay at the lodge, creating a tourist destination for anyone who could afford the rail fare. The Frisco and the federal hatchery at Neosho cooperated to stock the springs with thirteen thousand trout. Schlicht's three lakes, stocked with free government fish, were an additional incentive for women and children to learn to fish. Mrs. Schlicht's pet gobbler added to family entertainment. For company desiring continuity with the past, "Old Guide McGowan" had lived nearby since 1865 and rendered his opinions on the size of fish brought to the club. Every resort tried to have at least one native guide to impart local color and history.[24]

Guides coached the tourists on sporting techniques, sometimes even fishing the pools and eddies to give their catch to hapless St. Louisans. Proving their prowess to stay-at-home neighbors, Dixon Club members shipped barrels of bass and jack salmon to the city regardless of who caught them. On one Gasconade adventure, a party of six St. Louisans floated from Bartlett's Spring to Arlington, where they shipped three hundred pounds of fish. A mishap in which the river claimed their guns, cameras, and tackle did not lessen the anglers' enthusiasm—the pleasure was in great fishing. The "Rod and Gun" columns never dwelled on the negative but acted as the medium of exchange for compliments and challenges among the outing fraternities. Sporting friends also exchanged prize gifts as calling cards of their prowess, pleasure, and success on new sporting waters. For example, Judge William J. Hanley, attorney for the Dixon Club, sent his largest catch to a sporting friend, former state senator James Orchard in West Plains.[25] For years, Orchard had organized floating, fishing, and hunting trips for St. Louisans and Kansas Citians on the Eleven Point and North Fork Rivers.[26]

Clubhouses scheduled activities appropriate to the season. The Dixon Club celebrated their first Christmas with a deer roast at Schlicht Springs. For the coming year, members optimistically committed capital for extensive improvements, including a new barn, an icehouse, and an addition to the main building. The presence of stock at the resort led the press to call it "Emil Remmers' ranch," but "Rod and Gun" focused more attention upon the dual genders and multiple generations as "the broadest gauged of any of our angling organizations . . . Wives, daughters and sisters . . .

are the most charming part of the organization" and proficient in luring "the gamey bass." Families brought tents, "where the privacy of home [was] enjoyed."[27] The atmosphere at the Dixon Club and Schlicht Springs set the tone for bourgeois family tourism in the Gasconade valley with its fellowship of the sexes and welcome to children. Genial John Schlicht met the members at the Crocker railroad station, bringing his homemade wine for riders to sample on the way to the mill springs, where his wife had dinner waiting. The sporting Dixonites and the Schlichts quickly established their clubhouses as destinations on the social map of St. Louisans.

Pattison, Hanley, and others counted on a banner year at the Dixon in spring 1903. In the tradition of club openings, they reserved a special Frisco coach to bring guests to the freshly remodeled facilities. Convivial Dixonites sustained merriment and sport by inclusive preparations for all. Hanley challenged all anglers to a Gasconade "fishing race" (the most fish caught or the greatest weight in pounds). Genteel campfire entertainment featured the judge's song, "The Fisherman's Daughter," and Pattison's mandolin performance of "The Click of Papa's Reel" guaranteed to make the "stars grow more luminous and the croak of the frogs to assume a new and sweeter melody." As was customary, a local family—Mr. and Mrs. James Courson of Arlington—managed the resort. Exclusive to the Dixon Club, however, was a private telephone line for the use of members operated by club patron and Frisco physician R. T. Harrison. The Dixonites, with new telephone technology and, later, rural free delivery, maintained closer contact with their St. Louis businesses than any sporting tourists of the 1890s.[28]

The Dixonites' success spawned imitators in the Gasconade valley. One was the Two O'Clock Club, whose members visited the Dixon Club in 1903.[29] They sought advice on locating another preserve on the Gasconade and settled on a site at Brittain Eddy, a longtime favorite fishing pool for St. Louisans. The members engaged a St. Louis builder to draw plans, and John Brandon became the overseer for the construction. At Christmas 1903, the Two O'Clockers celebrated their success at their downtown St. Louis clubroom. They decorated Christmas trees and lit them with electric lights, but the main attraction was a tree ornamented by the trophies of quail, ducks, fish, snowbirds, possums, and pheasants.[30]

Club members determined to have a grand opening of the resort, renamed "Brandon's Bungalow" for its builder and club treasurer. Club president George Stumm and vice president Richard M. Johnson, two of St. Louis's most prestigious sportsmen, inspired another sporting poem for "Rod and Gun." Everyone at the mid-January frolic heard a reading of "At Brandon's Bungalow," a sentimental Arcadian performance.[31]

Figure 14. "Guides, Teams, Camp Outfitters" at Perry Andres's Boat House.
JOHN BRADBURY COLLECTION, ROLLA

The St. Louisans at Brandon's Bungalow quickly made friends with their neighbors. Pulaski County judge J. B. Harvey and his son, Henry, looked after the resort, reporting on spring rains and high water to the owners and keeping "an eye on the bungalow to see that it is not carried away by some marauding band of [tie] rafters." Members counted on Harvey for fresh milk, eggs, butter, and other farm produce; in return, the Two O'Clocks supplied the judge with extra bass, jack salmon, and catfish. The Harveys embellished the rustic simplicity of the property by planting flowers around the clubhouse. They also planted a garden with castor beans, lettuce, and sunflowers to attract birds, placed horseradish roots along the spring branch, and planted creeping vines to crawl over the fences. In season, club folks acquired watermelons and cantaloupes from valley farmers and cooled them in the spring. They built a "live pool" where members deposited fish for the viewing delight of all. Sportsmen feasted on fresh vegetables, frogs, and aquatic birds at their new epicurean center in the Ozarks. The men felled trees along the bank of Brittain Eddy so the leafy tops fell into the Gasconade River to attract crappie and bass to an arbitrary habitat. The bank along Brittain Eddy assumed a look that no suburban St. Louisan would find strange.[32]

St. Louis sportsmen typically assembled at fall camp hunts after the November elections; the Two O'Clocks were no different. Postelection trips to the Ozarks served another purpose as well. "Bungalow Brandon and Two O'Clock Stumm" wanted to hunt turkey, but they also wanted to monitor the seasonal firing of the open range—"'a sight to behold, and a menace to a great deal of property.'" Brandon and Stumm set backfires to combat flames advancing across the hills. The drama of the luminous nights included "long lines of fire that rolled down from the hills to die out at the river." But in sporting fashion, the Two O'Clocks gleefully reported the sight of live game that outdistanced the fire and came right upon them for a "social call" becoming the next trophies of the club members. In a caution to trespassers, manager Brandon claimed that range hogs had driven all the snakes into the resort's fenced enclosure, where they awaited unwanted prowlers.[33]

The Dixonites and the Two O'Clocks did a robust business while construction proceeded far downriver on the St. Louis and Colorado Railroad (later reincorporated as the Chicago-Rock Island line).[34] In fall 1903, the Rock Island and Frisco lines announced a cooperative transportation scheme for float trips beginning at Arlington and ending downriver at the Colorado crossing, dubbed "Riverside" camp, near Freeburg in Osage County. Here the Rock Island bridged the Gasconade, and floaters could board an eastbound train back to St. Louis. This circle of transportation from St. Louis by rail, water, and rail again proved ideal for landless urban clubs whose activities required convenient rail transport. Railroad pamphlets advertised local guides and their rates. Arlington outfitters profited by providing boats and guides for the downriver trip who hauled the boats and commissary back upriver. An inducement included packing fish at Riverside and shipping the catch to St. Louis on a two-hour freight. The railroads sold a $5.00 ticket good for thirty days, and tourist-sportsmen made the proposed loop regular business for the Arlington guides.[35]

The extension of the Colorado line westward toward Kansas City attracted another urban market to the Gasconade River. The *Globe-Democrat* began to promote opportunities in the Ozarks previously too inconvenient for Kansas Citians. The geography at Riverside presented an appropriate site for a new sportsmen's club. Rumors circulated that Perry Andres had considered and declined such a development, but urban sportsmen kept alive the idea of a new resort on the lower Gasconade. Maries County folks had just completed a clubhouse opposite Indian Ford, near Vienna, "furnished with the cold stuff in bottles and ice for packing fish," but the out-of-towners wanted a larger operation downriver from Indian Ford, where the great Rock Island bridge, the longest interior bridge in Missouri, spanned the river.[36]

Meade dramatized the possibilities in his "Rod and Gun" column by reporting game kills and fish catches near the bridge. Before long, Riverside crossing lured veteran Gasconade sportsman and Dixon Club promoter Hugh Pattison. He had been considering building a new club in Illinois, but in May 1905, he and fellow clubman Charles Zinn announced their lease of land near the "Colorado crossing" (Gascondy Station) and intention to erect a new resort. The next week a foursome from Saline County reported great success near Pattison's proposed development. T. H. Fisher and his pals spent a week catching 386 fish—126 bass, 84 jack salmon, and the balance in perch and catfish. The manager of the Freeburg hotel packed their fish for the return home. The grateful sportsmen, pleased with their trip to the Gasconade, recommended that all outdoorsmen keep up with the timely reporting in the *Globe-Democrat*. The Saline Countians, like the St. Louisans, knew that Meade's columns contained the best regional intelligence about new fishing waters in Missouri.[37]

Pattison began construction of his club on a summit overlooking the valley. The hotel, with a wide-sweeping veranda, and cottages stood within one hundred yards of the Gascondy depot and post office. His first order of business was to employ Glover Courson, a well-known Arlington guide, as keeper of the clubhouse and supplier of boats. By July, Pattison reported that the clubhouse had been completed, and he began accepting $10.00 memberships in the new Gascondy Club.[38] The establishment of the Gascondy Club was the final event defining "Lower Gasconade" (from Arlington downriver) and "Upper Gasconade" (upriver from Arlington) as terms for commonly understood geographical corridors. Vernacular speech and the outdoor press popularized their use among a wide audience.

Meade promoted the new club in "Rod and Gun" with regular features titled "Gascondy News" and "Gascondy Notes." The Gascondy Club had a novel appeal as a meeting ground for St. Louis and Kansas City tourist-sportsmen. Competitive trapshooters from the two cities already knew one another, but travelers made new acquaintances and business connections while fishing and hunting. Meade penned perhaps the longest of his sporting poems in Gascondy's honor. In it he offered special praise for W. J. Leahy, the passenger agent for the Rock Island Railroad who escorted Meade's journalist friends to inspect the new club. Sportsmen who patronized the new resort could not have improved upon Meade's laudable verse. The writer was a friend, professional peer, spokesman for the outdoors, and literary champion of access to Missouri's great natural resources.[39]

The 1905 Labor Day holiday provided an opportunity for Pattison to further advertise Gascondy. Meade and other journalists joined Judge Hanley, Pattison, and railroad executives of the Frisco, Rock Island, and Wabash Railroads at Union Station to board a "sportsmen's special car." After music and singing en route, the group met Pattison's two sisters at Gascondy, whom, with Mr. and Mrs. Grant (the domestic keepers of the clubhouse), served as hostesses and host for the outing. "Colored old boys . . . serve[d] up the good things to eat" and gave "strict attention to everything that was expected of them." The resorters, amid "fragrant fumes of the epicurean Havanas," listened to impromptu speeches delivered on the porch of the clubhouse, then walked the planked pathway from the high plateau down into the Gasconade valley to view the giant Rock Island bridge from below. Pattison's guests later toured the "royally fitted up apartments in the clubhouse" for family accommodations and the dormitory building "with its array of iron beds, and immaculate linen and restful equipment." C. C. McCarty, passenger agent for the Illinois Central, and his family had camped nearby on the Gasconade for ten days, and they came to join the holiday fun. Hanley awarded "trading stamps to the ladies of the Gascondy Club who [caught] bass or jack salmon weighing over three pounds"; Pattison's fashionable kitchen served up resort raised chickens and homegrown vegetables accompanied by sparkling spring water. Guests received packed lunches for day outings. The society and facilities at Gascondy Club promised luxury and sophistication, facilitated by the Rock Island's special club fare of $3.30 for round-trip tickets from St. Louis. Pattison's Gascondy Club became the largest sporting landmark on the Gasconade River.[40]

The fall season at Gascondy became a regular feature in "Rod and Gun." Each weekend dozens of St. Louisans poured in and out of the commodious resort. Pattison procured a gasoline launch to ferry hunters, fishermen, campers, and floaters up and down the river, which dramatically increased the traffic from Indian Ford downriver.

St. Louis merchants showcased trophies from the Gasconade in downtown store windows, and Pattison provided a gathering place for club members. He designed a large banquet hall in his building, made notable by a massive display of artists' renderings of "panel pictures in water colors of scenery along the classic rivers of the Ozarks." The businessman held meetings to elect annual officers and scheduled gala socials with music, dancing, and memorable feasts highlighted with wild game. In this setting, men and women recalled recent summer outings and happy days spent on the Gasconade, made wagers for an upcoming tennis match at the Gascondy Club, told hunting and fishing tales, and remembered youthful romances in the country. Guests assured one another that just as the robins would soon nest again in Ozark orchards, so they too would occupy resort cottages clustered in a picturesque Ozark valley.

Pattison rested and socialized throughout the winter in St. Louis; at the same time, he worked diligently to book reservations for the upcoming spring. His $10.00 annual fee exceeded that of some resorts but remained affordable for the traveling middle class. The fee entitled the member to "an elixir of life in the ozone of the Ozarks . . . Eat fried chicken, climb up the beautiful bluffs, take your gun and stroll down the Gasconade, or tramp up the shore, or pull a boat." Moreover, Pattison's new clubhouse superintendent, Charley Weston, had many tales to tell about his adventures in the American West. Storytelling was always popular at the clubhouse or on the gravel bar. Pattison, a longtime Irish tavern owner, had told tales for decades.[41]

As spring arrived in 1906, Pattison announced an exclusive innovation —prize-winning homing pigeons that had performed at the St. Louis World's Fair. Pigeon quartered in St. Louis and at the Gascondy clubhouse enabled hunters and anglers to report quickly about their backwoods success to friends at the clubhouse, though the affable Irishman claimed that their use was insurance in case of an emergency in the wilds. To advertise this novelty, Chris Von der Ahe, president of the Nineteenth Ward Democratic Rod and Gun Club (and the former owner/promoter of baseball's St. Louis Browns and Sportsman's Park), "liberated a bunch of Pattison's homing pigeons" in St. Louis to fly to the Gascondy coop, where Pattison and anxious guests welcomed them. Pattison, however, was not foolish enough to allow his pigeons free rein of the environs. When guests crowded his grounds, the Gascondy developer kept his pigeons cooped for fear that they would become targets. He felt relief when reading in "Rod and Gun" that game distributed by weekend sportsmen at the front entrance of St. Louis City Hall did not include his pigeons.[42]

Pattison, an innovator in the tourist-sportsmen trade on the Gasconade River, recognized that his commercial success was tied to the numbers of game and fish available. Although no one articulated a regulatory vision for wildlife without engendering opposing views, Pattison wanted stronger conservation laws. He brought self-conscious true sportsmen from the city who did not resist criticizing local farmers whom they observed "taking turkeys out of season." Missouri progressives passed the modern game law, known as the Walmsley Law for Kansas City state representative Harry Walmsley, who introduced it in 1905. The statute established game seasons and wardens with police power to arrest violators. Charles Meade called upon state government to send aggressive St. Louis game wardens, hired under the new law, to Osage County. In the same issue, Meade carefully reported that Gascondy guests "caught their fish on the square" and that the visitors observed the new and controversial game and fish regulations. A survey of the "Rod and Gun" column clearly indicates, however, that no consensus existed among natives or visitors about how game and fish should be regulated. There were many schemes for regulation as well as many critics. The controversy over conservation ethics and regulation, however, did not curtail the tourist trade in the Ozarks—visitors increased at all recreational clubs. And it did not diminish interest in hunting. In 1905, Pattison introduced another innovation at Gascondy—a trained setter to help guests in tracking fowl. The resort owner also offered "to teach all the club members and their families the art of trapping rabbits, minks, muskrats, coons, possums and foxes." Members already owned over one hundred gray and fox squirrel skins and planned to make them "prized packages" for the ladies who wished to wear fur in the city. Pattison used his popularity to attract large groups of sporting tourists, in and out of St. Louis, and provided his urban banquet hall and clubrooms for strategic forums held by the Missouri Game and Fish Protective League. The activist sportsman contributed to securing game and fish legislation in 1909.[43]

As business boomed, Pattison hired Russ Andres and two boys named Sheldon from Arlington to build eighteen "skiffs and flatboats" each for the spring 1906 season. No other site on the river, except Arlington, offered as many rental boats for sportsmen. Andres wasted no time in displaying his personal skill by killing ducks and catching an eighty-five-pound sturgeon near the Rock Island bridge. The fish was so large that Andres, prepared for any event, killed it with his pistol before bringing it to shore.[44]

With flatboat fleets available at Arlington and Gascondy Station, "Rod and Gun" published the names and approximate distances of landmarks along the eighty-five river miles between the two rail stations. Vacationers knew ahead of time to ask about conditions near Sock's Rock (also known as Thock's and Thox), Gaines Ford, Johnson's Ferry, Spring Creek, Indian Ford, and Hofman's Creek. In 1908, Till Andres, who had assumed the management of his brother Perry's outfitting business, added a new name to the river—"Gasconda"—the take-out point by the Rock Island bridge.[45]

The press, catering to clients who rode the Missouri Pacific, suggested that adventurers consider the longer trip from the Rock Island bridge downriver to the station at Gasconade City on the Missouri River. Floats on this stretch, requiring twice the time because of slower currents, never achieved the popularity of the Arlington-Gascondy Station corridor.

The expansion of recreational tours brought some difficulties. Landowners along the river were not pleased by either guides or their tenderfoot clients who loved to roam the woods. Artists and naturalists especially enjoyed wandering off for individual solace, sometimes becoming lost for a day or two. The increasing numbers of sportsmen and the police authority of the 1905 hunting law encouraged farmers to post their properties with "no trespassing, no hunting" signs. The *Globe-Democrat* printed its first warning about observing trespassing laws in 1906. Autumn floats carried as many hunters as fishermen, or more correctly, sportsmen fished and hunted from the water as always. Local law officers, usually justices of the peace, did not hesitate to arrest and fine the city folks. Sportsmen who arrived at St. Louis's Union Station with turkeys, ducks, quail, and rabbits complained of their lightened pocketbooks.[46]

Regardless of social adjustments along the railroad or on the Ozark rivers, vacationers grew in number and diversity. Sportsmen and tourists did not necessarily define themselves as belonging to one role or the other. Pattison's success with the Dixon and Gascondy Clubs and the subsequent establishment of clubs in the wake of the World's Fair excitement were followed by other new organizations on the Gasconade.[47]

Meade commented on the proliferation of recreational clubhouses on the Gasconade and elsewhere: "One of the most remarkable tendencies of the times among the sportsmen is to rush into clubs. It seems that every angler or hunter is promoting or joining the promotion of sportsmen clubs, where the object is shooting and fishing. It is becoming a fad to belong to eight or ten clubs . . . The idea is not bad, but there is such a thing as overdoing the club business."[48]

By 1908, Arlington had reached its peak as a recreational destination fed by the Frisco railroad. Only a generation earlier, the place had been an exotic locale advertised in *Forest and Stream.* It had been only fifteen years since St. Louisans had founded all-male sporting clubs geared for the Big Piney and Gasconade watershed. The 1904 St. Louis World's Fair and the generally robust national economy of the period promoted more clubs and, later, brought investors to build individual summer sanctuaries for families. Local businessmen from Rolla, Vienna, Freeburg, and Cooper Hill also built Ozark getaways. The out-of-towners, however, made Arlington and the Gascondy Club anchors in one of Missouri's earliest and most memorable "circle routes" of sporting—outdoorsmen left Union Station on the Frisco for Arlington, departed there and floated to Gascondy Station, and returned to St. Louis on the Rock Island.

Meade noticed a visible transition in the sporting business. Automobiles foreshadowed a decline of sporting tourism based solely upon rail transportation. John Brandon and the Two O'Clocks purchased an automobile for travel to and from the town of Dixon. More motorized vehicles began to cross at low-water fords throughout the Ozarks. Clusters of rentable cottages became fashionable for motorized visitors, whom Meade called the growing cult of nature worshipers. These mobile, middle-class families did not affiliate with clubs and represented the vanguard of the next great wave of tourists into the Ozarks. In September 1909, a St. Louisan drove the first automobile across the Big Piney River at Hooker Ford. During the same year, St. Louisans boarded gasoline launches on the St. Louis levee, boated up the Missouri River to Gasconade City, and then up the Gasconade River.[49] The long distance from the Gascondy Club to the Missouri River became much shorter. Automobiles and motorized boats headed for once-distant rivers, which were no longer easily hidden from the city.

Notes

1. Charles Meade, "Rod and Gun," *St. Louis Globe-Democrat,* October 20, 1907. At this time the mammoth sawmills operated by Missouri Lumber and Mining Company, Ozark Land and Lumber, Cordz-Fisher Lumber, and others were harvesting the largest marketable timber stands in Missouri and dumping loads of sawdust into the rivers.

2. Ibid., May 4, 1902. A safely anchored trotline, stretched across the river overnight, holds many baited fishing hooks dangling underwater and often yields a catch of several fish.

3. Ibid., May 17, 1903.

4. Ibid., August 3, 1902. Meade wrote this column with an Arlington dateline while sitting on Perry Andres's porch.

5. See ibid. for Meade's complete list.

6. Ibid.

7. William T. Hornaday, *Our Vanishing Wild Life: Its Extermination and Preservation* (New York: Charles Scribner's Sons, 1913), 263. The other two midwestern papers mentioned by Hornaday were in Chicago and Minneapolis.

8. Strawhun later moved to the Illinois River to manage the Prairie Slough Hunting and Fishing Club. Meade, "Rod and Gun," *St. Louis Globe-Democrat,* March 29, 1903, July 30, 1911.

9. Ibid., May 27, 1900. At this time, most guides had experience as tie-rafters on the river. It appears that Andres, a tie contractor, hired the same men for rafting crews and summer guides.

10. *Rolla Herald-Democrat,* July 30, 1903.

11. Meade, "Rod and Gun," *St. Louis Globe-Democrat,* August 23, 1903.

12. The Andres verse appeared in Meade's "Rod and Gun" column in the September 6, 1903, *Globe-Democrat.*

13. Ibid., April 7, 1901, September 7, 1902. Apparently, the investors did not commit to the preserve.

14. Ibid., August 24, 1902.

15. On the east side of the Frisco tracks, in the Meramec River basin, the development of sport fishing and family-oriented resorts on the Meramec River is discussed in Lynn Morrow, "St. Louis Tourist-Sportsmen and Meramec Valley Clubs," *Bulletin of the Illinois Geographical Society* 45 (Fall 2003): 48–64, and ibid. 45 (Spring 2004): 15–35. Regarding tie-rafts, see a definitive essay by John F. Bradbury Jr., "Tie-Hackers, Tie-Rafting, and the Railroad Crosstie Industry at Arlington and Jerome," *Old Settlers Gazette* (Waynesville: Old Stagecoach Foundation, July 30, 2005): 4–13.

16. Meade, "Rod and Gun," *St. Louis Globe-Democrat,* May 14, 1905. Rawlings managed the famous Rawlings Sporting Goods store in St. Louis; Fleming, a wealthy St. Louis businessman, was a mineral speculator in the Ozarks; and Pattison owned popular saloons in the city. Dennig, a local manager of Anheuser-Busch brewery from 1895 to 1910, later served as a director of the Conservation Federation of Missouri. In the late nineteenth-century, St. Louisans often hauled their St. Louis-made flatboats on the Frisco to use on the Gasconade. The Perry Andres outfitters provided the first commercial flatboats for tourism, known regionally as a johnboat. For an overview of the boats, see Lynn Morrow, "What's in a Name, like *Johnboat*?" *White River Valley Historical Quarterly* 37, no. 3 (Winter 1998): 9–24.

17. George W. Allen was mayor of St. Louis, January–April 1889, serving the last four months of David Francis's term, who had been elected governor. Izaak Walton, author of *The Compleat Angler,* is the patron saint of all anglers. The Izaak Walton League, a group of activist conservationists, was founded in 1922.

18. Some fifty St. Louis businessmen and a dozen Phelps County guests attended the opening of the Jerome Club designed by architect Louis E. Wessbecker. The event included the presentation of several specimens, including "eels, frogs, snakes, fishes, waterdogs, and lizards," to Julius Hurter of the St. Louis Naturalist Club. Jerome Club File, Kalen and Morrow Papers, in possession of author; Jerome Hunting and Fishing Club, Corporation Files, Missouri State Archives, Jefferson City.

19. Meade, "Rod and Gun," *St. Louis Globe-Democrat,* July 26, 1903.

20. Ibid., May 12, 1901.

21. By 1908, Charles Huber, formerly keeper of the Gilead Hunting and Fishing Club in Illinois, had assumed the management of the Jerome Club property. He sold postcards titled "Huber's on the Gasconade." Lynn Morrow, *St. Louis Globe-Democrat* index, and postcard, both in Kalen and Morrow Papers.

22. Pattison may have been influenced to look for new Missouri sporting grounds due to Illinois's enforcement of a nonresident hunting and fishing license law. After 1899 wardens began arresting noncompliant St. Louisans at rail depots, and "Rod and Gun" reported that some sportsmen had begun to patronize new club sites in Missouri. On October 21, 1901, Meade wrote that "over 800" hunters and fishermen left Union Station for Ozark destinations, most on the Frisco to the southwest.

23. Meade, "Rod and Gun," *St. Louis Globe-Democrat,* April 20, May 11, 1902. Organizers structured fees according to their vision of the openness or exclusivity of a

club. The Dixon Club was fairly exclusive, as most people would not pay $25.00 to join plus annual dues. At the same time, wealthy 8t. Louisans paid $200.00 at Cedar Crest Club on the Meramec River and $5,000.00 at the Dardenne Club in St. Charles County. Most clubs charged annual dues of $5.00 to $20.00.

24. Ibid., April 27, 1902. The Schlicht family and the Frisco began doing business together in 1902. The emergence of Forest Lodge is noted in the *Old Settlers Gazette* (Waynesville: KJPW Radio, July 20, 2002), 35.

25. William J. Hanley served as a justice of the peace for twelve years in the Eighth District Court. He held various city clerkships and ran unsuccessfully in 1908 for a local congressional nomination. *St. Louis Post-Dispatch,* August 8, 1910; *Gould's St. Louis Directory* (St. Louis: Gould Directory Co., 1904), 859.

26. Democrat James Orchard held several offices in Shannon County during the two decades prior to his election to the state senate from Howell County in 1894 and 1900. He became a frequent visitor to St. Louis and the Jefferson Club, telling stories from the backwoods. In winter 1902, he sent a deer to his pal William Hanley. The Missouri Audubon Society looked upon Orchard's political defeat in fall 1902 with great joy because he had refused to report the 1901 game bill from committee during the legislative session. Still, Hanley and Orchard socialized in St. Louis. In January 1906, they journeyed to the city's Laclede Hotel to promote a deer-hunting storytelling contest, where Hanley supported Orchard in a three-hour contest. Meade, "Rod and Gun," *St. Louis Globe-Democrat,* January 5, 1902, January 21, 1906; *Fish and Game Protector and Sportsmans Guide* (November–December 1902): 5.

27. Meade, "Rod and Gun," *St. Louis Globe-Democrat,* March 29, 1903.

28. Ibid., June 14, December 13, 1903.

29. Meade's August 16, 1903, column included a long verse by Mr. and Mrs. S. E. Barber devoted to two young children, a hero and a heroine who landed a twenty-pound catfish.

30. Meade, "Rod and Gun," *St. Louis Globe-Democrat,* December 13, 1903. By this time, St. Louis post office employees had established the Pulaski Rod and Gun Club at Mossy Spring Ford, and St. Louisan Harry Pinson had organized his clubhouse at Paydown Spring, both on the Gasconade. George Barbour of East St. Louis built the Piney Lodge near Shanghi Spring on the Big Piney.

31. Meade printed the poem in his February 7, 1904, column. Richard M. Johnson, known by friends as "Col. Dick Johnson," was a vocal and visible personality in the early game law movement. During the Civil War, he served as quartermaster's clerk at Pittsburg Landing throughout Ulysses Grant's western campaign. Grant later appointed him as post trader at Fort Dodge, Kansas, and as U.S. consul at Hankow, China. Beginning in 1876, Johnson practiced law in St. Louis and later served as assistant prosecutor and assistant circuit attorney. He spoke for the Missouri Game and Fish Protective League in fall 1902 in support of game law legislation, and in 1909 he was an unsuccessful candidate for the Missouri State Fish Commission. Johnson returned to China in 1903 for an extended fishing trip and took many hunting and fishing excursions to Minnesota, Michigan, Cape Cod, and the southern states and along the Cotton Belt railroad in Arkansas. He always voiced strong support for the sporting qualities of the Gasconade and Big Piney waters. Johnson may have named Shanghai Spring on the Big Piney. Meade, "Rod and Gun," *St. Louis Globe-Democrat,* October 26, 1902, September 20, 1903, January 24, 1909; *St. Louis Post-Dispatch,* September 10, 1922.

32. Meade, "Rod and Gun," *St. Louis Globe-Democrat,* April 24, June 5, 1904, April 2, 1905.

33. Ibid., December 11, 1904, July 23, 1905.

34. The Rock Island and Frisco Railroads sponsored common marketing promotions in tourism, real estate, and general commerce. For annual reports, see Brenda Brugger, compiler, *Guide to the Historical Records of the St. Louis-San Francisco Railway Company* (Rolla, MO: University of Missouri-Rolla, Western Historical Manuscript Collection, 1989), 79.

35. Meade, "Rod and Gun," *St. Louis Globe-Democrat,* September 27, 1903. During the 1920s, promoters used the same strategy for offering "circle drives" for automobile tourists. See Lynn Morrow and Linda Myers-Phinney, *Shepherd of the Hills Country: Tourism Transforms the Ozarks, 1880s–1930s* (Fayetteville: University of Arkansas Press, 1999), 188.

36. Meade, "Rod and Gun," *St. Louis Globe-Democrat,* August 28, 1904.

37. Ibid., May 14, 21, 1905.

38. Ibid., July 16, 1905.

39. Ibid., August 27, 1905.

40. Ibid., September 3, November 12, 19, 1905.

41. Ibid., February 25, January 7, 1906. Elite clubs had one-time membership fees of $1,000 and above. Meade identified the Dardenne, the Cuivre River, and the Maine Clubs as the most exclusive. The Dardenne and the Cuivre River were much older, two of the dozens of clubs located along the Chicago, Burlington and Quincy Railroad in St. Charles and Lincoln Counties. A selected list of well-known "Burlington clubs" included the Blue Wing, Brevator, Coleman, Dameron, Horseshoe Lake, Kampsville, King's Lake, Lemp, Prairie Slough, Richfield, Seaburger, Silver Lake, and Stringer. The main attraction was duck hunting on the Mississippi River wetlands prior to their draining and ditching. See Lynn Morrow, "St. Louis Tourist-Sportsmen: Urban Clubs in the Wetlands," *Missouri Historical Review* 97 (October 2002): 20–42.

42. Meade, "Rod and Gun," *St. Louis Globe-Democrat,* April 1, 1906.

43. Ibid., December 24, 1905. Pattison, a supporter of statewide conservation planning, maintained downtown offices at Ninth and Locust. His offices served as one of several forums for public debate for the conservation movement and the successful promotion of Governor Herbert Hadley's passage of the 1909 game law. Historically, George Rawlings had inaugurated the discussion for a statewide "protective association" and modern game law legislation in the "Rod and Gun" columns by 1900. P. H. Felker, publisher of the *St. Louis Fish and Game Protector* (c. 1899), and the Audubon Society of Missouri (founded in 1901) supported the suggestion for a statewide movement. Other advocates included the Missouri State Sportsmen's Association (founded in 1879 and known as the Missouri State Fish and Game Protective Association after 1888), which had Kansas City trapshooters at its core; the Missouri Sportsmen, Game and Fish Protective League, dominated by St. Louis businessmen and incorporated in 1902 specifically for the promotion of a modern game law; and the Missouri Fish and Game League, also dominated by St. Louisans, incorporated in 1912 to further stimulate activism for game law enforcement and the purchase of state lands for game refuges. See ibid., October 21, 1900, for credit to Rawlings.

44. Ibid., March 25, 1906.

45. Ibid., April 8. 1906. In the June 21, 1908, *Globe-Democrat,* Meade published a comprehensive fee schedule for Tilden Andres's business on the Big Piney and the lower Gasconade. Andres advertised costs from Arlington to take-out points based on distance. They ranged from $2.00 to $12.50 and included the haul by wagon, loads of supplies, and boat not to exceed 1,500 pounds; guides and cooks cost $1.50 each per day. Other daily charges included fifty cents for commissary tents and cooking outfits; twenty-five cents for living tents, fishing boats, minnow seine, and heating stove; and ten cents for cots. Examples of charges for wagon hauls were Arlington to Slabtown, $9.00; Arlington to Miller Spring, $6.00; Arlington to Thock's Rock, $3.50; and Arlington to Gasconda, $12.50. Perry Andres suffered from an extended illness, thus he took a secondary role in the guide business and worked on tie contracts and sold real estate. Local tradition holds that the two brothers may also have had personal disagreements.

46. Meade first noted "no trespassing" signs in his December 2, 1906, column.

47. For example, other Gasconade clubs formed in St. Louis included the Meramec and Gasconade Fishing and Hunting Club, the Pulaski Rod and Gun Club (at Mossy Springs), and the Globe-Democrat Fin, Fur, and Feather Club (at Kickapoo Lodge).

48. Meade, "Rod and Gun," *St. Louis Globe-Democrat,* June 3, 1906.

49. Ibid., September 26, 1909.

Whose Forest Is This?

Hill Folk, Industrialists, and Government in the Ozarks

DAVID BENAC

The timber boom of the 1890s and the first decade of the 1900s left the Missouri Ozarks with a depleted forest, a weak economy, and an uncertain future. In the face of these changes, timbermen, Ozarkers, and government officials adopted new attitudes and actions to meet the changing circumstances. The timbermen who remained in the area increasingly adopted the progressive mantle of conservation and worked to shape the forests for stable production. Local Ozarkers, rejected by the industry they had just recently embraced, sought a familiar relationship with their surroundings. The hill folk largely attempted to return to their preindustrial relationship with the woods, an economy based on woodsburning and open-range grazing, to which they now added a limited amount of local forest harvesting. Unable to summon the will or support to overcome the idealized visions of the forest offered up by these very different groups, the state and federal governments failed in their efforts to shape the forest through conservation policies. Consequently, governmental visions of forest policy remained beholden to highly motivated industrial benefactors. As Ozarkers, industrialists, and government officials all reevaluated their attitudes toward the state's resources, Missouri made the first steps toward establishing some state conservation policies during the first thirty years of the 1900s.

The impetus behind the efforts to protect forests throughout the nation emerged as early as 1868. There had been strong stirrings of conservationist thought in the preceding years, but the publication of George Marsh's *Man and Nature* crystallized many people's feelings toward forestland.

Based on his worldwide study, Marsh postulated that timber clearing led to direct and measurable increases in the severity of droughts, floods, and other catastrophic climatic conditions. Conservationists, following Marsh's work as well as that of many others, began to warn of an impending timber famine and pushed ever harder to protect valuable timber resources. Throughout the 1870s and the following three decades, several state legislatures passed measures to protect remaining timberlands. Tracing the progress of these efforts aptly illustrates the progression of the timber industry; as large-scale cutting ground to a close in each state, awareness of the exhaustion of forest resources rose.[1]

Conservation became an increasingly frequent topic of discussion shortly after the Civil War and achieved some significant victories within a couple of decades. By the late 1870s, the federal government began to consider ways to limit the rampant abuse of public domain land nationwide. In 1876, Franklin B. Hough became the first man hired by the federal government to investigate the nation's forests and determine potential courses of action. Contemporaneously with Hough, Carl Schurz, as secretary of the interior, lobbied the federal government to reserve and manage the nation's forests to avoid a future shortage of timber products. The German forester Bernard Fernow became head of the Division of Forestry in 1886 and furthered the actions of Hough by rapidly increasing the scientific underpinning of the study of the nation's forests with the goal of better management. Fernow successfully pushed to have forestry named as a division within the U.S. Department of Agriculture shortly after his appointment.[2] Forestry continued to evolve within the federal government and by the beginning of the twentieth century became a concern of widely recognized importance.

Wildlife conservation also entered the scene at the federal level during the late nineteenth century with the creation of the U.S. Biological Survey (in its earliest incarnation, the agency emerged in 1885) and the passage of the Lacey Act of 1900, which prohibited the interstate transfer of illegally taken game. By 1905 the agency had reached bureau status and was undertaking studies of fauna throughout the United States, Canada, and Mexico in an effort to better understand what confluence of factors led to the establishment of successful populations of unique species in specific locales. In the following decades, the Biological Survey followed a path similar to that of the Forest Service, the pursuance of the nation's economic well-being. The Biological Survey concentrated its efforts on regulating sport hunting and helping farmers efficiently manage the natural world.[3]

Another important factor in national conservation at the beginning of the century was the emergence of Progressivism. In the three decades before the Progressive era, some Americans began, for the first time, to

Figure 15. Lumbering was a controversial topic in the Ozarks in the late nineteenth and early twentieth centuries; view c. 1903.
STATE HISTORICAL SOCIETY OF MISSOURI-COLUMBIA

realize that the nation's forests were finite and a change in land/forest policy and use was necessary.[4] Progressives fought to bring efficiency and rational management to natural resources and social programs. Gifford Pinchot, a key Progressive leader in the field of conservation, began to serve as head of the federal Division of Forestry in 1898. The agency then became the U.S. Forest Service and gained control of the nation's forest reserves in 1905. Along with the growing influence of Pinchot, Theodore Roosevelt's rise to the presidency marked the arrival of Progressivism as the driving philosophy behind national resource policy. In the early years of the century, natural resource policy, including forestry, was directed by a desire to conserve resources through management so that present and future generations would be able to extract the greatest possible sustained yields.[5]

The timing of the development of Missouri's timber industry played a crucial role in the evolution of conservation policies in the state. By the 1820s, Missourians began operating sawmills in areas well situated along waterways to power waterwheels and to transport logs. The limitations of water power and transportation prevented these early mills from attaining large size, and they generally exhausted local timber supplies by the Civil War.[6] The situation changed dramatically during the 1880s. During that decade, the Missouri Lumber and Mining Company entered the state and began its operations at Grandin in Carter County. The combination of declining pineries in the Great Lakes and northeastern states and the entrance of railroads into the valuable, yet remote, pine forests of the Missouri Ozarks spawned a three-decade timber boom in the hills.[7] The push for forest conservation measures, as slight as it may have been, emerged in the state during the early twentieth century as Missourians began to perceive the destruction of the Ozark forests.

Missourians' acceptance of effective conservation policies generally lagged behind the creation of national policies. Because of efforts by the state's sportsmen, Missouri enacted some significant legislation to support wildlife conservation in the first decade of the twentieth century. It would be decades, however, before the state would devote significant resources to the cause. In terms of effective forest conservation, Missouri was about three decades behind the federal government and at least as laggardly in comparison to most other major timber-producing states. Missouri's slower pace resulted in part from resistance by Ozarkers to governmental involvement in the hill country and industrialists' desires to control the direction of conservation policies.

Throughout the nation, the early twentieth century was a time when the middle class increasingly began to see hunting as a sport regulated by ethical behavior and started to express outrage toward market hunters. As early as 1905, the state legislature made some headway in its efforts to gain control of Missouri's natural resources for the public good. In that year the Republican-dominated General Assembly approved a bill proposed by Representative Harry R. Walmsley, from Kansas City, and promoted with great fervor by sportsmen, to protect the state's game.[8] Because of the law's ban on the sale of game meat, businessmen involved in the transportation, storage, and sale of such meat in St. Louis, a powerful interest group, fought with great determination against the legislation. The Walmsley Law also established a system of game wardens in the state's employ, began the sale of licenses for hunting and fishing, regulated seasons for hunting, and protected nongame species. This law gave Missouri a foothold in the control of its natural resources.[9]

The issues contained within the Walmsley Law sat at the center of the state's deliberations over the nature of conservation in Missouri for decades. Close to ten years before passage of the law, Missourians, primarily from St. Louis, began lobbying the legislature for passage of a bill to protect game populations. On the other side of the issue stood a combination of rural legislators and urban merchants in the business of game meat. This antigame law faction utilized rural resentment toward urbanites to keep game laws from interfering with rural folks' liberties and urban merchants' business.[10] Businessmen and legislative representatives of rural Missourians kept up their pressure against the state's right to manage game populations through the 1940s and 1950s, introducing strong challenges in the legislative assembly at least three times.[11]

Missouri's early attempt at regulating usage of the state's game had limited success. The law gained its primary importance as a philosophical base for later efforts. In his first annual report (1905) to Governor Joseph Folk, the state's new game warden, J. H. Rodes, included a review of the evolution of Missouri's game laws by T. S. Palmer in which he expressed another key element of the Walmsley Law: "Under the new game law ownership of all birds, fish and game in Missouri is declared to be in the State and is held for the benefit of the people in common."[12] Rodes epitomized the conservationist ethic of the Progressive era. The office of the state game warden, created by the Walmsley Law, operated under the assumption that enlightened individuals could determine how to use resources to provide the greatest good for the greatest number of people. Implicit in this philosophy was the understanding that some individuals would disagree and that the state would possess the power to arrest and fine lawbreakers.

The sale of hunting licenses is one example of how the state attempted to control people's relationships with nature. In 1906, Rodes noted that Carter, Reynolds, and Shannon Counties (the counties this study addresses most directly, all of which are located in the most rugged portion of the Missouri Ozarks) accounted for fewer than twenty licenses each. The proportion of the population holding licenses in these counties was quite small. Based on the population count in the 1900 census, one in about three hundred residents of Carter County had purchased a license. The following year, 1907, the residents of the county refused to buy a single one. This was certainly tied to the legislature's decision that year to pass a new game management bill that took away almost all of the regulatory measures instituted under the Walmsley Law.[13]

Largely in response to the massive slaughter of game following the 1907 measure, the state reinstituted most of the protective measures of the Walmsley Law in new legislation in 1909. No one in Carter County got around to buying a statewide hunting permit until 1911, when one in just over six hundred residents bought one (based on the 1910 population census). In both 1910 and 1911, a significantly larger number of locals did buy county permits.[14] The annual reports of the state game and fish commissioner demonstrate that the rugged Ozark counties remained far behind the rest of the state in the purchase of fish and game licenses in the early twentieth century. The failure of hill folk to purchase permits suggests they may have recognized the system as an attempt by the government to increase its control in the region and thereby reduce locals' access to the bounty of the woods. It is also possible that Ozarkers simply refused to acknowledge state ownership of animals.

The state's efforts to gain control of its game populations and, by logical extension, to reduce Ozarkers' opportunities to hunt proved to be a major source of conflict. Hunting was a long-standing tradition that Ozarkers inherited from their Scots-Irish ancestors who had settled in the Middle Atlantic and the Upland South.[15] In *Southern Hunting in Black and White,* anthropologist Stuart A. Marks discusses the cultural importance of hunting for Scots-Irish immigrants to the Carolinas in the early and mid-eighteenth century.[16] The parents of approximately 60 percent of the heads of households in Johnson Township, Carter County (chosen here because of its importance to the timber industry), were born in Tennessee, North Carolina, or Kentucky according to the 1880 census. When Virginia and South Carolina are included in the count, the birthplaces of over 70 percent of those parents are identified.[17] Because many Ozarkers came from the same stock of people who had populated the Middle Atlantic and Upland South, it is important to recognize that state government was attempting to regulate an activity that locals and their ancestors had invested with cultural significance for close to two hundred years.

The state government was aware of the resistance it faced in the Ozarks and other rural areas of Missouri. In 1907, Rodes reported to Folk, "Unquestionably the greatest hostility to the present game law eminated [*sic*] from the south and southeastern part of the State."[18] Despite hill folks' opposition to state regulation of hunting and fishing, some of the most dramatic conflicts between hunters and the state occurred in the nearby wetlands of the Bootheel region. In this area of Missouri and the surrounding counties in Tennessee and Arkansas, market hunters, urban sportsmen, and local residents fought fiercely against governmental control over hunting.[19] Hill folk were no more accepting of private regulation of their use of the forest resources. Rangers hired by company president J. B. White to reduce timber poaching on Missouri Lumber and Mining lands expected armed resistance when meeting violators in the woods.[20]

Rodes worked against an entrenched system that favored Missouri's rural citizens and market hunters. Much of the antigame law success came about because of the way that Missouri selected its state legislators. Each of Missouri's 114 counties was guaranteed at least one representative, with the remainder of the House of Representatives' 142 members divided between the state's major metropolitan areas. This system awarded rural voters a disproportionate amount of power in comparison to voters in urban areas, a situation that continued to become more severe as Missouri's rural population declined and its urban population increased. In 1900 six representatives spoke for over 575,000 people in the city of St. Louis, which meant one representative per approximately 95,833 people. The 6,700 residents of Carter County in 1900, on the other hand, had sole claim on the attentions of their representative, George T. Lee.[21] This disparity in representation continued to widen until the voters of Missouri approved a constitutional amendment in 1966 that demanded adherence to the philosophy of "one man, one vote."

The conflict between rural and urban voters in Missouri mirrored similar nationwide conflicts over who would control resources. The Conference of Governors held in Washington, DC, in 1908 proved to be an important event for forest and waterway conservation throughout the nation. This conference was the first instance when the president assembled all of the state governors to address an issue of national concern. During the fourth session of the conference, Governor Folk addressed the assembly. In a short speech, he identified his positions on forest and waterway conservation and vowed, "As soon as I go back [to Missouri] I am going to appoint a State Forestry Commission."[22] The governor carried through with his intentions, and on December 1, 1908, he created the Missouri Forestry Commission.[23] Folk's participation in the conference was his first significant move to bring forest conservation to Missouri.

The Forestry Commission began amid an impressive state and national commitment to conservation, yet it fell short of establishing state forestry in Missouri. The original members—Dr. William H. Black, president of Missouri Valley College in Marshall, a Presbyterian minister, and a professor of psychology and ethics; Dr. Hermann von Schrenk, a forestry expert; David A. Latchaw, a Kansas City newspaper editor; and W. E. Barns, a St. Louis newspaper editor and timber industry spokesman—served pro bono.[24] Folk pushed a progressive agenda while governor, but ultimately his conservation legacy was spotty and overly responsive to the political winds that swept him up.

Deforestation, more than any other issue, prompted Folk to push for forest conservation. He discussed the consequences a sick timber industry could have on the general welfare of the state in his valedictory biennial message in 1909, stating that misuse of the state's forests would leave Mis-

Figure 16. Timber workers in camp cars being transported for July 4, 1911, celebration. KALEN AND MORROW COLLECTION

souri without "a foot of lumber left" within twenty-five years. Although he did not absolve timbermen of responsibility, he argued, "The greatest enemy of timber is not the axe, but fire."[25] It seems that Folk saw a benefit in identifying Ozarkers who burned their forests as more destructive than timber corporations that recklessly high-graded the state's woodlands.[26]

Despite growing concern over the health of the state's forests, efforts to protect Missouri's game and fish resources still dominated governmental conservation. As Missouri attempted to increase control over its resources, it had to expand its "protection" staff. In 1909 the game and fish commission employed twenty-one "regular deputy game and fish commissioners," stationed mostly in Missouri's cities, as well as fifteen "extra deputy game and fish commissioners," which it placed in the smaller Ozark communities of Poplar Bluff, Salem, Doniphan, Ellington, Van Buren, and Rolla, where help was needed. The commission also deemed it necessary to employ two individuals to detect "fish dynamiters" in Poplar Bluff and Doniphan.[27] The privilege of taking game in Missouri's forests was an early issue dividing the government and Ozarkers. Locals wanted to retain unfettered access to the resources at the heart of their subsistence strategies; the state government sought to protect natural resources for the good of the people throughout Missouri.

After spending its first year (1908–1909) studying forests throughout the state, the Missouri Forestry Commission produced a series of recommendations: (1) a permanent forestry commission, (2) a complete survey of the state for quantity and quality of timber, (3) a program of public education in support of forestry, (4) changes to current tax laws, (5) a fire-fighting and prevention program, (6) a state-sponsored nursery, (7) the ability to accept and manage lands for forestry, and (8) a substantial source of permanent funding.[28] The commission offered these recommendations to a state government headed by a strongly pro-conservation governor, Herbert Hadley. Both houses of the legislature considered conservation bills in 1909 with his full support. The Progressive ideology of conservation and rational and scientific management marked these recommendations. Dr. von Schrenk and the majority of the commission continued to argue that forests were an industrial resource and should be managed as such, not as parks for preservation.[29]

In the early years of the twentieth century, the state considered acquiring large cutover parcels of former timberland from owners who sought tax relief. In 1909, Governor Hadley appealed to the legislature to support the commission's recommendation for a bill that would authorize the state to obtain land for conservation. Hadley explained, "I am advised that the owners of large tracts of land in the southern half of this state from which the timber has been cut would be glad to deed the same to the State for such purposes [reforestation to check erosion]."[30] Although Hadley left the landowners unnamed, it is undoubtedly more than a coincidence that 1909 was the same year in which Hadley's friend and the state's most influential timber baron, J. B. White, was moving his Missouri Lumber and Mining Company out of Grandin.[31]

Despite facing resistance from powerful political figures and many rural Missourians, Hadley continued to assist Missouri's conservationists in their efforts to protect the state's forests. He took the initiative to set up a tour of the Ozarks with Gifford Pinchot and the Missouri Forestry Commission for 1910 but withdrew in the early stages of planning. This tour was intended to follow on the heels of a float trip "Hadley and a staff of land commissioners" took along the Current River in late 1909 to "ascertain the possibilities of this section of the State."[32] Pinchot was the acknowledged leader of forest conservation in the United States. In addition to serving as the first chief of the U.S. Forest Service, he had helped found the Yale School of Forestry, where he taught courses on federal forest reserves and forest policy. The school sent some of its students to Grandin to gain practical experience with the Missouri Lumber and Mining Company in 1906 and 1907.[33] After Hadley withdrew from the excursion, the governor turned responsibility for the trip over to J. B. White, who had a standing relationship with Pinchot.[34] The selection of White to head the excursion shows the increasing efforts of timbermen to play a key role in dictating the direction of conservation in Missouri.

The proposed Ozark tour apparently never happened. Many possible explanations exist, but the emergence of the Ballinger-Pinchot controversy is one of the most intriguing.[35] The controversy first emerged when newly appointed secretary of the interior Richard A. Ballinger refused to allow Pinchot to continue his customary bypassing of bureaucratic channels. After a series of minor skirmishes between the two men, full-fledged conflict occurred over the development of coal-rich lands in Alaska, with Pinchot trying to ensure that the resources remained earmarked for the public good. After Pinchot publicly attacked Ballinger's policies, President William Howard Taft dismissed Pinchot in January 1910. Pinchot's loss of political position during the planning stages for the Ozark tour posed a potential problem.[36] The former chief forester suddenly found himself thrust into a nationwide debate and increasingly at the center of a political maelstrom. Pinchot's political volatility may explain Hadley's decision to withdraw from the excursion and place responsibility in White's hands. The new challenges and demands may also have left Pinchot unable to meet his commitment in Missouri.

The planned tour of 1910 is one of many occasions when White's name appears in connection with Hadley's and with conservation. White and Hadley were two of Kansas City's most prominent citizens, and each voted the Republican ticket. This may have been enough to place the men in the same social circles, but their commitment to conservation certainly brought them together.

Although he continued to exploit the forests of the Missouri Ozarks with wanton disregard (reputedly operating the largest sawmill in the nation in 1899–1900), White had established a notable record as an advocate of conservation by 1910. He frequently called for reduced production in the industry, both to conserve timber for the future and to increase prices, but he did not cut his own production to extend the lives of Missouri's forests. Between 1905 and 1910, White directly advised President Roosevelt regarding the use of timber on an Indian reservation in Minnesota, accepted a presidential nomination to the National Conservation Commission, and served as chairman of the executive committee of the National Conservation Congress. White's involvement in conservation remained mainly advisory because he deemed it primarily the responsibility of the government, though he considered the manufacturers and consumers of timber products to hold some liability as well.[37]

Hadley attempted to advance conservation in Missouri, but he was unable to make significant progress. Several factors contributed to the governor's inability to achieve his conservation goals. One possibility is suggested by the important role played by White and other industrialists in activities such as the forestry commission and the proposed tour. Hadley may have relied on industrialists for support and been unable to establish policies counter to their needs. One result of this industrial leadership was the disinclination of Hadley and other conservationists in the first two decades of the twentieth century to consider the needs and desires of Ozarkers. This is a second likely reason Hadley failed in his efforts to promote conservation. Because Ozarkers only entered early conservation discussions in the context of woodsburning and poaching, they had little reason to support the efforts of a government that did not seem to have their interests at heart. A third, more concrete, explanation lies in party politics. Hadley, the first Republican governor in Missouri in approximately three decades, faced a penurious Democratic majority in both houses of the legislature.

A small group of influential individuals sought policies for conservation of Missouri's forests in the first three decades of the twentieth century, but the majority of Ozarkers refused to support the creation of a governmental presence in the region's woods. Even optimistic boosters of state forestry such as Samuel J. Record, who became forest supervisor for the Ozark National Forest in Arkansas when it was established on March 6, 1908, recognized the cultural inertia forest managers had to contend with in the Ozarks. In a 1908 report, Record acknowledged the damage the timber industry had wrought on the Ozark forests, but farmers who regularly burned the woods bore the brunt of the blame in his assessment.[38] Despite the reform efforts of several individuals (such as sportsmen, forestry professionals, and reform-minded legislators), Ozarkers refused to give up their generations-old dependence on the woods. A cadre of influential politicians, including Democrats Frank H. Farris (elected state senator for the Twenty-fourth District in 1898, 1902, and 1922 and state representative for Crawford County, 1906 and 1910, and Phelps County, 1914 to 1918), James Orchard (elected state senator for the Twenty-second District in 1894 and 1898), and George T. Lee (elected state representative for Wayne County in 1882 and 1886 and for Carter County in 1890, 1896, and 1898, and as state senator for the Twenty-first District in 1900), spoke on behalf of hill folk who may have feared that forestry legislation would lead to further interference with their traditions of woodsburning and open range by an outside source of authority that allowed them no voice in management strategies.

Woodsburning was a key element in Ozarkers' relationships with the hill country, and they refused to abandon it regardless of the state's wishes. Ozarkers relied on fire as a basic tool in their struggle to survive as independent farmers. Tom Martin, an Ozarker since he was born in Dent County in 1910, considered how his neighbors used fire, "They always burned out every spring. It didn't kill the timber then because there wasn't that many leaves. You let them leaves get knee deep and, lord it'll kill everything burned."[39] By annually employing fire, Ozarkers believed they could promote the growth of nutritive grass for their free-ranging livestock as well as create and maintain an ideal place for harvesting game, wild plants, and wood for building and heating their homes. Jack Toll, a resident of the Ozarks since the 1930s and a participant in the timber industry, considered why people burned the woods, "They burned it because it took the litter off, stimulated grass to grow, and a lot of the old timers said it killed all of the ticks."[40] Ozarkers burned out of a desire to shape the woods into a useful resource rather than to destroy a prominent element of their lives. Woodsburning and the open range were closely intertwined in Ozarkers' economic strategies and cultural attitudes toward the woods.

As subsistence farmers with small landholdings, Ozarkers included the commons of the free range in their economic strategies. Ab Dettwiler, born in Shannon County in 1903, recalled, "We used to always burn every spring. You had to burn every spring, 'cause you see there wasn't no stock laws. People just turned their stock out, it was free range."[41] Roy Baugh, born along the Jacks Fork River in 1907, shared Dettwiler's assessment of fire and the open range: "We had to [burn], because it was open range and stuff. We didn't have no pastures built up, we had that open range, we couldn't afford it [pasture land]."[42] From the earliest European settlement in Missouri until the 1940s and often later, woodsburning and the open range remained important in Ozarkers' culture, their patterns of subsistence, and their relationships with the woods.

The issue of the open range engaged many people in debate, most prominently in discussions of the South. The economist Shawn Everett Kantor provided an excellent analysis of the costs and benefits of enclosure throughout the South. As he considered the history of conflicts over open range, however, his logic fell short when he contended: "The debate [over closing the range] was not a class or cultural conflict, as some historians claim, but a battle between those who anticipated benefits from livestock enclosure and those who did not."[43] In the rugged Missouri Ozarks, those who perceived the closing of the range as beneficial were of a decidedly different class and culture than the proponents of open range. To benefit from enclosure, an individual had to possess the means and desire to acquire and improve land for pasture, cultivation, and participation in market agriculture. These were not the traits of Ozarkers in the most rugged portions of the hill country. Hill folks did not turn to agriculture or livestock raising to participate in the market economy. Before, during, and after the period in which Ozarkers participated in the cash economy driven by the timber industry, they viewed agriculture as a subsistence activity.

Americans frequently debated fence laws in the rural United States as farming shifted to market production. The historian Steven Hahn argues that the campaign to close the range in the upcountry of Georgia was in part motivated by race, but also by a clash of cultural attitudes. The region's elite sought to abolish common grazing and hunting rights in favor of more manageable and profitable enclosures during the 1880s. Robert C. McMath Jr., a noted historian, states that farmers on the Texas frontier, with a conscious reflection on the social and economic implications of enclosure on the lower classes in England, revolted violently against fence law advocates at the same time that the issue was under debate in Georgia.[44] Despite differing levels of philosophical objection to the idea of a closed range, preindustrial rural people across the United States refused to abandon common grazing rights.

Missourians who called for closure of the range demonstrated a difference in cultural attitudes from most residents of the rugged Ozarks. Counties throughout the state passed their first stock laws contemporaneously with similar nationwide movements in the 1870s, but these laws only closed the range in some areas and only on the basis of local option votes. Thomas T. Hathaway of St. Louis spoke for proponents of a closed range when he addressed his colleagues in the General Assembly regarding the option law, "It is a law acting by counties only, whereas I would have it a general law, compulsory in its character, embracing every foot of domain within the borders of our State." Hathaway's statements reveal that he felt he could dictate what was best for everyone in the state. This reformist attitude was at the center of many of the conflicts between Ozarkers and the government. Many Ozarkers resisted the efforts of proponents of the market economy like Hathaway, who claimed, "Speaking for the State of Missouri, nothing can be done to benefit the State so universally and to such an extent as the passage of a law which will compel owners of stock to herd or confine their stock within secure limits." Hathaway assessed the costs and benefits of fence laws based on a comparison of investments versus profits in field crops and free-ranged livestock.[45] This effort to turn rural Missouri into a more profitable resource for farmers demonstrates the cultural differences in outlook toward profit and resources that Kantor discounts.

Attitudes toward fire marked the most dramatic contrast between the beliefs of Ozarkers and governmental agents. Forest supervisor Samuel J. Record's assessment in 1908 demonstrated the beginning of the government's approach to fire in the Ozarks. He argued that the state must create programs to educate the public against woodsburning because laws alone would not convince locals to discontinue the annual setting of fires.[46] The issue remained a top priority for governmental agents attempting to manage Ozark forests. L. W. Pickens, a resident of Camden County, reported to the Forest Service in 1920 regarding his displeasure with locals who burned the woods: "The woods is kept burning at all times except when it is too wet or until the whole country is burned over. At any time during the winter or early spring months when the leaves is dry the light from the forest fires can be seen at night in every direction." He added: "The result is we now have neither grass or timber."[47] Woodsburning is a particularly instructive issue as the positions of government and Ozarkers remained static through the first third of the twentieth century.

Missouri's timbermen responded to the environmental and economic challenges they faced by organizing the Missouri Forestry Association in 1921 to seek a rational forest policy and thereby maintain the viability of the industry. The organization, membership, funding, and goals of the association revealed its basis as an industrialists' association. The timbermen came together at a dinner sponsored by the Lumbermen's Exchange of St. Louis and the Tie and Timber Division of the St. Louis Chamber of Commerce. Six of the association's founding officers (John H. Himmelberger, Himmelberger-Harrison Lumber Company; R. E. Lee, H. L. Tie Company; E. A. Nixon, Western Tie and Timber Company; Julius Seidel, Seidel Lumber Company; R. B. White, Exchange Sawmills Sales Company; and T. L. White, T. L. White Lumber Company) either owned or were employed by companies that manufactured or sold forest products.[48] Another member, Frederick Dunlap, had established a solid reputation while teaching forestry courses at the University of Missouri for most of the previous decade. Dunlap, a founding member and secretary of the association, admitted that the association owed a debt to the state's lumber dealers and producers as well as bankers and wholesalers.[49] The association's connection to the timber industry is unquestionable.

The association cast its net broadly in its initial search for capital. Individuals provided the bulk of the start-up money at a cost of two dollars per member. Approximately three hundred dollars of the association's initial capitalization, however, was loaned by timber companies. The association also obtained free office space and clerical assistance in St. Louis from the National Association of Railway Tie Producers.[50] The formation and activism of the Missouri Forestry Association marked yet another stage in the evolving concern of timbermen in Missouri for the state of the resource. As had J. B. White, the timbermen of the new association worked to gain and maintain control of conservation in the state. Timbermen did not want to restrict their profits through conservation; they wanted to increase efficiency, reduce taxation, and ensure a future timber resource.[51]

The Missouri Forestry Association's objectives led to the potential for conflicts with Ozarkers who wanted to return to their preindustrial lifeways and harbored a deep distrust of the industry that had abandoned the region, withdrawing the only significant employers. In the roughly three decades between the 1880s and 1910s while large-scale timber mills operated in the Courtois Hills of Missouri, Ozarkers grew accustomed to and partially dependent on the wage-labor system, only to have it yanked away, leaving no opportunities to work in the cash economy. The association recognized and was troubled by the general unwillingness of Ozarkers to cooperate with forestry measures. Although some promoters of forest policy believed the rapid deforestation of Missouri since 1880 prepared people to accept forest management, many forestry professionals remained pessimistic. Hermann von Schrenk, president of the Missouri Forestry Association, attributed Missouri's forestry problems to "a large back-wood farmer element in this State, with a more or less active politician leading them who is against everything."[52] Foresters and Ozarkers continued to struggle for control of the woods throughout the 1920s, without a resolution. The interactions between industrialists, Ozarkers, and the state's few citizens concerned with conservation left no group able to dominate the forests.

Industrial leaders and professional foresters opposed the establishment of national forests in Missouri, preferring instead to consolidate what support existed for forestry in the hands of a single state agency headed by educated forestry professionals. It is likely that industrialists within Missouri preferred a state rather than a federal agency because it would be more susceptible to their influence. Dunlap wrote to C. R. Tillotson of the U.S. Forest Service in 1922, "My own opinion is that we should first make an attempt to solve our forest problem through the agency of a state department rather than at this time to call in the Federal Forest Service."[53] William B. Greeley, chief of the Forest Service from 1920 to 1928, agreed, "It would be distinctly preferable not to press the idea of establishing a National Forest in the state." He explained, "To do so would confuse the issue and quite possibly injure the chances of securing legislation for the establishment of a State Forestry Board, which is now before the legislature . . . The first thing you need in Missouri is a State agency of your own which can study all of these questions and formulate a program for the best solution."[54] The leaders of both the state and the national forestry movements agreed that trained individuals with a stake in the future of the forests needed to author policy regarding Missouri's natural resources.[55]

To enlarge its opportunities for success, the forestry association undertook vigorous efforts to broaden its membership beyond its original foundation-industrialists. Dunlap and von Schrenk sought to gain support from the Missouri Horticultural Society, the Missouri Federation of Women's Clubs, and sportsmen's organizations.[56] The association also sent direct mailings, authored newspaper releases, and published at least a few issues of a magazine, the *Conservation Advocate*.[57] But the association never extended this membership drive to include Ozarkers living on small farms or operating small, portable sawmills among the forests in question—a crucial oversight common to early conservationists.

In 1925 the General Assembly finally agreed to provide for a state forester within the Board of Agriculture. But in late April, Dunlap had the duty of passing along bad news to a conservation-minded colleague: "Governor Baker indicates that he will veto the forestry bill enacted by the General Assembly this winter due to lack of funds to make it effective." Approximately two weeks later, Dunlap noted that "Governor Baker has signed our forestry bill and it now becomes law at midnight July 9, next."[58] It is unclear what caused the governor to change his mind. The most logical explanation, however, lies in funding.

Developments at the federal level may have influenced the state to finally allocate funds to forestry. In 1924 the federal government passed the Clarke-McNary Act to create a means of cooperating with states in fire prevention. The Clarke-McNary Act proved to be one of the most important pieces of legislation in the history of U.S. forest conservation. Under the act, the federal government had the authority to provide matching funds to states for fire protection and reforestation, to assist landowners who needed the advice of professional foresters, and to purchase land for the use and protection of timber. This was a dramatic departure from the Weeks Act of 1911, which only authorized the purchase of forest land to protect navigable streams.[59] By setting aside money for forestry in 1925 and instituting a fire protection program, however rudimentary, Missouri became eligible for funds from the federal government under the auspices of the Clarke-McNary Act. The availability of federal funds coincided directly with the efforts of Missouri's government to protect its natural resources. The state's political leaders were seemingly only willing to push for conservation when the state would bear a disproportionately small share of the cost.[60]

In August 1925 the Missouri State Board of Agriculture elected Frederick Dunlap as the first state forester at a salary of $3,000. The bill that created the new forestry division within the Board of Agriculture stated that the Missouri Forestry Association would pay Dunlap's salary. Furthermore, the University of Missouri Agricultural Extension Service and the U.S. Department of Agriculture would cooperate to contribute the money to cover Dunlap's expenses while he conducted fieldwork and promoted the planting of "farm timber patches." The State of Missouri created a state office for forestry without appropriating a dime.[61] The result was a state forester who was influenced by the needs of the industrialists who held the purse strings. Without the association's stipend, Missouri would not have been eligible for federal money, and the state was unwilling to establish a forestry program without significant federal support.

The duties of the state forester proved too numerous for a single individual, which led to the employment of Paul Dunn as the state's only district forester. He worked out of an office in Ellington in Reynolds County. Dunn described his role, "My assignment was to carry out a program with the school systems and timber companies in what we called fire protection education, introducing into the school system the need for prevention and control of fire." Persuading Ozarkers to abandon woodsburning dominated Dunn's efforts. He later assessed the program, "It was reasonably successful. However, most of the people in the area didn't consider the woods burning harmful."[62] This first incarnation of forest conservation in Missouri was designed to target the minds of Ozarkers as the key to ensuring the forest's future. Dunlap and Dunn believed they could end woodsburning by educating the next generation to discontinue the practice, but despite their efforts, the behavior remained culturally important to hill folk.

During the same years that the Missouri Forestry Association was seeking to establish a state forestry office, the state finally began to acquire some parks. The movement to create parks differed from calls for forest conservation primarily through their proposed use. According to Tim Birmingham, state game and fish commissioner: "The purpose of this act is to create a fund [by setting aside 5 percent of all funds from the purchase of hunting licenses] to acquire a large, well-watered tract of land somewhere in the state particularly adapted to game and fish where the work of propagation and protection can be carried on under the most favorable conditions."[63] As Birmingham pointed out, parks were not intended for trees; they were for game, especially game that could be caught or hunted. This 1917 measure created the legislative precedent for the later successful purchase of state parks.

The 5 percent diversion from hunting and fishing licenses established in 1917 proved insufficient, so in 1923 the legislature increased the amount of money set aside from license sales to 25 percent. This source of funds earmarked for parks enabled the state to begin purchasing land for public recreation. By 1925, Keith McCanse, the game and fish commissioner, was able to report to Governor Sam Baker, "Our system now comprises eight state parks with a total area of 23,224 acres." He identified the largest parks as Salem State Park in Dent County (12,868 acres), Ellington State Park in Reynolds County (4,920 acres), and Big Spring State Park in Carter County (4,258 acres), which combined to account for the majority of the system. The next largest park was Bennett Spring in Laclede County, also in the Ozarks, with a mere 574 acres. McCanse also noted that Alley Spring State Park with 427 acres and Round Spring with another 75 acres were both in Shannon County.[64] Missouri chose to locate the beginning of its state park system among the dramatic hills, bluffs, and rivers of the Ozarks. This region of natural splendor was central to some of the most intense opinions regarding governmental control of resources.[65]

Throughout the 1920s, forest policy remained under the influence of timbermen. The Missouri Forestry Association interpreted "farm timber" as woodlots that would ensure a source of timber well into the future. As the primary source of funding for state forestry through 1928, the association had at least some opportunity to influence the direction of state policy. Dunlap, accordingly, encouraged farmers to devote a greater percentage of their land to woodlots (a policy mostly directed toward northern Missouri) even though he was consistently unable to secure the support of the Missouri Farm Bureau. The elimination of woodland grazing and the annual burning of forests were such key issues for forest policy that Dunlap was willing to pursue them even without the support of the organization with the most influence over agricultural issues, the farm bureau.[66] The state forester's goals of "PREVENTION OF WILDFIRE and PLANTING FARM TIMBER" [emphasis in original] reflected the desires of industrialists.[67] Because Dunlap performed much of his work in northern Missouri, he valued woodlots for their dual purposes of timber production and protection from erosion in that part of the state.

The Missouri Forestry Association retreated from the public arena after 1928, though there are indications that the association may have survived in some form until 1937. Coincidently with the apparent collapse of the association, the General Assembly appropriated funds to support Frederick Dunlap's work as state forester in 1929.[68] It is unclear whether the disappearance of the timbermen's funds led to the state picking up the costs of the office or if the association melted away because it lost its defining rationale for existence once the state was willing to accept the costs of conservation. This appropriation was small and proved short lived, just a single biennium, but it was a key event, as the state finally agreed to fund a program of forest conservation. Even if the appropriation was temporary, the state moved its commitment to conservation forward by putting forth the necessary funds to encourage the movement.

Missouri's foresters still emphasized the prevention and fighting of fires in their interactions with the public. Dunlap theorized that fire was the most significant problem faced by Missouri's forests, partly because the public did not realize the damage such conflagrations caused.[69] The forester stated, "Our fires will be brought under control when these people [rural Missourians] know how to control them and in its work for the control of wildfire this Department is exercising no police power—it has none—but it is organizing local communities for the control of their own fire."[70] Once again, outsiders with the authority to call for changes in the Ozarks held a set of values concerning woodlands that was different from those of most residents of the hill country. Without proper protection from fire, Dunlap feared, Missouri's trees would lose their resistance to the growth of fungus, which led to rotten centers in timber.[71]

Efforts to prevent forest fires in the Missouri Ozarks went beyond the creation of fire lines and the construction of fire towers. Because of the agency's limited manpower, foresters ultimately relied on gaining the support of locals. By demonstrating "proper" forestry throughout rural Missouri and encouraging farmers to plant trees, Dunlap hoped to convince the public that fires destroyed the very forests they painstakingly planted and maintained.[72]

On June 1, 1931, Missouri reconsidered its funding for state-sponsored forest conservation and determined that the results did not warrant continued appropriations. The General Assembly concluded that it could no longer pay the salary of the state and district foresters. This decision undoubtedly bore some relation to the onset of the Great Depression. The state and district foresters each responded to Missouri's penuriousness by resigning in 1931. Historian Charles Callison suggested that Dunlap resigned in part because he felt it was impossible to get Ozarkers to abandon woodsburning.[73]

The Missouri Forestry Association, Dunlap, Dunn, and the state all worked to solidify state-sponsored forest conservation in Missouri, but they could not gather the necessary public support. The combination of a timber industry unwilling to allow the advancement of conservation it could not control and Ozarkers who sought to retain their independence to hunt, burn, and pasture the woods rendered conservation efforts in the Missouri Ozarks ineffective. For several years after the state and district foresters resigned, Missouri made no significant progress in gaining control of the Ozark forests. During the Great Depression and the New Deal of the 1930s, however, Missouri would witness a series of social and economic changes that would allow for a new beginning in conservation.[74]

Notes

1. George Marsh, *Man and Nature* (London: S. Low, Son and Marston, 1864); John Ise, *Use and Abuse of America's Natural Resources* (1920; reprint, New York: Arno Press, 1972), 28–29, 33–35, 96–97, 144–145.

2. Michael Williams, *Americans and Their Forests: A Historical Geography* (New York: Cambridge University Press, 1989), 394–401.

3. Kier B. Sterling, "Builders of the U.S. Biological Survey, 1885–1930," *Journal of Forest History* 33 (October 1989): 180–181.

4. Williams, *Americans and Their Forests*, 393–394.

5. Samuel P. Hays, *Conservation and the Gospel of Efficiency: The Progressive Conservation Movement, 1890–1920* (Cambridge: Harvard University Press, 1959), 121–125.

6. Milton D. Rafferty, *The Ozarks: Land and Life* (Norman: University of Oklahoma Press, 1980), 172–173. For the first Ozarks commercial timber boom, see Lynn Morrow, "Gasconade Mills: Daniel Morgan Boone's Piney Woods," *Newsletter of the Phelps County Historical Society* n.s. (October 2009): 5–26, and "Piney Sawmillers at Gasconade Mills," *Old Settlers Gazette* (Waynesville: Old Stagecoach Foundation), Issue 26 (July 26, 2008): 30–42.

7. David Benac, "This Land is all Terrible Rough: A History of Access to Forest Resources in Carter County, Missouri" (Ph.D. diss., University of Missouri, Columbia, 2003), 33–71.

8. John Bradbury and Lynn Morrow, "Honorable Frank Farris: Making a Bad Idea Look Good and a Good One Better," *Newsletter of the Phelps County Historical Society*, n.s., 30 (October 2004): 11–13, 22–23.

9. Charles H. Callison, *Man and Wildlife in Missouri: The History of One State's Treatment of Its Natural Resources* (Harrisburg, PA: Stackpole Company, 1953), 7–9.

10. Bradbury and Morrow, "Honorable Frank Farris," 11–13, 21–25.

11. "A New Attack on Conservation," *St. Louis Post-Dispatch*, March 29, 1945; "Committee Okays Measure to Curb Wildlife Agency," ibid., March 6, 1949; "New Grab at Conservation Agency Gets Started in Missouri House," ibid., March 6, 1953.

12. *Annual Report of the State Game and Fish Warden of the State of Missouri for the Year Ending December 31, 1905* (Jefferson City, 1906), 30.

13. *Annual Report of the State Game and Fish Warden of the State of Missouri for the Year Ending December 31, 1907* (Jefferson City, 1908), 6–8; U.S. Bureau of the Census,

Twelfth Census of the United States, Taken in the Year 1900, "Carter County" and "Shannon County" (National Archives Microfilm Publication T623, rolls 845 and 903).

14. *First Annual Report of the State Game and Fish Commissioner of the State of Missouri* (Jefferson City, 1910), 8–9; U.S. Bureau of the Census, *Thirteenth Census of the United States, Taken in the Year 1910,* "Carter County" and "Shannon County" (National Archives Microfilm Publication T624, rolls 775 and 824); *Second Annual Report of the State Game and Fish Commissioner of the State of Missouri* (Jefferson City, 1911), 15.

15. An effective discussion of the ethnic makeup of Ozarks settlers is available in Rafferty, *Ozarks,* 57–60.

16. Stuart A. Marks, *Southern Hunting in Black and White: Nature, History, and Ritual in a Carolina Community* (Princeton, NJ: Princeton University Press, 1991), 34–35.

17. U.S. Bureau of the Census, *Tenth Census of the United States, Taken in the Year 1880,* "Carter County" and "Shannon County" (National Archives Microfilm Publication T9, rolls 679 and 737).

18. *Annual Report of the State Game and Fish Warden . . . 1907,* 45.

19. Lynn Morrow, "A 'Duck and Goose Shambles': Sportsmen and Market Hunters at Big Lake, Arkansas," *Big Muddy: A Journal of the Mississippi River Valley* 4, no. 1 (2004): 77–79.

20. John A. Galloway, "John Barber White: Lumberman" (Ph.D. diss., University of Missouri, 1961), 184.

21. *Official Manual of the State of Missouri For the Years 1899–1900* (Jefferson City, 1899), 170–171.

22. Joseph W. Folk, "Address by Joseph W. Folk Governor of Missouri," in *Proceeding of a Conference of Governors in the White House, Washington, D.C., May 13–15, 1908,* ed. W. J. McGee and Newton C. Blanchard (Washington, DC: Government Printing Office, 1909), 159.

23. Hermann von Schrenk, "Report of the Missouri Forestry Commission," in *Appendix to the House and Senate Journals of the 45th General Assembly of the State of Missouri, 1909* (Jefferson City, [1909]), serial 48: 3.

24. For more extensive biographical information on Black, see *Missouri Historical Review* 25 (October 1930): 173; for Barns, see *The Book of St. Louisans: A Biographical Dictionary of the Leading Living Men of the City of St. Louis and Vicinity* (St. Louis: St. Louis Republic, 1912), 39; for Latchaw, see *Missouri Historical Review* 42 (April 1948): 289.

25. Folk, "Message: Waterways and Forestry," in *Appendix to the House and Senate Journals of the 45th General Assembly of the State of Missouri, 1909,* serial 1: 16–17.

26. High-grading is a process of removing trees of higher quality, leaving genetically inferior individuals and species. Future generations find a forest of smaller and less disease-resistant trees.

27. *First Annual Report of the State Game and Fish Commissioner,* 3–4.

28. Von Schrenk, "Report of the Missouri Forestry Commission," serial 48: 12.

29. Herbert S. Hadley, "Waterways and Forestry Commission, April 19, 1909," in *Appendix to the House and Senate Journals of the 45th General Assembly of the State of Missouri, 1909,* serial 6x: 3; Von Schrenk, "Report of the Missouri Forestry Commission," serial 48: 3–4.

30. Hadley, "Waterways and Forestry Commission, April 19, 1909," serial 6x: 7.

31. C. C. Sheppard to J. B. White, September 22, 1909, folder 737, Missouri Lumber

and Mining Co. Papers, Western Historical Manuscript Collection, University of Missouri-Columbia (hereinafter cited as WHMC-Columbia).

32. Munger Securities Company, advertising pamphlet (1916), 4, Western Historical Manuscript Collection, University of Missouri-Rolla (hereinafter cited as WHMC-Rolla).

33. Yale University, *Catalogue. 1906–1907* (New Haven, CT, 1906), 22, 26–27.

34. Hadley to Capt. James B. White, February 2, 1910, vol. 13; Hadley to Gifford Pinchot, March 12, 1910, vol. 13; Hadley to James B. White, February 14, 1910; all letters in Herbert S. Hadley Papers, WHMC-Columbia.

35. Hays, *Conservation and the Gospel of Efficiency*, 166–170.

36. The accounts of the Ballinger-Pinchot controversy are legion. For two concise discussions, see John Ise, *The United States Forest Policy* (New York: Arno Press, 1972), 201–205, and Harold K. Steen, *The US Forest Service: A History* (Seattle: University of Washington Press, 1976), 100–102.

37. Galloway, "John Barber White," 164–166, 168–169, 174–178.

38. Samuel J. Record, "Missouri's Opportunities In Forestry," in *Missouri State Board of Agriculture Annual Report, 1908* (Jefferson City, 1909), 4–6.

39. Tom Martin, interview by Alexander Primm, May 19–20, 1992, transcribed by author, transcript in author's possession, 13.

40. Jack Toll, interview by Alexander Primm, May 27, 1992, transcribed by author, transcript in author's possession, 14.

41. Ab Dettwiler, interview by Alexander Primm, April 23, 1992, transcribed by author, transcript in author's possession, 6.

42. Roy Baugh, interview by Alexander Primm, April 23, 1992, transcribed by author, transcript in author's possession, 28.

43. Shawn Everett Kantor, *Politics and Property Rights: The Closing of the Open Range in the Postbellum South* (Chicago: University of Chicago Press, 1998), 14.

44. Steven Hahn, "The Roots of Southern Populism: Yeoman Farmers and the Transformation of Georgia's Upper Piedmont, 1850–1890" (Ph.D. diss., Yale University, 1979), 331–376; Robert C. McMath Jr., "Sandy Land and Hogs in the Timber: (Agri)cultural Origins of the Farmers' Alliance in Texas," in *The Countryside in the Age of Capitalist Transformation: Essays in the Social History of Rural America*, eds. Steven Hahn and Jonathan Prude (Chapel Hill: University of North Carolina Press, 1985), 216–222 I.

45. Thomas T. Hathaway, "Speech in favor of a stock law in Missouri delivered by the Hon. Thomas T. Hathaway, of St. Louis, March 1873, Twenty-seventh General Assembly-Regular Session" (Jefferson City, 1873), 5–6.

46. Record, "Missouri's Opportunities in Forestry," 4–5.

47. L. W. Pickens to U.S. Forest Service, January 22, 1920, folder 66, Frederick Dunlap Papers, WHMC-Columbia; von Schrenk, "Report of the Missouri Forestry Commission," serial 48: 6. For more information on foresters' evolving attitudes toward fire, see Ashley Schiff, *Fire and Water: Scientific Heresy in the Forest Service* (Cambridge, MA: Harvard University Press, 1962).

48. "The organization meeting of the Missouri Forestry Association . . . ," December 1921; Missouri Forestry Association, articles of incorporation, December 7, 1921, both in folder 275, Dunlap Papers.

49. Dunlap to Clinton G. Smith, July 17, 1922, folder 160, ibid.

50. Report of the second annual meeting, February 3, 1922, folder 276, ibid.

51. A good statement on J. B. White's conservation philosophy is contained in Galloway, "John Barber White," 173–176.

52. Dunlap to von Schrenk, January 16, 1922, folder 166, Dunlap Papers; *State of Missouri Official Manual for the Years Nineteen Twenty-Seven and Nineteen Twenty-Eight* (Jefferson City, 1927), 663; von Schrenk to W. B. Greeley, September 25, 1922, folder 168, Dunlap Papers.

53. Dunlap to Tillotson, January 20, 1922, folder 159, Dunlap Papers.

54. Greeley to Charles F. Hatfield, February 10, 1923, folder 160, ibid.

55. The presence of public domain land in Arkansas, the other state comprising the bulk of the Ozark region, provides a prominent reason that the "Natural State" succeeded in obtaining a national forest decades earlier than Missouri, which disbursed its public domain land relatively early. Missouri's refusal to take part in the bill sponsored by the Committee of Public Lands to discontinue the private sale of public domain lands helped ensure that the state would dispose of those remaining lands. See Ise, *Use and Abuse*, 101.

56. Von Schrenk to Dunlap, February 2, 1923, folder 169; Dunlap to "The sportsmen of Missouri," November 13, 1924, folder 275, both letters in Dunlap Papers. The author has been unable to determine the effectiveness of these efforts to broaden the association's support base.

57. Dunlap to von Schrenk, November 19, 1921, folder 164; ibid., December 22, 1921, folder 165; ibid., October 17, 1921, folder 164; *Conservation Advocate* (September 1925), folder 1, all items in Dunlap Papers. There is no indication of the success or number of issues printed of the *Conservation Advocate.*

58. Dunlap to Foster Schreeder, April 22, 1925, folder 148; Dunlap to J. G. Peters, May 5, 1925, folder 163, both in ibid.

59. Steen, *U.S. Forest Service*, 188–189.

60. Mark J. Boesch, *The Role of the National Forests in Missouri*, pamphlet, August 1968; "Minutes of council meeting," November 13, 1924, folder 276, Dunlap Papers; *State of Missouri Official Manual for Years Nineteen Twenty-Five and Nineteen Twenty-Six* (Jefferson City, 1925), 823; *Official Manual . . . Nineteen Twenty-Seven and Nineteen Twenty-Eight*, 664.

61. *Official Manual . . . Nineteen Twenty-Five and Nineteen Twenty-Six*, 823.

62. Paul M. Dunn, "St. Regis Paper Company: An Oral History Interview," interview by Elwood R. Maunder (Santa Cruz, CA: Forest History Society, 1977), 4–5.

63. *Annual Report of the State Game and Fish Commissioner of the State of Missouri for the Year Ending December 31, 1917* (Jefferson City, 1917), 8.

64. *Annual Report of the State Game and Fish Commissioner of the State of Missouri for the Year Ending December 31, 1925* (Jefferson City, 1925), 47, 53–55. For more on the influence of McCanse, see Lynn Morrow, "Keith McCanse: Missouri's First Professional Conservationist," *White River Valley Historical Quarterly* 31, no. 2 (Winter 1992): 3–12.

65. There was strong support among some Ozarkers for conservation. Ellington, the location of Paul Dunn's office, was also home to Carter Buford and his brother, Wilbur. Carter, a strong advocate of state-sponsored conservation, served in the state senate from 1907 to 1918 and 1927 to 1930, and Wilbur served as state game and fish commissioner in the 1930s.

66. Dunlap to J. G. Peters, February 21, 1925, folder 163, Dunlap Papers; *Official Manual . . . Nineteen Twenty-Five and Nineteen Twenty-Six*, 959.

67. Dunlap, "What the Forestry Department is Doing," 1930, folder 274, Dunlap Papers.

68. *State of Missouri Official Manual for the Years Nineteen Twenty-Nine and Nineteen Thirty* (Jefferson City, 1929), 818.

69. Ibid.

70. Dunlap, "What the Forestry Department is Doing."

71. *State of Missouri Official Manual . . . Nineteen Twenty-Five and Nineteen Twenty-Six*, 959.

72. *State of Missouri Official Manual . . . Nineteen Twenty-Nine and Nineteen Thirty*, 818; Dunlap, "What the Forestry Department is Doing."

73. Callison, *Man and Wildlife*, 96; *State of Missouri Official Manual for the Years Nineteen Thirty-One and Nineteen Thirty-Two* (Jefferson City, 1931), 626.

74. See David Benac's book-length discussion, *Conflict in the Ozarks: Hill Folk, Industrialists, and Government in Missouri's Courtois Hills* (Kirksville: Truman State University Press, 2010).

Under Penalty of Death

Pierce City's Night of Racial Terror

JASON NAVARRO

In 1901 the town of Pierce City, Missouri, was the scene of a horrific triple lynching that drew national attention.[1] In one night, an attack by Pierce City citizens drove out the town's entire African American population under penalty of death. Bullets rained down, and innocent men died. Blacks fled into the night, leaving everything they owned behind, as their homes burned. Since that night, no substantial black community has existed in Pierce City. The violence even caught the attention of author Mark Twain, who lamented the lynchings: "And so Missouri has fallen, that great state! Certain of her children have joined the lynchers, and the smirch is upon the rest of us."[2]

Founded in 1870 as a division point on the St. Louis and San Francisco (Frisco) Railroad, Pierce City hosted a population of over 3,000 at its zenith. By 1900, due to the Frisco's decision to move the division point to nearby Monett in 1887, that number had dropped to around 2,200 people. Despite its decreasing size, Pierce City was still a thriving community at the dawn of the twentieth century. The town featured hardware and dry goods merchants, several hotels and saloons, and an opera house. Other businesses included a lumber mill, lime mining, a wagon shop, and a canning company. Farming in the Pierce City area consisted mainly of growing fruits and vegetables, with strawberries a featured crop.[3]

The violence brought about changes that were a radical departure from the town's traditions. A black population had been present since the founding of the town. Prominent African American families such as the Godleys, the Blys, and the Kelleys moved to southwest Missouri from Kentucky following the Civil War.[4] One of the first black settlers was Milia Godley. Born during the Revolutionary War and a survivor of slavery and the Civil War, Godley made the long trip from Kentucky with her family when she was in her nineties. She died on August 19, 1879, at one hundred and was one of a select few blacks to be buried in the Pierce City Cemetery alongside whites. An elegant headstone marked her grave. The Godley family remained in Pierce City, and more blacks moved to the area. By 1900 around two hundred African Americans lived in and around Pierce City.[5] They owned a few businesses in town, including a laundry and an icehouse. The black community also established two churches, one of which, St. Paul's Baptist Church, with its thirty-foot steeple, was highly visible to anyone entering the town by railroad from nearby Monett.[6] The church stood on the outskirts of the city and was a powerful reminder of the presence of a strong black community—a presence wiped out in one night of horrible violence that changed the city and the area forever.

Pierce City's foray into blood justice began on the morning of August 18, 1901. On that day, twenty-three-year-old Gisela Wild and her sixteen-year-old brother, Carl, attended Sunday services at the Methodist Church (South). The services ended at noon, and the siblings began the walk to their home a mile and a half southwest of town. Carl stopped to talk with friends, and Gisela continued alone.[7]

At 1:00 P.M., the community fire bell rang to announce a gruesome discovery. Outside of town, Carl had discovered his sister lying underneath a culvert with her throat cut from ear to ear and her body still quivering. The boy ran to the nearby Kane residence and the police were called. Pierce City doctor P. L. Freeland arrived and pronounced Gisela dead by one clean cut to the throat. He observed blood on the body, on the rocks, and spurted four to five feet high onto the sides of the bridge above. The citizens of Pierce City began a frenzied search for the killer as Carl went home to tell his parents the terrible news.[8]

The condition of the body and the murder scene suggested that the attack had begun as a sexual assault. Signs of a struggle were found, and Gisela's possessions were scattered and her dress torn. "We presume the fellow found Miss Wild too strong for him and thought to hide evidence of his crime by adding murder to it," the *Peirce City Empire* reported the following day. The young woman had suffered a compound fracture to the middle finger of her left hand during the struggle, but there was no evidence she had been raped.[9]

Gisela's body was carried home to her parents, Bernard and Elizabeth, German immigrants who owned a large farm outside of Pierce City where they had lived since the founding of the town. The community held the family in high esteem. The *Empire* promised the Wilds that "they have the sympathy of all in their bereavement, and that everything will be done to catch the guilty wretch."[10]

Suspicion soon fell upon Pierce City's black community. William Roark, a white man who owned a farm near the murder scene, reported that he and his wife had witnessed a "copper-colored negro" sitting on the bridge in the minutes before Gisela's murder. At the request of Washington Cloud, Pierce City mayor, search parties were dispatched to hunt for the killer. Weapons and ammunition were borrowed from the local National Guard armory for use in the scouting. The search parties returned empty-handed on Sunday evening, and more teams formed to look throughout the night. Lawrence County sheriff John Manlove arrived to oversee the operation, and John Conner, city marshal of nearby Aurora, came to Pierce City to assist in the manhunt. Conner recommended the procurement of bloodhounds, which arrived Monday afternoon from Lamar under the care of Barton County sheriff John Harlow.[11]

The search continued on Monday, and in the afternoon, "excitement in Peirce City was intense and threats of lynching certain negroes, that were thought to be implicated in the murder, were made openly." The *Empire* denounced the murder as "the most awful occurrence our people have ever had to contend with." Editor A. T. Boothe whipped up the mob mentality, declaring, "No such crime should ever go unpunished, and every citizen should constitute himself an officer for the time being to help down the murderer . . . every nick and corner of the city should be thoroughly searched, and when discovered no punishment is too bad." Similarly, the *Webb City Daily Sentinel* reported, "The people of Pierce City are greatly excited and threats of lynching and burning at the stake are freely made." Telegrams were reportedly sent to an Aurora druggist requesting oil because "there was not as much oil in Pierce City as they wanted if they caught the murderer." Two Pierce City banks offered hundred-dollar rewards for information leading to the capture and conviction of the murderer, and the reward was expected to increase to one thousand dollars by the end of the day. Against this tense background, two blacks, thirty-two-year-old William Godley and seventeen-year-old Eugene Barrett, were arrested and held in the city jail on suspicion despite a complete lack of evidence against them.[12]

An 1891 conviction for the rape of sixty-year-old Johanna Filo of Pierce City, based entirely on questionable eyewitness identification, had earned Godley a reputation as a sexual predator along with names including "godless Godley" and "mean nigger" that made him a natural target for the rioters in the absence of Gisela Wild's actual killer. Godley had barely escaped lynching after his arrest for the earlier rape and probably owed his life to Rueben J. Chappell, a Pierce City lawman and Confederate veteran who had managed to run Godley through a crowd of two hundred angry whites and put him on a carriage bound for the jail in Mount Vernon.[13] Godley received a ten-year sentence in the penitentiary for the rape but was released early for good behavior and returned to Pierce City. He did not have the benefit of Chappell's protection, who had been murdered in November 1900, on the night of his lynching.

As news of Godley's arrest circulated on Monday afternoon, two white girls stepped forward with allegations that he had attempted to rape them on their walk home from church a few months earlier. The crime was well known, but the identity of the perpetrator had not been established. The girls claimed that Godley had threatened to kill them if they disclosed his identity.[14]

The murder of Gisela Wild came in a year of national racial tensions. At least 135 blacks were lynched in 1901, and African American leader Ida B. Wells denounced lynching as the "national crime" of the United States. Booker T. Washington's dinner with President Theodore Roosevelt drew the fury of white southerners, forcing Washington to maintain armed guards at Tuskegee Institute. Senator Benjamin Tillman of South Carolina said that the dinner would require the killing of a thousand blacks "before they learn their place again," and a congressman from Alabama said it would have been a good thing if a bomb had been placed under the table to kill both Washington and Roosevelt. Congress became exclusively white in 1901 when Representative George H. White of North Carolina failed to gain reelection due to the disenfranchisement of black voters in that state. No African Americans served in Congress again until 1929.[15]

Local racial tensions were also on the rise in 1901. The white community blamed a series of crimes in Pierce City during the preceding years on the black population, but the allegations were not proven due to the perceived "impossibility to get a negro to testify against another negro." The most serious of these crimes was the unsolved murder of night watchman Rueben Chappell. These events contributed to the racial tension in Pierce City, but Gisela's murder provided the spark that ignited the town in what became known as "one of the worst pieces of mob vengeance and negro hatred ever known in the history of race war in the United States."[16]

On Monday evening, several hundred people gathered outside of the city jail and demanded possession of Godley and Barrett. Mayor Cloud and other city officials pleaded with the crowd to let the law take its course, and the gathering soon dispersed. The calm did not last long.

Around 9:00 P.M., the crowd reformed, with reinforcements from the countryside and nearby towns. This was no unruly mob but was instead an organized effort led by some of the town's more respected citizens. The group of over one thousand determined rioters stormed the jail and removed Godley and Barrett by force.[17]

The attackers placed a noose around the neck of each prisoner and demanded a confession of who was responsible for the crime. Barrett pleaded for his life and claimed to know who had committed the murder. He accused Joe Lark, a porter on the St. Louis and San Francisco Railroad who had been in Pierce City the day of the murder but had since departed. According to the *Empire,* Barrett also implicated another Frisco porter, William Favors. Barrett's statement saved his life. He was removed from the crowd, and Pierce City officials rushed him to the jail in nearby Mount Vernon. Unlike Barrett, Godley remained quiet throughout his ordeal. He never made a statement of innocence or guilt nor implicated others in the crime.[18] Apparently believing his situation hopeless, Godley accepted his fate.

Despite Barrett's implication of Lark and Favors, the rioters dragged Godley west on Commercial Street and attempted to hang him from a telephone pole. When the rope proved too short, Godley's captors yanked him to his feet and pulled him back down the street east to the Lawrence Hotel, one of Pierce City's oldest businesses. The rioters tied the rope to an iron banister on the hotel's second floor, and Godley was "swung off into eternity." The crowd immediately opened fire on the hanging body. One bystander reported, "The negro's body was perforated and as heavy bullets went through he swung with a force, and his clothes on the opposite side puffed out as though the wind were blowing through." The indiscriminate gunfire did heavy damage to the entire area. Stray bullets shattered most of the windows in the hotel and in several surrounding businesses and hit the depot behind the Lawrence Hotel, causing damage to the baggage rooms and scattering frightened passengers from the waiting room. The gunfire also reportedly injured a few bystanders. When the barrage ended, Pierce City attorney Joe French cut down Godley's body, which was "riddled almost to pieces."[19]

The racial violence did not end with the death of William Godley. The *Empire* reported that some rioters "thought of some other negroes who needed attention" after Godley's death. The crowd reformed and marched into the black district of Pierce City looking for Godley's cousin Pete Hampton. Although not implicated in the murder, Hampton was known in town as a "notorious negro criminal," and the rioters saw the opportunity to remove him and all other blacks from Pierce City. The attackers reached Hampton's house on South Elm Street and quickly determined that he was not there. They then set fire to the house, as well as to several surrounding black residences.[20]

The mob moved west to the home of seventy-year-old French Godley, stepfather of Pete Hampton and uncle of William Godley. There they found Hampton armed and ready to defend himself. An exchange of gunfire ensued in which several whites were hit. The white rioters, making use of an advantage in numbers as well as fifty Springfield rifles stolen from the National Guard armory after William Godley's lynching, quickly gained the upper hand. Pete Hampton and French Godley fell in the rain of bullets as other blacks hurried to escape from the rear of the house. Wiley Godley, a relative of the victims and one of nine men in French Godley's house when the shooting commenced, "saw Pete Hampton fall and knew he had been killed."[21]

A year before the lynching, Hampton had reported shots fired behind the Windsor Hotel to Reuben Chappell. He led Chappell behind the Windsor, where they met three men coming down the railroad tracks. When Chappell attempted to question the men, one pulled a revolver and shot Chappell's left eye. Hampton pulled his gun and exchanged fire with the men as they made their escape. Several men found Chappell and moved him to the Windsor Hotel saloon and eventually to his home. He died of the wound two days later. Chappell's murderer was never identified, and as time went on, Hampton became a suspect. This was the primary reason that the rioters sought Hampton on the night he was lynched.[22]

Unlike the other lynched blacks, French Godley did not have a bad reputation in Pierce City. The *Mt. Vernon Lawrence Chieftain* reported that "there was no desire to kill French Godley but he was unfortunately in the wrong place."[23] The report appears to be accurate; no other motive for Godley's murder was ever established.

First Lieutenant W. C. Gillen of Pierce City National Guard Company E watched the attack from the veranda of the nearby Windsor Hotel and thought it "the wildest mob I ever saw." Gillen stated, "There was a skirmish line drawn up . . . along the track, in front of the negro houses, with a considerable body of men at both left and right. The house of old French Godley was in the zone of a crossfire. It was peppered from two directions." Other guests at the Windsor Hotel hid in their rooms to avoid the stray bullets that riddled the building.[24]

After gunfire from French Godley's house ceased, the rioters burned the building. Gillen reported, "After the torch was applied the whole scene was brightly illuminated. Five houses were burning, those of Shack [or Doc] Brinson, Pete Hampton, French Godley, Mrs. Emma Carter, the Windsor Hotel cook, and another. This made a line of flames half a block long, which lit up Clear creek, in the rear, and the wooded ridge beyond." Despite the lack of return fire, the mob continued to terrorize black Pierce City "as long as one of the hated race could be found." Gillen believed that the white rioters fired at least six hundred shots, as that was the amount of ammunition missing from the looted armory. The number was probably much higher because numerous privately owned weapons were also used in the attack. One account placed the number of rounds fired at fifteen hundred.[25]

Blacks fled Pierce City throughout the night, avoiding the certain death that awaited them if they remained. The escapes were narrow and dramatic. Two black preachers, S. S. Pitcher of Carthage and L. M. Smith of Lamar, had the terrorizing experience of being trapped in the path of the rioters. The preachers, in Pierce City to lead a church camp, wisely chose not to continue with services after hearing of the Wild murder. The men retired to the home of James Cobb, a black Pierce City resident who was French Godley's neighbor. When Godley's house was attacked, the Cobb residence took much of the fire. Pitcher later described the events: "When the first volley came crashing in we all dropped flat on the floor to keep from being hit. In a few minutes the shooting seemed to let up a little and we all crawled to the cellar. There we felt safer, but the shooting continued for a long while and many bullets hit the house." Realizing that the houses around them were on fire, the occupants of the Cobb home decided to escape out the back door and into the woods. "Every time one of us would jump out in sight to make a run a volley of shots would come after us and some of the balls hit pretty close. It was the greatest wonder in the world we were not shot." The preachers walked back to Carthage after their ordeal, leaving their church tent in Pierce City. Pitcher estimated that two hundred shots hit the Cobb residence before they made their escape. The Cobb family fled to Springfield.[26]

The charred bodies of Pete Hampton and French Godley were discovered in the ruins of Godley's house the following morning. Overnight, the city's entire black population of over two hundred had gone into exile. The *Joplin Globe* reported, "The very best citizens in this city say that they are satisfied that the negro population has been removed, and that henceforth Peirce City shall be a white man's town." Most of the blacks moved to Joplin, Carthage, or Springfield. Springfield African Americans assisted those uprooted from Pierce City. The *Globe* noted, "A colored man by the name of Abernathy has constituted himself a committee of safety and meets every westbound train on the Frisco and warns all colored

Figure 17. Side street in Pierce City, c. 1910.
POSTCARD VIEW, KALEN AND MORROW COLLECTION

passengers not to go nearer the danger line. He has filled up his house with passengers thus stopped and refugees from Peirce City." The Cobb family was among the refugees who found sanctuary at James Abernathy's house in Springfield.[27]

On Thursday, the murdered men were buried in the potter's field of the Pierce City Cemetery with no services and no mourners present.[28] Throughout the week, exiled blacks returned to town to retrieve their possessions but were not allowed to remain. They found themselves obliged to sell anything they could at any price they could get. "Uncle" Ben Kelly was forced to sell his chickens for forty dollars and commented, "Them chickens was wuth mo'. A heap sight mo', sah, but dey had to be sol at a sac'fice."[29] Another woman complained that she had to sell her cow for ten dollars, despite the fact that it was worth three times that much. The *Globe* reported, "The white men stand ready to buy their [the African Americans'] real estate. After this is done, they must vacate the town."[30] With these matters finished, the Pierce City black community ceased to exist.

Although Gisela Wild's murder sparked the racial violence, the people of Pierce City did not let the issue drop after the vengeful triple lynching. Residents regarded Frisco porters Joe Lark and William Favors as likely to have committed the crime, and officials sought the men's arrests. Pete Hampton and French Godley were never connected to the murder, and although William Godley was arrested on suspicion, he was not a strong suspect. Each of the three men had a proven alibi for his whereabouts at the time of the murder.[31] These men met their deaths for reasons that had contributed to the white community's hostility toward the entire black population of the city.

The composition of the crowd that lynched William Godley and led the attack on Pierce City African Americans was typical of most lynchings. The lynchers were not entirely from the lower class; they came from various social and economic backgrounds and varied in age. No one wore a mask to conceal his identity. The leaders were businessmen and merchants, including well-known businessman Jack LeGrand, a forty-four-year-old coal dealer, and William Abbott, a twenty-seven-year-old laborer, as well as twenty-one-year-old shop worker John Rogers, and former city marshal William Guthrie. At least one lawyer was present; Pierce City attorney Joe French was at the front of the crowd that lynched William Godley. *Peirce City Empire* editor A. T. Boothe, probably an eyewitness, credited French with cutting down Godley's body.[32] It is unknown if Boothe took an active part in the lynchings, but his editorials in the *Empire* were pivotal in inciting the mob violence.

Also typical was the denial of involvement by the Pierce City elite. Residents adopted the southern myth that poor whites carried out lynchings and that the elite despised the practice. In an attempt to blame someone else for the lynchings and to save their town's reputation, some prominent citizens formed the Pierce City Citizens Committee, which issued a report placing the blame on Bernard Wild's "farmer friends," asserting that they "came to avenge the crime by the hundreds." The report also claimed: "Many people from neighboring towns were here to assist. It is safe to say that a larger number of people from outside the city limits were among the mob than from within."[33]

A more honest description of the crowd's composition came from a prominent Pierce City businessman. In an interview with the *Joplin Globe,* a Mr. Perrott described the rioters as a "well organized body of determined men." He added, "The crowd that meted out justice was composed of some of Peirce City's most honorable citizens, not the wealthiest class, understand, but men of good reputation. Of course a few of the lower rank joined the delegation, but they were not the leaders." Another eyewitness noted that the crowd was "composed largely of young men, 20 to 30 years old, but there were also many older heads."[34]

Women came to watch the events. After William Godley's body was cut down, "a dozen or so women, in twos and threes with escorts came and gazed." This is not unique. White women often attended lynchings, shouting encouragement to the male participants.[35]

The role of the National Guard in the riot is unclear. The local unit was not called out to defend the black community, and some members of the guard were rumored to have participated in the lynchings. It was widely known that the mob breached the armory without resistance and used rifles and ammunition belonging to the guard in the attack. The rumors prompted Missouri governor Alexander Dockery to send W. T. Dameron, adjutant-general of the Missouri National Guard, to Pierce City to secure state property and investigate the involvement of the local company in the riot. Dockery was prepared to disband the company pending Dameron's findings.[36] The investigation led Dameron to the conclusion that "none of the officers or men of Company 'E,' aided or assisted directly or indirectly, the mob in the execution of their unlawful acts." He declared that the company "stood ready to assist the civil officers to protect life, property, to restore order and keep the peace, had they been called on to do so" and that he did not "feel warranted in recommending the disbandment of the Company." Instead, Dameron stated that the "men are entitled to much credit for the manner in which they conducted themselves during the exciting hours in the city, and they should be exonerated from unjust criticism based on mere rumors."[37] The report satisfied Governor Dockery, and Pierce City Company E remained intact.

One of the most appalling aspects of the lynchings was the fact that the lynchers knew that their victims were probably not the killers of Gisela Wild. Once a decision to lynch was made, determining guilt or innocence was not as important as making an example of the victim in front of the black community. A young Pierce City man remarked, "'The people of Peirce City believe that the life of one girl like Miss Wild is worth more than the lives of all the 'niggers' in the United States.'" The *Mt. Vernon Lawrence County Record* reprinted an *Aurora Argus* editorial applauding the lynchings: "'There is no punishment great enough to atone for such a crime. The argument is often put up that an innocent victim is liable to suffer. Perhaps so, but if they have to hang 25 to get the guilty one they will have an object lesson before the eyes of the nigger population. We say keep up the good work, Pierce City, until you get the right nigger.'"[38]

On the Thursday following the lynchings, Pierce City residents were alarmed by rumors of a counterattack by hundreds of African Americans hiding in the woods. The *Globe* reported: "At this hour there are a large number of armed negroes encamped to the south of this city [Pierce City] and trouble is apprehended. Pickets has been thrown all around the town and precautions are being taken to guard against any outbreak." Panicked city officials sent a telegram to nearby Carthage, exclaiming, "A large number of negroes are coming up from Neosho and Joplin; please send sheriff and policemen." Mayor Cloud also sent a telegram to the Jasper County sheriff in Carthage asking if any blacks were missing from that city. Carthage investigators could not account for the whereabouts of twenty-five to thirty blacks, contributing to the hysteria. The nervous mayor, who had earlier neglected to use the National Guard to protect blacks in Pierce City, called up Company E to protect whites from the possible attack. The company immediately sent out an order for ammunition because most of the rounds in the armory had been used in the attack on the black citizens.[39]

The rumors proved groundless; no attack ever ensued. According to the *Sentinel,* "Not a nigger was found, seen nor heard of about Pierce City last night. Conservative people laugh at the idea that the colored population of southwest Missouri has courage or vindictiveness enough to attempt a mob attack." One black resident of Carthage confirmed that the rumors were unfounded: "'I aint got no business at Pierce. There was nobody there last night but low down white trash from Monett.'"[40]

In the months following the violent night, two black men accomplished something extraordinary—Joe Lark and Will Favors won their freedom in a court of law.

Following the Monday night attack, whites in Pierce City began searching for the real killer of Gisela Wild. In his statement just before the lynching of William Godley, Eugene Barrett saved his own life by implicating Lark and Favors in the murder. The case against Lark began on Monday afternoon before the lynchings, when search parties put bloodhounds on the trail of the killer. Although the trail was old, the bloodhounds led lawmen to Lark's home. Lark was out of town working as a Frisco porter by this time, but officials sent word to surrounding towns to hold him if he was found. Authorities in nearby Springfield placed Lark under arrest but did not send him to Pierce City because of threats to lynch him. Will Favors was arrested at about the same time in Tulsa, Oklahoma. A battle ensued for custody of Favors, soon jailed in Oklahoma City. Several Tulsa African Americans raised money to hire Favors an attorney and to prevent his release to Missouri officials. After gaining assurance that Favors was safe from lynching, Oklahoma officials released him from custody. Missouri officers immediately arrested him as a fugitive and jailed him in Kansas City.[41]

The evidence against Lark appeared strong, leading most Pierce City residents to believe that he was the murderer. As prosecutors built the case, however, they met with difficulty. Authorities believed that an eyewitness identification of Lark as the man sitting on the bridge just before Gisela Wild's murder would be condemning evidence in the upcoming trial and sent four witnesses from Pierce City to Springfield to identify Lark. Police prepared a lineup of fourteen men, including Lark and thirteen blacks known to have been in Springfield when the murder took place. William Roark, who had originally reported seeing a man on the bridge, could not identify anyone in the lineup who looked like the man he remembered. Roark's wife picked two men who were in Springfield at the time of the murder. The other witnesses also failed to identify Lark. One witness pointed Lark out as a "man I have frequently seen in Peirce City, but I did not see him on the day of Miss Wilds' [*sic*] murder."[42]

Despite the failure of the lineup to implicate him, Lark went to trial in Mount Vernon for the murder. Without the testimony of eyewitnesses, prosecutors focused on items taken from the murder scene and evidence found in Lark's house. Barton County sheriff John Harlow testified that his bloodhounds had led him to Lark's house on the day after the murder and that Gisela Wild's bloody handkerchief was found halfway between the murder scene and the house. A search of Lark's residence on the Tuesday after the murder had yielded a knife, possibly stained with blood, and the burned remains of a shirt. Another search of the house a month later had yielded a blood-stained shirt, but the defense attacked the find because the shirt was not present during earlier searches. Subsequent tests revealed that the stain on the knife was rust rather than blood. Despite this weak evidence, the *Peirce City Empire* reported: "The State had about rested its case, and had presented a strong one. In fact it is about conceded by parties who had heard the evidence that there would certainly be a conviction. There has been a general opinion among our people that Lark was the guilty man ever since he was arrested, and the web woven around him at Mt. Vernon has not weakened that opinion one bit."[43]

On November 26, the jury voted eight to four to acquit Lark. The decision angered the *Empire's* editor, who wrote: "News came to us over the telephone this morning that the jury in the Joe Lark case at Mt. Vernon had brought in a verdict of Not Guilty, which means that the negro has been turned loose on the community to again meet some lady on the public highway and cut her throat as he did that of Miss Gazelle [*sic*] Wild." The *Empire* declared, "It is just such verdicts as this which cause mob violence."[44]

Figure 18. Jasper County Courthouse, Carthage.
POSTCARD, POSTMARKED 1914, KALEN AND MORROW COLLECTION

After the decision, prosecutors saw little chance of convicting Will Favors. Because the case against him was far weaker than the one against Lark, charges were dropped. When told of his impending release, Favors was said to have exclaimed, "For de Lawd sake, is dat so?" and declared his intention to hereafter be a "good niggah." Marshal Eyler, deputy in the jail where Favors was held, declared, "There never has been a better prisoner in the jail than he."[45] The release of Lark and Favors made this case unique during the early twentieth century.

Who killed Gisela Wild? Only one other suspect was ever mentioned, and the story caused controversy. A little over a week after the murder, the *Joplin Globe* reported that Gisela's life had been insured and that Carl would soon be arrested for murdering his sister to collect on the policy. The *Globe* later retracted the allegation after learning from sources in Pierce City that no insurance policy existed for Gisela. The *American-Tribune* from nearby Sarcoxie, home to several members of the Wild family, refuted the story and accused the *Globe* of "yellow journalism." The *American-Tribune* stated: "The young man, Carl, was left prostrate from the news . . . There is not one penny's worth of insurance on any member of Bernhard Wild's family." Carl Wild died in 1966, and rumors of a deathbed confession continue to circulate in Pierce City, but the story appears to have no merit.[46]

The final development in the Pierce City episode was a remarkably bold action on the part of the city's former black community. In an unprecedented move, the widows of the lynched men filed civil suits against the leaders of the riot. In early August 1902, nearly a year after the lynchings, America Godley, Sarah Godley, and Beedie Hampton each filed $5,000 lost support suits in the Jasper County Circuit Court against twenty-one citizens of Pierce City. After fleeing Lawrence County, the widows lived in Joplin. When John Rogers, one of the presumptive riot leaders, moved to Carthage, the women filed the suits in Jasper County, rather than in Lawrence County where they did not believe they could win. The pretrial depositions eliminated most of the suspects named in the suits, but four defendants remained. Rogers, who had worked in a store near the site of William Godley's lynching, remained a suspect because he was shot during the riot and therefore had no alibi to place him elsewhere. The three remaining defendants were Jack LeGrand, William Abbott, and William Guthrie.[47]

On February 18, 1903, Sarah Godley, the widow of French Godley and the mother of Pete Hampton, took her case to trial in Joplin. The plaintiff's attorneys presented their case first. It quickly became obvious that LeGrand was the primary defendant as a parade of witnesses, all of them African American, identified him as the principal leader of the riot. Godley testified that she had seen LeGrand, Abbott, and Guthrie in the crowd that attacked her house. Her neighbor Doc Brinson, the owner of one of the houses burned during the riot, also identified LeGrand and Abbott as rioters. Charles Hunter, a black schoolteacher from Joplin, stated that he had been in Pierce City on the night of the lynchings and had "recognized LeGrand in the mob and said he was in the lead when he first saw him."[48] Hunter further testified that LeGrand was carrying either a gun or a club.

Several witnesses reported recognizing LeGrand's distinctive voice in the crowd, and many pointed him out in the courtroom. Two witnesses recounted incriminating conversations with LeGrand. Will Young testified that LeGrand had stopped him before the riot and asked him who had killed Gisela, telling him, "'If you know you had better tell, for if we find out who committed the act it will go as hard with you as any of them.'" According to the *Joplin Globe,* Jessie Hampton, perhaps a relative of Pete Hampton, testified that when the bodies were removed from the Godley house on Tuesday morning, LeGrand stated that "they did not intend to kill French Godley; they wanted to kill Pete Hampton."[49]

The plaintiff's attorneys also built a strong case against William Guthrie. In addition to his identification by Sarah Godley as a member of the crowd, Guthrie took a bullet in the arm during the riot, and like John Rogers, could not place himself elsewhere due to his injury. Guthrie, a former marshal of Pierce City, owned a gun shop in town. The plaintiff's attorney attempted to establish Guthrie's ill will toward the black community by introducing reports that "the local hardware stores sold out of their arms early, but several applications from negroes were refused." Other reports claimed that the guns and ammunition had been handed out to whites free of charge. The case against William Abbott depended on eyewitness accounts and the weakness of his alibi in the pretrial depositions.[50] After one day of testimony, the plaintiff's attorney rested his case.

The next day, defense attorneys tried to end the case by arguing that no proof existed that French and Sarah Godley had been legally married; therefore, Sarah was not entitled to a settlement. Each had been married previously, and proof of annulment or death of the previous spouses could not be produced. The judge disapproved of the motion, allowing the trial to continue.[51]

Each of the defendants took the stand in his own defense, with Jack LeGrand testifying first. He explained his presence at Godley's house by saying that he had been deputized that afternoon and had entered the riot that night to try to prevent trouble. LeGrand stated that "he went to a man who seemed to be the leader and asked him not to harm the old people. To this he said the fellow shoved a gun in his face and asked: 'Who the —ll is running this affair?'" LeGrand admitted that he then called the city electrician and requested that power to the streetlights be shut off so the blacks could not target the white rioters. He testified that he did not have a gun when he was at Godley's house and that he did not recognize any of the rioters as citizens of Pierce City, believing that they were "from the east."[52] LeGrand denied making the statements attributed to him by the black witnesses.

William Guthrie took the stand and testified that he also had been in the crowd as an officer of the law when he was shot. He said that he did nothing to prevent the riot because he was greatly outnumbered and that he left immediately to see a surgeon after he was wounded. The defense then produced many witnesses who testified that the defendants were all men of good reputation and that the black witnesses had bad reputations in Pierce City.[53]

After the defense finished calling witnesses, the attorneys for Sarah Godley argued to the jury that the defense had formed its arguments only after hearing the testimony of the preceding day. Godley's attorney George Grayston also argued that the pretrial depositions were tainted because the witnesses for the defense had been allowed to sit in the room together and hear the statements of other witnesses, thereby keeping their stories consistent and protecting the lynchers. Grayston had tried to stop this practice, but the defense continued to allow it despite his objections. Grayston argued that "an attorney who had faith in his witnesses to tell the truth would not have objected to the rule." Defense attorney Joe French countered Grayston's arguments by appealing to the jury that the case was "in a way a criminal one; that if the defendants were implicated in the killing of French Godley to the extent that they should pay his widow one dollar, they could be prosecuted for murder and convicted." French also asked the jury if "they were going to believe the testimony of crap-shooting negroes or that of good, reputable citizens." He disputed Sarah Godley's financial loss, declaring that "French Godley was not physically able to earn a day's wages and that Sarah Godley . . . was better off by reason of his having been killed."[54] These statements were typical of French, who was among the rioters who lynched William Godley and was credited with cutting down Godley's body from the hotel banister.[55]

Plaintiff attorney Stonewall Pritchett then gave a passionate closing statement to the jury in which he repeatedly shouted at the defendants. "Why did you not attempt to protect the colored people from the mob by requesting the mob to go to their homes?" he yelled at LeGrand. "Abbott, why didn't you remain at home and protect your own family?" Pritchett screamed.[56] After this theatrical closing statement, the case went to the jury.

On the following morning, the all-white jury acquitted the defendants of all charges and awarded Sarah Godley nothing. The decision was a great relief to the local people who feared "many other cases of a similar nature would be brought" if Godley's suit succeeded. Godley's attorneys filed a motion for a new trial on the grounds of jury misconduct. They presented witnesses who testified that they had observed members of the jury discussing the case in Joplin during the trial, despite specific instructions from the court not to do so. The appeal proved unsuccessful, and the case was closed. America Godley apparently lost heart after the first verdict and failed to appear for her trial. Her case was dismissed, as was Beedie Hampton's suit.[57] Although filing the civil suits were a courageous move by the widows, they proved unsuccessful.

The end of the court cases began many years of near-silence about the Pierce City affair. An examination of local histories shows that the events of 1901 are rarely mentioned. With the notable exception of a series of articles in the 1991 *Monett Times,* the incident merits no more than a sentence or two in any city or county history. A 1974 history of Lawrence County included the incident in a section on population loss, stating only that the problem was compounded by the black population leaving and noting that "at these years occurred the unfortunate difficulty of the murder of the young daughter of a white family, and the uprising of outsiders, bent on trouble making, that led to the withdrawal of the Negro Population." A 1992 county history ignored the extralegal violence entirely, instead focusing on the execution of convicted criminals in what were referred to as "legal hangings." A book written for the Pierce City centennial in 1970 failed to cover the city's past racial violence, instead providing a few pages under the heading of "Negroes Assist Peirce City to Develop." The only mention of the events of 1901 occurs in a section on economic hardships: "There were hard times for most everyone. So that after disturbing situations, the Negro population left Pierce City as well as most other small towns in the border states; economics were not such as to offer much work for Negro families."[58] These vague assertions fail to capture the gravity of the event, leaving the local histories nearly silent on Pierce City's bloody past.

The violence in Pierce City played a pivotal role in a larger regional story. A series of lynchings in southwest Missouri between the years of 1894 and 1906 drove away most of the region's black population. These lynchings were unlike lynchings in the Deep South, where the main goals were to uphold white supremacy and to keep a compliant and intimidated force of agricultural laborers. In the decades after the Civil War, southwest Missouri saw a vast immigration of southern blacks into the region.[59] This population was not economically important to a local economy that did not depend on cash crops such as cotton and tobacco. Blacks instead found themselves competing with poor whites for mining and railroad employment. This condition led to racial tensions, and when the lynchings took place, their aim was not only to intimidate but also to remove the region's black population.

An 1894 lynching in Monett led not only to the expulsion of the town's black population but also to the removal of most African Americans from Barry County. The 1901 triple lynching and race riot in Pierce City finished the process in Barry County when Willis Dehoney sold his farm and moved, leaving the county without a single black resident. In Lawrence County, all of the blacks left Pierce City, and blacks farming at nearby Jolly Mill "received a 'request' from a number of white citizens of that part of the country to vacate, decided that discretion was the better part of valor, sold their property at a sacrifice and started out to hunt another home." The black population left Sarcoxie as well, fearing hostility from the many Wild family relatives there. After the Pierce City violence, the *St. Louis Post-Dispatch* reported: "Southwest Missouri is gradually growing into a colorless community. Down here they call it the white man's heaven." The account listed Aurora, Cassville, Newburg, and Webb City as additional places where blacks were not welcome within city limits.[60]

Other southwest Missouri towns contributed to the pattern of violence. A lynching and race riot in Joplin in 1903 turned much of the city's black population into refugees, although many returned within a few days. Springfield continued the violent chain of events when three blacks were hanged and their bodies burned and mutilated in the town square in April 1906.[61] On that occasion, removal of the black population was called for but prevented when a sympathetic white man armed the black community with dynamite and the state militia organized to prevent further violence. Many of Springfield's African American leaders and professionals left and did not return. Taken collectively, these events removed most of southwest Missouri's black population. Every county in the region reported a decline in black population between the years of 1890 and 1910.[62]

The Godley family's troubles were far from over. On April 16, 1903, just a few weeks after the conclusion of Sarah Godley's civil trial, Joplin erupted in racial violence. The murder of police officer Theodore Leslie by a black man on the preceding night led to the lynching of suspect Thomas Gilyard. A crowd numbering in the thousands then stormed the African American sections of Joplin, setting fire to houses and cutting the hoses of firemen who tried to extinguish the blazes. The *Peirce City Empire* cheered the lynching, reporting, "The black brute who shot to death Officer Leslie in Joplin Tuesday night was hanged by a crowd of righteous citizens in that town Wednesday and another name was added to the list of good negroes."[63] The Godley family fled Joplin that night, veterans of this all-too-familiar event.

Notes

1. The original spelling of the town's name is Peirce City, honoring railroad tycoon Andrew Peirce, who donated the land on which the town was founded. The modern spelling of Pierce City started as a postal error and was eventually adopted. Miriam K. Brown, *The Story of Pierce City 1870–1970* (Cassville, MO: Litho Printers, 1970), 21. The author has used the modern spelling in this article, except for primary sources that refer to the original spelling.

2. Charles Neider, editor, *The Complete Essays of Mark Twain* (Garden City, NY: Doubleday, 1963), 673.

3. *Twelfth Census of the United States, 1900, Population Schedule,* "Lawrence County" (National Archives Microfilm Publication T623, roll 870); Jessie C. Miller et al., editors, *Lawrence County Missouri History* (Mount Vernon: Lawrence County Historical Society, 1974), 203.

4. Murray Bishoff, "Monett's Darkest Hour: The Lynching of June 28, 1894," *Monett Times,* June 27–28, 1994.

5. Murray Bishoff, "The Lynching that Changed Southwest Missouri," *Monett Times,* August 14–16, 1991.

6. Map, *Peirce City, Lawrence County Mo., May 1902* (New York: Sanborn Map Company, 1902).

7. *Neosho Times,* August 22, 1901. Many variations of the spelling of Gisela appear in the primary sources. The author has used the spelling that appears on her tombstone, except when quoting documents that spell it otherwise.

8. *Mt. Vernon Lawrence Chieftain,* August 22, 1901; *Missouri* v. *Lark,* 1901, Lawrence County Circuit Court, Lawrence County Courthouse, Mount Vernon; Bishoff, "The Lynching that Changed Southwest Missouri."

9. *Peirce City Empire,* August 19, 1901; *Carthage Evening Press,* August 19, 1901.

10. Brown, *Story of Pierce City,* 21; *Peirce City Empire,* August 19, 1901.

11. *Mt. Vernon Lawrence Chieftain,* August 22, 1901; *Report of the Adjutant-General of the State of Missouri for the Year 1901* (Jefferson City: Tribune, 1902), 17; *Joplin Daily Globe,* August 20, 1901; *Peirce City Empire,* August 20, 1901.

12. *Report of the Adjutant-General,* 17; *Peirce City Empire,* August 19, 1901; *Webb City Daily Sentinel,* August 19, 1901; *Mt. Vernon Lawrence Chieftain,* August 22, 1901.

13. *Carthage Evening Press,* August 20, 1901; Bishoff, "The Lynching that Changed Southwest Missouri."

14. *Peirce City Empire,* November 29, 1900; September 6, 1901.

15. Darlene C. Hine, editor, *Black Women in United States History* (Brooklyn: Carlson, 1990), 279; Donald L. Grant, *The Anti-Lynching Movement, 1883–1932* (San Francisco: R and E Research Associates, 1975), 39, 66–67.

16. *Peirce City Empire,* September 6, 1901; *Carthage Evening Press,* August 20, 1901.

17. *Report of the Adjutant-General,* 17; *Joplin Daily Globe,* August 21, 1901.

18. *Joplin Daily Globe,* August 21, 1901; *Peirce City Empire,* August 21, 1901; *Report of the Adjutant-General,* 18.

19. *Peirce City Empire,* August 21, 22, 1901; *Carthage Evening Press,* August 20, 1901; *Joplin Daily Globe,* August 21, 22, 1901.

20. *Peirce City Empire,* August 20, 1901; *Mt. Vernon Lawrence Chieftain,* August 22, 1901.

21. *St. Louis Post-Dispatch,* August 25, 1901; *Peirce City Empire,* August 22, 1901.

22. *Peirce City Empire,* November 29, 1900; September 6, 1901.

23. *Mt. Vernon Lawrence Chieftain,* August 22, 1901.

24. *St. Louis Post-Dispatch,* August 25, 1901; *Peirce City Empire,* August 22, 1901.

25. *St. Louis Post-Dispatch,* August 25, 1901; *Mt. Vernon Lawrence Chieftain,* August 22, 1901; *Carthage Evening Press,* August 20, 1901.

26. *Carthage Weekly Press,* August 22, 1901; *St. Louis Post-Dispatch,* August 25, 1901.

27. *Joplin Daily Globe,* August 22, 23, 1901; *St. Louis Post-Dispatch,* August 25, 1901.

28. *Joplin Daily Globe,* August 22, 1901.

29. *St. Louis Post-Dispatch,* August 25, 1901. Newspaper accounts from the period often used phonetic spelling when quoting African Americans and proper grammar in quotes from whites. Quotations appear in their original form throughout this article.

30. Ibid.; *Joplin Daily Globe,* August 22, 1901.

31. *Peirce City Empire,* August 20, 1901; *Missouri v. Lark.*

32. *Sarah Godley v. Rogers,* 1902, Jasper County Circuit Court, Jasper County Courthouse, Carthage; Bishoff, "The Lynching that Changed Southwest Missouri"; *Peirce City Empire,* August 22, 1901; *Twelfth Census . . . 1900,* "Lawrence County."

33. *Peirce City Empire,* September 6, 1901.

34. *Joplin Daily Globe,* August 29, 1901; *Carthage Evening Press,* August 20, 1901.

35. *Carthage Evening Press,* August 20, 1901; Michael J. Pfeifer, "The Ritual of Lynching: Extralegal Justice in Missouri, 1890–1942," *Gateway Heritage* 13 (Winter 1993): 27.

36. *Joplin Daily Globe,* August 24, 1901.

37. *Report of the Adjutant-General,* 18–19.

38. Leon F. Litwack, *Trouble in Mind: Black Southerners in the Age of Jim Crow* (New York: Knopf, 1998), 290; *St. Louis Post-Dispatch,* August 25, 1901; *Mt. Vernon Lawrence County Record,* August 29, 1901.

39. *Webb City Daily Sentinel,* August 24, 1901; *Joplin Daily Globe,* August 23, 1901; *Report of the Adjutant-General,* 18; *Carthage Evening Press,* August 23, 1901.

40. *Webb City Daily Sentinel,* August 24, 1901.

41. *Joplin Daily Globe,* August 22, 23, 25, 1901; *Carthage Evening Press,* August 20, 1901; *Peirce City Empire,* August 20, 1901.

42. *Peirce City Empire,* September 19, 1901; *Joplin Daily Globe,* August 27, 1901.

43. *Mt. Vernon Lawrence Chieftain,* November 28, 1901; *Peirce City Empire,* November 25, 1901.

44. *Peirce City Empire,* November 26, 1901.

45. Ibid., December 19, 1901.

46. *Sarcoxie American-Tribune,* August 30, 1901; Bishoff, "The Lynching that Changed Southwest Missouri."

47. *Mt. Vernon Lawrence Chieftain,* February 26, 1903; *Sarah Godley v. Rogers; Peirce City Empire,* August 20, 1901; Bishoff, "The Lynching that Changed Southwest Missouri."

48. *Joplin Daily Globe,* February 19, 1903.

49. Bishoff, "The Lynching that Changed Southwest Missouri"; *Joplin Daily Globe,* February 19, 1903.

50. *New York Times,* August 22, 1901; *Joplin Daily Globe,* August 21, 1901; *Sarah Godley v. Rogers.*

51. *Joplin Daily Globe,* February 19, 1903.

52. Ibid., February 20, 1903.

53. Ibid.

54. Ibid.

55. *Peirce City Empire,* August 20, 1901.

56. *Joplin Daily Globe,* February 20, 1903.

57. *Mt. Vernon Lawrence Chieftain,* February 26, 1903; *Sarah Godley v. Rogers; America Godley v. Rogers,* 1902, Jasper County Circuit Court, Jasper County Courthouse.

58. Miller et al., editors, *Lawrence County Missouri History,* 203–204; Kathy S. Fairchild, editor, *Down Turnback Trails: A Sketch Book of Lawrence County, Missouri* (Mount Vernon, MO: Lawrence County Historical Society and Lawrence County Record, 1992), 44; Brown, *Story of Pierce City,* 45, 47.

59. Litwack, *Trouble in Mind,* 307; *Tenth Census of the United States, 1880, Population Schedule,* "Lawrence County" (National Archives Microfilm Publication *T9,* roll 698).

60. Bishoff, "The Lynching that Changed Southwest Missouri"; *Neosho Miner and Mechanic,* September 19, 1901; Lanny J. Headley, *Gilbert H. Wild, his ancestors and related families, Allen, Brindle and Hase* (Gwinn, MI: by the author, 1989), 194; *St. Louis Post-Dispatch,* August 25, 1901. See the excellent regional study, Kimberly Harper, *White Man's Heaven: The Lynching and Expulsion of Blacks in the Southern Ozarks, 1894–1909* (Fayetteville: University of Arkansas Press, 2010).

61. Burton L. Purrington and Penny L. Harter, "The Easter and Tug-of-War Lynchings and the Early Twentieth-Century Black Exodus from Southwest Missouri," in *Visions and Revisions: Ethnohistoric Perspectives on Southern Cultures,* ed. George Sabo III and William M. Schneider (Athens: University of Georgia Press, 1987), 60.

62. Burton L. Purrington and Judith A. Brooks, "Adaptation, Repression, Resistance and Flight: African Americans in Southwest Missouri, 1865–1920" (paper, American Society for Ethnohistory, Chicago, November 4, 1989), 2, 6.

63. *Peirce City Empire,* April 19, 1903, quoted in Purrington and Harter, "The Easter and Tug-of-War Lynchings," 70.

"Our Company Feels that the Ozarks are a Good Investment"

The Pierce Pennant Tavern System

KEITH A. SCULLE

On July 16, 1928, in Springfield, Missouri, Pierce Petroleum Corporation formally opened an $80,000 highway terminal comprising three buildings, the largest of which was a bus station housing a restaurant, soda fountain, and restrooms. A gasoline station and a grease house with car-washing facilities completed the complex. Nothing comparable to Pierce Petroleum's terminal existed anywhere else in the United States, according to both the *National Petroleum News*, the petroleum industry's foremost trade magazine, and the head of the nationwide Pickwick bus company. Edward D. Levy, president of Pierce Petroleum, appeared in Springfield on the eve of the terminal's grand opening. He explained that the city had been picked to anchor a chain of elaborate facilities named "taverns" in both Missouri and Oklahoma because it was "the gateway to the Ozark region." Though grandiose for its time, Levy nonetheless was convinced of the value of Pierce's plan, "Our company feels that the Ozarks are a good investment and we are all for making them the most popular playgrounds in the United States." "Pennant" was an additional name Pierce dubbed its products, hence the name affixed to all the facilities selling them.[1]

As one of the nation's oldest petroleum companies, Pierce Petroleum had long been one of the leaders in the industry. Pierce Petroleum's forerunner, the Waters-Pierce Oil Company, which had been founded in 1871 by two St. Louis businessmen, W. H. Waters and Henry Clay Pierce, was run by Pierce. He developed a reputation for exceptionally aggressive, independent, and sometimes ruthless entrepreneurship. Pierce bought John Finlay and Company, his father-in-law's St. Louis refinery, the first west of the Mississippi River. Eyeing the sparsely settled area of southern Missouri, Arkansas, western Louisiana, Texas, and the Oklahoma Territory in the 1870s, Pierce foresaw it was on the verge of rapid growth. From his St. Louis headquarters, he rapidly established control of the petroleum market throughout the region. In the process, he quickly drove his company to national prominence in the era of industrialization.[2]

After 1878, when Standard Oil eagerly acquired 40 percent ownership of Pierce's company, it ranked as one of the most important independent distributors during the Standard Oil trust's duration. By the 1880s, the Pierce refinery in St. Louis was among the nation's largest, and by the early 1900s, Pierce used railroads to establish a sterling reputation for innovative marketing. He had introduced bulk handling, being the first to use special wooden barrels for delivering oil in St. Louis. Then, in cooperation with the railroads opening the southwestern territory, Pierce had been the first to use tank wagons to unload oil from railcars at local destinations and deliver it to a network of oil company bulk stations. He had also been the first to market in Mexico, where he eventually built three refineries.[3]

Pierce also became a leader in tapping an important new petroleum demand: the automobile. In typical advertising hyperbole, Pierce said his company led the way in "abandoning 'shanty' service stations for architecture and convenience." Indeed, the Atlantic Refining Company, an important eastern oil company, studied a Pierce station before launching a chain of stations that have been known as some of the finest early designs. Although Pierce had made Missouri an important place in the petroleum industry throughout the early days of the automobile, his fortunes foundered in 1925 when he lost control to new owners in a spectacular financial fight.[4]

Renamed Pierce Petroleum, the company was placed under the direction of Edward Levy, a former vice president of the St. Louis-San Francisco Railroad, popularly known as the Frisco. Levy drew on three Pierce traditions to improve profits: targeting the Ozarks for economic development, using innovative marketing techniques, and—to achieve both—exploiting established railroad practices. The latter included advanced ticket sales, trip maps, and radio advertising.

Levy envisioned a series of roadside services that would grow by increments in and around the Ozarks. People outside the region were just beginning to tap the recreational assets of this splendid highland. Since the late nineteenth century, special weekend railroad rates had helped lure businessmen from Kansas City and St. Louis for hunting, fishing, and camping trips. Resorts provided diversified retreats for family city dwellers during the summers. The Frisco railroad branch to Memphis began to draw tourists early in the twentieth century. Lodging ranged from numerous small cottages to a few fine resort hotels. Looking like an "accident wandered out there and happened" when twelve hundred visitors descended on the health spa at Eureka Springs, Arkansas, one weekend in 1879, the site boomed in 1882 with the construction of a Frisco railroad spur south from Springfield and again four years later with construction of the Crescent Hotel. Styled in the period's florid eclecticism, with broad porches on each of its four stories and built of native stone, the Crescent Hotel was regarded in looks and service as the showplace of northwest Arkansas. Railroads serving splendid hotels in the Ozarks became commonplace, much like in the American West. It was the middle-income family, seeking bargain prices and traveling by automobile, yet hungering for the pretenses of patrician services and settings, who swelled the tide of the Ozarks tourist boom of the 1920s.[5]

Developers of highways in the Ozarks hoped to tap the region's potential for outsiders. William Hope Harvey, a real estate developer commonly known as "Coin" for his interest in monetary reform, started a resort hotel for midwestern businessmen at Monte Ne in northwestern Arkansas about 1900. He launched the Ozark Trails Association in 1913 to promote regional highway development after the railroad to his resort closed.[6] The association, a loosely knit group of local boosters that promoted a marked highway to California, broke into factions due to bickering about the exact route in the Southwest and disappeared in 1924. The Ozark Trails Association's alignment lay through the Ozarks between St. Louis, Rolla, Springfield, and Miami, Oklahoma, an early route followed as the most convenient upland trail across several ridges of the Ozarks. The Frisco railroad had used this same alignment as did Route 66 after its creation in 1926.[7]

Perceived as the gateway to the Ozarks from this pathway, Springfield served as Pierce's initial location for an elaborate set of highway facilities, anchoring the company's latest regional exploitation. Springfield had long been a good target for outside investors. By the 1920s, it was the state's fourth largest city, growing by almost twenty thousand inhabitants during the decade. Site of Southwest Missouri State Teachers College and the Frisco's extensive shops and switching yards, national headquarters for the Assemblies of God Church, base of operations for an estimated one thousand traveling salesmen, and depot for the timber, fruit, vegetable, cattle, and poultry industries of the Ozarks as well as manufacturer

Figure 19. Pennant Tavern System, Rolla.
POSTCARD, POSTMARKED 1934, KALEN AND MORROW COLLECTION

of many commodities used in local agriculture, Springfield was a very prosperous city, centering the regional economy for 150 miles around. Into this profitable mix, Pierce added a terminal to service the fifteen bus lines passing through the city and automobile travelers, including tourists, traveling businessmen, and local residents. Attempting to assure success by employing experienced key personnel, Levy hired R. W. Lochrie from the management of the Harvey House restaurant in Frisco's station in Springfield to run Pierce's restaurant at the bus terminal. Harvey House restaurants had long represented the standard in railroad restaurants.[8]

Rolla's tavern opened next. Although it was a far smaller town, numbering slightly over five thousand residents by 1930, Rolla was an advantageous setting for Pierce's second stake in the new Ozarks strategy and reflected the same pattern of regional development as did Springfield. Platted in 1855 by Frisco railroad contractors seeking private profit along the old interior ridge route, Rolla's constant traffic seemed assured as the county seat and home to the Missouri School of Mines and Metallurgy. Roughly halfway eastward between Springfield and St. Louis along the new U.S. Highway 66, Rolla was, according to Pierce's reckoning, within a convenient drive out of St. Louis, about one hundred miles, for an evening meal. Pierce bought the highest point on the edge of Rolla to house the terminal, allowing travelers to gaze for miles in any direction across the surrounding Ozarks.

Like the Springfield terminal, Rolla's tavern boasted not only food service and a soda fountain but spacious and clean restrooms, a gasoline station, and grease and oil services for automobiles. Rolla, however, merited a three-story building with a second-floor restaurant and dance floor. The third floor housed the manager and his family. The contrast with Springfield's one-story terminal probably seemed justified by the possibility of drawing private dinner parties from the fraternities of the Missouri School of Mines in addition to tourists. These upscale services were clearly designed for recreational outings as much as for the routine highway trade. Opened two weeks after the Springfield facility, the formal opening of Rolla's tavern on August 1, 1928, amid pomp and pageantry was "an event that marked a new period in the life of Rolla," in the words of the local newspaper. With officials from Pierce's headquarters in St. Louis as well as local notables present, an "elegant reception and dance" with a buffet was held until midnight. Pierce thus laid the basis for an innovative exploitation of the new automobile trade in the two Ozarks cities, with services attuned to the respective needs of each.[9]

Pierce's experiment soon exceeded the company's expectations. Not only did Pierce sell large quantities of gasoline at Rolla—as much as one of its most profitable bulk stations—it averaged 400 noon meals served during the first summer in Rolla. After Labor Day, when business was expected to decline, as many as 185 meals were served.[10]

Expansion seemed warranted. Hence, Pierce announced in January 1929 the plan for additional grand facilities in Columbia, on the northern edge of the Ozarks, and in Miami and Tulsa, Oklahoma, on the western edge. By February 1929, an unexpected degree of success in the Ozarks inspired Pierce to declare even larger plans, a chain of taverns coast-to-coast. A site on the outskirts of Oklahoma City would receive the first tavern outside the Ozarks. Because the location at Rolla had excited customers with a view of the countryside, Pierce reasoned that its newest facilities should also be built on the edge of their respective cities. Considerably more would be spent on each of these taverns, $20,000 and $30,000 over the cost at Springfield and Rolla, respectively. At least ten-acre lots would be purchased for each site, again more than for the first two. A parking lot for two hundred cars and considerable room for future expansion would also be provided at the new terminals. The buildings would be "white-washed brick colonial structures built to resemble a large country home," in the words of the *National Petroleum News.* Moreover, an emergency hospital with an operating table and a nurse in regular attendance would be added; experience in Rolla made the availability of medical help expedient. And, alert to the latest means of transportation as an income source, Levy selected a site for the Columbia tavern across the highway from the city's airfield. He hoped customers would be at the front door immediately after leaving their airplane flight. The completed network would provide the automobile traveler with "first class restaurants" every 125 miles and, with the addition of Pierce service stations with superior restrooms halfway between each restaurant, would comprise the most elaborate roadside services owned by any company. But still more would come.[11]

The finishing touch to Pierce's innovative tavern system of automobile services would be hotels. Rolla and Columbia, both in the Ozarks and with available land for purchase to expand, would be the first recipients. Springfield and Tulsa and Miami, on the Ozarks' fringe, would receive hotels in the future.[12]

The *National Petroleum News* lavished more attention on Pierce's roadside services in a fifth and final article detailing the company's unrivaled "motorist hotels." Each cost $150,000 to build. "Equal in . . . appointments to modern hotels in large cities," according to the *News,* Pierce's hotels far surpassed the ordinary roadside lodging of the time.[13] The facilities offered free garages for guests on the first floor. Upon arrival, they drove into the garage, gave orders for service if they wished, and retired to their rooms. Pierce personnel vacuumed every car's upholstery, washed the windows, and replenished the water and air—all overnight. The first floor also housed the office, a foyer, and sixteen guest rooms; the second floor sixteen guest rooms; the third floor a foyer, eight guest rooms, and quarters for the hotel hostess and other attendants; and finally, ten rooms on the top floor provided space for the guests' chauffeurs. Each guest room was spacious (sixteen feet by twelve feet, and eight and one-half foot ceilings) by the standards of roadside lodging at a time when the fledgling motel industry had a reputation for "shacks." Pierce's hotel rooms were incomparably provisioned with two full-sized beds; a writing table; a dresser with mirror; lights for the ceiling, beds, dresser, and writing table; upholstered chairs; a carpeted floor; a telephone; steam heat; an electric wall fan; a folding ironing board; an electric iron; and a clothes dryer. Each room had a private bathroom with tub, shower, electric fan, hot and cold running water, and floor and walls lined with rubber tile. Bronze plaques in each room portrayed the impression Pierce coveted, "The quality of this institution is indicative of the quality of Pierce Pennant Products."[14]

At this time, advertising through images came of age. Companies designed images with favorable impressions for the purpose of enticing shoppers to buy their goods and services. Business historian Thomas

Figure 20. Henry Clay Pierce.
STATE HISTORICAL SOCIETY OF MISSOURI-COLUMBIA

Dicke has argued that petroleum sales were especially susceptible to image advertising because the newness of the commodity, the absence of tangible differences among competitors' commodities, and the numerous outlets could readily profit from catchy signs, slogans, and service. As calculated loss leaders, Levy hoped the high cost of the taverns would be recouped in increased petroleum sales, candidly acknowledging that Pierce's petroleum products were no better than their competitors'.[15]

Pierce's bronze plaques spoke these vanities, but it was the architectural styling that visually aimed at clinching the sale. Beverly T. Nelson, a respected St. Louis residential architect deft in the colonial revival motif, designed the hotels crowning Pierce's empire of roadside services for the hinterland Ozarks. Each hotel's exterior included a moderately pitched gable-end roof covered in slate, gable-end chimneys of squat proportions, cornices with returns, and most often, flat-arched windows. Semicircular arched windows on both sides highlighted the fireplace. In the dining room and bedrooms, delicate moldings delineated rectangular panels on each wall, and inside the terminal, a fireplace mantel complete with entablature and fluted columns distinguished the public space. Flower stands, mantel clocks in colonial revival motif, and paintings of early American scenes helped trigger the sentiment for gentility that inspired the colonial revival style. Pierce's strategy with those elegant objects and a patrician setting was twofold. First, the company tried to distinguish itself from competitors in a business where makeshift and modest buildings characterized the norm. Second, Pierce hoped to appeal to motorists' vanity in a mass market where the consumers' selection of goods and services with highbrow imagery implied the consumers' own high status. Feeling, not critical reflection, was at the root of the strategy.[16]

In the rustic Ozarks, moreover, Pierce's colonial revival snob appeal perhaps was aimed at creating an even more glaring contrast. Vance Randolph had been making photographs throughout the 1920s for his first book, *The Ozarks: An American Survival of Primitive Society,* whose subtitle reflected the impression many would subsequently share about the region. Local people too played to the popular sense of "otherness" by lining Route 66's roadside to sell folk crafts to curious tourists. Pierce Petroleum was not alone in capitalizing on the Ozarks' evolving sense of place.[17]

Hoping to wring the fullest profit from the Ozarks market, Pierce adapted familiar railroad strategies to the new automobile trade. Tickets reserving a specific room at a Pierce Pennant hotel were sold in advance of arrival at the hotel, much like a Pullman ticket, Pierce claimed. "Time-table trip maps" were distributed free at Pierce stations. Claimed to be almost identical to those used by railroad engineers and passengers, these maps measured four by twelve inches and illustrated the type of road surface on a trip of one hundred to three hundred miles between major cities in the Pierce market. Calibrations along each side showed intermediate distances between the major destinations. The reverse side provided the names of all the towns along the route, with the distances between them, and spaces for the motorist to log his time en route. These maps became so popular that almost every passenger wanted one, although only one per car had been intended. Pierce craftily provided no station with all fifty maps in order that "station attendants" could tell customers where the next Pierce station was to obtain maps for the succeeding leg of their trip.[18]

Pierce also used sound trucks and radio broadcasting to entwine public service with commercial messages. The trucks, each with eight loud speakers, traveled to special events in communities throughout Pierce's market, playing phonograph records to entertain and carrying microphones for local representatives to make public speeches promoting their community's distinctions. The company emblazoned each truck with advertising and scoreboards announcing inning-by-inning results of St. Louis's two major league baseball teams, both popular throughout Missouri. On radio station KMOX in St. Louis, Pierce sponsored various broadcasts, including the home games of the city's major league baseball teams and programs that lasted from 9:00 to 9:30 each evening except Saturday. The latter opened with fifteen minutes of music and closed with fifteen minutes of promotion for the Ozarks. Guests ranged from Missouri's game and fish commissioner giving tips on the best fishing spots to local spokesmen describing their area's attractions. Pierce freely admitted that it gained a commercial advantage by acquainting itself with local leaders. Questions were also invited from listeners seeking recreational opportunities in the Ozarks, and brochures describing destinations accessible by car were offered by mail.[19]

By introducing signs that reached beyond the railroad experience, Pierce innovated again. Some ten thousand signs showing mileage to and from principal cities were placed every two miles throughout Missouri, Oklahoma, Texas, and Mexico. Other signs included large billboards apparently placed only along Missouri's major highways. Located at the entrance to towns and at major highway intersections, these billboards listed the distances to important cities and featured a state map showing road surface types and a Pierce advertisement. The company hoped that a public service for all drivers might bait some trade for Pierce's private gain. Billboards like these foreshadowed the look of the future roadside, producing an eventual backlash against them by people wanting to beautify rather than unduly commercialize the landscape. In the meantime, gawking motorists who slowed or stopped to read Pierce's billboards produced complaints about traffic hazards from the Missouri highway department. Heedless of such disgruntlement, Pierce planned to increase the profit flowing from petroleum sales at its grand tavern system, which billboards stimulated throughout the Ozarks.[20]

By the early 1920s, the Ozarks was well on its way to becoming a major tourist attraction. Pierce boasted of having been "largely instrumental" in bringing nearly one and a half million tourists to the Ozarks in 1929 alone. Although perhaps a bit exaggerated, the company nonetheless had been an important factor. For example, the Rose Cliff Hotel in Van Buren reported that five of the seven tourist parties staying at the hotel on one weekend in 1928 had come because they had heard Pierce's promotional radio programs. Despite this success, the Pierce hotels promised at Springfield, Miami, and Tulsa were never constructed, and the complete complex at Oklahoma City was never built.[21]

Pierce's system of taverns, indeed, nearly died aborning. In June 1930, eight months after the last facility, the Rolla hotel, opened, Pierce Petroleum proudly made public its talks to sell out to Sinclair Consolidated Oil Corporation. Pierce had been unable to make satisfactory profits in the preceding six years, principally because it did not own any petroleum supplies. Having survived because of its strong marketing, however, Pierce was eagerly acquired by Sinclair in its drive to become a fully integrated and nationwide company. Although Sinclair never added taverns, it used Pierce's marketing techniques in the Ozarks, even down to retaining the name "Pennant" for the taverns in Missouri. The first page of a six-page Sinclair brochure elaborated twelve reasons for stopping at the newly renamed Sinclair Pennant Taverns: restaurants and hotels offering complete accommodations of the "finest kind, at low rates"; tasty dinners and breakfasts; curb service for sandwiches and soda fountain goods; clean restrooms; prompt laundry and valet service; and facilities for doing small amounts of laundering in the rooms. For the tourists' cars, some automotive service was available twenty-four hours a day, and hotel guests could park in the garage free. "Diversions for young and old" included road maps with tour information; miniature golf facilities at Des Peres and Tulsa; playgrounds at Columbia and Rolla; a nine-hole golf course free to guests at Columbia; and radio rentals for a nominal fee in Columbia and Rolla. "And all these [are] in or near the famous Ozark Mountain Country—one of the loveliest spots in the whole world," hawked the brochure. Sinclair added its own tourist proposal to its system of acquired services: "An extremely interesting triangle tour of Missouri may be had with St. Louis, Columbia and Rolla as the turning points, and with Sinclair Tavern service at each corner. The trip is approximately 335 miles long from downtown St. Louis."[22]

As late as 1933, Sinclair highway maps of the area prominently identified the six locations of the system with large pennants. During the Depression, however, the taverns' elegance probably became less of an asset. Their rates of $1.50 for a single with a "nearby bath" and $3.00 for one person, $5.00 for two, $6.50 for three, and $8.00 for four with bath inside the room certainly made them more expensive than the ubiquitous cabins of spare simplicity charging from 50¢ to $1.00 for lodgers.[23]

The system slowly disintegrated. The Greyhound bus company purchased the Springfield terminal by 1936, and both the Columbia and Rolla hotels were sold to a local businessman by 1942. Eventually, all the buildings were razed except for the complex at Columbia, which survives as an assisted living facility at the time of this writing.[24]

Pierce's system of taverns, although short lived, was eloquent testimony to the circumstances in which it arose. After the Ozarks provided home to permanent residents, their recreational delights began attracting outsiders with a passing yet passionate interest, first sportsmen coming by railroad, later families coming by car. Businessmen traveling through the area by car complemented the demand. Modestly housed services were adequate for most travelers, but the Ozarks also engendered renowned palatial hotels at health spas remote from railroads and highways. The Ozarks thus witnessed splendid settings combining wooded and hilly retreats at which all the civilities of fine urban hotels could be enjoyed. Pierce Petroleum matured with this regional tradition as it expanded the new petroleum trade from the company's base in Missouri to the South and Southwest.

During the twentieth century, when the greatest profit in petroleum turned from kerosene sales to gasoline sales due to the automobile's increasing popularity, Pierce adapted traditional techniques of regional sales to its new customers. Car travelers were hosted at Pierce's taverns where fine food, commodious lodging, and reliable automotive work were available. The Ozarks tourist landscape began slowly to be homogenized, with aspects of the isolated, elegant spas applied to Pierce Pennant's taverns on the national highways. Pandering to the mass appetite for patrician surroundings at the proverbial affordable prices, Pierce built its taverns in upscale architectural pose, visual symbols of refinement belying their common origins. The taverns also benefited by contrast with the region's rustic identity. Roadside signs and radio programs complemented the advertising as Pierce drew tourists to the Ozarks while profiting from the products and services they purchased.

Pierce's contributions to the early phases of Ozarks automobile tourism held national meaning as well. The 1920s and 1930s witnessed the start of the roadside service industry for automobile travelers—gas stations, motels, and restaurants. A few places outside the Ozarks, principally in California, popped up to serve lodgers, diners, and their cars in one place.[25] These resembled Pierce's taverns, and like the Pierce taverns, they were the creation of big corporate investment. Mom-and-pop services, however, predominated almost everywhere in the nation through the late 1940s. When big corporations invested in the roadside again, they flooded it, pushing the small businessperson to the margins of profitability. Pierce's services seem commonplace now, further reason for placing them in the historical perspective of evolving roadside services for automobile travelers.

Notes

1. J. C. Chatfield, "Now It's Transportation By Oil and Gasoline Station at Springfield, Mo.," *National Petroleum News* 20 (August 1, 1928): 20; *Springfield Sunday News and Leader,* July 15, 1928.

2. William Hyde and Howard L. Conard, editors, *Encyclopedia of the History of St. Louis* (New York: Southern History Company, 1899), 3: 1731–1733; *The Book of St. Louisans: A Biographical Dictionary of Leading Living Men of the City of St. Louis and Vicinity,* 2nd ed. (St. Louis: St. Louis Republic, 1912), 474; Harold F. Williamson and Arnold R. Daum, *The American Petroleum Industry: The Age of Illumination, 1859–1899* (Evanston, IL: Northwestern University Press, 1959), 541, 545; Allan Nevins, *John D. Rockefeller: The Heroic Age of American Enterprise* (New York: Charles Scribner's Sons, 1940), 1: 438, 658–659.

3. Williamson and Daum, *American Petroleum Industry,* 532, 542–543; Roger B. Stafford, "Sinclair to Take Over Business Of Pierce Petroleum Corp.," *National Petroleum News* 22 (May 21, 1930): 27.

4. *Springfield Sunday News and Leader,* July 15, 1928; John G. McLean and Robert W. Haigh, *The Growth of Integrated Oil Companies* (Cambridge: Harvard University, Harvard Graduate School of Business Administration, Division of Research, 1954), 268–269; Keith A. Sculle, "Jenney Manufacturing Company: A Proper Bostonian Appeal Along the Roadside," *Pioneer America Society Transactions* 19 (1996): 19; Stafford, "Sinclair to Take Over," 28.

5. Carl O. Sauer, *The Geography of the Ozark Highland of Missouri* (Chicago: University of Chicago Press, 1920), 231–232; *Fayetteville Arkansas Sentinel,* October 8, 1879, June 2, 1880, cited in H. Craig Miner, *The St. Louis-San Francisco Transcontinental Railroad: The Thirty-fifth Parallel Project, 1853–1890* (Lawrence: University Press of Kansas, 1972), 114; Milton D. Rafferty, *The Ozarks: Land and Life* (Norman: University of Oklahoma Press, 1980), 194–195.

6. For a history of the Ozark Trails Association, see Clara B. Kennan, "The Ozark Trails and Arkansas's Path Finder, Coin Harvey," *Arkansas Historical Quarterly* 7 (winter 1948): 299–316; Nan Lawler, "The Ozark Trails Association" (Master's thesis, University of Arkansas, 1991); Arthur Krim, "The Ozark Trails: The Original Mother Road," *Society for Commercial Archeology Journal* 14 (spring 1996): 21–26.

7. Sauer, *Geography of the Ozark Highland,* 139, 223.

8. H. Craig Miner, "Hopes and Fears: Ambivalence in the Anti-Railroad Movement at Springfield, Missouri, 1870–1880," *Bulletin of the Missouri Historical Society* 27 (January 1971): 129–146; Rafferty, *The Ozarks,* 75; Sauer, *Geography of the Ozark Highland,* 226; *Missouri: A Guide to the Show Me State* (New York: Duell, Sloan and Pearce, 1941), 323–333; Dick Grosenbaugh, *A Million Hours of Memories: A Condensed History of Springfield, Missouri Published on its 150th Birthday* (n.p.: Springfield Sesquicentennial Committee, [1979]), 30–31, 33; Chatfield, "Now It's Transportation," 20; *Springfield Sunday News and Leader,* July 15, 1928.

9. *Missouri: A Guide,* 411–412; J. C. Chatfield, "Pierce Undertakes New Experiment In Caring for Motor Tourists," *National Petroleum News* 21 (February 13, 1929): 92; Chatfield, "Now It's Transportation," 23; *St. Louis Globe-Democrat,* January 10, 1929; *Rolla Herald,* August 9, 1928.

10. J. C. Chatfield, "Three More Tourist Terminal Stations To Be Built by Pierce Petroleum," *National Petroleum News* 21 (January 2, 1929): 105.

11. Ibid., 105–106; *Miami [Oklahoma] Daily News-Record,* February 12, 1929; Chatfield, "Pierce Undertakes New Experiment," 91.

12. Carleton Whiting, "'Gas' Stations Grow to Motorist Hotels Under Pierce Terminal System," *National Petroleum News* 22 (March 19, 1930): 153; Norman Coats, son of Jake Coats, Pierce Petroleum warehouse foreman in Springfield, 1922–1930, telephone interview by author, April 11, 1997; *Miami [Oklahoma] Daily News-Record,* February 12, 1929.

13. Chatfield, "Pierce Undertakes New Experiment," 90; Warren James Belasco, *Americans on the Road: From Autocamp to Motel, 1910–1945* (Cambridge: Massachusetts Institute of Technology Press, 1981), 134–142, passim; John A. Jakle, Keith A. Sculle, and Jefferson S. Rogers, *The Motel in America* (Baltimore: Johns Hopkins University Press, 1996), 232–240, passim. For a review with illustrations of Route 66's roadside services in Missouri, see C. H. (Skip) Curtis, *The Missouri US 66 Tour Book* (Lake St. Louis, MO: Curtis Enterprises, 1994).

14. "Roadside Cabins for Tourists," *Architectural Record* 74 (December 1933): 457; Whiting, "'Gas' Stations Grow," 157.

15. Stuart Ewen, *Captains of Consciousness: Advertising and the Social Roots of the Consumer Culture* (New York: McGraw-Hill Book Company, 1977), 100–102; Stuart Ewen, *All Consuming Images: The Politics of Style in Contemporary Culture* (New York: Basic Books, 1988), 6–8, 14–16, 78–79; Thomas S. Dicke, *Franchising in America: The Development of a Business Method, 1840–1980* (Chapel Hill: University of North Carolina Press, 1992), 88; *Miami [Oklahoma] Daily News-Record,* August 4, 1929.

16. Esley Hamilton, letter to author, February 25, 1997. Hamilton is the former architectural historian for the Department of Parks and Recreation, St. Louis County, Missouri. Whiting, "'Gas' Stations Grow," 157.

17. John R. Hensley, "Vance Randolph's Photographic Views of the Ozarks," *Missouri Historical Review* 82 (April 1988): 251–266; Elbert I. Childers and John F. Bradbury Jr., "Basketville and the Roadside Craftspeople on Route 66," ibid. 91 (October 1996): 24–34. Emergence of the Ozarks' stereotype around Branson is traced in Damien Francaviglia, "Branson, Missouri: Regional Identity and the Emergence of a Popular Culture Community," *Journal of American Culture* 18 (Summer 1995): 57–73.

18. Chatfield, "Pierce Undertakes New Experiment," 92; J. C. Chatfield, "Radio Tourist Bureau Builds Sales As Well As Good Will," *National Petroleum News* 20 (August 8, 1928): 26–27.

19. Chatfield, "Radio Tourist Bureau," 25–26. Pierce attracted contemporary visionaries in his radio promotion. In 1929, KMOX hired Missouri game and fish commissioner Keith McCanse, as director of Ozark broadcasting, and another former game and fish commissioner, Jesse Tolerton, was district manager in Springfield. In 1930, McCanse, Senator Harry B. Hawes, and other St. Louis sportsmen sponsored legislation to create a "commission control of game and fish" based upon a Pennsylvania model; Missouri voters agreed to the commission concept in governance for conservation in 1936; see Lynn Morrow, "Keith McCanse: Missouri's

first professional conservationist," *White River Valley Historical Quarterly* 31, no. 2 (Winter 1992): 3–12.

20. *Springfield Sunday News and Leader,* July 15, 1928: Daniel M. Bluestone, "Roadside Blight and the Reform of Commercial Architecture," in *Roadside America: The Automobile in Design and Culture,* ed. Jan Jennings (Ames: Iowa State University Press, 1990), 172, 175–176; Chatfield, "Radio Tourist Bureau," 26–27.

21. Whiting, "'Gas' Stations Grow," 161; *Springfield Sunday News and Leader,* July 15, 1928. For the Rose Cliff Hotel, see Lynn Morrow, "Rose Cliff Hotel: A Missouri Forum for Environmental Policy," *Gateway Heritage* 3, no. 2 (Fall 1982): 38–48.

22. Stafford, "Sinclair to Take Over," 27; "Sinclair Pennant Hotels & Taverns" (n.p.: Sinclair Refining Company, c. 1931), 2, 7.

23. "1933 Sinclair Missouri Highway Map"; "Sinclair Pennant Hotels & Taverns," 4.

24. *Polk's Springfield (Greene County, Mo.) City Directory,* 1936 (Kansas City: R. L. Polk and Company, 1936), 159; John F. Bradbury Jr., compiler, "Phelps County During World War Two," *Newsletter of the Phelps County Historical Society* (April 11, 1995): 6.

25. For example, see W. E. Green, "Chain Stations De Luxe, By Highways, Are California Venture," *National Petroleum News* 20 (August 22, 1928): 25–26; Lester B. Colby, "Standard Oil, Swift, National Dairy to Aid Chain of 1,000 Wayside Inns," *Sales Management* (May 23, 1931): 313; "National Motor Inns Will Establish Chain of 'Super-Camps,'" ibid. (October 3, 1931): 30.

Lake Placid

"A Recreational Center for Colored People in the Missouri Ozarks"

GARY R. KREMER AND EVAN P. ORR

On October 8, 1934, during the heart of the Great Depression and in the second year of Franklin Delano Roosevelt's first term as president of the United States, two white men from Morgan County, Missouri, sold a 346-acre plot of land in the Missouri Ozarks to two black men from Kansas City. The sellers were a prominent county physician, Dr. C. A. Wiest, and his son-in-law, a local farmer named Reed J. Blackman.[1]

The buyers were Dr. P. C. Turner and J. M. Sojourner. Dr. Turner served as superintendent of General Hospital No. 2 in Kansas City—the publicly supported, but racially segregated, hospital for African Americans in Missouri's second-largest city. A printer, Sojourner ran the Sojourner Press at 1604 East Nineteenth Street in Kansas City. The business served only a black clientele. Segregation defined the world occupied by Turner and Sojourner. State and local laws and customs dictated that African Americans live, work, shop, worship, and even play in separate facilities, away and apart from whites.[2]

Magnificent Swope Park, comprising more than thirteen hundred acres, served as the major public recreational area for Kansas Citians during the 1930s. The land had been donated to the city for recreational use in 1896 by real estate developer and philanthropist Thomas Hunton Swope. In accordance with plans drawn up by George Kessler, the landscape architect and designer who helped to make Kansas City a shining example of the

Figure 21. The P. C. and Mayme Turner cabin.
LEONARD PRYOR COLLECTION, KANSAS CITY

Progressive era's so-called City Beautiful Movement, the city developed the land as a park during the early 1900s.[3] No amount of landscaping, however, could hide the ugly fact that Swope Park was racially segregated, with blacks forced to go to a small section of the park widely referred to by members of both races as "Watermelon Hill.

Dr. P. C. Turner, the driving force behind the purchase of the Morgan County land, wanted a place to relax without having to suffer the indignities of racial segregation. This eliminated Swope Park and the segregated city park in his hometown of Independence, where Turner had grown up as the son of a postal worker and his wife at the turn of the century.[4] Turner, a hunter and a fisherman, loved the outdoors and dreamed of the opportunity to roam the hills of the Ozarks, unfettered by the rules and racism of reigning whites. He had been looking for just such a place since at least 1932. The Morgan County property seemed to fit his needs.[5]

Turner and Sojourner visualized the land as more than a place for their own personal use. According to the contract signed by the parties in 1934, ninety-six acres of the land were "to be used and set aside for a l[a]ke, Dam, Golf course, Park ETC [*sic*]." Individual lots measuring 33 1/3 x 100 feet would be sold at prices ranging from fifty dollars to one hundred dollars, depending upon the location. Thus, from the very beginning, the purchasers conceived of the area as "a recreational center for colored people."[6]

Turner and Sojourner had little cash available, which was not surprising in the fifth full year of a national depression. Their lack of cash but eagerness to buy, combined with Blackman and Wiest's keenness to sell the land and the absence of other buyers, led to a creative way to finance the sale. Turner paid the sellers two dollars in cash (Sojourner apparently never provided any cash for the project) and agreed to pay Blackman and Wiest 40 percent of the amount earned from the sale of lots, "which sum is to be used to payoff a mortgage now existing against the said land." Once $2,000 had been paid, the buyers would then pay 20 percent of gross sales, "until the sum of $6,650.00 more has been paid." At that point, the sellers were to receive "thirty per cent of the gross sales until the sum of $13,350.00 more has been paid, making a total payment of $22,000.00 in all." Thus, Turner and Sojourner agreed to pay the considerable sum of more than $63.58 per acre for rocky, hilly, tree-covered, northern Ozarks land. This represented at least three times the per acre cost of similar land in the area. The advantage to Turner and Sojourner, of course, was that they could payoff their indebtedness to the sellers from the proceeds earned from selling lots. The contract placed no time limit on the arrangement, except that the buyers had to pay the sellers $2,000 by August 31, 1935.[7]

Almost immediately after purchasing the Morgan County property, Dr. Turner arranged to have a rustic cabin built by a local craftsman on the land as a "getaway." Here he and his wife could relax, and he could pursue his hobbies of hunting and fishing and allow his favorite dogs to roam. At first, the cabin had no modern conveniences such as central heat, indoor plumbing, or electricity. Initially, the Turners either brought food with them from Kansas City and/or relied on Dr. Turner's skills as a hunter and fisherman to sustain them. An active spring, perhaps one hundred yards from the cabin, provided fresh water and served as a storage place for perishable foods while the couple stayed at the cabin.[8]

From the very beginning, Turner intended to build a lake on the property. He clearly built his cabin at a point on a sloping south hillside that would give him a commanding and attractive vista of the lake. Turner, however, could not afford the cost of building a large dam. He began seeking federal support through the Works Progress Administration (WPA) for the construction of a dam sometime in late 1935 or early 1936. The WPA had been established by executive order of President Roosevelt on May 6, 1935, with an initial appropriation of nearly five billion dollars. The money was to be spent for relief work: creating public works projects that would serve the common good (roads, schools, hospitals, parks, reservoirs, etc.) while employing millions of unemployed Americans.

Workers spending their wages, government officials hoped, would help to stimulate the stagnant depression economy. The building of a dam on private property owned by Turner and Sojourner was construed to be a "public" project because, it was argued, if water supplies continued to be difficult to maintain in the drought-ridden years of the mid-1930s, the lake formed by building the dam could be opened to "the public."[9]

Each state employed an administrator for WPA projects within its borders. According to historian Robert H. Ferrell, "The choice of a state's WPA administrator lay with its senators." Missouri's senators, Bennett Champ Clark and Harry S. Truman, supported the appointment of Matthew S. Murray, a longtime, loyal associate of notorious Kansas City boss Thomas J. Pendergast. As Ferrell points out, this placed Murray and, by extension, Pendergast, in control of eighty thousand jobs in Missouri.[10]

The Murray-Pendergast connection raises the intriguing but difficult-to-answer question of what role, if any, Pendergast played in helping Turner to obtain WPA funds for construction of the dam. Contemporaries of Turner remember that the doctor and the boss knew each other well and sometimes did favors for each other. None, however, remembers a specific oral tradition overtly connecting Pendergast to the allocation of WPA funds to the Lake Placid project. A number of these contemporaries are inclined to think that Pendergast likely played a role in the building of the dam since the two men sometimes assisted each other. Also, Turner's desire to obtain federal support would have meshed with the boss's willingness to do favors for black leaders in the hope of securing black votes for his causes and candidates.[11]

Another important connection between Turner and Pendergast appears to have been Dr. William J. Thompkins, an African American doctor who preceded Turner as superintendent of General Hospital No. 2. A native of Jefferson City and a graduate of Lincoln Institute, Thompkins earned his medical degree from Howard University, Washington, D.C., in 1905. He began the practice of medicine in Kansas City in 1906 and in 1915 was appointed the "first Negro superintendent of General Hospital No. 2." One of the most prominent African Americans in Kansas City during the first three decades of the twentieth century, Thompkins was also a businessman and a newspaper publisher who launched and edited the *Kansas City American* during the mid-1920s. According to Pendergast biographers Lawrence H. Larsen and Nancy J. Hulston, Pendergast helped to finance the newspaper's publication. In 1927, Thompkins was appointed assistant commissioner of health in the Department of Hygiene and Communicable Diseases in Kansas City. His high profile in the city's African American community made him a natural ally of political boss Tom Pendergast. By the early 1930s, Thompkins had become widely known as a power broker among black Democrats throughout the Midwest. According to his obituary, "In the campaign of 1932 [Thompkins] had charge of the colored contingent for all states west of the Mississippi river for the Democratic party. The National Colored Democratic association, of which he was president consists of clubs in Missouri, Oklahoma, Kansas, Nebraska, Colorado, Iowa, California, and 19 other states." Thompkins's active support of the Democratic Party led President Roosevelt to appoint him to the prestigious position of recorder of deeds for the District of Columbia in 1934. This position had previously been held by other prominent African Americans, including Frederick Douglass, Monroe Trotter, and Blanche K. Bruce. Thompkins's appointment came at the recommendation of senator-elect Harry S. Truman, in recognition of the doctor's strong and active involvement in Democratic Party politics.[12] In a late 1980s reminiscence on the founding of Lake Placid, Girard T. Bryant, one of the early investors, wrote that he believed Thompkins had helped Turner obtain WPA funding for the Lake Placid dam.[13]

Even before construction of the dam commenced, other Kansas City African Americans began building cabins on the property. One of the first was veteran teacher H. O. Cook, who built a cabin southwest of Dr. Turner's cottage. Cook served as principal of Lincoln High School for more than twenty years. His wife, Myrtle, was a former teacher at Lincoln High School and an active member of the National Association of Colored Women.[14] Dr. Turner allowed one of his patients, Ketchum E. "K. E." Snell, to live in an old cabin at the property's entrance. Sent by the doctor to the lake to recuperate from an illness in the fresh Ozarks air, Snell helped build the Turner cabin. Snell liked the outdoors of Morgan County so well that he decided to stay, despite the fact that he had relatives, including a wife, in Kansas City. In addition to providing him with a cabin, Turner periodically purchased an old car for Snell's use and supplied him with clothing and food. Snell earned small amounts of money by doing maintenance work for cabin owners and occasionally charging hunters for their use of the property.[15]

Snell quickly became a fixture in the Stover area. A black person in Stover during the mid-1930s was a rarity. According to the federal census, only 236 African Americans lived in Morgan County in 1930, more than half of whom resided in the county seat of Versailles. The number of African Americans who called Morgan County home dropped to 185 by 1940.[16]

One of the first local white families to befriend Snell were the Wrays, who lived several hundred yards south of his cabin. Although not one of the WPA workers, Jodie Wray had done contract work on the Lake Placid dam for the WPA. Snell sometimes purchased farm produce, including eggs, chickens, and garden vegetables, from the Wrays. Alice Wray Jones, an adolescent at the time, remembers Snell as a gentle, polite man who initially declined the Wrays' invitation to dine with them. He eventually accepted and came to be regarded as almost one of the family. He had a "place" at the family table and often ate with the Wrays multiple times a week. On many occasions, Alice and her sister, Betty, would either walk or ride their horse to Snell's cabin to visit. At an earlier point in his life, Snell had been a schoolteacher, and the Wray daughters found him to be a never-ending source of information. He always asked them about their schoolwork and encouraged them to do their best in school. Snell had also worked as a meat cutter, a job that made him a skilled assistant when it came time for the Wrays to butcher hogs, beef, or chickens.[17]

The Lake Placid dam was under construction by late 1936 or early 1937. An article in the May 21, 1937, *Stover Tri-County Republican* noted that "the J. F. Martin family spent Sunday visiting the Turner Dam which is under construction on the old Reed Blackman Place." The paper observed, "It is being constructed of native stone and cement and is worthy of the attention of the people of the surrounding country."[18] Emma Jean Clark, who

Figure 22. Lot owners took great pride in the addition of the dam to the Lake Placid area. LEONARD PRYOR COLLECTION, KANSAS CITY

as a young girl often visited the property with the Turners, recalls, "We took a great deal of pride as the dam was being built because this would enable us to have water. The older people were looking forward to being able to fish in the new lake."[19]

The dam was completed during the summer of 1937, and the lake quickly filled, covering approximately fifteen acres. By 1940 six cabins stood near the lake. In addition to the Turner, Cook, and Snell structures, Dr. Joe Houston Lewis had built a cabin he called "Jest-a-mere." A dentist, Lewis had graduated from Sumner High School in Kansas City, Kansas, the University of Minnesota, and Meharry Medical College.[20] Steve Blantyre, a Kansas City businessman, also built a cabin. Early in 1940, Girard T. Bryant's cabin was completed some distance from the water. Uninterested in hunting, fishing, or water sports, schoolteacher Bryant simply wanted a place where he could read in peace. During the first two summers that he owned a lake cabin, however, Bryant was forced to take jobs as a dining car waiter on the Union Pacific Railway to supplement his meager teacher's salary. Thus, his wife, Louise, and daughters, Betty and Barbara, spent most of their time at Lake Placid without him.[21]

At least two of the early cabin owners at Lake Placid were druggists. Leonard Hughes, who ran a pharmacy at 2519 Tracy, had become acquainted with Turner through his business. Leonard's wife, Eva, operated a business known as Eva's Wardrobe Exchange. The Hugheses built one of the largest cabins at the lake, a place that would accommodate several families. Their former daughter-in-law, Mayme Hughes Rodgers, recalls that she and her husband, also named Leonard, spent their honeymoon at the lake in September 1949. More than a decade later, Rodgers purchased her own cabin at Lake Placid.[22]

William Houston, who operated a pharmacy at 2300 Vine Street in Kansas City, built an early cabin at the lake. An 1897 graduate of Lincoln High School, the very light-skinned Houston had "passed" for white as a University of Kansas student during the first decade of the twentieth century. Upon his graduation from college, Houston was licensed as a pharmacist by the state of Missouri. After Houston's death in May 1941, his cabin, which he had named "My Blue Heaven," passed on to his half-brother, Arthur "Chic" Pullam.[23] Pullam was a longtime postal worker in Kansas City and a former player on the Kansas City Monarchs baseball team. Pullam's daughter, Barbara Pullam Thompson, recalls that "it was quite prestigious" to have a cabin at Lake Placid during the 1940s. One of her most vivid memories of Lake Placid while a teenager, however, is a negative one: an automobile accident enroute to the lake with the Carlis Evans family (who operated a bakery at Twenty-fourth and Vine in

Kansas City). Just south of Sedalia, their car rolled over three times before coming to rest on the driver's side. Barbara was holding a big pot of chili beans at the time, and the beans were strewn all over the car and its occupants. Although no one was seriously injured in the accident, all of the car's occupants received medical attention from the doctors when they finally arrived at the lake. After Chic Pullam's death, "My Blue Heaven" was passed to his son, Richard, a former "Tuskegee airman," who lived year-round in retirement at Lake Placid until his death in August 1997.[24]

By late 1939, Turner and Sojourner decided to formalize their effort at creating what they envisioned as "a recreational center for colored people" in the Missouri Ozarks. In December they drafted articles of incorporation for Lake Placid, Incorporated. According to the document, "the amount of capital" was $50,000, "divided into 50,000 shares of stock of the par value of One dollar, ($1.00), each." Twenty-seven thousand and five hundred shares of the stock were divided among five stockholders: Dr. P. C. Turner (15,844 shares); J. M. Sojourner (6,000 shares); Mayme Turner (5,000 shares); K. E. Snell (500 shares); and Josephine Abbie Sojourner (156 shares). Presumably, the remaining 27,500 shares of stock were to be divided among future purchasers of Lake Placid property. The corporation subsequently hired Kansas City businessman, and Lake Placid property owner, Steve Blantyre as its agent to promote and sell lots. The lots were to range in price from $65 to $159 (although some would later be sold for as little as $30), the amount to be paid in cash or "on time," with financing arranged through the black-owned People's Finance Company, located on Vine Street in Kansas City. Turner was a principal stockowner in the People's Finance Company. On January 31, 1940, Missouri secretary of state Dwight H. Brown issued a "Certificate of Authority to Commence Business" to Lake Placid Resort, Incorporated.[25]

Later that same year, property owners organized the Lake Placid Lot Owners' Association, which initially met at the African American YMCA in Kansas City. The association, first presided over by Girard T. Bryant, assessed each lot owner a $3.00 fee "to provide funds for stocking the lake with fish, for upkeep of roads, and other necessary improvements." In addition, each cabin owner was assessed an annual $5.00 fee "for caretaker services." In September 1941, the association adopted "regulations for fishing," which prohibited "out-board motor boats" on the lake and declared: "Outsiders are forbidden on this private property." Guests who came to Lake Placid were stopped at the entrance, gained Snell's approval for entry, and signed a guest register kept by the caretaker. The guest register for the late 1930s and early 1940s documents a steady stream of visitors to the lake, mostly from the Kansas City area.[26]

Although the number of cabins increased during the early years of the 1940s, the growth was not as quick or as great as either Turner or the men he had purchased the land from had hoped. By 1942, with money still due for the purchase of the land, Blackman and Wiest sued Turner and the Lake Placid Corporation, charging them with breach of contract and seeking to repossess the land with its improvements, including the lake and the cabins. Turner and his associates employed Carl Johnson, a prominent black Kansas City attorney (and later judge), to argue the case in the Morgan County Circuit Court. Early in 1943, the court decided in favor of the defendants, arguing that Turner and Sojourner had not violated the original contract because no time period, other than "reasonable," had been set to achieve its terms.[27]

Lake Placid boomed during the post–World War II era. A rapidly expanding economy in which a growing number of middle-class blacks shared and a persistent white racial recalcitrance that hung on to Jim Crowism throughout Kansas City, Missouri, and the Midwest fueled its growth. One of the people who began regularly visiting Lake Placid during the postwar period was Leonard Pryor, who first met Turner while dating the doctor's niece, Maxine Turner. Pryor had grown up in Topeka, Kansas, with a father who was an avid outdoorsman. He met Maxine while attending Washburn College in Topeka. After a stint in the navy during World War II, Pryor married Maxine, and the two of them became like surrogate children to the childless Turners.[28]

Among Leonard Pryor's fondest memories is the excitement of preparing for a late Friday night trip to the lake. Pryor would try to have the car packed, filled with gas, and ready to go so that he and the Turners could leave immediately after Dr. Turner got off of work. Sometimes it would be 10:00 P.M. before Turner finished his rounds at the hospital. Regardless of the time, Pryor recalls, when the doctor had fulfilled his responsibilities, the three of them would drive out of town on U.S. Highway 50, leaving the bright city lights behind and heading for the quiet peace of the Missouri Ozarks. "You could not find this kind of place in the inner city," Pryor remembers. "You are with nature and if you love nature, you would love [Lake Placid]." The trio always traveled well dressed, hoping that wearing fine clothes would reduce trouble with whites they might encounter if their car broke down.[29]

At Sedalia, Pryor and Turner would turn south on U.S. Highway 65 until they reached Missouri Highway 52, which took them east, through Cole Camp, to County Road FF. At County Road FF, they would stop the car, whereupon Turner or Pryor would get out, armed with a .410 shotgun, and lie across the right front fender with his feet resting on the running board.

Ready to shoot any game (usually rabbits) that might cross the road, the Turners and Pryor proceeded the last few miles to the lake. By the time they reached the lake, Pryor recalls, they had always killed enough game for at least one meal.[30]

Word spread within and beyond Kansas City that Lake Placid provided recreational opportunities for African Americans. Church groups began to visit, as did fraternities and sororities. Many blacks from St. Louis, most of them teachers, began coming to Lake Placid after World War II. Among the St. Louisans who bought property at the lake was Andrew S. Jackson, G. T. Bryant's brother-in-law. Jackson taught at Sumner High School, the oldest high school for African Americans west of the Mississippi River. Affectionately known as "Papa Jack," Jackson had been born on December 4, 1900, in Decatur, Illinois. He originally aspired to become a doctor but decided to become a teacher when it became clear that his family could not afford to send him to medical school. He moved to St. Louis in 1926. Like the vast majority of Missouri's African Americans during the 1930s and 1940s, Jackson worked and lived in a segregated world. He lived in a St. Louis neighborhood known as "the Ville," with other African American teachers, doctors, lawyers, preachers, and middle-class residents.[31]

With limited access to public places of recreation, other African American Sumner teachers and Ville residents began to visit Lake Placid. Among them were a number of couples who had formed a group known as "The Travelers," a "couples club" whose members had vacationed together at Kentucky Lake prior to their discovery of Lake Placid. William Wyatt, known to the club as "Chink," was one of the first of the group to buy a cabin at Lake Placid. Clarice Dreer Davis, the daughter of prominent community leader Herman Dreer, lived across the street from "Papa Jack" in the Ville and also taught for a while at Sumner High School. She visited Lake Placid many years before she and her husband, John, also a teacher, purchased a cabin there. She still remembers Lake Placid as "our little island of paradise."[32] Vivian DeShields Rasberry, another member of "The Travelers," also visited Lake Placid for many years before purchasing a cabin there. Rasberry liked to play cards (pinochle and poker), and she found in Lake Placid a place of peace, where she and her fellow "Travelers" could literally play cards all night long.[33]

The Fourth of July always attracted a large crowd of people to the lake. Children and adults swam off of a concrete dock just below Dr. Turner's cabin. Fishing and boating were also popular. Meals were taken communally, with all present gathering at Turner's cabin, called there by the ringing of a dinner bell that hung from a pole near the cabin's front door. During the evenings, prior to electricity arriving at the lake during the 1950s, adults sometimes danced to music provided by a local band brought in to add to the revelry. One of the favorite bands from the early years was known as the Whiskers Band, because all of its members wore artificial whiskers when they played. The Whiskers Band "played mostly 'Rag Time' music, but they could play any kind." Among the band members was Warren Cooper, who owned Cooper's Store in Stover, where many of the Lake Placid visitors bought groceries during their weekend trips. In later years, after the arrival of electricity, vacationers brought record players and their favorite records for listening and dancing. A flyer for a July 4, 1953, picnic at Lake Placid announced a full day of activities, including swimming, boating, dancing, fishing, card playing, singing, and "Clay Pidgeon Shooting."[34]

The annual "Lot Owners' Association" meeting, held on the third Sunday in August, provided another important gathering time. A barbecue capped the weekend's activity. Emma Jean Clark recalls a trip with Dr. and Mrs. Turner from Kansas City to the lake, during which she held a live lamb on her lap the entire way, unaware that the animal was to be slaughtered and barbecued at Lake Placid.[35]

Local whites were sometimes present when African Americans gathered at the lake. Occasionally, Jodie and Alta Wray and their daughters, Alice and Betty, came to the lake, always at the invitation of the Turners or K. E. Snell. Turner's providing medical treatment to Mrs. Wray and the couple's daughters sealed the friendship between the Wrays and the doctor.

During the late 1930s, Alta Wray began to experience gynecological problems that her family physician, the same Dr. Wiest from whom Turner had purchased the Lake Placid land, felt unable to treat adequately. Wiest recommended that she consult Turner during his next visit to the lake. She readily agreed. Subsequently, Dr. Turner visited the Wray home, examined Mrs. Wray, and encouraged her to be admitted to Wheatley-Provident Hospital in Kansas City, a privately operated hospital for African Americans established in 1914 by Dr. J. Edward Perry. The Turners transported Mrs. Wray to Kansas City in their car. Dr. Turner performed a hysterectomy on Mrs. Wray at Wheatley-Provident, then took her into his home for several weeks of recuperation before returning her to Morgan County. In December 1999, an ailing and frail Alta Wray, ninety-two years old, still smiled warmly at the mention of the Turners' names and remembered them as "good people—they were good people."[36]

When the Wrays' daughters, Alice and Betty, then teenagers, needed their tonsils removed a few years later, the family again turned to Dr. Turner. Alice and Betty remember that they had the utmost faith in Dr. Turner and found their stay at Wheatley-Provident to be a comfortable and reassuring experience. That pleasant experience notwithstanding, Betty developed complications from the surgery and became seriously ill. Turner cared for the young woman and nurtured her through a life-threatening illness. After Betty was discharged from the hospital, she and her mother stayed in the Turner home for *months,* so that the doctor could monitor her recovery.[37]

The Wrays are only three of many persons, both black and white, who remember the Turners with what can be described as adulation. Dr. Carl Peterson, a turn-of-the-century octogenarian, recalls being inspired by Turner's mentoring while serving a medical internship at General Hospital No. 2. He resolved to work for and with the man who treated him like a son. Not surprisingly, Dr. Turner often brought young doctors and nurses to Lake Placid for rest and recreation.[38]

Turner's involvement with Lake Placid diminished during the early 1960s. Plagued by health problems, he ended his active medical practice in 1963, after thirty-seven years in medicine. Dr. Turner's wife, Mayme, a longtime nurse at General Hospital No. 2, died in 1964. Friends and family members recall that her death left her husband dispirited and less interested in the lake. Dr. Turner died on January 19, 1966, at Wheatley-Provident Hospital, as the result of a spinal injury he had suffered two days earlier in an automobile accident at the intersection of Linwood and Benton in Kansas City. His last visit to Lake Placid had occurred one week prior to the accident.[39]

Lake Placid experienced a decline in prosperity during the early 1960s —a decline that paralleled Turner's decreased involvement with the resort. No doubt the absence of his forceful and charismatic personality had an impact. The successes of the civil rights movement in Kansas City and elsewhere also played a role. By the mid-1960s, the passage of public accommodations laws in the state and nation opened many public recreational places to African Americans. Mayme Hughes Rodgers recalls that her children often complained about being "required" to go to Lake Placid during this period, preferring instead the urban entertainments available to them.[40]

The lake area seemed to decline even further after K. E. Snell died in 1973 at the age of eighty-three. His death left the lake without a permanent resident and caretaker. Although elderly, Snell seemed to be in reasonably good health until his short, final illness. He was still a close friend of the Wray family. Although he had family members living in the Kansas City area, Snell chose to be buried in Morgan County. He had been a longtime member of Stover's First Baptist Church, but he asked that his final resting place be in the Methodists' Mount Pleasant Cemetery because it lay along the road to Lake Placid. He had said to many people that even in death he wanted to be where he could watch who came and went to "his" lake. Mrs. Wray and her daughters remember Snell fondly, as does Evelyn Cooper. She and her husband owned Cooper's Store in Stover where Snell did most of his shopping for nearly forty years. During an interview on January 19, 2000, Mrs. Cooper described Snell as "a very precious man. He traded with [us] and he had a wonderful personality. He was just good."[41]

The past two decades have witnessed renewed activity at Lake Placid with a newly energized commitment to carrying on the traditions begun there more than six decades ago. Second- and third-generation vacationers to the lake have picked up where their parents, grandparents, aunts, and uncles left off. Among the leaders in the revival of the lake has been Robert Wilson of Des Moines, Iowa, who served as president of the Lake Placid Lot Owners' Association through much of the 1990s. Wilson's father, Paul L., and his mother, Dorris D., also previously served as presidents of the association. Robert Wilson recalls that he first visited Lake Placid during the early 1950s, when his aunt, Ione Coleman, a former school nurse at Lincoln High School in Kansas City, purchased a cabin at the lake. Wilson remembers: "I enjoyed extended weekends and long periods during the summer visiting my aunt . . . In the old days kids dived and swam from Dr. Turner's pier, we had community meals, there were bells to call the kids to eat, there was a party line telephone system, kids from everywhere met kids from everywhere. If there was a utopian situation for the young this was as close as you might expect to get and still be among the living." In 1994, Wilson's parents deeded their lake property to him; he, in turn, carries on the Lake Placid tradition.[42]

Another Lake Placid property owner who carries on the tradition is Dr. Keith Turner, a psychiatrist who practices in Riverside, California. Dr. Turner's parents, L. C. "Chris" and Mrs. Turner, have been coming to the lake since the 1940s. Chris Turner, whose father was Dr. P. C. Turner's brother, is a retired postal worker from Topeka, Kansas. In recent years, Keith purchased a cabin next to the one owned by his parents; he has also recently bought some acreage adjoining the Lake Placid property and plays a leadership role among those trying to preserve the memory of the lake and its founders. In turn, his teenage son, Miles, has also taken an interest in Lake Placid.[43]

Among the younger persons to show a deep interest in Lake Placid are Craig Pryor and Renee Pryor Newton, the children of Leonard and Maxine Pryor. As a boy of five or six during the early 1970s, Craig would often accompany his parents and his sister to Lake Placid on summer weekends. He remembers it as being "always peaceful . . . being down there was timeless. There was no concern for what you had to do and when you had to do it and near the end of the weekend you hated to leave, but you knew you would come back again on another weekend." The young boy often rode his mini-bike, wandered through the woods, and played in the lake. "It was almost an unrestrictive 'Fantasy Land,'" he recalls. "Everyone was family down there so you knew your neighbors and as a child my parents never worried about me running around the area because they knew everybody."

Craig's sister, Renee, also fondly remembers Lake Placid, especially overnight trips there with friends from the Jack and Jills, a group formed in the pre–World War II period when African Americans did not have access to Kansas City's white YMCA facilities. Renee especially remembers the sounds of nature at Lake Placid—the frogs croaking and the summer night sound of nearby crickets. She now takes her adolescent daughter to the lake. Whatever happens to Lake Placid in the future, she hopes that it will always be "a quiet place, so people [who] want to be there can enjoy nature and not feel the pressure of the world."[44]

Much has changed in American society since the day, more than sixty years ago, that Mr. Sojourner and Dr. Turner purchased land for their "recreational center for colored people" in Morgan County. Lake Placid no longer serves as the hub of summer activity; African Americans can now go to the Lake of the Ozarks or any other place of public accommodation that they choose. Still, it is important to remember the society that created Lake Placid and the paradoxical side effects of racial cooperation that flowed from its presence in the Missouri Ozarks. Lake Placid remains what, in a sense, it has always been: a place of beauty that stands as a silent reminder of the ugliness of American racism. It stands, too, as a testimony to the perseverance, energy, and creativity of multiple generations of African Americans who refused to allow Jim Crow to deny them the opportunity to find recreation in peace.

Notes

1. "Contract for sale of land," in Case File No. 2479, Morgan County Circuit Court Records, April 1942 term, Morgan County Courthouse, Versailles, Missouri. This parcel of land included 271 acres in Morgan County and 75 acres in adjoining Benton County.

2. The story of segregation in Kansas City during this era is well told by Sherry Lamb Schirmer, "Landscape of Denial: Space, Status and Gender in the Construction of Racial Perceptions, 1900–1958" (Ph.D. diss., University of Kansas, 1995).

3. For more on the City Beautiful Movement, see William H. Wilson, *The City Beautiful Movement in Kansas City* (Columbia: University of Missouri Press, 1964),

and William S. Worley, *J. C. Nichols and the Shaping of Kansas City: Innovation in Planned Residential Communities* (Columbia: University of Missouri Press, 1990).

4. For more on P. C. Turner, see William H. Young and Nathan B. Young Jr., *Your Kansas City and Mine* (Kansas City: privately published, 1950). Also helpful is a late-in-life interview with Turner in the *Kansas City Call*, December 6, 1963.

5. Young and Young, *Your Kansas City and Mine, 58.* The Lake of the Ozarks came into being in 1931 and many Kansas City investors committed to Depression-era projects in the Osage River valley, south of the Lake Placid development. For a view of white resorts during the same time in southwest Morgan County, see Dwight Weaver, *History & Geography of Lake of the Ozarks, Volume Two* (Eldon, MO: Osage River Trails, 2008).

6. "Contract for sale of land."

7. Ibid.

8. Emma Jean Clark, interview by Gary Kremer and John Viessman, tape recording, November 10, 1999.

9. Regina Akers, "Welcoming Waters," *Kansas City Star Magazine,* July 26, 1992; Leonard Pryor, interviews by Kremer and Viessman, tape recordings, August 3, 17, September 1, December 1, 1999.

10. Robert H. Ferrell, *Truman and Pendergast* (Columbia: University of Missouri Press, 1999), 30.

11. Lawrence H. Larsen and Nancy J. Hulston, *Pendergast!* (Columbia: University of Missouri Press, 1997), 105. According to Dr. Carl Peterson, when Pendergast wanted to hide an associate who was having trouble with the law, he would ask Turner to admit him as a patient to General Hospital No. 2. Carl Peterson, interview by Kremer and Viessman, tape recording, August 17, 1999. Pryor, interviews, August 3, 17, September 1, 1999.

12. William L. Thompkins obituary, *Kansas City Call,* August 11, 1944.

13. Girard T. Bryant to Keith Turner, June 23, 1988, copy in possession of authors.

14. Young and Young, *Your Kansas City and Mine,* 104; *Kansas City Call,* June 6, 1941.

15. Pryor, interviews, August 3, 17, September 1, December 1, 1999.

16. Gary R. Kremer and Donald H. Ewalt Jr., *Missouri's Black Historic Sites: A Preliminary Survey of the State* (Jefferson City: Missouri Department of Natural Resources, 1980), 18, 26.

17. Betty Wray Curnutt and Alice Wray Jones, interview by Kremer and Viessman, tape recording, December 17, 1999.

18. *Stover Tri-County Republican,* May 21, 1937.

19. Clark, interview. See also work papers filed with the WPA in Record Group 69.5, Records of Works Progress Administration Projects, Morgan County, roll 856, National Archives, Washington, D.C.

20. Young and Young, *Your Kansas City and Mine, 97.*

21. Bryant to Turner.

22. Mayme Hughes Rodgers, interviews by Kremer and Viessman, tape recordings, December 12, 1997; September 22, 1999; Pryor, interview, August 17, 1999.

23. William Henry Houston death certificate, Missouri Department of Health, Division of Vital Records, Jefferson City; *Kansas City Call,* May 23, 1941.

24. Barbara Pullam Thompson, interviews by Kremer and Viessman, tape recordings, May 5, June 11, 1998.

25. Lake Placid Resort, Inc., incorporation papers, File No. 62981, Corporations Division, Office of the Secretary of State of Missouri, State Information Center, Jefferson City.

26. H. O. Cook, financial secretary, Lake Placid Lot Owners' Association, to Lake Placid Lot Owners, September 30, 1941; *Kansas City Call,* June 19, 1942; Lake Placid guest register, copy in possession of authors.

27. Case File No. 2479, Morgan County Circuit Court Records, April 1942 term.

28. Pryor, interviews, August 3, 17, September 1, December 1, 1999.

29. Ibid., September 1, 1999.

30. Ibid.

31. Andrew "Papa Jack" Jackson obituary, *St. Louis Post-Dispatch,* April 13, 1993. For information about the Ville, see Gary R. Kremer and Donald H. Ewalt Jr., "The Historian as Preservationist: A Missouri Case Study," *Public Historian* 3 (Fall 1981): 5–22.

32. John and Clarice Davis, interview by Kremer and Viessman, tape recording, August 22, 1999.

33. Vivian DeShields Rasberry, interview by Kremer and Viessman, tape recording, August 13, 1998.

34. All of the interviewees talked about Fourth of July celebrations. The most elaborate descriptions came from multiple interviews with Leonard Pryor. "July 4, 1953, at Lake Placid," copy in possession of authors.

35. Clark, interview.

36. Alta Wray, interview by Kremer and Viessman, tape recording, December 17, 1999.

37. Curnutt and Jones, interview.

38. Peterson, interview.

39. *Kansas City Call,* January 28–February 3, 1966; Dr. Percy C. Turner, obituary, memorial service program, January 23, 1966, copy in possession of authors.

40. Rodgers, interviews, December 12, 1997; September 22, 1999.

41. Evelyn Cooper, interview by Kremer and Viessman, tape recording, January 19, 2000.

42. Robert Wilson to Gary Kremer, e-mail, January 17, 2000.

43. Keith Turner and Miles Turner, interview by Kremer and Viessman, tape recording, August 22, 1999.

44. Craig Pryor, interview, January 18, 2000; Renee Pryor Newton, interview, January 12, 2000. Both interviews by Kremer and Viessman, tape recording.

Reflections on Public Welfare in Washington County, Missouri, 1939–1941

CLARENCE R. KEATHLEY

During the Great Depression in the 1930s, major changes occurred in social welfare legislation designed to assist people in need. Congress, for example, enacted the Social Security Act on August 14, 1935. President Franklin D. Roosevelt signed this landmark in social legislation on the same date.[1] The Missouri General Assembly passed a related act two years later, establishing the State Social Security Commission of Missouri to administer the Old Age Assistance, Aid to Dependent Children, General Relief, and Child Welfare Services programs.[2] Federal and state agencies developed written policies to implement the legislation that had a profound effect upon the lives of needy Missourians. An examination of the welfare activities in Washington County provides insight into the experiences of county welfare agents in Missouri.

The program of the Washington County welfare office progressed with the aid of a county court (with limited funds), an advisory County Social Security Commission, the county superintendent of schools, a public health unit staffed by two registered nurses, a child welfare worker, the federal Forest Service office in Potosi staffed by two men, a Farm Security Administration agent, a Business and Professional Women's Organization in Potosi, other state and federal agencies and organizations, and a supportive community. During the Depression years, the welfare office provided help for the poor, ill and aged, the unemployed tiff miners, strikers, farmers, and underprivileged children.

Figure 23. Mining tiff by hand.
CRESWELL FAMILY PAPERS, STATE HISTORICAL SOCIETY-ROLLA

Washington County appeared one of the most economically depressed areas in Missouri. Located in the Ozark region of southeast Missouri, Washington County's rich mineral deposits and other natural resources encouraged settlement of the area. The first county seat, named St. George in 1813, later became Potosi, to honor the silver-mining town in Bolivia. Potosi's location at the center of the barite production area led to its recognition as the barite capital of the world.[3] The deposits of barite, usually referred to locally as tiff, are extensive in Washington County and probably the largest in the world.[4] Mining of tiff in the area began in 1850.[5]

By the early 1900s, several thousand people engaged in tiff mining in the county. Although employing many workers, tiff mining provided little economic security for its workers, but it also created a need for public welfare services. Company houses, little more than shells with dirt floors, sprang up quickly for the miners. Many people had no work, but the influx of people into the county looking for work during the Depression years complicated community problems and increased unemployment in the county. Some former residents returned from the city having been unable to find jobs there. Workers hoped to gain employment in tiff mining, but this industry was declining. Those moving to the country usually had little education or lacked skills for the limited number of jobs available during the Depression. And so, people faced immediate need for food, clothing, and improved shelter. From the mid-1930s to the early 1940s, the *St. Louis Post-Dispatch* and the *St. Louis Globe-Democrat* gave extensive coverage to conditions in Washington County and the plight of the tiff miners. In 1939, Henry B. Lieberman, writing for *Ken* magazine, described the living conditions among the Creole tiff mining families living in the Old Mines community of Washington County:

> When a miner takes his place on someone else's land he and his family are given a ramshackle shanty in which to live rent-free, if one is available. Hundreds of families are now living as many as eight and ten in one of these one, two and three-room shacks—bundles or log slabs, some without floors, all without gas, electricity and sanitation facilities of any kind, pasted up with oiled newspapers to keep out the wind and rain. In these huts furnished with crude pine beds, nail keg chairs and huge wood-burning stoves which serve for cooking and heating, the average Creole family lives on a steady diet of fried dough-bread, beans and potatoes. A few of the miners have truck gardens, and the diet of the Creoles is also varied occasionally with Squirrels and quail shot in the woods.[6]

A miner decided the number of hours he wanted to work. Short hours intensified his poverty. Others labored hard, farmed on the side and, by comparison, prospered. The rise in barite demand brought an end to the tiff miner's way of life when mechanized mining entered Washington County in 1924. The greatest boost in the industry occurred in 1926 when barite began to be used as a weighing agent in oil-well drilling. Drilling demanded immense quantities.[7]

During the 1930s, the tiff mining industry suffered from the severely depressed economy. Employers again increased the use of hand mining to provide jobs that mechanization had taken away. However, unemployment remained high.[8] As a result, by July 1939, approximately one-fourth of the people in Washington County received General Relief, Old Age Assistance, surplus commodities, or child welfare services. At that time, tiff miners voted to strike for higher pay and improved working conditions. Labor leaders from outside the county encouraged them in their demands. Union members in various communities of the tiff mining area of the county served on local committees. These committees had earlier been asked to recommend the families living in their community that they believed to be in need of help.

One morning the chairmen of the county union committees stood in a semicircle in front of the welfare office. The spokesman for the group at one end of the line said to the director, "We hear you are not going to use our committees anymore." When asked, "Who told you that?" he turned to the man next to him and said, "He did." This routine continued down the line to the last man who responded, "No, I didn't."[9] Thus ended the confrontation.

In the early 1940s, a legal decision had a profound effect on those engaged in hand tiff mining. The International Union of Mine, Mill and Smelter Workers, Local 113, affiliated with the Congress of Industrial Organizations, filed charges. The National Labor Relations Board through the acting regional director for the Fourteenth Region (St. Louis, Missouri) issued its complaint October 20, 1940, against respondents R. A. Blount, Hearst B. Blount, Lonnie Flinn, and Eunice Simpson, of Potosi. This action alleged the respondents had engaged in unfair labor practices affecting commerce. They had violated specific sections of the National Labor Relations Act, Sec. 49, Stat. 449. Landowners and union employees had engaged in hand mining and hauling tiff at the Paw Paw Patch, Richwoods, Missouri. This case, no. C-1817, was resolved December 16, 1941. Two key issues decided in the case were (1) the union employees engaged in hand mining and hauling tiff at the Paw Paw Patch, Richwoods, had been employees of the landowners; and (2) the landowners had failed to bargain collectively with the union. The impact of this decision resulted in a decline of hand tiff mining and hauling in the county.[10] As tiff mining began to recover, mechanization of the industry increased. In early 1942, about twenty strip mines and washers operated in the county.[11] World War II and the remaining decade saw final transition from hand mining to mechanized mining and washing.[12] Changes in work and wages also caused unemployment.

In spite of early assistance programs, needy families still received small and inadequate relief orders and surplus food commodities. Miners and their families dramatized their plight by holding group meetings, parading on the main street in Potosi, and camping on the courthouse square. One Saturday afternoon, word reached the district welfare supervisor, John F. Pletz, preparing to leave on vacation, and Clarence Keathley, the secretary-director, that the sheriff wanted to see them. They went to his office. Fifteen to twenty tiff miners followed them into the office and sat on the floor. At that point the sheriff said, "These people want to talk with you." Then he left.

The miners demanded relief orders that day and insisted they would stay until they got them. The explanation by Pletz and Keathley, that relief funds allocated to the county for the month had been spent and additional orders could not be written, did not satisfy them. Pletz called the state administrator, George I. Haworth, by phone and explained the situation. Haworth stated that the request for additional funds could not be approved. At that

Figure 24. George Haworth, administrator of the Missouri Social Security Commission.
STATE HISTORICAL SOCIETY-COLUMBIA

point the supervisor handed the phone to the spokesman for the miners group to present their case. He convinced the administrator of their plight and need for food. The phone call resulted in securing an additional allotment of funds. Pletz and Keathley proposed that the orders would be issued the following Monday. The group insisted orders be written that evening, saying some families had no food and could not wait until Monday. The question arose as to which families needed assistance immediately. The tiff miners proposed that a committee from their group could decide, as they knew the people. They were asked what they would do if all the people did not agree with their decisions. The plan suggested by Pletz and Keathley proved to be acceptable.[13] Cooperation among county and state welfare agents helped resolve many such conflicts.

Police and a representative of the local union sometimes attended county agency meetings. Edward Richeson, a visitor (later called caseworker) on the county welfare office staff and a resident of the county, knew many of the union members: He attended the mass meetings of the union and reported the discussions to the secretary-director. This kept the secretary abreast of developments and proved helpful in planning with office staff and the county social security commission. Chairman of the commission, William H. Martin, station agent for the Missouri Pacific Railroad at Irondale, Missouri, appeared well known and highly respected in the county. His advice and counsel in dealing with local problems proved most beneficial. Through the efforts of county, state, and federal agencies, the plight of the tiff miners improved.

Those people employed in agriculture, another major sector of Washington County's economy, also needed relief and aid. Palmer, a small community west of Potosi, had once been a thriving mining town but the Forest Service had acquired the land. In an effort to help county farmers, the Palmer Project developed to relocate families to better farming land.[14] More fertile soil near Palmer helped farmers improve their living conditions. The Forest Service offered to help people build new houses and farm buildings. The Farm Security Administration, in keeping with its 1937 directive to help low-income farm families, agreed to provide loans and give consultation. The county welfare agency assisted those who met eligibility requirements. Representatives of the three agencies developed an interview questionnaire to help plan with each family involved. The Forest Service staff in Potosi made the initial approach. Even though the relocation sites did not extend more than five or ten miles from Palmer, some families resisted the move because of emotional ties to the home place and the community cemetery. Those who did relocate benefited from agency cooperation in providing aid.

Young workers first entering the employment market during the Great Depression faced hardship. Inexperienced and unskilled, these men could not find jobs in areas where employment opportunities already were scarce. On April 5, 1933, President Franklin D. Roosevelt established a new program of emergency conservation work aimed at this national situation. Two weeks later, the Civilian Conservation Corps (CCC) was organized and the first men enrolled. In Missouri, officials named the Relief and Reconstruction Commission as the certifying agency. It held this responsibility until the State Social Security Commission took over its duties. The CCC helped unmarried men between the ages of eighteen and twenty-five by giving them work. Each county received a quota allotment for sending young men to camp. The county welfare office processed the applications, giving preference to those receiving assistance. Young men from nonassistance families completed quotas. The office also arranged transportation to Camp Berryman, Company 3733, located eighteen miles west of Potosi. The number of young men enrolling each time depended on the number needed to fill the county quota.

The camp doctor gave complete physical examinations for each applicant. Those enrolled received a modest monthly salary of $30.00. Out of that some young men also made allotments to their families. In addition to lodging, clothing, educational programs, employment, and medical and dental services while in camp, they received a well-founded work program and valuable training. Major work projects included erecting telephone lines, building roads (still in use), and fire lookout towers; planting white oak, pine, and walnut trees; general Forest Service work in several hundred acres of standing timber; and fighting forest fires prevalent in those days. Lester R. Hogoboom, educational adviser, developed a comprehensive program, and R. D. Crawford, superintendent of the Forest Service personnel office in the Courtois Ranger District, along with his staff, planned and supervised the work program.[15]

Everett V. Mead, commanding officer of the Berryman CCC Camp in 1940,[16] had attended Wentworth Military Academy, Lexington, Missouri,[17] and the University of Nebraska-Lincoln.[18] He understood the value of learning skills. Between one-fourth and one-third of the Washington County boys could neither read nor write. Their CCC camp work experience, coming just before World War II, undoubtedly helped these young men in military service.

Besides benefiting from employment, CCC camp workers enjoyed leisure time together. When the county welfare office staff took the boys to CCC camp, they visited with staff members from other county offices to exchange ideas and experiences, and engaged in light-hearted conversation. A worker from one county bet Mead a carton of cigarettes that Missouri would defeat Nebraska that year in football, win the conference football title, and Paul Christman, quarterback of the Missouri team, would make All American. On the next trip to the camp she collected the bet.[19]

The CCC camp at Berryman provided the setting for a most successful group dinner meeting. Staff of the Washington County office planned the event as an interagency meeting to exchange ideas and improve services. CCC enrollees, under the supervision of their main chef, prepared and served the dinner. One hundred and fourteen persons attended, including the Washington County welfare staff, related agency personnel, public officials, and guests from Washington and adjoining counties. Guest speaker, Bill Silkett, of the Bureau of Agricultural Economics, secretary of the Land-Use Planning Board, United States Department of Agriculture, spoke on "Cooperation of Agency Programs."[20] Similar interagency staff meetings occurred in other rural counties during the Depression when most agency programs were relatively new. They helped staffs get acquainted and to learn more about agency program organization, about becoming more knowledgeable of services provided, and about making appropriate referrals to other agencies. Of course, this proved beneficial in providing more effective services to the clientele.

The plight of underprivileged children in Missouri led to legislation for their aid before the Depression. In 1913 and 1921, the state authorized foster homes, and later a state home, for neglected and homeless children. However, inadequate funding plagued these programs. In addition, many children of low-income families received no aid under those legislative acts. The state Social Security Act established the Aid to Dependent Children program to provide financial grants to families with children in need under the age of sixteen. For some families in Washington County, receipt of this aid helped children complete their high school education.[21]

The first applications for this aid program were processed in the late 1930s. Unmarried parents, especially the mother, faced stigma by the community. Some thought unmarried parents should not receive assistance. An honored occurrence, Dr. Catherine Lenroot, chief, U.S. Children's Bureau, Washington, D.C., visited the Washington County Welfare Office in Potosi. While there she talked with a young unmarried mother who had her baby with her. Pleased to see how an Aid to Dependent Children grant and counseling by the child welfare worker had helped the family, Dr. Lenroot commented that the baby appeared one of the best developed and healthiest children she had seen. Under this program, an average of forty-one needy families in Washington County received $18.92 a month in 1939 for the care of their children.[22]

Marcia Chadwick, the county child welfare worker under the Child Welfare program, provided for the protection and care of homeless, dependent, and neglected children. She also helped children in danger of becoming delinquent, and those not benefiting in the Aid to Dependent Children program. Chadwick worked toward a full case program for normal children, adjudged by juvenile courts to be neglected, abandoned, or ill-treated and needing state guardianship in the state home for children.[23]

Inadequate educational facilities and poor school attendance also deprived many Washington County children. In 1938, Mary Bolland Taussig wrote a thesis on "Factors Influencing School Attendance in Washington County, Missouri." Her study included a brief history and description of the community. It described the educational facilities and the laws affecting school attendance and the problems of their enforcement. Taussig also noted the relationships between poor school attendance and certain social and economic factors. Four school districts represented the tiff mining area in the study. On the basis of information collected, Taussig concluded that (1) statistics for Washington County showed the mining area had the highest illiteracy rate in the state; (2) a small sample of one hundred children made up of fifty regular and fifty irregular attendants, showed that poor attendance brought retardation in school; and (3) the degree of social and economic distress correlated with school attendance.[24]

One of the major problems that befell public welfare in Washington County, especially during the Depression period, concerned irregular school attendance. The average daily school attendance in the tiff mining area related, at least in part, to the children who helped mine tiff. County superintendent of schools Fred Cole enlisted the help of the schoolteachers. Fortunately, Washington County was one of the few rural counties in the state to have a professionally trained child welfare worker as a member of the county welfare office staff. In addition, the county was one of the few rural areas selected to have a demonstration public health unit. Chadwick and two registered nurses assigned to the county unit played an important role in improving school attendance. The county prosecuting attorney cooperated by enforcing the school attendance laws. Their efforts reinforced those of agency staff that held regular interviews with the families.

A county school lunch program encouraged regular school attendance. Mae Burford, a local public health nurse, supervised this program, with the help of Works Progress Administration (WPA) and National Youth Administration (NYA) federal employees. The State Social Security Commission furnished a wide variety of surplus food commodities allocated for the school lunch program. Teachers, school board members, and community persons requested commodity distribution by the county welfare office in Potosi. In some schools, families with children donated food for the program. In one district, the children asked to have school during Christmas vacation so they could eat hot lunches. Nearly all of the public and private schools in Washington County participated in the program. Children learned to eat foods they had not eaten previously. The well-prepared lunches contributed to nutritional education and good health of the children and encouraged school attendance.

In addition to county, state, and federal programs, concerned private citizens joined the effort to aid children in Washington County. A distinguished churchman, Bishop William Scarlett of Christ Church Cathedral in St. Louis, Missouri, was one such individual. An outstanding leader with wide influence, he visited Potosi and other communities in Washington County, consulted community leaders and observed the needs of the people first hand. He worked in cooperation with the county welfare office, and members of his parish collected, donated, and delivered much-needed clothing and shoes to Washington County's needy children.

Other citizens focused their attention on the Old Age Assistance program. County welfare officers had a good working relationship with Wilson Bell, the editor of the *Potosi Independent Journal.* Bell, later elected as state treasurer, showed special interest in assisting the elderly while campaigning for office. As state treasurer, he respected agency policy and problems while considering requests made to him. In 1939, over $84,000 went to Washington County elderly under this program.[25]

The General Relief program provided financial help to the unemployed. The Missouri legislature appropriated funds for this program of the Social Security Commission. The commission allocated funds to county welfare offices based on the number of persons receiving General Relief. County officers wrote relief orders based on the number of persons in each household. The relief orders could be traded for food at the local grocery store. As a rule, the merchants helped the families get the most for their money. Likewise, the Social Security Commission allocated surplus food commodities to the county welfare offices. Then, the county offices distributed the items, such as butter, cabbages, potatoes, peanut butter, dried milk, oatmeal, dried beans, whole wheat flour, and fruits in season. Nutrition training and recipes helped ensure wise use of these foods. A full-time commodity clerk, Fannie Belle Stamper, supervised the school lunch program and the distribution of surplus food commodities to families. To facilitate handling of the food, the agency issued identification cards to eligible families and individuals. When clients, often women, called for commodities in Potosi, they presented their cards. Occasionally, when unable to locate their identification card, they would say, "We forgot and left our Modesty-Card at home."[26]

The county welfare office, in cooperation with related agencies and organizations, provided certain types of health service. Trachoma, a contagious eye disease caused by poor sanitation and medical care, occurred often in Washington County. Instructions and referral for treatment helped to lessen this problem. Public health nurses held clinics in the schools to identify children with trachoma. The Missouri Trachoma Hospital at Rolla, under the administration of the State Board of Health, provided diagnostic service, instructions, and treatment. The county welfare office arranged transportation for the patients to and from the hospital. This service extended over a period of many years.

Another health problem again related to ignorance of proper nutrition. One case that drew the attention of the county welfare office dramatized the need for medical care and information. A young couple brought their infant to the office. He appeared badly dehydrated and skeleton-like. The secretary-director phoned the public health nurse. She came and examined the boy, called a St. Louis hospital and made arrangements for the child's admission. The parents took the boy to the hospital immediately and after treatment he fully recovered. Public health information and referral services helped improve health conditions in the county.

The administration of these diverse programs early suffered from a lack of staff. However, the county welfare agency began to employ additional caseworkers and clerical staff. The National Youth Administration provided clerical help on a part-time basis. Reba Choate, assistant to Director Arthur Nebel, Division of Public Assistance, State Social Security Commission, spent time in the county office. She helped to evaluate the administrative situation and to recruit needed staff members. George I. Haworth met with the Washington County Social Security Commission and helped to evaluate possible office sites for distribution of aid.

Due to the large number of people receiving relief and surplus food commodities, agency staff met clients at different locations in the county. Staff members often arrived at the location by 7:30 A.M. and found people waiting to be helped. Agency staff wrote relief and commodity orders using a preplanned list for eligible clients. Staff assisted new applicants in filing applications.

Sometimes irate and demanding persons confronted staff members; occasionally angry clients threatened workers. One group of men demanded that Leavy Thomas, county welfare office worker, write relief orders for them. She had completed writing orders for those on her list and had used all the order forms in her book. She tried to explain why she could not write their orders. As they continued their demand, she finally gave them paper and said, "You may write your own orders." This ended the confrontation, with no orders written.[27]

The need to review the caseload soon became evident. This resulted in deleting the names of persons no longer living in the county, the employed or the deceased. However, the number of applicants for Old Age Assistance, Aid to Dependent Children, and General Relief enlarged due to the increase in unemployment. Some applicants for Old Age Assistance had difficulty securing the age verification required. Members of the Catholic Church had no problem obtaining a baptismal certificate to verify their age.

Other problems faced the county welfare office. State agency policy required that persons receiving assistance present a doctor's statement that no one in the household could ably work. People went by a local doctor's office to secure the statement that did not give a diagnosis nor state why the persons could not work. The secretary-director discussed this with a doctor who recognized the problem, but giving the brief statement saved time in handling a large number of people. Of course, this failed to solve the problem. The county welfare staff had to secure additional medical information or work history.

In 1941, several coordinated committees developed a master plan to study the economic and social problems in Washington County. Governor Forrest C. Donnell appointed the committee to make the study. Hubert Harris of the Social Security Commission, Jefferson City, chaired the Committee on Immediate Relief. The study culminated in a meeting in the governor's office, April 14, 1941, with Washington County committee members and representatives of tiff miners in attendance. Governor Donnell presided and gave all participants full opportunity to present their views. Secretary-Director Keathley presented a report entitled "Social Problems of Washington County." The report helped serve as a background for the group discussion.[28]

Public welfare in Washington County during 1939–1941 appeared similar to other counties in the state, but differences existed due to special economic, health, and social problems. Social programs during these times helped people improve their quality of life. Residents raised their standards of living by taking advantage of opportunities to improve life for themselves and their children. Food and General Relief aid helped meet immediate needs and improved nutritional standards. School attendance improved through the Aid to Dependent Children program. And the school lunch program gave children meals while teaching them about nutrition. Health care improved from the efforts of local doctors and the public health unit. The enrollment of young men in the Civilian Conservation Corps provided the necessities of life, such as food, clothing, and shelter and medical and dental care. In addition, the young men received educational opportunities, discipline, supervision, and work experience. Each county and city in Missouri had public welfare agencies during the Great Depression. These reflections on the work in Washington County, however, provide a glimpse of life in one area of Missouri during the difficult years of the 1930s and early 1940s.

Notes

1. *Compilation of the Social Security Laws* (Washington, DC: U.S. Government Printing Office, n.d.), Volume 1, p.v.
2. Fern Boan, *A History of Poor Relief Legislation and Administration in Missouri* (Chicago: University of Chicago Press, 1941), 122.
3. George W. Showalter, *Potosi, Missouri Bicentennial 1763–1963, A Bicentennial Scrapbook* (Potosi, MO: Independent-Journal reprint edition, 1975).
4. Allen W. Clark, *The Story of Barytes*, Illustrations by O. E. Berninghaus (St. Louis: Delore Baryta Company, J. C. Finck Mineral Milling Company, 1920), 1–2.
5. Heyward M. Wharton, "Barite Ore Potential of Four Tailings Ponds in the Washington County Barite District, Missouri," Missouri Geological Survey and Water Resources, *Report of Investigations, Number 53* (Rolla, MO, 1972), 6.
6. Henry R. Lieberman, "Les Miserables in Missouri," *Ken*, March 9, 1939, 26.
7. Jo Buford, "Underground Treasures, The Story of Mining in Missouri," *Official Manual of the State of Missouri, 1977–1978* (Jefferson City: Von Hoffman Press, Inc., n.d.), 23–29.
8. Wharton, "Barite Ore Potential," 10.
9. This personal experience of the author, then secretary-director, with union leaders illustrates the value of asking an appropriate question to resolve a problem.
10. 37 National Labor Relations Board No. 107, 662–673.
11. Wharton, "Barite Ore Potential," 10.
12. Showalter, *Potosi.*
13. This experience shows how representatives of the State Social Security Commission of Missouri at the county, district, and state office level worked together and resolved, to the satisfaction of tiff miners, a problem posed by the Washington County sheriff.
14. Clarence Keathley, "The Palmer Project, An Example of Coordinated Agency Action at the Local Level" (paper prepared for extension course, Washington University, George Warren Brown School of Social Work, St. Louis, April 23, 1943).
15. Missouri, State Social Security Commission of Missouri, "Some Backgrounds of Public Welfare In Missouri With Special Reference to Public Relief," *Aiding Needy Persons in Missouri* (Jefferson City, 1939), 10. Information about CCC Company 3733, Berryman, Missouri, in a publication loaned to the author by Charles F. Kitchen, Ironton, Missouri. Kitchen, from Graniteville, Missouri, served as an assistant leader in Company 3733 in the late 1930s.
16. Carmelita S. Ryan, National Archives and Records Service, Washington, DC, to the author, April 7, 1983.
17. Mrs. Ryland Hough, registrar, Wentworth Military Academy, Lexington, to the author, May 2, 1983.
18. Shirley Thomsen, University of Nebraska-Lincoln, to the author, April 22, 1983.
19. This incident illustrates how staff members from county welfare offices, who accompanied young men to the Berryman CCC Camp, developed a good working relationship with administrative staff at the camp.
20. "Washington County Organizations Meet," Potosi *Washington County News*, July 31, 1941.
21. Boan, *History of Poor Relief*, 120–122.

22. Missouri, State Social Security Commission, *Public Assistance in Missouri: A Biennial Report of the State Social Security Commission 1939–1940* (Jefferson City, 1941), 83 and 97.

23. Missouri, State Social Security Commission, *Manual of Instructions* (Jefferson City, 1938), 7–8.

24. Mary Bolland Taussig, "Factors Influencing School Attendance in Washington County, Missouri" (Master's thesis, Washington University, St. Louis, 1938).

25. Social Security Commission, *Public Assistance,* 74.

26. The identification cards resembled the identification cards carried in billfolds or purses today.

27. An experience related to the author by Leavy Thomas, visitor in the Washington County welfare office, to illustrate how one worker resolved a difficult problem.

28. Clarence Keathley, "Social Problems in Washington County, Missouri" (unpublished report, April 14, 1941).

Agricultural Change in the Western Ozarks

MILTON D. RAFFERTY

The western Ozarks, and most particularly the section known as the Springfield Plain, is designated as the Ozark Highland Section of the East and Central General Farming and Forest Region.[1] Because of conditions of terrain, accessibility, and marketing, Ozark agriculture has been marginal and many experiments have been tried. While an unusually large number of agricultural systems have been practiced, it is apparent to even the casual observer that great changes have occurred toward standardization and elimination of many specialty crops. Cursory inquiries into evolution of the present farming systems of the Springfield Plain revealed that the historical agricultural geography of the area was piecemeal and incomplete. Eight counties in the vicinity of Springfield were selected for more detailed study: Christian, Dade, Dallas, Greene, Lawrence, Polk, Stone, and Webster.[2]

The first settlers from Tennessee and Kentucky entered the area in the early 1800s and Springfield, soon to become the leading city, was founded in 1830. True agriculture in the pioneer stage developed slowly, partly because the markets were inaccessible and partly because the first settlers were as much woodsmen as cultivators. The cultivation of crops was an adjunct to hunting, fishing, and the gathering of honey, berries, nuts, fruits, and greens from the forest.

Compared to the hardships of pioneer life on the plains, the life of the Ozark pioneer must have been relatively easy. A log house could be erected in a very few days. An unlimited supply of game and fish was close at hand. Pigeon, wild turkey, and deer were plentiful. An abundance of mast and prairies of bluestem grass provided for the cattle and hogs so that it was unnecessary to cultivate more than a few acres of basic crops.

Statistics for the very early years are unavailable. As for the number of livestock, a farmer's own account would have been an approximation, for practically all stock ran at large on the open range. Hogs, in particular, were killed for meat according to the need with no accounting expected.[3] Gradually, livestock came to be "marked," usually with a cut in the ear, to denote ownership.

Corn, a staple for man and beast, became the most important crop grown by the first settlers. They grew wheat for white bread and biscuits. Because of the isolated area and the primarily subsistence economy, nearly all the pioneer farms produced some tobacco, flax, hemp, and cotton for domestic use. The women spun wool or cotton for clothing. As late as 1869, Lawrence County farmers grew sixty-six bales of cotton.[4]

General farming began about 1870. By that time much of the area had become well settled and the native grass, which had been an important factor in the agriculture of the area, began to disappear. Prior to this, it had been the custom to burn over the prairies and woodlands each spring. As the country became more heavily settled and fenced, this custom had to be abandoned. A thick growth of underbrush, which had been kept down by the annual fires, then sprang up in the open fields and choked out the grass. At the same time, settlement and cultivation began to reduce the acreage of the natural range to a marked degree.

A second important factor in general farming, the comparatively cheap railroad transportation, became available after 1870. Prior to that time, the only possible commercial agricultural product was livestock, which could be driven north to markets on the Osage and Missouri Rivers. Railroad transportation meant that wheat, corn, and other grain, as well as livestock, could be produced for market.

The transition from subsistence and livestock farming to general farming occurred quickly, as indicated by the rapid adoption of improved machinery for cultivation. In 1868, for example, the firm of McGregor and Murray in Springfield sold more than 700 "turning" plows.[5]

The rapid shift toward general farming was most pronounced in the immediate vicinity of Springfield because of the smoother topography, better soils, and better transportation facilities. Grain growing proved profitable, especially on the "red soils" of the Springfield Plain. In the interior Ozarks, residents practiced general farming in the valleys where conditions were favorable, but in the hilly parts the farms continued to be of subsistence or livestock types. By 1900 general farming dominated the agricultural system in the Springfield Plain, and it was regarded as a desirable and secure form of agriculture, as witnessed by one observer's remarks:

> Greene County is especially blessed in not being a region where the farmer has to place his reliance almost wholly on any one particular crop. He can choose for his specialty, if he so wills, almost any standard crop of the temperate zone. Or he can have crops of any and all grains, fruits and vegetables. Thus, with more than one string to his bow, he can feel sure that if disaster befalls one or two of his crops, the others will hold him safe from harm.[6]

General farming and its diversity of crops and livestock led to smaller farms, especially in the area near Springfield. A 1915 county history stated that "small farms and diversity, of crops" well could be adopted as the motto of Greene County.[7] Another commentary noted the extent to which this subdivision of land had progressed by 1915:

> Take a late map of the county, which shows the names of each land owner, and the size of his holdings, and you will be surprised to see how far this subdividing of land has already gone. In one government township, taken haphazardly from the map, I find one hundred and forty-four farms. Of these, ninety-six, exactly two thirds of all, are tracts of eighty acres or less. Fifty-one are forty-acre tracts.[8]

Of course, a few large farms existed at that time, and some large timbered tracts were held by individual owners, but the tendency toward smaller farm units is evident. As the more intensive use of the land occurred there was a natural increase in land values.

Between 1890 and 1900 the number of farms in the eight county area around Springfield increased from 13,540 to 23,311 an addition of nearly 10,000 farms.[9] For the next twenty years the number of farms remained fairly stable, but a marked decline occurred after World War II.

The chief field crops were corn and wheat. Corn, used primarily as livestock feed, at all times exceeded other grains in acreage. The soil of the river bottoms and the upland prairies were regarded as emphatically "corn land."[10] Wheat was the standard cash crop, although unusual weather conditions, chinch bugs, or Hessian flies sometimes caused reduced yields. Oats, barley, feed sorghum, and forage crops provided livestock feed.

Cattle and hogs, along with horses and mules, were raised widely; however, sheep were not as popular as in earlier years when they supplied wool for homespun clothing. The general farmer usually kept two types of cattle: those raised for meat and those raised for milking purposes. In

Figure 25. Railroads, dairies, apples, and strawberries in the Ozarks.
POSTCARD, POSTMARKED 1936, KALEN AND MORROW COLLECTION

the "cream can" stage of dairying the general farmer could obtain a profit from a few dairy cows, and by "stall feeding" a few head of beef stock he could add to his income. Hogs, raised in large numbers for a time, were fattened for market and profitably sold.

Considerable improvement in methods of production took place in the era of general farming. Smaller farms called for greater care and more intensive cultivation of cropland and improved livestock husbandry. Higher land prices and smaller acreages per farm required a greater per acre yield in crops and livestock.

During the pioneer stage of agriculture when land was plentiful and cheap, maintaining land fertility received little attention. It was common practice to tear down log stables and move them to new locations when the accumulation of manure made it impossible to use the stable. It was easier to move the stables than the manure.[11] With the adoption of more intensive land use farmers hauled manure to fields to be spread as fertilizer.

The general farm retained its position of leadership until the 1940s when the dairy farm became the leading type of farm. In the period 1930 to 1964 the general farm fell from first-place to fourth-place ranking in number of farms. The decline from 11,172 in 1930 to 420 in 1964 constituted a decrease of 10,742 general farms.

Several forces contributed to the decline of general farming. Crop specialty farming introduced in the 1890s attracted some farmers from general farming to the production of apples, peaches, strawberries, or tomatoes. Shortly after 1900 even more farmers turned to dairy farming. In recent years many general farmers have switched to livestock farming, often in conjunction with part-time employment in nonfarm jobs. However, the overriding forces contributing to the decline of general farming have been the improvements in transportation, organization, and integration for the marketing of agricultural products throughout the United States. Increasing area specialization and the economies of large-scale production have made general farming largely uncompetitive.

The decline of general farming was witnessed by the decrease in wheat and corn acreages, crops that were largely products of general farms. Data from the U.S. Census of Agriculture illustrates that, in the eight counties, there were substantial declines in corn and wheat acreages by 1940, and by 1964 corn and wheat acreages had declined, respectively, to 17.6 percent and 19 percent of the 1910 levels.[12]

As general farming began to decline, fruit growing increased in importance. From the earliest time to the present, apples and peaches have been the most popular and most successfully grown fruits. Apples were grown so widely in small household orchards that the Ozarks had earned the title, "Land of the Big Red Apple," even before the coming of the railroads and the development of commercial orchards.[13] The "Knous," "Huntsman's Favorite," and "Ben Davis" apples became popular in the early orchards.[14] Most of the peaches were seedling or "Indian peaches," the kind that come up where peach pits are dropped. Seedling peaches grew in fence rows, in roadside ditches, among apple trees, and around the back doors of farmhouses where the pits had been discarded. Seedling peaches are common today. Even though they vary greatly in size and taste they are sometimes picked and eaten in season.

Railroad officials encouraged fruit growing. During the 1880s and 1890s thousands of trees were planted, mainly along the railways in the western part of the Missouri and Arkansas Ozarks.[15] Large orchards were set out in 1892 near Seymour in the southern part of Webster County.[16] However, a major stimulus to fruit growing came in 1901, when the apple season produced an extra good crop. Because of drought, farm crops were generally a failure that year, and the farmers found the small household orchards an important source of income. Interest in apple culture increased, and the orchard acreage was greatly extended. By 1905 orchards of from 500 to 2,000 and 3,000 trees, two and three years old, became common.

Plantings were numerous near Seymour in Webster County, in the vicinity of Springfield and Republic in Greene County, and around Marionville in Lawrence County. About twenty years later, in 1923, within a radius of six miles of Marionville, there were 2,500 acres in commercial apple orchards capable of producing 100,000 barrels of apples.[17] In Greene County, orchards of 40 and 100 acres were common, while those containing from 200 to 400 acres were not unusual.[18]

The period of important acreage and production of fruit was between 1910 and 1940. While large orchards were set out prior to 1910, most of the trees did not reach bearing age until after that time. By 1940 the majority of the orchards had fallen into disuse, or had been cleared and converted to other uses.

During the "apple era" much of the crop went by rail to St. Louis and points east. Apple barns were built close by railroad sidings where apples were sorted and graded before shipment. Many of the larger fruit farms also operated cider presses. Commercial "evaporators" produced dried apples and peaches on a large scale, thereby saving year-end surpluses just as pioneer families had saved their surpluses by sun-drying them on the roof of a shed.

Fruit growers associations were established as a means of dealing with the problem of marketing and securing labor to harvest the crop. A large production of apples around Marionville and Logan in 1914 and 1915 glutted the fruit market at picking time, resulting in low prices and loss to the growers. Faced with this condition, the growers organized a stock company and erected a large cold storage building on the Frisco railroad at Marionville.[19]

Fruit growing began to decline in the early 1930s, a time of important geographic and economic adjustment in fruit growing throughout the United States.[20] Increasing commercialization, mechanization, organization, and technology demanded greater specialization if fruit growers wanted to maintain their individual shares of an increasingly discriminating competitive market. Gradually, the kitchen orchards and small farm orchards disappeared from the landscape of the United States, and fruit growing became concentrated in scattered specialized locations.[21] Fruit growing in the western Ozarks declined because of the reluctance or inability of the growers to make necessary adjustments to remain competitive. Within the eight counties, the number of fruit farms decreased from a high of 426 to only 20 in 1964.

Through the developmental years, as the number of apple trees in the area increased, the orchards became infested by the codling moth or apple worm. At first, the moths were controlled by repeated treatments of arsenic of lead or a mixture of lime, sulphur, and water, but gradually the sprays became ineffective.[22]

Other factors also contributed to the decline of apple growing. A depressed economy during the 1930s greatly curtailed the market for apples. Drought persistently caused severe failure of the fruit crop in 1934 and 1936. Although the war years of the 1940s stimulated a stronger demand for apples, orchardists suffered from higher labor costs and outright labor shortages during the harvesting season. During the 1930s and 1940s fruit acreage gradually diminished. Few new plantings were made, and other crops replaced the aged and less productive trees. In the outskirts of Springfield, orchards were cleared to make room for new houses as the city experienced unprecedented growth during the 1940s and 1950s. By the end of the severe drought that extended for several years during the 1950s, virtually all of the large orchards had disappeared.

At present, fruit growing on a commercial basis is highly localized. Although commercial orchards of some importance are in production near Seymour in Webster County and near Springfield, the largest acreages in fruit are in the Marionville area.

Several factors have contributed to the persistence of fruit growing in the Marionville area. (1) Orcharding had reached its greatest development there during the 1920s. Marionville had adopted the title of "The Apple Capital of Missouri" by that time. Since there was a larger fruit acreage to begin with, more has persisted to the present. (2) The Orchard Growers Vinegar Company established a vinegar plant there in 1924. Later taken over by Speas Vinegar Company, the plant used locally grown apples until 1957. Low-quality apples could be sold to the vinegar plant during periods of drought or heavy insect infestation. In this way growers near Marionville derived some income from their apple orchards while producers in other areas became discouraged and converted orchard land to other uses. (3) The large cold storage plant, built in 1916 and expanded in 1929, continued to handle apples until it was converted to store poultry and meat during the war years. The apple storage plant offered growers near Marionville a somewhat improved market over that of other growers during the Depression years of the 1930s. (4) A tradition of fruit growing became better established in the Marionville area. Knowledge concerning the care of trees and the handling and marketing of fruit has lasted over the years; most of the present-day growers are old-time fruit growers or the descendants of early fruit growers.[23] A few roadside fruit stands have persisted up to the present.

The growing of tomatoes for canning purposes was introduced around 1900 and expanded very rapidly.[24] For several reasons tomatoes were well suited to the time and setting. First, tomatoes could be grown on very rough and rocky hillside farms. Second, the whole family could help in setting plants, tending them and harvesting the crop. Third, tomatoes hauled to the nearest cannery brought in badly needed cash at a time when many farmers suffered reduced income because of the decline of the timber industry. Fourth, women and girls found employment in the canning season to bolster family incomes.

The raising of tomatoes and truck crops rarely became the sole farming operation, but fields of one to three acres of tomatoes became common on farms near the canneries. Most of the tomatoes for a given cannery were raised within a radius of eight or ten miles. Near Springfield and Marionville tomatoes were grown in conjunction with fruit orchards to help defray the cost of cultivation and care of the orchard until the trees reached bearing age.[25]

Tomato farming required little investment other than labor and the profits were at times substantial. In 1905 upland tomatoes in Webster County yielded an average of 72 bushels per acre for a gross return of $16.39 per acre.[26] For this reason tomatoes were grown widely on small upland subsistence farms in the rougher parts of southwest Missouri and northwest Arkansas.

Figure 26. Strawberry field and pickers, Lawrence County.
POSTCARD PHOTOGRAPH, KALEN AND MORROW COLLECTION

Apparently many of the early Ozark canneries were often no more than family enterprises that operated only when prices were high. Any favorable combination of supply and demand brought a marked increase in "shade tree canneries."[27] Normally, the product of these small ventures was sold to larger canneries located in a nearby town.

Wild blackberries, beans, and a few other vegetables also were packed, but the main product was tomatoes.[28] The canneries fit into an economic niche created by time and place, taking advantage of the availability of cheap surplus seasonal labor from the farms and the lack of rigorous competition from other producing areas.

Economic forces and adverse climatic factors brought the decline of tomato farming. Droughts of the 1930s and blight in the wet years caused the crops to fail and canneries to close down. World War II precipitated a labor shortage, probably the most important factor for the closings. Stoop labor was almost impossible to hire when better paying and less demanding work could be obtained in nearby cities. Thus, surplus farm labor, the main support of tomato farming and the cannery industry, was diverted toward urban employment. The products of the small canneries could not match the quality and prices of larger plants in more favored growing areas. By 1955 tomato farming, and the canneries it supported, had all but disappeared from the landscape. Only a few small commercial patches of tomatoes are now planted near Springfield and other towns to supplement locally grown tomatoes for the table and home canning.

The growing of strawberries on a commercial scale developed in the late 1890s in two Ozark localities, in southwest Missouri and on the lower south slope of the Boston Mountains near Van Buren, Arkansas. By the 1920s strawberry growing had spread through southwestern Missouri and northwestern Arkansas.[29]

Strawberry cultivation flourished for the same reasons that tomato farming became important. Strawberries grew well on the chert-choked soils of the hillsides; in fact, the stone covering in cherty soils provided an excellent mulch for strawberries, holding the frost in the ground in the spring so that the plants did not bloom too early and providing a dry surface on which the berries could ripen free of mildew. Freshly cleared land was preferred for strawberries because of the greater humus content. The care and harvesting of strawberries consumed much labor, a surplus commodity on the small Ozark farms of the early 1900s. Also, strawberry farming required little in the way of land and capital outlay, and when stories circulated of sales in excess of five hundred dollars from strawberry patches of less than an acre, farmers in increasing numbers set out strawberries to bolster their incomes.[30]

Grown usually no more than ten miles from point of shipment, the strawberries were marketed through growers associations that set up railside receiving and crating sheds at the main shipping points. Where rail facilities were not available grocery or feed dealers purchased the berries and resold them at these points.

The strawberry picking season normally lasted five weeks, from the end of May to the first of July. Since most of the production came from family farms where women and children could help with the harvest, little outside labor was used. In a few cases, where fields of 50 acres or more were set out, laborers from Arkansas were brought in to help with the harvest.[31]

During the peak production, in the 1920s, strawberry growing had spread throughout the area and several towns had become important shipping points. At Logan, the most important of these points, there were two large strawberry barns, and it was not unusual for 150 carloads to be shipped during a season. Ozark, Springfield, Marshfield, Aurora, and Monett were other important points of shipment. Most of the strawberries were transported to St. Louis and other eastern cities.

The growth and decline of strawberry farming paralleled that of tomato production; the virtual cessation of strawberry growing for distant markets following World War II resulted from labor shortages.

Figure 27. Model dairy barn, along the Frisco.
POSTCARD VIEW, KALEN AND MORROW COLLECTION

The pioneers who had settled the Ozarks usually led one or more cows as they migrated. Most of these cows were of nondescript characteristics, largely of the beef type, but a few were crossed with dairy breeds. These cattle supplied both milk and meat; some were used as oxen. Good quality livestock, representing the various dairy breeds, did not reach the area in any great numbers until after 1900.

Only a small amount of trade in dairy products occurred at an early date. With the end of the Civil War and the coming of the railroads, Springfield grew rapidly, so that a sizable local market developed for milk, cream, and farm-churned butter. By modern standards this early trade was conducted in an extremely crude and unsanitary manner. General merchandise stores maintained cream stations that purchased cream from farmers and sent it to market in Springfield every few days. The stores also bought churned butter from the local farmers, dumped it into a common butter tub, and when ready for market the lid was nailed on and it was sent along with the other products. Tuberculosis and brucellosis testing was unheard of, and the products were produced under any number of unwholesome conditions.

Commercial dairying began shortly after 1900. By 1905 several Springfield cream and produce dealers shipped to markets in the East and South.[32] At that time four creameries were established in Webster County. Lawrence County also experienced a similar growth in dairying. The first large-scale dairy manufacturer in the area, Springfield Creamery Company, founded in 1910, inaugurated the practice of picking up cream from the farms.[33]

Several factors stimulated the growth of the dairy industry. First, good markets became available in St. Louis, Kansas City, and several towns that had grown up in the Tri-State Mining District. High prices for dairy products encouraged its extension. Second, as the area became better settled and landholdings became smaller it required that each acre receive intensive use, or that some other outlet for labor be afforded. Dairying provided a means to both ends. Third, the nature of the area's topography made it necessary to keep much of the land in pasture. Most of the grass and forage crops, such as orchard grass, bluegrass, timothy, clover, and sorghum grew well and furnished an eight- or nine-month grazing season for stock. Innumerable springs supplied plenty of good, clear water.[34]

At first, very few farms made a specialty of dairying, but a number of farms had as many as ten to fifteen milk cows. Gradually, farmers began to specialize. Because dairying developed before there were large numbers of automobiles and trucks, most of these dairy farms were located close to the railroads. Springfield, with a substantial local market and several railroad lines, formed a nucleus about which dairy farms were established.[35]

Thus, in the early years, commercial dairy farming tended to be concentrated around Springfield and along the railroads that radiated from the city. Each major shipping point on the railroad served as the market for a cluster of dairy farms in that area. Later, as roads improved and trucks picked up dairy products from the farms, the dairy farm became more widely distributed. However, because of poor roads, the extremely rough topography, and limited forage, dairying never became as important in the Ozark interior.

The demand for dairy products from markets outside the area became more discriminating and competitive, requiring herd improvement, better management, and better feeding. Many herds were developed from purebred Holsteins and Jerseys, but other popular dairy breeds included Brown Swiss, Guernsey, and the Milking Shorthorn.

Remarkable growth of commercial dairy farming occurred from its inauguration until 1940. In 1910 dairy cattle in the eight county area surrounding Springfield totaled 64,361, but by 1940 the number had increased to 113,200.[36] The growth during the 1920s was especially rapid. Lawrence County rose from twenty-ninth-place to third-place ranking among Missouri counties in number of dairy cattle in only three years. Between 1921 and 1924, the number of dairy cattle in the county increased from 9,640 to 14,530.[37] By 1934 Springfield ranked fourth in the nation in churned butter, and eleven large creameries in that city employed over 650 workers.[38]

The shift to larger and more efficient dairy manufacturing plants, along with improvements in farm technology, management, and cooperative marketing, contributed to fewer but larger dairy farms with improved methods of production. In the early days milk was separated on the farm, the skimmed milk fed to calves and hogs, and the cream traded for household and farm supplies. In contrast, modern dairying has geared to cheap, fast, and efficient transportation. Today, most of the cows are milked in inspected milking sheds using the most modern equipment. The cream can, though still seen, is fast disappearing from the roadside and farmyard as it is replaced by bulk milk tanks serviced by fast and efficient tank trucks.

In recent years, milk production in Missouri has declined slightly. Most of the decline occurred in areas outside the old, established, and highly specialized production areas. Either highly efficient production or strong market orientation seems to be required. Efficiencies of area specialization are apparently more important than cheap labor and underemployment.

The developments in poultry production over the past century have been phenomenal. There is little relation between the methods of handling poultry in the early days and those of the increasingly "foot-loose" production methods of modern times. The pioneers rarely brought in poultry of distinct breeds. Because they allowed poultry to run wild in the lots around the house and barn, there was no opportunity to develop pure strains, and mixed breeds were typical. A few farmers had guineas; some had small numbers of turkeys, geese, and ducks. On most farms the chickens and turkeys were expected to find their own food. Simple poultry houses or sheds were built before the Civil War, particularly for chickens, but for many years the turkeys and guineas roosted in the trees.

Farmers raised chickens for meat and eggs. Fried chicken, mainly in the summer months, was a favorite food, just as it has always been farther south. Turkeys were eaten on special occasions such as Thanksgiving and Christmas, as were small numbers of ducks and geese.

Certainly the methods of production and marketing of poultry and poultry products were primitive by modern standards. In the early years eggs, incubated by "setting hens," provided the new stock of "fryers" and "laying hens." The first incubators, which appeared shortly after 1900, were the small box-type. Heated with a kerosene lamp, they held from 50 to 100 eggs. Later, the size increased and electric incubators were introduced. Thus modern hatcheries gradually developed with great batteries of egg trays.[39]

With the introduction of the incubator, brooders came into use to replace the hen. Small boxes kept in a warm place, often beside the fireplace or stove in the home, first served this purpose. Later, brooders used kerosene, gas, and electric heat.

Ozark poultry farming developed contemporaneously with dairying. Usually the marketing of poultry and dairy products was combined; cream, eggs, and poultry were collected at produce houses and general stores in the small towns for shipment to the large creameries and larger produce houses in Springfield.

Farm women usually cared for the chickens and turkeys. Children assisted in the task of "gathering" eggs. Because the chickens had the run of the farmyard, the chore consisted of locating all the potential "laying spots." Eggs were sold ungraded, and rarely cleaned. Because they were marketed irregularly, with little protection from the heat, many of them spoiled.

Prior to the invention of the egg crate, eggs were hauled to market in farm wagons. A heavy layer of straw was placed in the wagon bed on which was placed a layer of eggs, and other layers of straw and eggs alternated until the wagon was filled to the top. A layer of boards covered the whole and a "boom pole," fastened down in front and back, kept the eggs from jolting around.[40] Almost universally, farmers exchanged poultry products for groceries, leaving little record of the magnitude of the business.

By 1920 broiler production became widespread on the general farms throughout the Springfield Plain and poultry production assumed an important place in the agricultural economy. Each farm had at least one small shed, where laying hens or broilers were sheltered, particularly during the night when predators were at large. By 1934 production of eggs and poultry products achieved such importance that Springfield adopted the somewhat ambitious title, "The World's Poultry Capital."[41]

Poultry farming has experienced great changes in recent years. The semiwild and nondescript flocks that foraged for themselves and laid their eggs in the loft or in the woods, by 1930, had given way to a flock of some 100-200 hybrid birds. These flocks were kept in modern poultry houses built according to plans recommended by the state experiment station.[42] These small family-sized flocks, then in turn, yielded to highly specialized production systems with flocks of 20,000 or more birds.

Most contemporary poultry farmers specialize in one of the modern breeds or hybrids. The principal utility breeds of chickens now raised include White Leghorn, White Plymouth Rocks, New Hampshires, Rhode Island Reds, and Inbred Hybrids.[43] The main breeds of turkeys are the Bronze, White Holland, and Beltsville. The U.S. Department of Agriculture developed the latter breed to meet the growing demand for smaller turkeys. The changes in poultry farming are strikingly evident in the landscape. Many abandoned barns, representing an intermediate stage in the trend toward larger production units, stand in various stages of disrepair and decay. This anomalous mixture of farms with abandoned poultry barns, side-by-side with apparently prosperous poultry farms, is repeated again and again throughout the western Ozark poultry region in southwest Missouri and northwest Arkansas.

Prior to the coming of the railroads, livestock husbandry was the only possible system of commercial agriculture. The cost of shipping grain or other bulky products over rough terrain to distant markets outside the Ozarks was prohibitive. Cattle could be driven from the Springfield area to St. Louis and even to New Orleans. Warsaw, the head of navigation on the Osage River, and Boonville on the Missouri River, served as the main shipping points prior to 1870, when the first railroad reached the area. Salt meats, cured hides, tallow, and lard were major exports via the river route.[44]

In addition to the cattle and half-wild hogs that ran at large on unfenced commons, early stock farmers also raised horses and mules. Horses were in strong demand both locally and in northern cities, and most of the mules were sold in the southern states where they were used in the cotton fields.[45]

As open range livestock farming gave way to general farming, cultivated crops, particularly corn, received more emphasis, and farmers gave greater attention to raising hogs and poultry. In 1912 Greene County shipped 35,732 hogs and 11,346 head of cattle, and for several years hogs had exceeded the value of cattle in the county.[46] Also, stall feeding cattle, to produce a finished animal, became more common. From about 1900 to 1940, when general farming reached its height, a "corn belt" type of livestock economy became popular. However, corn production was never great enough to make the area really important for production of finished hogs and beef. Production of beef cattle attained its greatest importance in the Springfield Plain where the natural conditions were better suited to the production of corn and other feeds.

In the years since World War II, there has been a marked shift back to a livestock economy based on the production of unfinished feeder cattle. In the last few years, this shift in emphasis has reached major proportions and constitutes one of the most significant economic changes in the Ozarks. As a result, land use and landscape patterns have been greatly altered, and the changes promise to continue for some time to come. High cattle prices made conversion of timberland to pasture profitable. Between 1966 and 1969 more than 73,000 acres were defoliated and aerially seeded to pasture by one southwest Missouri farmers cooperative.[47]

The trend to beef cattle is nationwide, but the percentage growth rate in beef cattle in the Ozarks is substantially above the national average. Numbers of beef cattle in Missouri increased 75 percent from 1958 to 1967, considerably more than the 43 percent increase in the United States. In the Springfield vicinity of southwest Missouri, the increase in beef cattle amounted to 136 percent.[48]

Only recently has part-time farming received the attention of researchers, and because these farms have received little study, there is confusion concerning their place, importance, and permanence in the process of agricultural evolution.[49] Part-time farming has increased markedly in the Ozarks over the past few decades. The number of part-time farms in the eight-county area around Springfield increased from 1,593 in 1930, 7 percent of the total number of farms, to 4,394 in 1964, 28 percent of the total number of farms. This increase in the number of part-time farms is in contradiction to the general decline in the number of farms in the Springfield vicinity.

Ozark farmers have always looked to alternate sources of income to bolster their standard of living. The early hunter-woodsman, who gained as much of his living from the wild game and the forests as from agriculture, may be considered as the prototype farmer.

The first settlers of necessity were largely self-sufficient, so that in addition to producing nearly all their food and clothing, they manufactured a large part of the farmstead furnishings and tools. Some farmers manufactured furniture, tools, leather products, or other essential commodities to supplement their incomes.[50] Tanyards, whiskey distilleries, stave and barrel works, ax handle and tool works, furniture and coffin manufacture, sorghum mills, and numerous grist mills often were run as adjuncts to agriculture. In some cases, farm manufacturers persisted through several generations.

Gradually as towns matured, sufficient capital was accumulated by the middle- and upper-income business and professional people. This additional capital led to the establishment of "country gentlemen" part-time farms.[51] Many who occupied such farms were former rural inhabitants who had made good in the city, but still yearned for country living.[52] In the period 1900 to 1930 and following World War II, "country gentlemen" part-time farms near Springfield were used as places for recreation and casual country living, and only incidentally for agricultural purposes.

Part-time "subsistence" farms appeared during the economic depression between 1930 and 1940. As economic activity declined, the centripetal pull of the urban centers transformed into a centrifugal force, causing unemployed workers to seek open country where they could at least subsist. Because of low land prices, low-cost rural rental property, and low living costs, the Ozarks became a popular place to establish subsistence homesteads.[53] Strawberry and tomato harvesting, logging, and work in the canneries provided seasonal employment that provided income to purchase those things that could not be produced on the farm. In some cases, those who went back to the cities after the Depression returned to the Ozarks to reestablish part-time retirement farms.

In recent years the part-time farmer has moved to open country in response to improved roads, mobility of the rural population, and increased cost-price squeeze on farming operations. Ozark farmers found that enlargement of the farm unit is not always easy because the conditions of slope and topography are not well suited to mechanization. The alternative to expansion has been to earn income from nonfarm employment. This has been particularly true of dairy farm operators who, in order to remain competitive, are faced with the need for larger farm units and increased amounts of expensive equipment. Numerous dairy farms in the Springfield area have been converted to part-time stock farms, a transition that involves no large capital investments, and allows more time to be spent off the farm.

Ozark agriculture appears to have come full circle. The original Ozark farmer was a part-time agriculturalist, a keeper of livestock, and a hunter. The land he plowed was safe and secure in stream bottoms. His economy was more in tune with the existing natural resources than some of the subsequent types of farming. Development of commercial agriculture in the Ozarks has been a long and sometimes destructive process replete with experimentation and constant adjustments in man-land relations. Large-scale contemporary agriculture in the Ozarks leans heavily on livestock with cultivation ancillary to livestock production. The general farm has all but disappeared, dairy farming continues under heavy pressure, while only vestiges of fruit farms and truck farms remain. Like his forebear, the less progressive contemporary Ozark farmer often finds greater reward in alternate pursuits than in attempting to wrest his total livelihood from reluctant soils. One can speculate that mutual benefit may accrue to man and land.

Notes

1. Morris E. Austin, "Land Resource Regions and Major Land Resource Areas of the United States," *Agricultural Handbook No. 296*, Soil Conservation Service, U.S. Department of Agriculture (Washington, DC, 1965).

2. Data sources included interviews, direct observation, U.S. Census reports, and a variety of historical records.

3. Walter O. Cralle, "Social Change and Isolation in the Ozark Mountain Region of Missouri" (Ph.D. dissertation, University of Minnesota, Minneapolis, 1934), 269.

4. *Ninth Census of Wealth and Industry of the U.S.* (Washington, DC, 1872), III.

5. Johnathan Fairbanks and Clyde Edwin Tuck, *Past and Present of Greene County, Missouri* (Indianapolis: A. W. Bowen & Company, 1915), I:198.

6. Ibid.

7. Ibid.

8. Ibid.

9. *Eleventh Census of the United States: Statistics of Agriculture* (Washington, DC, 1895), 216-217; *Twelfth Census of the United States: Agriculture* (Washington, DC, 1901), Vol. VI, Part II, 96-151.

10. Fairbanks and Tuck, *Past and Present of Greene County,* 200.

11. Ibid., 198.

12. *Thirteenth Census of the United States: Agriculture* (Washington, DC, 1913), Vol. VI, 900-904; *Sixteenth Census of the United States: Agriculture* (Washington, DC, 1942), Vol. I, Part 2, 299-308; *United States Census of Agriculture:* 1964, *Statistics for the State and Counties, Missouri* (Washington, DC, 1967), Vol. I, Part 17, 14-19.

13. Walter B. Stevens, *Missouri, The Center State* (Chicago, 1915), 617. In 1882, New York investors owned 177,000 acres of land, centered in Laclede County, and employed Absalom Nelson as marketing agent for their Ozark Plateau Land Company.

Nelson and his Missouri colleagues established fruit orchards, built a barrel manufacturing plant, and exported carloads of fruit on the Frisco railroad. Nelson's efforts led to a region-wide expansion of the term, "Land of the Big Red Apple." See Phyllis Rossiter, "Land of the Big Red Apple," *Briarwood* 1, no. 2 (November 1988): 17-23.

14. Ibid., 616.

15. Curtis Marbut, *Soil Reconnaissance of the Ozark Region of Missouri and Arkansas* (Washington, DC, 1915), 22.

16. J. A. Drake and A. T. Strahorn, *Soil Survey of Webster County, Missouri* (Washington, DC, 1904), 6.

17. A. T. Sweet and Howard V. Jordan, *Soil Survey of Lawrence County, Missouri* (Washington, DC, 1928), 1150.

18. H. H. Krusekopf and F. Z. Hutton, *Soil Survey of Greene County, Missouri* (Washington, DC, 1915), 12.

19. Lee Collier, "A History, of Marionville, Missouri," 40, unpublished manuscript available in Marionville and Springfield public libraries.

20. Clarence W. Olmstead, "American Orchard and Vineyard Regions," *Economic Geography* 32 (July 1956): 213-227.

21. Ibid., 214.

22. C. E. Jackson, retired fruit grower, personal interview, September 14, 1968.

23. R. L. Head, owner of Head Orchards, Marionville, Missouri, personal interview, September 17, 1968.

24. F. W. George, *History of Webster County* (Springfield, MO, 1955), 81.

25. Krusekopf and Hutton, *Soil Survey of Greene County*, 13.

26. Drake and Strahorn, *Soil Survey of Webster County*, 17.

27. Irene A. Moke, "Canning in Northwestern Arkansas: Springdale, Arkansas," *Economic Geography* 28(April 1952): 55. By 1905, small investors could purchase a model canning factory in Springfield and counties such as Stone had as many as thirty-eight canneries at one time. See Lynn Morrow and Linda Myers-Phinney, *Shepherd of the Hills Country: Tourism Transforms the Ozarks, 1880s-1930s* (Fayetteville: University of Arkansas Press, 1999), 169-172.

28. J. E. Curry, A *Reminiscent History of Douglas County, Missouri, 1857-1957* (Ava, MO, 1957), 147.

29. Moke, "Canning in Northwestern Arkansas," 156.

30. C. K. Renner, "Strawberry Culture in Southwest Missouri," *Missouri Historical Review* 64 (October 1969): 18-40.

31. Milton D. Rafferty, "Persistence Versus Change in Land Use and Landscape in the Springfield, Missouri Vicinity of the Ozarks" (Ph.D. dissertation, University of Nebraska, Lincoln, 1970), 151.

32. Krusekopf and Hutton, *Soil Survey of Greene County*, 14.

33. Fairbanks and Tuck, *Past and Present of Greene County*, 680.

34. C. H. Hammar et al., "Types of Farming in Missouri," *University of Missouri Agricultural Research Bulletin No. 284* (Columbia, May 1938), 96.

35. Lewis F. Thomas, "A Geographic Study of Greene County, Missouri" (Master's thesis, University of Missouri-Columbia, 1917), 51.

36. *13th Census of the U.S., 1910, Agriculture,* Vol. VI, 896-900; *16th Census of the U.S., 1940, Agriculture,* Vol. I, Part 2, 274-282.

37. Sweet and Jordan, *Soil Survey of Lawrence County*, 1129.

38. Virginia Hogg, "Urban Pattern of Springfield, Missouri" (Master's thesis, Washington University, St. Louis, 1934), 55-56.

39. Rafferty, "Change in Land Use," 168.

40. Cralle, "Social Change," 281.

41. Hogg, *Urban Pattern*, 51.

42. Cralle, "Social Change," 181-182.

43. Rafferty, "Change in Land Use," 181-182.

44. Carl O. Sauer, "Geography of the Ozark Highland of Missouri," *The Geographic Society of Chicago Bulletin No. 7* (Chicago, 1920), 46.

45. Fairbanks and Tuck, *Past and Present Greene County*, 202.

46. Ibid., 210-212.

47. O. L. Claxton, Area Community Development Agent, Ava, Missouri, comments to the author, July 18, 1969.

48. *A Guide for Growth in Missouri's Food and Fiber Industry* (Columbia, MO, 1960), 9.

49. W. N. Ross and A. R. Gagan, *Part-time Farming, Its Role in a Changing Agriculture* (Columbia, MO, 1965), 3.

50. Ibid., 4.

51. Ibid., 6.

52. F. Hart, "The Changing American Countryside," in *Problems and Trends in American Geography*, ed. Saul B. Cohen (New York, 1967), 73.

53. Milton D. Rafferty, "Population and Settlement Change in Two Ozark Localities," *Rural Sociology* 38 (Spring 1973): 46-56.

The Origin and Development of the Ozark National Scenic Riverways Project

STEPHEN N. LIMBAUGH

King John signed the Magna Carta at Runnymede in June of 1215. Perhaps the most important provisions were that "no free man shall be seized or imprisoned, or stripped of his rights or possessions, or outlawed or exiled, or deprived of his standing in any other way, nor will we proceed with force against him, or send others to do so, except by the lawful judgment of his equals or by the law of the land. To no one will we sell, to no one deny or delay right or justice."

Five hundred fifty years later, those colonists established in the North American continent were still urging the monarchy to follow these principles. Private land was freely confiscated by the king for debt, disobedience, or virtually any other reason. Sam Adams in Boston addressed his followers, saying that the king and the Tories must fight him before they could take his home. Patrick Henry in Virginia urged revolt because of confiscatory taxes set by the king resulting in loss of real estate as a result of the inability to pay the taxes. Thomas Paine, the pamphleteer of the Revolution, urged in his *Common Sense* the right of free people to retain their interest in property and avoid government confiscation without just cause or due process.

Although the need for centralized government in some areas was evident, most colonists wanted no government interference in their personal lives. They wanted the opportunity to own land, develop it as they pleased, and live and work on this land without government interference.

This was as innate in the feeling of people as was any basic right to liberty and freedom.

Thus, it was enacted in the last portion of the Fifth Amendment to the Constitution that no person shall "be deprived of life, liberty, or property, without due process of law; nor shall private property be taken for public use, without just compensation." This perhaps was one of the great compromises in the enactment of the Bill of Rights. It enabled people to own property without government interference. The exception was that government could interfere and take someone's property provided that the taking was for the public use and provided that just compensation be paid for the taking.

In fact, the government through Congress quickly began to make use of the right of eminent domain. This is the right of the United States through its regular organization to reassert either temporarily, or permanently, its dominion over any portion of the soil of the individual or a state on account of public exigency and for the public good. Eminent domain is commonly referred to as condemnation or expropriation.

At the outset, private land as well as that owned by the states or municipalities or other public bodies was taken, principally, to advance commerce and transportation. Canal rights-of-way were formed for the public good. Later, land was confiscated for railroads and, today, for highways. Land is taken for the construction of public buildings or for other important public purposes.

Although the United States condemning authorities as authorized by Congress have had their judgment questioned in litigation as to the need for the public taking, it is rare that any court has determined the judgment of Congress to be inappropriate for a public taking. When this determination is made, the only remaining issue is to calculate what constitutes just compensation for the taking.

One of the great motivations of the westward surge of expansion in North America was to avoid the eminent domain rights of the United States. Even today, it is innate in our feeling that our home, our land, our buildings should not be subjected to government taking—even with just compensation.

This point of view was manifest in the hearts and minds of the settlers in the Missouri Ozark region. The early Scotch-Irish settlers and later German immigrants wanted nothing more than to have a small tract of land in the Ozark wilderness where they could live untrammeled by government interference.

The rural Ozark area is sparsely populated, hilly, rugged with timber, and alive with game, waterfowl, and fish. The area was only slightly

Figure 28. Fishing in a johnboat, the Current River.
GERALD MASSIE COLLECTION, MISSOURI STATE ARCHIVES

touched in the last century and the early part of the twentieth century by railroad expansion and the growth of modest communities. While there was some agriculture, it too was sparse, and transportation was by roads and trails. Timber was important, and both yellow and white pine as native timber were harvested by teams of mules pulling the felled logs along logging trails. There was a modest social, religious, and educational exposure, but most people lived by home rule, and they desired it. It was against this backdrop of public feeling, sentiment, and attitude that the first seed of government intervention into the lives of the citizens of the Ozark area was sown.[1]

In the late 1950s and early 1960s, the inhabitants of Dent, Shannon, Reynolds, Carter, Oregon, and Ripley Counties began to feel the power of the federal government. In this area flow three of the most majestic streams in the country. The principal one is named the Current River. It begins at Montauk State Park in Dent County, a few miles southwest of Salem, Missouri. It flows in a southeasterly fashion past the former Round Spring State Park into Van Buren in Carter County, past the former Big Spring State Park area, meanders to Doniphan in Ripley County, and then travels south into Arkansas.[2]

The second stream begins in Texas County, a few miles north of Mountain View, and flows in a northeasterly direction past former Alley Spring State Park, through Eminence in Shannon County, and then converges with the Current River. This stream is named the Jacks Fork.[3] The third stream is called the Eleven Point River. It runs in a southeasterly direction north of Alton in Oregon County and meanders its way into the state of Arkansas.

The beauty of these rivers is indescribable. The rivers are fed by hundreds of springs and produce waters that are exceptionally cold. There are so many springs that the water is abundant and produces a swift flow; hence, the name Current River. In the upper and middle sections of the Current and Jacks Fork, the streams are more narrow and fast flowing. At some points, the rivers are twenty-five to fifty feet wide. After the Current River flows past Van Buren, it widens, and the current is less swift. At this point, the river may be three hundred feet across.

At various points along the river, the banks are adjacent to farmland. The more prevalent areas are tree lined, and in many instances, cliffs two hundred feet high rise straight up from the edge of the river. Many trees bend over the river. Some of the area is rocky, and there are many sandbars in other portions. On numerous points, large caves meander in the side of a cliff, with the swift-flowing stream passing by. For the most part, in the 1950s the area seemed untouched by modern intrusions. There were deer and wild turkey in abundance as well as an occasional black and brown bear and panther or mountain lion. Fox, bobcat, mink, muskrat and beaver, rabbit, squirrel, opossum, and raccoon were evident, as were ducks, geese, quail, and some pheasants. The rivers were naturally stocked with largemouth and smallmouth bass, trout, perch, catfish, an occasional walleyed pike, and a host of other species.

People drove for miles to see the splendid mill and spring area at Round and Alley Springs.[4] Others would come to Van Buren to visit the Big Spring area, which purportedly produces 280 million gallons of water a day.[5]

This rugged area basically limited to timber production and some farming was emerging as a recreational paradise. The state of Missouri had already established parks at Round and Alley Springs and Big Spring and at nearby areas. The federal government had acquired much of the adjacent forest land and converted it into the Mark Twain National Forest preservation area.

In 1959, Missouri senators Thomas C. Hennings and Stuart Symington, Missouri governor James T. Blair Jr., and officials of the National Park

Service, Forest Service, and Fish and Wildlife Service met for the purpose of studying a proposed Ozark Rivers National Monument. Later, Congressmen Thomas B. Curtis and Richard H. Ichord presented bills to perpetuate the rivers into the national park system. Secretary of the Interior Stewart Udall floated the Current River with St. Louis journalist and conservationist Leonard Hall and National Park Service officials. The power of eminent domain was swiftly pervading this once-quiet part of the Missouri Ozarks.

There was a hue and cry from the landowners along the rivers who wanted nothing more than to be left alone. All of the residents bore arms in their hunting and fishing pursuits, but on these occasions, the arms were always loaded. The restaurants, such as the famous one in the Rose Cliff Hotel in Van Buren,[6] and the small, sparsely situated stores were abound with angry citizens and conversation. The government was about to take their land. The old colonial spirit arose like a fire out of control one final time in the heart of rural Missouri.

It was to no avail as the senators and congressmen and the secretary of the interior determined that the government had a need. The need was established as one of preservation of the natural and scenic beauty of the area. The floor of Congress was filled with eloquent talks about the expansion of commercialism along these famous streams and the ultimate ruination of them absent some kind of control to preserve their natural beauty. In the final analysis, the government won, and it is only for the beholder today to make the decision as to whether government intervention was or was not proper.[7]

On August 27, 1964, the law establishing the Ozark National Scenic Riverways was passed and signed by President Lyndon Johnson. As is usual in the passage of national legislation, there was a compromise. The condemnation of the Eleven Point River was eliminated from the overall plan. The lower portion of the Current River in Ripley County as it flows through Doniphan was also eliminated. Thus, the project included the Current River beginning at Montauk State Park in Dent County and flowing past Van Buren to the southern line of Carter County. All of the Jacks Fork River was also included.

The legislation authorized the secretary of the interior to acquire sixty-five thousand acres of land held mostly in private ownership. The land roughly included a mile strip, with approximately one-half mile on each side of the Current and Jacks Fork Rivers. An area where the Jacks Fork River flowed through Eminence was excluded for two miles on each side of the community, with the same provision being made for Van Buren as the Current River flowed through that community. The secretary of the interior was given the power to acquire the private land in the areas mentioned by agreement with the landowners or by the condemnation process.

The measure also included a provision that authorized private owners to occupy their real estate as it might be included in the condemned area for life. This meant that a husband and wife who had a home or structure in the condemned area could keep this for their natural lives and use it in conformity with the regulations established by the Ozark National Scenic Riverways Commission. Such a life estate, obviously, would decrease the value of the property taken.

The secretary of the interior was given the authority to negotiate with the state of Missouri for the acquisition of the state parks at Big Spring, Round Spring, and Alley Spring for the inclusion of such lands in the Ozark National Scenic Riverways. With the cooperation of state authorities, these park lands were, in fact, transferred to the secretary of the interior on January 1, 1970. Congress appropriated $10,804,000 for the acquisition and interest in the riverways' lands involved.

The act provided for the establishment of the Ozark National Scenic Riverways Commission, which was to cease to exist in ten years. Four members of the commission were to be appointed by the county courts in Carter, Dent, Shannon, and Texas Counties; two were to be appointed by the governor of Missouri; and one by the secretary of the interior. The commission was to be the sounding board for the secretary, and at the end of ten years, the operation and control of the project would be solely in the hands of the secretary of the interior.

The act called for the secretary to evolve land use development programs, to preserve and enhance the natural beauty of the landscape, and to conserve the outdoor resources in the watersheds of the Jacks Fork and Current Rivers. The secretary was given the authority to permit hunting and fishing on lands and waters within the area in accordance with applicable federal and state laws. The secretary could designate zones where no hunting would be permitted because of public safety and in cooperation with the Conservation Commission of the State of Missouri.

An Iowa congressman, John Kyl, took issue with the project, and in a powerful floor speech, he stated that the government was setting up a park-like preservation of 86,500 acres if state-owned lands and federal forest lands were included. The area was 140 miles in its entirety. He continued: "With national recognition the project will become a mecca for tourists, recreation seekers and part-time or permanent residents. There will undoubtedly be commercial and residential development overlooking the narrow strip. My greatest objection is the strong possibility that we will hasten destruction of the very values that we seek to preserve."

Nonetheless, the legislation was enacted, and the secretary of the interior began to implement the project. Government real estate appraisers surveyed the entire area in accordance with the various abutting tracts of land owned by individuals. The acreage in each individual tract was identified, and estimates were made of the value of each parcel of land to be taken. This was a difficult project and took some time to complete. Fortified with the identification of owners and quantities of land in all tracts to be taken, the acquiring officials began the laborious process of meeting with landowners to discuss an agreeable price for the purchase of the land. Absent agreement, the tracts were condemned by court proceedings. The process was made even more difficult when there were multiple owners and some would agree on a price and others would not agree. In these instances it would be necessary to acquire some interest in the land by agreement and then condemn the remaining ownerships.

The United States Courts in Missouri are divided into the east and west sections, with the east being principally located in St. Louis. There is a northern division in Hannibal and a southeastern division in Cape Girardeau. Most of the land involved lay in counties that were in the southeastern division. A few were located in the greater St. Louis division. As the condemnation cases would be tried in the United States District Court in Cape Girardeau, many landowners went to Cape Girardeau or other southeast Missouri attorneys for counsel. The first inquiry by all irate landowners was how to defeat the project. All lawyers indicated to their prospective clients that this was not possible, that Congress had the authority to enact the law that it had passed, and that the landowner had only one remedy—to obtain the highest possible compensation for the land taken.

After a series of negotiations, there remained two hundred to three hundred tracts of real estate for which the compensation could not be agreed upon. Accordingly, suits in condemnation were filed, most of them having their venue in Cape Girardeau.

The first cases were slated for trial in 1967. The two judges assigned to handle the condemnation cases were James Meredith and Roy Harper. They called a meeting of all of the lawyers representing landowners. As there were so many cases involved, and in order to save time, the judges persuaded many lawyers to try their cases before the court without a jury, although in condemnation proceedings, the landowner has a right to a jury trial for the purpose of establishing value. The issue in a condemnation case is the determination of the fair market value of the land taken. In the case of those persons reserving a life estate in the land, the issue would be the fair market value of the land taken subject to the value of the life estate reserved.

The first case was to be tried before Judge Meredith, and a jury was waived. My father, Rush H. Limbaugh, seventy-four years of age at the time, represented the landowner in that case.[8]

As a result of the Ozark community hostility to the entire project, Judge Meredith suggested a plan in an attempt to assuage the passion of the community. He proposed a temporary transfer of the United States Court from Cape Girardeau to the county courthouse at Van Buren. If the case were to be tried in the heart of the area to be condemned, Judge Meredith felt that might in some way pacify the concerns of the people involved. Accordingly, with the consent of the state judicial system and the parties, the United States case was tried in the courthouse in Carter County in Van Buren.

The preparation on behalf of the landowners of this type of condemnation was somewhat unprecedented. There are few condemnation cases of

Figure 29. Canoes at Bales Boating Company, Eminence, 1978.
KALEN AND MORROW COLLECTION, JEFFERSON CITY

record in recent origin where land is taken for preservation purposes. Accordingly, the landowners and their attorneys were faced with the dilemma of determining how best to present the evidence to show the highest and best use of the land, which was the standard required for calculating value. Unfortunately, farming was sparse, and if the highest and best use was for farming, there would be little evidence to establish substantial values. Some of the land had improvements such as homes, barns, or other buildings, but generally these were of modest value. Much of the land had timber. White or yellow pine and walnut could produce some value. The only other realistic highest and best use of the land was for recreational purposes. There were few precedents on which real estate appraisers could rely to base substantial values because of recreational potential. There were few business recreational uses. The rental of canoes was the principal business recreational use. Accordingly, the real estate appraisers were resigned to setting a value for recreational use only, plus any value for timber and improvements.

Several persons were used to advantage by many landowners and attorneys to establish real estate value. The first was Dub Crutcher, a real estate appraiser from Essex, Missouri. The second was Robert Hedden from Cape Girardeau, a timber expert formerly with the old Armstrong Cork Company. The third was Nellie Burrows of Van Buren, who was an inveterate fisherman, knowledgeable of the entire area, a local, and the owner of the principal abstract company in the area.

Bob Hedden would examine the timber on a particular tract. He called it "cruising the timber." He would search out valuable timber and estimate its height and width and then be prepared to testify as to the value of that timber, were it to be harvested. Dub Crutcher would examine a tract of real estate for the purpose of testifying to its highest and best use and then establish values on the basis of comparable sales, which is a technique used by many real estate appraisers.

Ordinarily, when people acquired land along the river, they retained ownership, and it would pass through various generations. Accordingly, there were not a substantial number of comparable sales, and those that were found did not involve great sums of money. It made the landowner's job extremely difficult.

When the timber expert and the real estate expert would survey the lands for appraisal purposes, the attorneys generally accompanied them. It is exceedingly difficult to describe how one would gain access to a particular tract of land. In some instances, the owner would gain access by boat; in other instances, there would be only old logging trails. The roads, if any, were few and walkable rather than usable by vehicles. Tramping over these lands was an arduous task and yet a beautiful one. It was virtually like walking through an uncharted wilderness in many respects. On many occasions, deer would scurry by, or a wild turkey would flap his wings and run. The sounds of the area were unmistakably lovely.

After a two-and-one-half-day trial before the court in Van Buren, Judge Meredith ruled on the spot. He awarded one hundred dollars per acre for the land taken in this particular tract, plus a small amount for a log home there and a modest amount for some timber. After announcing his decision, Judge Meredith left the courthouse in the company of three U.S. marshals and made his way back to Cape Girardeau. This was the only case tried in Van Buren, and the remainder were tried principally in Cape Girardeau, and a few in St. Louis. The judge had made his point in the heart of the riverways project that the land was not worth more than one hundred dollars per acre, plus improvements and timber. The case had its desired effect on many landowners, and numerous ones from that point on capitulated and negotiated successful prices with the government for their property.

The point was also made that, hereafter, further cases should be tried by juries, and most attorneys subsequently submitted their cases to juries. Numerous attorneys were involved with the condemnation litigation. One was Dorman Steelman, who was later to become a Missouri state judge in Salem. One of his clients owned a cave fronting on the Current River in Dent County. The landowner charged admission for access to the cave, so he lost a business because of the taking. The case was tried in the St. Louis court, and the landowner received a substantial verdict.

H. Kenneth Wangelin, a Poplar Bluff attorney at the time, tried a case involving a tract in the Current River area immediately below Van Buren and obtained a satisfactory jury award in the Cape Girardeau court. In this case, the owner was able to establish farming as the highest and best use, and damage could be calculated more readily. Wangelin was appointed judge of the very court in which this case was tried only a few months after the trial.

I had the privilege of trying approximately thirty-five separate cases in Cape Girardeau before a jury. As one might expect, the range of verdicts varied substantially. Some juries would lay great faith in the landowners' real estate valuations and, when doing so, awarded fairly substantial sums to the landowners. Other juries put more belief in the conservative assessment of values by the government's appraisers. When this occurred, the valuation was more modest. The last cases were tried in 1969 and early 1970, and the taking was complete. The government now had ownership, subject to some life estates, of the entire area described along the Current and Jacks Fork Rivers.[9]

Since that time, the National Park Service has taken over the implementation of the project and its management. The officers of the National Park Service have done a splendid job in the operation and management of the park areas and the maintenance and control of the rivers. Although there is heavy usage of the rivers, principally by fishermen or floaters in canoes or johnboats, the principal object of Congress has been carried out in the preservation of the original and natural beauty of the area. On a weekend in the summer, it is not unusual to see canoes bumper-to-bumper going down the river. The occupants of the canoes are as diverse as the whole citizenry of this country. Some will have their pet dog or cat or other animal in the canoe with them. All are enjoying immensely this precious area in the heartland of Missouri.[10]

It has been thirty-two years since the bill establishing the Ozark National Scenic Riverways Project was argued on the floor of Congress and twenty-five years or more since the National Park Service began operating the project. The sentiment against condemnation has dwindled. Whatever one's personal feeling is about obtrusive government, the service has operated well in implementing this project.[11]

On a personal note, may I recall two interesting experiences: the first occurred while interviewing witnesses while preparing for one of the condemnation trials. A witness and I had spent an afternoon tramping over one of the river tracts to be condemned. It was the middle of January, extremely cold, with snow and ice on the ground. As we finished dinner at a Van Buren restaurant, three men entered the restaurant, all of whom were known to my friend. They were a disheveled group who appeared to have been in the wilderness for days. They encouraged my friend and me to come outside in the inclement weather and view something they had in the bed of a large pickup truck. The bed of the truck was covered with a tarpaulin, and as it was rolled back, we saw seventeen beaver. Obviously, the men had been in the Ozark wilderness trapping the beaver and were prepared, legitimately or otherwise, to sell the skins. It was reminiscent of those pioneer trappers who explored the Northwest and made their living trapping animals for hides. Yet, this was in the 1960s in the Missouri Ozarks. It was one more illustration of the need for the preservation of this wild territory and its inhabitants.

The second experience occurred approximately ten years ago when my wife, Anne, and I floated a portion of the Current River. We put in for a day's float north of Van Buren on a lovely October day. The weather was still mild, but the scarlet, orange, and yellow leaves adorned the countryside. The current was swift enough so that it was frequently unnecessary to paddle. The water was intensely chilled, but the stream, at some points, was so clear that at six feet in depth, the bottom of the riverbed was quite visible. It was in the middle of the week, and there were no other canoers on the river in our vicinity. The whispering breeze and the sounds of the wildlife and the trickle of the stream added to the zest of the adventure. We felt as close to God as one might come, enjoying the magnificence of this spectacular Ozark stream. As the great conservationist Leonard Hall remarked, it was truly "stars upstream."[12]

Notes

1. See Donald L. Stevens Jr., *A Homeland and a Hinterland, The Current and Jacks Fork Riverways* (Omaha, NB: National Park System, Midwest Region, 1991) for a well-illustrated prehistoric and historical overview of the area. A variety of interests had envisioned reservoir dams on the Current River since World War One. After World War Two, the dam issue became a warm-up controversy prior to the proposal for a free-flowing river park. See "The Damnable Current River Dam and other topics, A Conversation with Dan Saults, 1982," interview by Robert Flanders and Lynn Morrow, *OzarksWatch* 2, no. 4 (Spring 1989): 26–28, and 3, no. 2 (Fall 1989): 26–28.

2. The Missouri state park board conveyed ownership of Round Spring, Alley Spring, and Big Spring state parks to the Ozark National Scenic Riverways on January 1, 1970. See the excellent overview of Missouri's state park system in *Exploring Missouri's Legacy, State Parks and Historic Sites,* ed. Susan Flader (Columbia: University of Missouri Press, 1992), especially "Evolution of the System," 1–24. Ironically, decades later in 2008, the former private Alton Club on the upper Current River became state property, the Current River State Park, to be managed by the Missouri Department of Natural Resources; see "Gov. Blunt Announces Name of Missouri's Newest State Park," press release, May 13, 2008, Matt Blunt Papers, Missouri State Archives.

3. For an aesthetic view and description of the Current and Jacks Fork Rivers, see Steve Kohler, *Two Ozark Rivers, The Current and Jacks Fork,* photographs by Oliver Schuchard (Columbia: University of Missouri Press, 1984). The origin of the name Jack's Fork has never been proved. A plausible tradition related to Lynn Morrow during the late 1970s in Shannon County was that it stood for a "Capt. Jack," a leader among the Delaware Indians during their 1820s emigrant residence.

4. For an extended historical treatment of Alley Spring, see Robert Flanders, *Alley, An Ozarks Mill Hamlet, 1890–1925, Society, Economy, Landscape* (Springfield: The Center for Ozarks Studies, Southwest Missouri State University, 1985); and for archaeology, Mark Lynott, James E. Price, and Roger Saucier, "The Alley Mill Site & the Early Prehistory of the Current River Valley, Southeast Missouri," *Missouri Archaeologist* 67 (December 2006): 1–47.

5. The hydrology of the springs is in Jerry D. Vineyard and Gerald L. Feder, *Springs of Missouri* (Rolla: Missouri Geological Survey and Water Resources, 1974). The publisher is now the Department of Natural Resources, Division of Geology, Rolla, MO.

6. For the Rose Cliff Hotel as a meeting place for professionals, see Lynn Morrow, "Rose Cliff Hotel: A Missouri Forum for Environmental Policy," *Gateway Heritage* 3 (Fall 1982): 38–48. The Missouri Department of Transportation razed this National Register of Historic Places site to widen modern highway 60.

7. Nonresidents normally applaud the results of the Ozarks National Scenic Riverways; however, many residents still resent the intrusion of the federal government, hordes of canoeists (increasing from tens of thousands in the 1960s to hundreds of thousands annually), and the loss of family lands along the rivers.

8. See the biography by Dennis K. Boman, *The Original Rush Limbaugh: Lawyer, Legislator, and Civil Libertarian* (Columbia: University of Missouri Press, 2012).

9. Attorneys litigated over two hundred cases. A controversial issue was the varying appraisals, often conspicuously low, given by private contractors to the federal government. Litigation commonly resulted in higher awards to the plaintiffs. Historian Will Sarvis concluded that "The poor method of appraising OSNR lands became a very unfortunate aspect of establishing the wider public use, leaving OSNR with a difficult legacy it will not soon overcome." For a comprehensive discussion on the origins of the Scenic Riverways, see Sarvis's companion articles, "Old Eminent Domain and New Scenic Easements: Land Acquisition for the Ozark National Scenic Riverways," *Western Legal History* 13, no. 1 (Winter/Spring 2000): 1–37, quote above on p. 37, and "A Difficult Legacy: Creation of the Ozark National Scenic Riverways," *The Public Historian* 24, no. 2 (Spring 2002): 31–52.

10. For another nonresident view, inspired in part by the beauty of the area, see the documentary film interpretation, *Shannon County: Home,* Robert Flanders, executive director, and Robert Moore, producer director (Springfield: Center for Ozarks Studies, Southwest Missouri State University, and Veriation Films, Palo Alto, CA, 1981), and its companion, *Shannon County: The Hearts of the Children. Home* earned a blue-ribbon first-place award in the American Film Festival, 1983.

11. The management of the Riverways has created its own history. During the half-century of National Park Service implementation of management plans, public constituencies have battled the Park Service in the use and future vision for the Riverways. Among them, two areas have received prominent press—what to do about wild horses and "wild people" on the water. For example, see Mark Bliss, "Judge rules wild horses must stay in Ozark country," *Cape Girardeau Southeast Missourian,* June 18, 1992; Keith White, "Ozarks' wild horse free to roam, at least for now," *Springfield News-Leader,* October 8, 1993; "Congress passes bill protecting horses in Missouri Ozarks," *Jefferson City Daily Capital News,* October 4, 1996; Mike Penprase, "DNR worried about Jacks Fork, and that worries locals, Shannon County's canoes, horses, septic tanks and more threaten river's water quality, state says," *Springfield News-Leader,* April 6, 2003; a 3-part series by Michelle Friedrich, in the *Poplar Bluff Daily American Republic,* "Zero Tolerance, Regaining Control of the River," August 12, 2005; "Joining forces to regain control of the river," August 14, 2005; and "Bluff Jumpin', It's not a good idea," August 15, 2005; Chad Livengood, "Riverway bill targets drunken debauchery," *Springfield News-Leader,* February 3, 2009; "National Park in Crisis!" press release, Missouri Parks Association, July 16, 2009, said that "Over the past more than 40 years this park has not lived up to the expectations that we and the country had"; and "The Current Controversy, The future of the Ozarks National Scenic Riverways is uncertain," *Columbia Daily Tribune,* September 6, 2009. Other issues include such topics as the placement and use of

county-built roads, size of outboard motors, horse trails across public lands, various hunting and fishing regulations, etc.

12. The author's reference is to Leonard Hall's influential book, *Stars Upstream, Life Along an Ozark River* (Columbia: University of Missouri Press, 1969), originally published in 1958. Read and quoted by government officials (some of whom floated the Current River with Hall), conservationists, naturalists, and citizen promoters for a new approach in the preservation of American rivers, *Stars Upstream* became a famous narrative, but one often cursed by resident Ozarkers. Leonard Hall and his wife owned an idyllic country home in Bellevue Valley, north of Caledonia.

Appendix

All essays from the *Missouri Historical Review*

1. Lynn Morrow, "Trader William Gilliss and Delaware Migration in Southern Missouri," *MHR* 75, no. 2 (January 1981): 147–167.

2. Barbara L. Green, "Slave Labor at the Maramec Iron Works, 1828–1850" *MHR* 73, no. 2 (January 1979): 150–164.

3. John F. Bradbury Jr., "'Good Water & Wood but the Country is a Miserable Botch': Flatland Soldiers Confront the Ozarks," *MHR* 90, no. 2 (January 1996): 166–186; rpt. *A Rough Business: Fighting the Civil War in Missouri*, ed. William Garrett Piston (Columbia: The State Historical Society of Missouri, 2012): 124–144.

4. Charles K. Piehl, "The Race of Improvement: Springfield Society, 1865–1881," *MHR* 67, no. 4 (July 1973): 484–521.

5. Stephen L. McIntyre, "The City Belongs to the Local Unions": The Rise of the Springfield Labor Movement, 1871–1912," *MHR* 98, no. 1 (October 2003): 24–46.

6. H. Roger Grant, "The Ozark Short Line Railroad: A Failed Dream," *MHR* 100, no. 4 (July 2006): 197–211.

7. Lynn Morrow, "Before Bass Pro: St. Louis Sporting Clubs on the Gasconade River," *MHR* 99, no. 1 (October 2004): 1–23.

8. David Benac, "Whose Forest Is This?: Hillfolk, Industrialists, and Government in the Ozarks," *MHR* 101, no. 1 (October 2006): 17–35.

9. Jason Navarro, "Under Penalty of Death: Pierce City's Night of Racial Terror, *MHR* 100, no. 2 (January 2006): 87–102.

10. Keith A. Sculle, "'Our Company Feels that the Ozarks are a Good Investment . . . ': The Pierce Pennant Tavern System," *MHR* 93, no. 3 (April 1999): 293–307.

11. Gary R. Kremer and Evan P. Orr, "Lake Placid" A Recreational Center for Colored People in the Missouri Ozarks," *MHR* 95, no. 1 (October 2000): 68–85.

12. Clarence R. Keathley, "Reflections on Public Welfare in Washington County, Missouri, 1939–1941," *MHR* 82, no. 1 (October 1987): 51–70.

13. Milton D. Rafferty, "Agricultural Change in the Western Ozarks," *MHR* 69, no. 3 (April 1975): 299–322.

14. Stephen N. Limbaugh, "The Origin and Development of the Ozark National Scenic Riverways Project," *MHR* 91, no. 2 (January 1997): 121–132.

Acknowledgments

The contributors to this volume collected many debts over the last generation—fellow historians, archivists, librarians, collectors, spouses and significant others, and our personal informants have all influenced our work. A special thanks goes to the two readers for the press who gave their time to offer excellent suggestions.

The current publication also owes gratitude to a number of veterans for the diverse tasks necessary in production and dissemination of Missouri history. The University of Missouri Press editor-in-chief Clair Willcox, managing editor Sara Davis, and Debbie Upton invested their considerable skills during development. At the State Historical Society of Missouri, Gary Kremer, Lynn Gentzler, Gerald Hirsch, John Bradbury, and Ann Cox quickly produced scanning and OCR of the *Missouri Historical Review* essays, digital pictures, and insightful observations. It is a distinct pleasure to work with so many sociable colleagues. As always, my wife, Kristen, deserves her own merit badge.

As editor, I have applied a light hand on the authors' original essays. The primary tasks included a cleanup of the digital capture of competing fonts, formats, and general gibberish, and then I placed additional sources or commentaries in discursive endnotes that broadened the context of the original essay

All of us hope that newcomers to Missouri history will discover an intriguing story in this volume and want to explore additional authors, or perhaps examine and record their own life histories. And, all readers surely have historical resources that you can donate to a Missouri repository, as someone will want to know your story, too.

Contributors

David Benac teaches American and environmental history and manages the public history program at Southeastern Louisiana University. He earned his doctorate at the University of Missouri in 2003. His article became part of *Conflict in the Ozarks: Hill Folk, Industrialists, and Government in Missouri's Courtois Hills*, Truman State University Press, 2010.

John Bradbury is the associate director for the State Historical Society of Missouri, Missouri University of Science and Technology, Rolla. Since 1980 he has worked to support preservation efforts in many historical societies, authored regional history books, and published dozens of articles about the Ozarks and the trans-Mississippi Civil War.

Roger Grant spent part of his youth working in the Western Historical Manuscript Collection–Columbia. Since then he became one of the world's leading authorities on transportation history and American railroads, writing or editing two dozen books and scores of articles. In spring 2005, he was the Maxwell C. Weiner Visiting Professor in the Humanities at the University of Missouri–Rolla, when he did the research for his article.

Barbara Green earned a doctorate, *The Slavery Debate in Missouri, 1831-1855*, at the University of Missouri in 1980. Dr. Green teaches at Wright State University.

Clarence Keathley spent a career in state government social services before retiring as a training supervisor for the Missouri Division of Welfare. As an officer and member of the Iron County Historical Society, he authored several publications. (Deceased)

Gary Kremer has sponsored historic preservation surveys and national register of historic place nominations while writing interpretive reports for the Department of Natural Resources' cultural departments. Kremer is executive director of the State Historical Society of Missouri. Evan Orr, one of his students at William Woods University, participated in research and development of this essay as both sought additional insights to Missouri's ethnic history.

Stephen Limbaugh Sr. of Cape Girardeau served in the Navy after World War II, earned a B.A. at Southeast Missouri State University, and a J.D. at the University of Missouri in 1951. He spent thirty-two years in private practice, including three as a prosecuting attorney and four as a city attorney for Cape Girardeau. In 1983 he became a federal judge in the Eastern District of Missouri.

Stephen McIntyre teaches Missouri and American labor history at Missouri State University. McIntyre earned his doctorate at the University of Missouri–Columbia in 1995. He is the editor of *Springfield's Urban Histories, Essays on the Queen City of the Missouri Ozarks*, Moon City Press, Missouri State University, 2012.

Lynn Morrow developed his article on William Gilliss while working as a public historian at the Center for Ozarks Studies, Southwest Missouri State University. He managed his historic preservation firm in the 1980s, and was director of the Local Records Preservation Program, Missouri State Archives, Office of Secretary of State, 1990–2012.

Jason Navarro, a public schoolteacher at Wheaton High School in Barry County, earned his degree at Missouri Southern State University and pursued a significant event left out of local history books.

Evan P. Orr works at High Caliber Stables, Greensboro, North Carolina.

Charles Piehl is a Nebraskan who earned an A.M. degree at Washington University. Dr. Piehl is professor emeritus at Minnesota State University, Mankato.

Milton Rafferty taught several years in the Kansas public schools, but joined the Missouri State University faculty at Springfield in 1966. His pathbreaking *The Ozarks, Land and Life* book, first published in 1980 and significantly revised in 2001 at the University of Arkansas Press, is the most influential work for understanding broad patterns in Ozarks history.

Keith Sculle has published widely on the relationship between automobile travel and place, including several articles about the Ozarks. For thirty-five years he served as a public historian in Springfield at the Illinois Preservation Agency. He and geographer John Jakle have coauthored three books in The Road and American Culture series at Johns Hopkins University Press.

Index

About the Editor

Lynn Morrow is the former Director of the Local Records Preservation Program, Missouri State Archives. He is the author or editor of three books, including *Shepherd of the Hills Country: Tourism Transforms the Ozarks, 1880s–1930s*. He lives in Jefferson City, Missouri.